Politeia

SUNY series in Ancient Greek Philosophy

―――――

Anthony Preus, editor

Politeia

New Readings in the History of Philosophy

Edited by

ANNE J. MAMARY and
MEREDITH TREXLER DREES

Published by State University of New York Press, Albany

© 2025 State University of New York

All rights reserved

Printed in the United States of America

No part of this book may be used or reproduced in any manner without written permission. No part of this book may be stored in a retrieval system or transmitted in any form or by any means including electronic, electrostatic, magnetic tape, mechanical, photocopying, recording, or otherwise without the prior permission in writing of the publisher.

Links to third-party websites are provided as a convenience and for informational purposes only. They do not constitute an endorsement or an approval of any of the products, services, or opinions of the organization, companies, or individuals. SUNY Press bears no responsibility for the accuracy, legality, or content of a URL, the external website, or for that of subsequent websites.

EU GPSR Authorised Representative:
Logos Europe, 9 rue Nicolas Poussin, 17000, La Rochelle, France
contact@logoseurope.eu

For information, contact State University of New York Press, Albany, NY
www.sunypress.edu

Library of Congress Cataloging-in-Publication Data

Names: Mamary, Anne J. M., 1964– editor. | Trexler Drees, Meredith, 1984– editor.
Title: Politeia : new readings in the history of philosophy / edited by Meredith Trexler Drees and Anne J. Mamary.
Description: Albany : State University of New York Press, [2025] | Series: SUNY series in ancient Greek philosophy | Includes bibliographical references and index.
Identifiers: LCCN 2024051661 | ISBN 9798855803013 (hardcover : alk. paper) | ISBN 9798855802993 (ebook)
Subjects: LCSH: Philosophy, Ancient.
Classification: LCC B108 .P65 2025 | DDC 180—dc23/eng/20241202
LC record available at https://lccn.loc.gov/2024051661

Contents

Introduction: *Politeia: New Readings in the History of Philosophy* 1
   Anne J. Mamary and Meredith Trexler Drees

Plato on Laughing at People 13
   D. Z. Andriopoulos

Plato's Dialogues: Educating the Mind for 2400 Years 29
   Martha C. Beck

Different Ways of Being Different, Different Ways Not to Be:
Parmenides and the Critical Relativism of Alain Locke 43
   Rose M. Cherubin

The Art of Training the Black Horse: The "War within the Soul"
and Socrates' Palinode 67
   Meredith Trexler Drees

"Riches without Envy": Picturing the Words of *Philebus* 40a10 83
   Mateo Duque

Karl Marx and the Riddle of the *Nicomachean Ethics* 5.5 99
   Howard Engelskirchen

The Tragedy of Natural Philosophy 115
   Myrna Gabbe

"Turn the Brightness Outward": *Muthos* and *Paideia* in
Pindar and Plato 131
   Hyun Höchsmann

Don't Be a Drag, Just Be a Queen 149
    Anne J. Mamary

Plato on Hate and the Limits of Morality 165
    Phillip Mitsis

Neither an "Exact Grasp" Nor a "Complete Falsehood":
The Truth Status and Rhetorical Function of the
Tripartite Model of City and Soul in the *Republic* 181
    Mark Moes

The Unity of Being 195
    Parviz Morewedge

The Double Meaning of Strife in Hesiod 211
    Joyce M. Mullan

The Myth of Er and Pamphylia's Polyglossia 227
    Nickolas Pappas

Between *Numen* and *Nous*: Bachelard on the Awakening
of Consciousness 243
    Eileen Rizo-Patron

Justice, Accountability, and Its Limits in Plato's *Republic* I 263
    Anne-Marie Schultz

Beauty Dethroned? Plato's Symposiasts on What We Love 277
    Thomas M. Tuozzo

Forms as Causes in *On Coming to Be and Passing Away* II.9 291
    William Wians

Contributors 305

Name Index 311

Introduction

Politeia: New Readings in the History of Philosophy

ANNE J. MAMARY AND
MEREDITH TREXLER DREES

Politeia: New Readings in the History of Philosophy began as a special issue of the journal *Politeia* in honor of Anthony Preus, edited by D. Z. Andriopoulos. Unfortunately, Dr. Andriopoulos became too ill to complete the project. As a former student of Dr. Preus (Anne) and friend of, and collaborator with, Dr. Andriopoulos (Meredith), we are offering *Politeia: New Readings in the History of Philosophy* as a libation to Dr. Preus. The anthology also shares its name with Plato's *Politeia*, which has come to us in English as the *Republic*. The Greek title, *Politeia*, suggests a mutually constitutive interaction between engaged individuals and a dialogic, inquisitive community striving to enliven the excellence (*arete*) of each participant and the whole. Both Dr. Andriopoulos and Dr. Preus inspire just such interactions, and the eighteen essays in *Politeia* both grow from and honor their generous, open, and broad-ranging work.[1]

D. Z. Andriopoulos was an international scholar of Ancient Philosophy. He lived and inspired a true *Politeia* by bringing together the scholars and students with whom he worked. He served by example, promoting collaborative philosophical progress in the classroom, through his leadership as a journal editor, and among his colleagues. Dr. Andriopoulos edited *Philosophical Inquiry* until it closed and then re-opened as *Politeia: International Interdisciplinary Philosophical Review* in 2018. He served as lead editor of *Politeia* for three years and was dedicated to organizing and publishing honorary works for his colleagues. We hope that *Politeia: New Readings in the History of Philosophy* serves as a mark of respect for, and a tribute to, Dr. Andriopoulos's legacy. Dr. Andriopoulos served as a professor of philosophy at the Aristotle University of Thessaloniki throughout most of his career; however, he also spent part of his tenure at the University of Missouri in Kansas City. Dr. Andriopoulos impacted philosophy on a personal and global level, encouraging individuals to seek the best in themselves in collaboration with others.[2]

Anthony Preus has mentored countless graduate students at the State University of New York at Binghamton, has edited the series in ancient philosophy at SUNY Press for decades, and has facilitated the *politeia* that is the Society for Ancient Greek Philosophy (SAGP) for as long. He edited six volumes of *Essays in Ancient Greek Philosophy* (the first five with John Anton), which ranged in focus from the pre-Socratics to Plato to Aristotle's ontology and ethics. Dr. Preus is a prolific scholar, writing on topics as diverse as medical ethics in the ancient and contemporary worlds, nutrition in the ancient world, the manifold Mediterranean influences on Greek thought, the natural philosophers and neoplatonists, mythology and philosophy, and on a wide variety of topics related to Aristotle, to name just some of his many areas of scholarship. Dr. Preus has the curiosity and patience to welcome all comers, as Plato's Socrates met his interlocutors where they were. And, like Socrates, Dr. Preus challenges scholars to take that work to new heights or to greater depths. This collection facilitates a *politeia* of the varied, broad ancient Greek world and its Asian neighbors, and on influences of these ancient worlds with some contemporary philosophers and issues. Some of the essays are meditations, while others reflect on teaching ancient philosophies as a practice of developing ethical and intellectual virtues. Some of the authors have an analytical bent, while others are more phenomenological. Like its eponymous journal and Dr. Preus's wide-ranging work, *Politeia* is not organized thematically or chronologically. Instead, the volume's contributors bring together a diversity of voices that both shine individually and encourage conversations collectively; they do not write about Professor Preus's work but rather in celebration of the unique insights and multiple and overlapping discussions inspired by Dr. Preus. We hope the book's many voices will welcome a diversity of readers, who will continue the conversations in their own work.

This book opens with D. Z. Andriopoulos's "Plato on Laughing at People," which argues that, for Plato, laughter plays an important ethical role in discourse. Through a new analysis of both the dialectic and drama of the dialogues (especially the *Philebus*), Andriopoulos suggests that Plato distinguishes between specific forms of bad and good laughing at people; the former harms the soul and stifles human inquiry, whereas the latter benefits the soul and furthers human inquiry.

Martha C. Beck's "Plato's Dialogues: Educating the Mind for 2400 Years," explores some practical implications of inquiry on the human soul in her discussion of what college students can gain from reading and reflecting on Plato's dialogues. Drawing on the *Ion*, the Seventh *Letter*, the *Phaedrus*, and the *Republic* as but a few examples, Beck argues that students who have read Plato can take the lead in modeling an examined life, knowing how quickly the freedom they enjoy can be lost. Her hope is that they will learn from the dialogues that they will have to change their minds in order to preserve the goal of maximizing human flourishing. Everything that makes life worth living is at stake: free scientific inquiry, free artistic expression, freedom to say what you think publicly and be held accountable by others so that citizens can collectively become wiser, freer, and more engaged in public life and in private pursuits. Living in and inheriting a society that provides citizens the freedom to develop as human beings, Beck explains, is the greatest gift we can nurture in each other and pass on to the next generations.

Combining scholars from across the millennia, Rose M. Cherubin reads Alain Locke through a Parmenidean lens in "Different Ways of Being Different, Different Ways Not to Be: Parmenides and the Critical Relativism of Alain Locke." Cherubin writes that Parmenides' account of difference in the account of the opinions of mortals is a potentially helpful contribution to today's discussions about rendering differences without subordination or presenting one side as a norm and the other as its negation. His account poses difference in a way that does not involve the kinds of hierarchies or denials of otherness that Val Plumwood has termed "dualisms." Nor does it support the denials of history and valuation that Alain Locke showed to be central to invidious modern constructions of race. In fact, Parmenides' formulation calls for the acknowledgment and investigation of these kinds of conditions. In that way, Parmenides helps us to envision the kind of inquiry that Locke's "critical relativism" might require. Cherubin suggests that the goals of Locke's critical relativism may be better understood through the notion of *alētheia* (ἀλήθεια) than they are through the notion of truth.

Meredith Trexler Drees's "The Art of Training the Black Horse: The 'War within the Soul' and Socrates' Palinode" examines Plato's descriptions of the tripartite soul in the *Republic* and the *Phaedrus*. Drees argues that a more thorough understanding of the "training of the black horse" in the famous myth of the charioteer sheds light on the relationship between these two dialogues, specifically in the context of Plato's view of the relationship between aesthetic experience and moral progress. Drees suggests that not only is it possible to train the black horse of the *Phaedrus* but also that this training is precisely the aesthetic education described in Books II and III of the *Republic*.

Mateo Duque, too, engages the riddle of Plato's images of (and on) the soul and their implications for human and moral goodness. In "'Riches without Envy': Picturing the Words of *Philebus* 40a10," Duque reminds readers that in the *Philebus*, Socrates describes what we might call "internal representation" with the metaphor of two craftspeople: inside of us, there is a scribe who writes words on our souls as if in a book and a painter who paints images in our soul as if on a canvas. Duque shows that Plato is both characterizing and exemplifying the concept of ekphrasis. He complicates an implication of the analogy that we think primarily in words *first* and *then* images. He argues that interpretation is necessary for imaging words, and uses the reading of the phrase "*chruson gignomenon aphthonon*" at 40a10, which he contends is a written riddle, as an example. 40a10, Duque suggests, has traditionally been read as if the good person will come to have a lot of money; instead, he reads it as the good person will come to have goods *without envy*—the literal meaning of *aphthonon*. Someone morally good will possess an abundance, especially virtue, without feeling envy or ill-will toward others.

Howard Engelskirchen is also a rich reader of riddles in "Karl Marx and the Riddle of the *Nicomachean Ethics* 5.5." Engelskirchen notes that in *Nicomachean Ethics* 5.5 Aristotle acknowledged defeat. He asked why goods in the market exchange on the basis of equality—one house for five beds in his example—and admitted he was unable to provide a fully persuasive reason for the phenomenon. In order to exchange on the basis of equality there had to be some property all such goods shared that rendered them commensurable. Conscious of the vast natural diversity of things offered for sale or purchase, Aristotle concluded, "in truth it is impossible that things differing so much should become commensurate" (1133b18–19). But, he added, "with reference to demand they may become so sufficiently." Confronted with the global reality of market relations triumphally dominant, Engelskirchen shows how we can readily imagine Marx's meditations on the riddle of the *Nicomachean Ethics*

5.5, suggesting a sketch for the entire trajectory of his project. Forms of exchange depend on forms of association, not the reverse, and it is the privation of a structure of separation piled on separation that must be overcome by our rich and freely developed association with one another (Marx and Engels, *German Ideology* 80).

Myrna Gabbe addresses the mysteries of the human soul in the face of mortality through the lens of tragedy. In "The Tragedy of Natural Philosophy," Gabbe writes that, in Plato's *Phaedo*, Socrates offers a series of arguments for the immortality of the soul to defend his optimism in the face of death. Gabbe's essay critically examines the first in the series, the so-called Cyclical Argument, which Socrates presents as a philosophical interpretation of the ancient mystery doctrine that the soul comes from, and returns to, Hades. It is a fitting start, as the mysteries promised initiate a light heart in life and good hope in death. Yet against the view that Plato endorses the universal principles of change laid out in the Cyclical Argument, Gabbe contends that the argument establishes these principles as claims to be refuted in subsequent arguments. Examining the theories of Anaximander and Empedocles, the essay shows that these principles underwrote such tragic views as: justice requires injustice, love is no better than strife, and human flourishing is born from, and destined to collapse back into, chaos. Gabbe's claim is not that Plato abandons the doctrine tied to the mysteries but that he seeks to ground it in principles genuinely capable of explaining how we can be of good cheer throughout our lives and why we should have hope on our deathbeds.

In "'Turn the Brightness Outward'—*Muthos* and *Paideia* in Pindar and Plato," Hyun Höchsmann also offers hope for living a good life in the face of discord through her reading of Pindar's *epinikia* (victory odes). Pindar sets the frame of reference of his *epinikia* by drawing upon myths and maxims, establishing the parallels between the events of victory and divine or heroic achievements, and enhancing the individual consciousness beyond a transient moment of celebration. Pindar does not commemorate the victors as individuals but transforms them into the representatives of the highest *arete* (excellence/virtue). In endowing individual achievements with an enduring purpose and meaning in the context of shared traditions and knowledge, Pindar's *epinikia* point to the sphere of possible transcendence of regional dissidence and strife.

Pindar's distinction between the traditional narrations of myth and his interpretations of myths as *logos* (*Olympian* 7.21, *Nemean* 1.34) brings Pindar closer to Plato's view of myths and supplies a defense of his odes against Plato's criticism of the poets in the *Republic* 2.363–67. In *Pythian 3*, Pindar affirms the vigor of moral capacity to surmount adversities to "turn the brightness outward" (3.83).

Riding the three waves of Plato's "female drama," Anne J. Mamary's "Don't Be a Drag, Just Be a Queen" brings Homer's poetry into conversation with the *Politeia* as it brings to light the *metis* (courage and craft) required both to plumb the depths and attempt the ascents of *The Republic* in order to reweave interlocutors and readers. Plato's Socrates proposes that justice is the harmony of *epithumia* (appetitiveness), *thymos* (spiritedness), and *andreiea* (courage/manliness), held together by an erotically wise *sophrosune* (moderation, temperance)—whether in an individual or society. When Socrates "went down . . . to the Peiraeus with Glaucon, the son of Ariston," for the festival of the newly introduced Thracian goddess, Bendis, Socrates makes the strange familiar when he praises the Thracian contingent and Athenian citizens alike (327a). Waylaid on his return to Athens, Socrates makes the familiar strange, using conventional names for the virtues, yet recomposing their meaning. Plato suggests Socrates' interlocutors must shift their view of justice through an examination of what it means to be affluent men. Socrates reminds them there is a female drama played out in three waves that threaten to wash the men ashore. He urges them to examine "the beach rubble" (Sappho) that Socrates makes of their conventional masculine and class assumptions in a journey that resonates with Odysseus' fraught voyage home. Instead of returning to Ithaka and Penelope, Plato's men might sail home to Athens and Socrates, who has been waiting for them and exhorting them all along.

In "Plato on Hate and the Limits of Morality," Phillip Mitsis suggests that hate, along with its benefits, is regularly coupled with love at several key junctures in Platonic texts, and they are lauded together as mutually supporting mechanisms in education, virtue, knowledge, the state, religion, and so forth. Given that Plato's endorsements of hate are apt to seem worryingly suspect to most contemporary ears, Mitsis argues it behooves us to look a little more closely at why Plato seems so convinced about hate's importance for our lives, especially since that conviction is an integral part of his (and not just a particular interlocutor's claims) entire philosophical theory. Even with careful attempts from youth to instill the proper loves and hatreds, not everyone can become a philosopher capable of loving the nature of true justice. Accordingly, it appears that hatred may be ultimately more effective in drawing the limits that help prevent us from being morally incurable. Indeed, the overall moral of Plato's passages on hate seems to be a banausic consequentialist conclusion that money cannot buy non-philosophers love, but it can induce them to hate what they should hate, at least enough to keep them out of jail or worse, thus transforming them into something useful to themselves and others.

Mark Moes's "Neither an 'Exact Grasp' Nor a 'Complete Falsehood': The Truth Status and Rhetorical Function of the Tripartite Model of City and Soul in the *Republic*" attempts to clarify what rhetorical work Plato and Plato's Socrates aim to accomplish in using the theoretically deficient model of the tripartite soul in the *Republic*. It attempts to explain, with the help of Mitchell Miller's views about the rhetorical aims and the compositional structure of the Platonic dialogue, why Plato has Socrates introduce the tripartite model in the first place, why it disappears in the *Republic*'s digression on philosophy, and why it reappears in Books VIII and IX doing several kinds of rhetorical work. Finally, it attempts to harmonize Socrates' remark that the tripartite model does not give us an "exact grasp" of the soul's structure with his remark that the tripartite model is "not a complete falsehood." The harmonization, Moes argues, relies on a distinction between epistemological truth and ontological truth.

Parviz Morewedge also highlights contrasting epistemological and ontological truths as he explains that much of Western philosophy frames alienation as a problem of, and for, humanity. Drawing on Zoroastrian and Shi'a texts, "The Unity of Being" shows that, by contrast, in Central Asian, Islamic, and Iranian models, alienation is expressed as an unsensed unity of being. Contractual agreements between God and people in Abrahamic traditions consider God and people as separate from each other, leading to a sense of alienation, mortal from divine. There is no such alienation in Islamic mysticism and its Middle Eastern and Central Asian precursors: the Soul seeks the One. The vocabulary of a reed being cut from its root—from its source—shows this same longing for reunification as the analogy of the daughter, who, recognizing the absolute love for, of, and with the father, wants no otherness, no alienation. In the Zoroastrian phase, as the Divine or Wise Lord (*Ahurā Mazdā*) needs humanity to achieve its goal of providing the best possible world, a human will and the Divine plan are de-alienated. In the Archaic-Shi'a tradition, the ultimate being (the God of monotheism) is neither a being nor a substance. It posits no creation out of nothing, no divine will, no divinely revealed meta-nature source of norms, no independence from, and alienation with, human beings. Rather than a sense of alienation from the One or from God, these traditions show a Unity of Being.

In "Strife in Hesiod's *Works and Days*," Joyce M. Mullan also shows the possibility for unity in what might seem at first glance to be a divisive concept. Mullan shows that there has been a renewed interest in recent years on the specifically Greek concept of *Agon* as contest or struggle and its role in preserving democracy. Hannah Arendt in her *Human Condition* started a cottage industry of agonistic democratic theorists. More recently, *Law and Agonistic Politics*, and in particular in that work, Andreas Kalyvas's "The Democratic Narcissus: The Agonism of the Ancients compared to that of the Post-Moderns" continues the trend. Mullan argues that in the depiction of *Agon*, Hesiod revisits and revises the idea to defend a more productive use of Strife. This will be quite influential in the domestic and international thought and politics of Ancient Greece.

Nickolas Pappas's "The Myth of Er and Pamphylia's Polyglossia" continues the themes of justice in philosophy and in action, in the Greek and non-Greek. Pappas starts with a question: Could the journeying in the *Republic*'s myth of Er carry philosophical significance? As a comment on the dialogue as a whole, Pappas suggests that it might illuminate the *Republic*'s ambivalence regarding justice among the foreigners. Afterlife journeys may promise to erase ethnic difference. But a closer look at Pamphylia problematizes that expectation. Real-life Pamphylia was polyglot, both Greek and non-Greek; in the myth, non-Greek afterlife focuses on punishment or reward for past deeds, while the Greek heroes depicted focus on their choices of lives to come. Those two parts of the myth correspond respectively to ordinary justice in actions and philosophical justice in souls. It would seem to follow that Pamphylia lets Plato divide types of justice unequally among the world's population.

In "Between *Numen* and *Nous*: Bachelard on the Awakening of Consciousness," Eileen Rizo-Patron writes that the Latin *numen*, root of adjectives *numinous* or *numinal*, is understood as a spiritual force felt presiding over a natural phenomenon or place. Derived from *nuo+men*, "a head nod," it connotes an assent to "divine influence." Some have suggested that the term *noumenon* and its adjective *noumenal* (Gk. *nous*, reason)—describing a purely intellectual intuition—was imported into early Latin as the word *noumen* (becoming *numen* in classical Latin). Rizo-Patron contends that Bachelard's *Intuition of the Instant* marks his "initiation" into the mysteries of *numinal* insight (revelation) to which *noumenal* intuition (reason) must yield before it can be reborn in the face of unprecedented experience. Further, he pursues his discovery of reason's dependence on such advents of inspiration through his study of "poetic reverie" in the writings of select philosopher-poets from Ancient Greece to his days. A parallel process even finds its way into Bachelard's epistemological studies in *The Philosophy of No*, as the adventitious undoing and transformation of science's epochal paradigms, via "anagogic reverie" and experimentation. Hence Bachelard's apparent conviction regarding the dependence of human reason on a vibrantly numinous world and, conversely, of this numinous world on reason's ethical responses to its persistent calls, as they emerge in time.

Anne-Marie Schultz suggests in "Justice as Accountability in Plato's *Republic* I" that most readers of Plato regard *The Republic* as a sustained inquiry into the nature of justice (and injustice) on both the individual and the political level. This view is not surprising, given the project Socrates sets out in Book II after "Glaucon and the others begged [him] not to abandon the argument but to help in every way to track down what justice and injustice are and what the truth about their benefits is" (*Republic* 368c). While Schultz in no way wishes to argue against this well-justified view, she reconsiders Plato's philosophical masterpiece as an exploration of accountability, which she, following the Office of Juvenile Justice and Delinquency Prevention, regards as a disposition or activity involving "taking responsibility for your behavior and taking action to repair the harm." To make her case, Schultz first surveys some recent literature on accountability followed by an examination of the opening scene and the three definitions of justice offered in *Republic* I. These aspects of the text explore both individual and collective accountability. Third, Schultz examines the historical fates of Glaucon, Cephalus, Polemarchus, and Socrates to illustrate the importance of accountability in the face of civic unrest. Finally, Schultz considers the disastrous results that can arise when we lack this virtue on both the individual and collective level.

The beautiful (*kalon*) is the object of love (*eros*): this is the overwhelmingly dominant view of the ancient Greeks, writes Thomas M. Tuozzo in "Beauty Dethroned: Aristophanes vs Diotima in Plato's *Symposium*." Whether something is beautiful because it is loved, however, or loved because it is beautiful, was a matter of debate—both among the Greeks and in the cultures inheriting their legacy. The Platonic Socrates' magnificent speeches in the *Symposium* and *Phaedrus* leave no doubt that he falls into the second camp. But Plato himself supplies what has been perhaps the most influential case for the other side: Aristophanes' speech in the *Symposium*. Indeed, so little does beauty play a substantive role in that speech's account of *eros* that no form of the word *kalon* appears in it at all.

In this essay, Tuozzo gives an interpretation of Aristophanes' speech that highlights this fact and examines the ways in which the beautiful figures in the speeches preceding his. Doing so reveals conceptions of love in which the beautiful does not play so central a role as it does in Socrates', conceptions that may, for that reason, have something to recommend them.

William Wians's "Forms as Causes in *On Coming to Be and Passing Away* II.9" closes the collection. Wians writes that in a passage late in *On Coming to Be and Passing Away*, Aristotle argues that Platonic forms are inadequate to serve as efficient causes of generation (*On Coming to Be* II.9, 335b9–24). An adequate account—something "every philosopher dreams of" (335b7–8)—must be able to explain a fundamental phenomenon of generation: the generator does not always generate, but only at some times at not others. Forms as described in the *Phaedo* cannot explain why. Several scholars have recently examined *On Coming to Be* II.9's argument against the Forms. But none sufficiently attends to the essay's larger structure, within which the anti-Platonic argument is just one stage. The essay considers three types of cause of generation in nature—efficient, material, and formal. Within this context, it becomes clear that Plato's account is not entirely wrong-headed. What the *Phaedo* account does do, Wians argues, is identify one of the necessary conditions for coming into being in nature. But more than one condition must be satisfied. A second condition is found in the strictly materialist account Aristotle goes on to reject in the continuation of II.9. So, in good Aristotelian fashion, a portion of the truth is found in each of the opposing accounts.

In good Preusian fashion, the volume's eighteen contributors bring together a diversity of voices that both shine individually and encourage conversations collectively in the spirit of Dr. Andriopoulos's journal and Dr. Preus's work in the classroom, in print, and with the Society for Ancient Greek Philosophy. It is our hope that this collection will inspire readers to engage in the ideas that are presented and to join in the *Politeia* from which they were formed.

Notes

1. We would like to extend a special thanks to Michael Rinella, Diane Ganeles, and everyone at SUNY Press for their helpful collaboration throughout the course of this project. Our thanks to Jacob Buckman for his eagle eye, help, and support. We would also like to thank Peter Klosky, Director of Exhibitions

at the Roberson Museum and Science Center in Binghamton, New York, who created a draft cover design for the book, and Monmouth College Administrative Assistant Caitlin Eberle and Monmouth College 2018 alumnus and former Administrative Assistant Amjad Karkout for their time and dedicated work on stylistic edits to the manuscript.

    2. We thank Anastasia Marionopoulou of Hellenic Open University, the Philosophy Documentation Center, and, especially George Leaman for consulting with us about permission to publish Dr. Andriopoulos's essay.

Plato on Laughing at People

D. Z. Andriopoulos

According to Plato's *Apology*, Socrates' most dangerous accuser is the comic poet Aristophanes, who maliciously convicted Socrates in the court of public opinion (18b–d). Laughter is not only dangerous for the soul (ψυχή) but also socially and politically dangerous. However, contrary to one prominent line of interpretation, Plato does not oppose laughing at people.[1] Plato's views on laughter and comedy are more complex and more interesting.[2] After all, Plato is a comic poet of sorts. As others have noted, striking stylistic and thematic similarities occur between Plato's dialogues and ancient Greek comedies.[3] Like Attic comedy, the dialogues are a mimesis of contemporary people, touching on plebian topics in colloquial language, often for the sake of political critique. Aristotle even compares Socratic dialogues to the farcical mimes of Sophron and Xenarchus (*Poetics* 1447b).[4]

In this essay, I argue that, for Plato, laughter plays an important role in discourse. In both the *Republic* and the *Laws*, Plato introduces regulations on comedy and laughter. The *Philebus* provides a psychological justification for such regulation: maliciously laughing at people, in comedy or otherwise, corrupts the soul. Plato distinguishes between specific forms of bad and good laughing at people; the former harms the soul and stifles human inquiry, whereas the latter benefits the soul and furthers human inquiry.

Laughing at People: Intentional and Representational

Plato does not develop a general theory of laughter. Instead, given Plato's interest in the social, ethical, and political dimensions of laughter, it makes sense that the dialogues present the ethical implications of the pleasurable affectation [πάθος] that arises from judging or imagining people to be self-ignorant and powerless. Such laughter is "intentional," not in the sense that it is voluntary but rather in the sense that it is about an object and represents an object (unlike, say, nervous giggling or laughing automatically in response to tickling).

Intentional laughter is also norm-governed. One important norm is "fittingness." According to Plato, one laughs fittingly at people, if one accurately believes or imagines them to lack (a) self-understanding of their own financial, physical, epistemic, or moral failings (especially ignorance) and (b) the power to defend themselves when laughed at (*Philebus* 47e–50e).[5] The self-ignorant and powerful person is frightening, not funny. For example, there is nothing funny about a powerful and self-ignorant tyrant, because they have the potential to do great harm. So, laughter does not "fit" the powerful tyrant. Although laughable people believe they are better and more self-aware than they are, they are powerless to defend themselves when laughed at. When we laugh at such people, our laughter is fitting in the sense that it arises from our appreciating the genuinely laughable features of another person or group of people (i.e., their self-ignorance combined with powerlessness).

Sometimes laughter is not a fitting response. For example, when we laugh at men and women exercising naked together, we are laughing at the wrong people, because reason reveals naked, co-ed exercise to be good for us (*Republic* 452c–d). Thus, naked exercisers are not self-ignorant; rather, they are wiser than we are. Moreover, engaging in unfitting laughter reveals one's own foolishness. Only fools laugh at naked, co-ed exercisers. Similarly, it is foolish to laugh at the enlightened soul, who is confused in virtue of coming from the light to the darkness, instead of the dimwitted soul, who is confused in virtue of coming from the darkness to the light (*Republic* 518a–b).[6] Whereas the former has wisdom, the latter does not.

Plato's *Theaetetus* further expands on this point: the object of fitting laughter is someone who really is, rather than merely appears to be, self-ignorant and powerless. When the philosopher laughs at his companions for overvaluing noble ancestry, the philosopher is "scornfully laughed at" [καταγελᾶται] by the many (174e–175b). In such cases, the philosopher appears to the many to be without resources, arrogant, and ignorant—in effect, a powerless and laughable [γελοῖός] figure who is ignorant of his own ignorance. However, the lawyers, at whom the "free and the educated" laugh, are the objects of fitting laughter. For the lawyer falsely believes they are "clever and wise" [δεινοί τε καὶ σοφοί] when, really, they are ignorant of the most important matters (175d). When questioned about kingship, happiness, and misery, the lawyer is stumped, a laughable figure amid a comic chorus of clouds (175d). In short, laughter is a wise and fitting response to lawyers. By contrast, laughter is a foolish and unfitting response to philosophers.

Because laughter can be foolish or wise, fitting or not, comedy plays an important role in Platonic moral education. For example, in the *Laws* the Athenian Stranger proposes a law that permits some comedy in Magnesia, on the grounds that virtue requires "practical wisdom [φρόνιμος] about vice," that is, recognizing and hating vice (816e). Magnesia's citizens are to laugh at slaves' comic imitations of vicious people to become habituated in discerning and disdaining the vicious among us. However, so as not to become vicious themselves, citizens should not perform comic mimesis; or if they do, they should not do so "seriously" [σπουδῇ] but only satirically" (*Republic* 397a).[7]

In conclusion, wisely laughing at people is part of practical wisdom about vice. On the face of it, this is a strange result. How can a wise person laugh at people? It may seem that laughing at people is morally wrong even when it is a fitting response. Plato is aware of this problem. Indeed, good laughter must meet additional ethical norms: it must not be serious or malicious. The sort of laughing at people that Plato recommends—laughing at people who are represented as self-ignorant and powerless—not only fits its object but has important implications for political and philosophical discourse. That is, it is playful (unserious) and benevolent in nature.

Serious Laughing at People

Serious laughter is a form of abusing [νεικείων], that is, a way of harming or threatening to harm someone in a social or political setting. A scene from Homer's *Iliad* brings out the ways in which violence, politics, and laughter intersect (215–82). Thersites, an old cripple, scolds Agamemnon for weakening the Achaean army by angering Achilles, a man better than he, whose concubine (a war prize) Agamemnon stole. In verbally abusing Agamemnon, Thersites attempts to channel the Achaeans' fury into laughter directed at the ridiculous Agamemnon, whom Thersites represents as a man more interested in bedding women than winning the Trojan War.

"Let us go home in our ships and leave this man [Agamemnon] here in Troy to ponder his prizes," Thersites jeers (240–42). However, Odysseus successfully turns the weapon of laughter back on Thersites.

To the laughing Achaeans, Thersites, not Agamemnon, is ignorant of his own ignorance and powerless to defend himself. The officers may be ignorant—since "no one knows how this will all turn out"—but they are also powerful, a fact Odysseus violently impresses on Thersites (249–75). Laughter resolves a potential threat to Agamemnon's power, effectively stabilizing that power. Such laughter is not playful. It is serious.

Like Thersites, Thrasymachus in Plato's *Republic* attempts to use laughter as a weapon against Socrates, after Socrates claims to be ignorant about what justice is (337a2–6). Thrasymachus sees Socrates as a laughable pretender to knowledge, a powerless fraud who cannot defend his own view of justice. Thrasymachus' terrifying laugh contains a threat, which Socrates acknowledges when he twice remarks that the roaring Thrasymachus inspires fear. However, the ensuing philosophical discussion exposes Thrasymachus to be ignorant of justice and incapable of defending himself. Although Socrates emerges as the wiser and more powerful dialectician, Socrates does not use laughter as a weapon against Thrasymachus. For, as Socrates remarks in the discussion, pity, not violence, is an "appropriate" response to human ignorance (336e9–10). Although serious laughter may be politically expedient, it does nothing to ameliorate human ignorance. To be sure, Thrasymachus is genuinely laughable, and the dialogue represents him as such. But if we, the readers, are to laugh at him, we should not laugh at him in the violent way that he laughs at Socrates.

What I am calling "serious" or "violent" laughter permeated many aspects of Greek culture. Aristophanes and Hypereides even portray bullying crowds gathered in the agora, laughing and jeering at a shamed person (Halliwell, *Greek Laughter* 237; "Uses" 286).[8] In his book on the cultural psychology of laughter in antiquity, Stephen Halliwell dubs such laughter "consequential laughter," that is, laughter that harms or threatens to harm ("Uses" 281–96). While consequential laughter is abundant in Greek tragedy, its consequences are consequences for tragic characters. The terrible actions of Euripides' Medea spring at least in part from her desire to avoid consequential laughter.[9] In contrast, by directing serious laughter at contemporary people, Attic comedy had serious consequences for Socrates, his accusers, and the jurors who convicted him.

In the *Republic*, however, Socrates disparages serious laughter, instead, for its harmful effects on the laugher himself. Indeed, the *Republic* proposes we do away with "violent laughter" [ἰσχυρῷ γέλωτι], which produces a violent "change in mood" [μεταβολήν] (388e–389a). Similarly, in *Laws XI* comedians are permitted to make fun of people "not in angry seriousness [σπουδῇ . . . ἅμα καὶ θυμουμένοισιν], but in a playful spirit [μετὰ παιδιᾶς] and without anger [ἄνευ θυμοῦ]" (936a5–6). The worry is that serious, angry laughter devolves into "real hatreds and quarrels of the most serious kind" (935a2–3), transforming the laugher into a reckless beast (934e–936b).

In contrast, mirthful or playful laughter—common at Greek festivals, symposia, and even the assembly and law courts—was a form of communal play, fostering a sense of togetherness and joint relaxation (Halliwell, "Uses" 281–96). Though the dialogues say little about playful laughter, Plato's characters laugh playfully. For example, at *Phaedo* 115c6–116a2, Socrates laughs in response to Crito's question about how to bury him. Instead of laughing seriously at Crito, Socrates laughs at himself for failing to teach Crito that his soul is immortal. He then implores his companions to teach Crito, expressing concern for Crito's soul. Unlike serious or consequential laughter, playful laughter is unifying, inclusive, and benevolent in nature.[10]

Maliciously Laughing at People

Containing an inherent comedic drama, Plato's *Philebus* also contains Plato's most sustained discussion of laughter, nested within a complex argument about pleasure and its role in the good life. At *Philebus* 49d–50a, Socrates claims that malicious laughter is a mixed psychic pleasure, combining in the soul elements of pleasure and pain. Plato writes:

> Malicious laughter is a mixed psychic pleasure, combining in the soul the pain of unjust malice (itself a mixed pleasure) toward neighbors and the pleasure of enjoying and laughing at "bad things" belonging to neighbors (i.e., various forms of self-ignorance). The pain stems from unjust malice [φθόνος] toward neighbors [φίλοι],[11] and the pleasure is the pleasure of enjoying [καίρειν] and laughing at the bad things [κακοῖς] belonging to neighbors. Many passions (if not all) produce mixed pleasures of the soul (47e).[12] Malice is "a sort of unjust pain and also a pleasure" [λύπη τις ἄδικός ἐστί που καὶ ἡδονή]. (49d1)

While the object of malicious laughter is a weak neighbor, the object of the pleasure of malicious laughter is more complex, deriving from the comparison malicious laughers make between their neighbors and themselves. In maliciously laughing at neighbors, we enjoy their presumed badness not in and of itself but rather insofar as it seems to augment our own excellence by comparison. In particular, in maliciously laughing at our neighbors, we enjoy our own supposed financial, physical, and/or spiritual superiority, as well as our own supposed epistemic superiority—that is to say, we think we know our worth, whereas our oblivious neighbors laughably overestimate their own. Because malice [φθόνος] is the desire for "bad things belonging to neighbors" (hereafter, "BBN"), malice is serious; it harms or threatens to harm its object, either directly or indirectly. The desire for BBN stems from the desire to be financially, physically, and/or psychically better off than one's neighbors—a desire whose satisfaction produces the pleasure of malice.[13]

While Socrates does not explicitly invoke the malicious laugher's enjoyment of her presumed superiority, without this piece, Socrates' account of the pleasure of malicious laughter does not make sense.[14] Why would we take pleasure in the badness of our neighbors for its own sake? Also, as we have seen, serious laughter is used to establish or reinforce one's superior status. Moreover, going this route explains Socrates' otherwise puzzling claim that the enjoyment of bad things belonging to enemies is neither malicious nor unjust: we enjoy our enemies' faults and misfortunes not insofar as they seemingly elevate our own greatness by comparison but rather because deriding their weaknesses protects us from harm.[15]

At this stage, malicious laughter is problematic because it is serious; it arises out of a desire that one's neighbor be harmed. This desire could result from envy, in certain cases. The issue, however, is that that such laughter harms or threatens to harm its object, either directly or indirectly. This is what makes this sort of laughter serious and what makes it problematic. To appreciate its effect on the soul of the laugher, we must now turn to Socrates' discussion of anticipatory psychic pleasures, which precedes his discussion of the pleasure of malicious laughter. Like the psychic pleasure of malicious laughter, false anticipatory pleasures are also vicious pleasures of the soul (40a–c). In explicating false anticipatory pleasures, Socrates develops a rich moral psychology, on which I draw to sketch the kind of problematic falsity inherent in the pleasure of malicious laughter.

At 39d–40e, Socrates discusses the psychic pleasures of anticipation, for the purpose of explaining a type of falsity applicable to all psychic pleasures, including the pleasure of malicious laughter. Socrates maintains that such pleasure involves beliefs and imaginings that represent the pleasure-experience and pleasure-object in certain ways (39a–c). While scholarly debate is enormous regarding what aspect of the content of these representations makes their corresponding pleasures true or false, my primary aim is not to take a hard line in these debates. Rather, I argue that however we understand the falsity of anticipatory pleasures, such falsity is ethically problematic in the case of the pleasure of malicious laughter.

After claiming that "writings in the soul" (i.e., beliefs) and "paintings or pictures in the soul" (i.e., imaginings) attend pleasures (38e–39d), Socrates and Protarchus discuss false anticipatory pleasures at (39d6–40e9).[16] This passage is famously ambiguous, dividing interpretations of what kind of falsity Socrates means to invoke. Is the false anticipatory pleasure for gold false because the belief and imagining "I will get gold" is false (call this "non-hedonic falsity")? Or rather, is it false because the belief and imagining "Getting gold is pleasant" is false (call this "hedonic falsity")? It seems Socrates implicates both kinds of falsity. Non-hedonic falsity does not threaten the reality of the pleasure in question; the anticipatory pleasure is still a real pleasure, despite its predictive failure, that is, despite the fact that the subject will not obtain the gold he anticipates for himself. Hedonic falsity provides clear support for Socrates' primary point: the vicious or wicked are prone to false pleasures. The vicious, who value wealth over virtue, have hedonically false pleasures; they are wrong about what is pleasant. The predictive failure of an anticipatory pleasure does not obviously imply its viciousness; its hedonic falsity does. So, while Socrates selects the gold example to draw our attention to two types of falsity, only hedonic falsity supports his larger point that false anticipatory pleasures belong to the vicious.

This is puzzling. Why should Socrates pinpoint two types of falsity, when only hedonic falsity supports his larger point about anticipatory pleasure? Both hedonic and non-hedonic falsity apply more widely to all psychic pleasures (and possibly all pleasures), including the non-anticipatory pleasure of malicious laughter. Following the gold example, one belief-imagining pairing must represent the pleasure-object, and the other must represent the pleasure-experience. Keeping in mind that a malicious laugher takes pleasure in her neighbor's presumed badness relative to her own presumed goodness, the beliefs and/or imaginings attending malicious laughter represent the following two contents:

(1) I am better than my neighbor in virtue of my financial, physical, and/or psychic worth and in my superior knowledge of my worth.

(2) My neighbor's inferiority and inferior knowledge thereof are pleasant.

The pleasure of malicious laughter is non-hedonically false on the Platonic picture, because the belief representing content (1) is false. The malicious laugher is foolish and unjust in desiring that bad things befall her neighbor, so, in maliciously laughing at her neighbor, she is not genuinely better than her neighbor, despite what she inaccurately believes or imagines, even if she is better off financially. Plato privileges qualities of soul above all other measures of human worth. Recall, in Socrates' words, a non-hedonically false pleasure is not "about anything that either is the case or ever was the case" (39d6–40e9). The false pleasure of malicious laughter is also not about anything that is the case, because the malicious laugher is not really superior to the object of her foolish and unjust laughter.

While malicious laughter is pleasurable, it is vicious, since its non-hedonic falsity stems from folly, not mere predictive error (as in the case of false anticipatory pleasure). Just as malicious laughter is serious, malicious laughter is foolish because the pleasure of malicious laughter is normally non-hedonically false. A malicious laugher is rarely, if ever, superior to the person at whom he laughs, at least not in the moment of her unjust laughter. As a result, malicious laughers do not take pleasure in any real state of affairs—that is, their own real goodness relative to their neighbor's real badness. Why should this be? Recall, malicious laughter is serious and unjust in that it satisfies the desire for BBN, establishing power or strength based on harm or threat of harm. However, it is never just to "harm" [κακουργεῖν, κακῶς ποιεῖν, βλάπτειν] anybody, friend or enemy (*Crito* 49c; *Republic* 335b–d). To imagine and believe in one's own human superiority, while simultaneously being unjust, is, for Socrates, the pinnacle of self-ignorance.

Indeed, the irony of malicious laughter is this: the malicious laugher is herself laughable. Deluded by a false comparison, she is oblivious to her own self-degradation and self-ignorance. One might object that it is possible for one to maliciously laugh at someone who really is inferior to oneself—and so, in that case, the malicious laughter is non-hedonically true. But I take Socrates' point to be: when we maliciously laugh at someone, in that very moment we cannot simultaneously claim to be a superior human being; that is, we cannot claim that we possess more "occurrent" goodness, even if we have the disposition of a moral saint. For, in the moment of our unjust laughter, we lower ourselves to their level. What is more, our malicious laughter backfires. One need only consider the lowness of certain political commentators who maliciously deride politicians. While they may be morally superior, when they maliciously laugh at politicians, in that moment they forfeit any claim to moral superiority. This is one of the reasons why their malicious jibes so often fail to convince. Perhaps there are exceptions to this rule—cases in which an instance of malicious laughter is non-hedonically true. The point is that, in general, malicious laughter is non-hedonically false.

What makes the pleasure of malicious laughter hedonically false? To be sure, the malicious laugher initially experiences some real pleasure, just as the wicked man who receives gold. Both the malicious laugher and the wicked wealth acquirer are wrong about their estimation of the pleasure; both judge the pleasure to be far greater than it actually is.

This discussion of anticipatory pleasure sets us up to see the ways in which the pleasure of malicious laughter is false. Like false anticipatory pleasures, the pleasure of malicious laughter takes false mental judgments or imaginings as its object. And like false anticipatory pleasures, the pleasure of malicious laughter is non-hedonically and hedonically false; the malicious laugher wrongly supposes that she is superior and that her pleasure experience is more satisfying and more happiness-making than it really is.

In conclusion, regarding the pleasure of malicious laughter, both kinds of falsity, non-hedonic and hedonic, point to the viciousness of the pleasure of malicious laughter. To be wrong in our assessments of our own goodness relative to our neighbors' presumed badness implies our foolishness. To be wrong about what we take pleasure in—to suppose that the world, and not our own fantasies thereof, furnishes the objects of our pleasures—implies our ignorance about the world, ourselves, and the disconnect between the two. Ultimately, though, what accounts for the twin falsity of the pleasure of malicious laughter is the injustice and seriousness at its core—that is, that it arises from the desire that our neighbors be harmed. Far from supporting our actual superiority (as it is intended to do), the vicious pleasure of malicious laughter undermines our real worth as human beings, effectively falsifying the self-affirming fantasies that attend the pleasure of malicious laughter.

So far, the ensuing discussion might seem to recommend the view that laughing at people is always bad. However, only maliciously or seriously laughing at people is bad, in virtue of its relation to outward injustice and violence, inner psychic sickness (i.e., ignorance, injustice, and foolishness) and falsity. In the next section, I will show that the comedic drama of the

Philebus—in particular, the joking interactions among Socrates, Philebus, and Protarchus—reveals a form of good laughing at people.

The *Philebus*: Good Laughing at People

Comedy and laughter abound in the *Philebus*. While I cannot give a full analysis of the comedy of the *Philebus* here, focusing on a few passages will reveal what a salutary form of wise, playful and virtuous laughter looks like. Good laughter crucially involves the laugher laughing at himself, in addition to his companions. In this way, good laughter is inclusive—an emotional acknowledgment of our shared human flaws and limitations. Instead of deluding us with fantasies of superiority, good laughter enables us to confront our own human limitations honestly, especially regarding knowledge. In effect, good laughing at people helps us know what we do not know, inspiring us to inquire jointly through discourse. In this way, good laughter involves the development of wisdom.

In what follows, I will advance the view that the *Philebus* is a dramatic comedy about discourse. The comedy itself is complex, in that two comedies run side by side. One the one hand, Socrates and Protarchus act out a satire of eristic discourse, combatively pitting themselves against each other in jest. On the other hand, Socrates and Protarchus laugh at themselves and their position as non-eristic truth seekers, laughing at their own Sisyphean efforts to marshal the machinery of philosophic dialectic to put a limit on unlimited human discourse. In other words, a comedy about eristic discourse runs alongside a comedy about philosophic discourse. Both forms of comedy elicit laughing at people, albeit in a wise, playful, and virtuous way.

The dramatic context of the *Philebus* is funny. Protarchus, Philebus, and their youthful gang are supposedly holding Socrates hostage, while they all settle the relative roles of reason and pleasure in the good human life. Given this superficially hostile situation, Socrates encourages Protarchus not to be a childish lover of victory [φιλόνεικος] but an ally in seeking the truth (13c–14e). Socrates worries that in staking out one's position from the start and childishly inventing absurdities (e.g., one-many puzzles), eristic discussants will ultimately forfeit the discussion, with each side refusing to concede out of love of victory. Indeed, the eristic Philebus has already bowed out of the discussion, just as soon as he found himself unable to defend his Hedonist position. Even when spoken to, Philebus remains mostly mute throughout—a constant reminder of an eristic discussion gone wrong. While setting out to discuss whether pleasure is the good or whether knowing, understanding, remembering, right opinion, and true calculation is the good (11b–c), Socrates presents one-many puzzles and attempts to guide Protarchus toward a resolution (15d1–16a4).

Seeing himself implicated in this depiction, Protarchus jokingly replies with a threat in playful jest—suggesting that his gang will only release Socrates once the discussion reaches a satisfactory limit (16a5–b3, 19e, 23b). Meanwhile, Socrates makes fun of eristic discussants; if they could, these lads would dominate nonhuman animals in discourse! In his reply, Protarchus merely plays the part of the victory-loving eristic; in reality, he is desperate for Socrates to reveal the truth about the human good (19c–20a), even if such revelation requires that he, Protarchus, laughably hand over Philebus' thesis to Socrates (19a–b).

One major indication that the discussion is not genuinely eristic is that nobody (except eristic Philebus) staunchly stakes out a position. Protarchus reluctantly defends Philebus' Hedonist position (38a), and Socrates revises his own initial position, allowing pure pleasure to be an ingredient in the good life. Indeed, after acknowledging that Protarchus' combative threats are unserious, Socrates introduces a promising new thesis, belonging to the gods—that is, that a third thing (neither pleasure nor knowledge) is the human good (20b–c). Despite this noncombative spirit of cooperative inquiry, Philebus aggressively clings to his Hedonist position, accusing Socrates of extolling his own God (27e–28b)—that is, intelligence, knowledge, and reason. Protarchus interrupts Philebus' ad hominem attack, beseeching Socrates to be spokesperson, lest they invite a "false note" into the discussion (28b6–8). Socrates, in turn, defends a view attributed to earlier thinkers—namely, that reason is ruler of the cosmos (30d). Socrates emphasizes that this discourse is not idle but proves the important point that reason belongs to the "fourth kind," which is cause of that mixture that is the good human life (30d–e). Clearly, the cooperative pursuit of truth underlies the eristic theatrics.

If we laugh at these eristic caricatures, we laugh wisely. Eristic discussants like Philebus are the proper object of laughter—dialectically powerless, ignorant, and ignorant of their own ignorance. However, despite the fact that Philebus is genuinely laughable, Socrates and Protarchus do not laugh at him. In fact, Protarchus defends Philebus' position, and Socrates repeatedly invites Philebus back into the discussion. Thus, the purpose of this playful eristic satire is not to degrade eristic discussants like Philebus maliciously (in order to establish one's own superiority) but rather to service the philosophic pursuit of truth through avoiding an eristic breakdown of discourse. Such playful satire (and the laughter it elicits) is virtuous in that it helps people pursue wisdom and spiritual advancement.

As I suggested in section 3, benevolently laughing at people (here, eristic discussants) involves laughing at oneself (here, philosophic dialecticians). Including oneself in the sphere of the laughable communicates the benevolent, non-malicious intention of one's laughter. Even more important, playfully laughing at oneself fosters knowledge of oneself and one's position in the world, in stark contrast to malicious laughter, which is delusional. Whereas the pleasure of malicious laughter derives from a painful state of spiritual sickness, the pleasure of playfully laughing at oneself may be understood as a pure pleasure of learning about oneself and one's real position in the world. Such pleasures are salutary, not harmful.

What is so laughable about the position in which Socrates and Protarchus find themselves? Protarchus correctly interprets Socrates as requesting that they investigate the various kinds of pleasure and knowledge, both their number and their nature (19b, 20a). The pair sets out to do just this, lest, through discourse, pleasure and knowledge become unlimited, plunging them into boundless ignorance. However, Protarchus repeatedly flounders, entreating Socrates to take over the discussion or else clarify matters (e.g., 20a, 51b–c, 53e, 54b, 57a), at one point alluding to the laughable nature of his own dialectical ineffectiveness (19a). At the conclusion of Socrates' discussion of cosmic wisdom (which initially confounds Protarchus), Socrates remarks, "sometimes joking is a relief from seriousness" (30e6). The "joke" is Socrates' feigned ignorance of the obvious, namely, that reason rules the cosmos. Indeed, taking Socrates' apparent ignorance of the obvious seriously, Protarchus is initially incredulous (28e, 29c–d).

Why would Socrates want the discussants (or us) to laugh at him? At 23c11–d2 Socrates again represents himself as laughable, albeit in virtue of a real aspect of his position as a philosophic dialectician. Notably, Socrates does not succeed in limiting the discourse. In fact, the very structure of the *Philebus* underscores this failure. Strangely, the discussion begins in the middle (after a substantial conversation with Philebus) and ends in the middle. The dialogue's discourse is not limited, reflecting the unlimited nature of the domain of inquiry. This is not to suggest that knowledge is unlimited; rather, the domain of inquiry and human discourse are unlimited. The philosopher's attempt to limit the discourse with distinctions and enumerations is comically futile. Read in this light, the final lines of the *Philebus* are hilarious. Socrates asks Protarchus whether he will release him, and Protarchus replies, "There is still a little missing, Socrates. Surely you will not give up before we do. But I will remind you of what is left!" (67b9–11). While the mindless pleasure-seeker is stuck in the limitlessness of his pleasures, the philosopher Socrates is trapped in the limitlessness of his discourse, held hostage by his young interlocutor's boundless ignorance! In effect, the dialogue makes fun of the philosopher and in particular the futility of providing a limited discussion of an unlimited domain of inquiry, so as to save oneself (and others) from boundless human ignorance.

However, in acknowledging his own funny situation by laughing at himself and inviting others to do the same, Socrates does not become a genuinely ridiculous figure, for the ridiculous are ignorant about their own human ignorance. As Protarchus aptly exclaims, "while it is a great thing for the wise man to know everything, the second best is not to be mistaken about oneself, it seems to me" (19c1–3). The example of Socrates suggests an alternative to malicious laughter—and with it, an alternative to becoming genuinely laughable. When confronted with the pain of our own human deficiencies (especially regarding knowledge), instead of fantasizing about our supposed superiority, we should join our peers in laughing at ourselves and our shared human situation of dialectical weakness in the face of an unlimited domain of inquiry. Only then can we know what we do not know, acquiring a "second best" sort of wisdom (i.e., self-knowledge). And only then can the real, cooperative work of never-ending human inquiry get started.

Notes

1. See Keith-Spiegel and Morreall.
2. See De Vries, Shelly, Miller, Perks, and Austin.
3. For example, the *Gorgias* and Aristophanes' *Knights* and the *Protagoras* and Eupolis' *Flatterers*. See Brock, Craik, and Nightingale.
4. Syracusans Sophron and Xenarchus wrote "mimes" in prose, that is, farcical sketches of everyday occurrences.
5. While Plato does not explicitly use the language of "fittingness" to describe laughing at people, his discussions clearly capture this concept. Laughter is warranted or unwarranted depending on whether the laugher correctly conceptualizes her object.

6. Here Socrates suggests that the best response is to admire the enlightened soul and to pity the dimwitted one. Socrates suggests that, in some cases, it may even be unwise to laugh at the dimwitted soul.

7. While *Laws* 816e mandates that only slaves perform comic mimesis, the *Republic* allows citizens to perform unserious or satirical comic mimesis. See Ferrari (118–19) for the argument that un-serious mimesis is satirical mimesis.

8. Aristotle classes verbal abuse as a form of violence (*Nicomachean Ethics* 1131a9; *Politics* 1262a27).

9. See Dillon (345–55).

10. In a similar vein, the *Symposium* portrays Diotima playfully laughing at the youthful Socrates, whom she teaches about love (202b–d). Performing Socratic elenchus on Socrates, Diotima gently (and with a laugh) steers Socrates to see the contradiction in his theory of love. This gentle learning moment is foil to the dialogue's depiction of pedagogical pederasty as disempowering and spiritually destructive.

11. Following Hackforth, Frede, Taylor, and Austin, I translate "φθόνος" as malice. Those who translate "φθόνος" as "envy" (Tuozzo, Miller, and Bury) face the following problem, noted by Russell: the characters of Attic comedy are simply not of the sort we would envy (189n47). Russell goes on to explain that "φθόνος" means "envy" in Aristotle, because Aristotle is focused on the phenomenon of being pained by good things belonging to neighbors (n49). In contrast, Plato is focused on the phenomenon of being pleased by bad things belonging to neighbors. Both phenomena share the same psychic source, i.e., a desire that our neighbors fare poorly, not well.

12. This leads some to speculate that, for Plato, all emotions involve mixed pleasures (Frede and Hackforth). Plato chooses to focus on the emotion of malicious laughter, because laughter and comedy are a dramatic theme in the dialogue.

13. Pleasure may indicate the pleasure-experience (as in, "the pleasure of eating") or the pleasure-object (as in, "the pleasure of food"). So, when I say "the pleasure of malice," I am referring to the pleasure-experience (i.e., the experience of taking pleasure in BBN) rather than the pleasure-object (i.e., BBN and malicious laughter). See Harte (113–30).

14. Indeed, humor theorists attribute a "superiority theory" of laughter to Plato—for example, Perks (126), Shelly (352), Keith-Spiegel (6–7), and Morreall (4–5). Plato does not have a superiority theory of laughter so much as a sense that bad, malicious laughter involves feelings of superiority.

15. And possibly all pleasures, though this is a matter of debate. When, at 36e, Socrates starts to articulate what it means to say a pleasure is true or false, he goes on to cite only examples of psychic pleasures (no bodily pleasures). See Fletcher "Divine Method" (179–208) and "Deceptive Pleasures" (379–410).

16. See Evans for a good summary of the literature. Socrates does say, at 40b2–5, that the pictures in the soul are "true" in the case of good people, because

they are dear to the gods. But even this comment does not definitively imply that non-hedonic truth/falsity is at issue here. The gods could just as easily give good people the right values as they could give them material resources. This ambiguity between hedonic and non-hedonic falsity is intended; both forms of falsity are implied, and we need not suppose that only one kind of truth/falsity is implicated here.

Works Cited

Austin, Emily. "Fools and Malicious Pleasure in Plato's *Philebus*." *History of Philosophy Quarterly*, vol. 29, no. 2, 2012, pp. 125–39.

Brock, Roger. "Plato and Comedy." *'Owls to Athens': Essays on Classical Subjects for Sir Kenneth Dover*, vol. 5, edited by Elizabeth M. Craik, Clarendon, 1990, pp. 39–50.

Bury, R. G. *The Philebus of Plato*. Cambridge UP, 1987.

De Vries, G. J. "Laughter in Plato's Writings." *Mnemosyne*, vol. 38, no. 3, 1985, pp. 378–81.

Dillon, Matthew. "Tragic Laughter." *The Classical World*, vol. 84, no. 5, 1991, pp. 345–55.

Evans, Matthew. "Plato on the Possibility of Hedonic Mistakes." *Oxford Studies in Ancient Philosophy XXXV*, 2008, pp. 89–124.

Ferrari, G. R. F. "Plato and Poetry." *The Cambridge History of Literary Criticism* 1, 1989, pp. 92–148.

Fletcher, Emily. "The Divine Method and the Disunity of Pleasure in the *Philebus*." *Journal of the History of Philosophy*, vol. 55, no. 2, 2017, pp. 179–208.

———. "Plato on Incorrect and Deceptive Pleasures." *Archiv für Geschichte der Philosophie*, vol. 100, no. 4, 2018, pp. 379–410.

Hackforth, Reginald. *Plato's Examination of Pleasure: A Translation of the* Philebus, with Introduction and Commentary. Cambridge UP, 1945.

Harte, Verity. "The *Philebus* on Pleasure: The Good, the Bad and the False." *Proceedings of the Aristotelian Society* (New Series), vol. 104, no. 1, 2004, pp. 113–30.

Homer. *The Iliad*. Translated by Barry Powell, Oxford UP, 2014.

Keith-Spiegel, Patricia. "Early Conceptions of Humor: Varieties and Issues." *The Psychology of Humor: Theoretical Perspectives and Empirical Issues*, edited by J. H. Goldstein and P. E. McGhee, Academic Press, 1972, pp. 4–39.

Miller, Mitchell. "The Pleasures of Comic and Socratic Inquiry: Aporetic Reflections on *Philebus* 48a–50b." *Arethusa*, vol. 41, no. 2, 2008, pp. 263–89.

Morreall, John. *Taking Laughter Seriously*. SUNY Press, 1983.

Nightingale, Andrea W. *Genres in Dialogue: Plato and the Construct of Philosophy*. Cambridge UP, 1995.

Perks, Lisa G. "The Ancient Roots of Humor Theory." *Humor*, vol. 25, no. 2, 2012, pp. 119–32.
Plato. *Philebus*. Translated by Dorothea Frede, Hackett, 1993.
———. *Philebus*. Translated by R. Hackforth, Cambridge UP, 1972.
———. Plato *Philebus* and *Epinomis*. Translation and Introduction by A. E. Taylor, edited by Raymond Klibansky, with co-operation of Guido Calogero and A. C. Lloyd. Thomas Nelson and Sons, 1956.
Russell, Daniel C. *Plato on Pleasure and the Good Life*. Oxford UP, 2005.
Shelly, Cameron. "Plato on the Psychology of Humor" *Humor*, vol. 16 no. 4, 2003, pp. 351–67.
Tuozzo, Thomas M. "The General Account of Pleasure in Plato's *Philebus*." *Journal of the History of Philosophy*, vol. 34, no. 4, 1996, pp. 495–513.

Plato's Dialogues

Educating the Mind for 2400 Years

MARTHA C. BECK

Introduction: Reading Plato's Dialogues in Context

There are a number of contexts within which to understand our experiences with Plato's dialogues. We know that somehow Plato's dialogues are one of Western civilization's "foundational" texts. We know Greek civilization and culture has been considered the bedrock of a cultural tradition that, until recently, has been the torchbearer in the drive toward creating societies that provide more and more citizens with opportunities to flourish and to participate in social and political life. If true, what is it about Plato that should enable us today to preserve the faltering democracies around the world?

First, Plato's own experience. Plato was born in Athens when, as far as they knew, Athens had the most sophisticated culture anywhere. The Greeks defeated the Persians twenty years earlier. When Plato was a toddler, the Peloponnesian War began; it ended when he was thirty-two. He witnessed the decline and then the total collapse of his "great" democracy. Worst of all, his beloved mentor, Socrates, was condemned to death by the democrats for "corrupting the youth" and "not believing in the city's gods" (*Apology* 23c–d). Socrates performed his duty as a citizen in a free society. He asked powerful people to explain what they knew that justified the power they were given by the public. The sons of the privileged class followed Socrates and saw that the leaders they had trusted were incompetent or corrupt, and they lost respect for them. Socrates, however, did not allow the youth just to rebel. Instead, he asked them to seek wisdom and justice, so that when they took over they would use their power justly. After deciding that all the political leaders were corrupt, Plato started a school, the Academy. He brought together the best and brightest from everywhere, the future leaders, trying to motivate them to seek wisdom rather than pleasure, wealth, power, or glory. Even today, students who read Plato are among the privileged, those with the natural capacity, motivation, and opportunity to go to a college that offers liberal-arts classes, including philosophy.

Second, Plato's dialogues describe the characters and setting from his own historical experience but then tells a story that describes a pattern that he knew would occur over and over again. Plato followed the same pedagogical technique as the other Greek poets. He created a story, a myth, about how his city fell, showing the many, many ways that leaders in every sector of society used the "freedom" they had to get money, power, and glory. Plato is not accusing any one person or social sector of causing the downfall of Athens. Instead, he shows us that there were enough Athenians in leadership positions who abused their power enough for a long enough time to eventually lead to the collapse of social order and the election of a dictator, Critias. None of them thought Athens could ever revert to authoritarianism, but it did. Plato is showing future leaders what they might be tempted to do but must avoid if they want their societies to be stable for their children and grandchildren. Like Homer and the tragedians, and following many of the patterns in tragedy described by Aristotle in the *Poetics,* Plato's dialogues are written to motivate us to identify with the characters and fear for our own capacity to make similar mistakes. We need to flush from our minds the irrational emotions and opinions that motivated the characters to make such serious mistakes. We can then use our minds to create laws, institutions, and a quality of life that will preserve individual and collective flourishing over time.

Third, Plato's legacy for future leaders and citizens. Somehow, for whatever reason, enough people with enough privilege have been able to preserve Plato's work and pass it down to the next generation. Each generation, each individual, tells a different story about Plato and Plato's dialogues. Each generation tends to project its own customs and intellectual training onto the texts. Sometimes this is done unintentionally. When readers do not know the cultural tradition in which Plato grew up, they will not recognize the way he has adapted the tradition he grew up in to suit his own context. Most Greek poetry focuses on the way monarchs and aristocrats abuse the power they inherited. Plato had to educate the citizens of Athens, a society with a constitutional government, where citizens took turns ruling and being ruled. Plato's readers have to match their own political situations to Plato's lessons. Good leaders will use the power they have to help citizens flourish, not for personal gain. Citizens in any form of government have to stay informed about public affairs and recognize both abuses of power and statecraft among their leaders.

Fourth, Plato's legacy for future educators. Among the intellectual elite, sometimes Plato's work is deliberately forced to fit the trendy intellectual categories of an era in order to somehow legitimize it, assuming Plato did not know what more recent scholars know about the natural world, human nature, or human culture. Many stories in Greek poetry show that knowledge without wisdom gives smart people the power to do good or evil. The god of reason, Apollo, is smart but not wise. Oedipus was smart—he solved the riddle of the Sphinx—but not wise; he did not know himself. The sophists in Plato's dialogues were smart and developed sophisticated techniques for teaching students to speak persuasively, but their reasoning powers were dedicated to helping themselves and their students gain power, fame, pleasure, and wealth. Today, the worlds most gifted and powerful STEM leaders, such as Mark Zuckerberg, Bill Gates, and Charles Koch, are using their knowledge to promote opposite goals. Gates wants to end fossil fuel consumption while the Charles Koch political machine promotes fossil fuels, ignoring all the scientific knowledge about the effect of carbon in life on earth. Zuckerberg claims to save the world by expanding freedom of speech but with no concern for whether that speech is motivated to manipulate or educate Facebook users. We should know that more STEM will not save us. We still need mythological education because it educates our emotions. It shows why our intellectual capacities need to be guided by a strong moral character. Readers of Plato, including my students from around the world, have identified analogies between Plato's stories and their own lives for 2400 years.

Fifth, Plato's legacy as one system of education that educates the power of the mind, apart from the particular historical circumstances. Plato argues that the power of the human mind (*nous*) is a natural capacity of the human soul (518c–519a). Socrates describes when he first heard about Anaxagoras, who supposedly claimed that Mind is the ultimate force behind the universe as we experience it. Before reading Anaxagoras, Socrates speculates that if Anaxagoras' view is correct, then, "the directing

Mind would direct everything and arrange each thing in the way that was best . . ." (97d). If this is so, then in order to fulfill our natural purpose, we must use our own minds to always ask what is best in any given situation, "[therefore] it befitted a man to investigate only, about this and other things, what is best" (97d). When asked why he is about to die, Socrates makes clear that every aspect of his life has been driven by his mind, his idea of the best choice in a given situation: "After the Athenians decided it was better to condemn me, for this reason it seemed best to me to sit here and more right to remain and to endure whatever penalty they ordered. . . . [In everything I do] I act with my mind" (98d–99a). The natural object of the mind is the Idea of the Good, both the Divine force that holds everything in place in the best ways possible, and the human mind's capacity to choose the best option possible in any given situation.

Plato's dialogues are written to activate the power of our minds. They *are* the dialectical education we are seeking. Socrates represents how people think and act when their minds are the cause of every aspect of their lives. As we read what Socrates says and how his interlocutors reply, we are supposed to ask, "Why is that the best thing to say or do in this situation? Why would this be what the mind perceives as best?" Although I have not studied every dialogue carefully, from the eight or so I have examined, there are a number of patterns that keep repeating themselves. These are the types of situations, characters, arguments, and choices that people living in free and open societies often experience. These are also situations where the most serious questions are addressed and decisions made. These are the choices that lead toward more authoritarianism or toward more citizen self-governance. If we can learn to recognize when our lives are caught up in one of these types of situation, we can recognize what mistakes people have made in the past, avoid those mistakes, look at what Socrates did, and try to adapt that type of response to our own situation. We can save the very freedom that enables us to read Plato's dialogues. No authoritarian societies would allow Plato to be read. The dialogues as a whole are trying to link all the other intellectual powers of soul to the mind, so that they are turned in the right direction and are able to determine what is, in fact, best, in a given situation.

Patterns in Plato's Dialogues

The *Republic* explains explicitly many of the patterns that occur in the other dialogues. In Book I, Socrates asks Cephalus about the "road of life (328d–e)."

Cephalus talks about sex and drinking. He earned his money from selling military equipment, and because he is afraid of death, he is also concerned about passing on his fortune to his son. So, pleasure, wealth, power, and the fear of death are his view of "the road of life." At the beginning of Book II (357b–368c), Glaucon and Adeimantus describe their elders as telling them that human beings are by nature irrational and seek irrational goals. They want Socrates to convince them that they should pursue wisdom and justice both for their own sake and for what they contribute to the human community—as the natural and necessary way for human beings to flourish. Throughout the dialogues, Socrates is on the "high road" while the interlocutors are on the "low road." To put it another way, the interlocutors are in the "Cave" of opinions about life, while Socrates has escaped from the Cave, seen the light, has now returned, and is trying to turn the souls of his interlocutors around from the darkness to the light.

The dialogues are carefully organized. They begin with Socrates asking his interlocutors their views on the issue at hand. The interlocutors have false opinions based on the assumption that human beings are by nature irrational. About one-third of the way through, they come to an impasse (*aporia*). Socrates says they must start all over, from a different foundation (*arche*), this time the love of wisdom as the natural goal of human life. They begin the path outside of the cave. About two-thirds of the way through is the climax. Socrates asks the most critical question. The interlocutor rejects the path out of the cave. The dialogue returns to the cave, and Socrates reverts to irrational reasons for the interlocutors to pursue justice or wisdom, such as fear of punishment after death. Readers, however, can learn what the interlocutors failed to learn. They can recognize that this dialogue focuses on one aspect of the overall corruption that eventually led to the fall of Athenian democracy and that will lead to the decline of any free and open society.

Many of the dialogues are named after a character who makes a mistake in judgment about a serious question. Many of the characters themselves come to a bad end because of this mistake. Their ideas are connected to a way of life. The problem with their opinion becomes the problem that causes them to make the wrong choice. Since they are members of the powerful elite, their personal mistakes also contribute to Athens' decline and fall. Plato is showing us that our ideas mold our characters; our characters determine our choices, and our choices lead us and the societies in which we live to happiness or unhappiness. There is no gap between theory and practice. Opinions (*logoi*) are incarnated into a way of life (*ergon*).

The dialogues are often named after a historical person, but Plato has made the transition from the particular details about their lives to telling a story (*mythos*) that portrays them as types of people in types of situations making types of mistakes that lead to a bad end. Because the stories represent patterns, readers can identify with the pattern, think of their own examples of similar types of people making similar types of mistakes, and learn the lessons the dialogue is trying to teach. Many of the dialogues have a character who is better than most, Socrates, a character who is worse than most, often but not always a sophist, and people who are intermediates. Sometimes the intermediates are the youth, who have not yet decided for what they want to live. Socrates is fighting against another interlocutor for the souls of the future leaders, which will determine the future of the society. Sometimes other Athenians are listening who also have to make this choice. Readers are also the intermediates who have to decide how to live.

The dialogues as a whole include many types of intellectual capacities: arguments, definitions, knowledge of different objects, opinions, skills (*techne*), calculation of means to one's ends, persuasive speaking, logical reasoning, etc. On the Divided Line, the dialogues activate all of the powers of soul in the four parts of the Line: imagination (*eikasia*), trust (*pistis*), dianoia (many types of intellectual activity), and the highest level is mind (*noesis*). Socrates' nemesis, often a sophist, is driven by an idea of the good based on imagination, on the love of pleasure, wealth, power or glory, things based on the physical world, and tangible goals. Socrates' conversation is driven by his mind.

Both the sophists and Socrates are engaged in the power of rhetoric. In the *Phaedrus*, Socrates distinguishes between the sophists, who use rhetorical speech to manipulate the wealthy elite into paying them to educate their sons, and the true rhetorician, who uses speech to lead the people she is talking to toward the love of wisdom. The dialectical rhetorician, Plato writes:

> will classify the kinds of speech and of soul there are . . . He will then coordinate each kind of soul with the kind of speech appropriate to it, [and] . . . on meeting someone he will be able to discern what he is like and make clear to himself that the person actually standing in front of him is of just this particular sort of character he had learned about in school—so that he must now apply speeches of such-and-such a kind in

this particular way in order to secure conviction about such-and-such an issue. (271b–272a)

The goal of this "laborious effort" is to be able "to speak and act in a way that pleases the gods as much as possible" (273e). This is what Socrates does throughout the dialogues.

It should be no surprise if Socrates says things that are contradictory if taken out of context. If understood within the context, however, readers must ask themselves why Socrates says what he does to that person at that time and why that is Plato's idea of the best possible way to try to lead that interlocutor at that time toward a love of wisdom, justice, and truth. What Socrates does might appear to be no different from a sophist. He uses many of the same techniques. Earlier in the *Phaedrus*, he talks on both sides of a question, as a sophist does. In his first speech, he claims Eros is by nature irrational. Then he purges himself of that false opinion and delivers his long speech that celebrates Eros as divine. At the end of that speech, he says he has delivered "the best and most beautiful palinode we could, . . . especially in light of the rather poetical choice of words Phaedrus made me use" (257a). In the last section, he describes the dialectical rhetorician as one who does what Socrates has just been doing.

This way of reading Plato is important at this moment in human history because a major cause of the political polarization around the world is the abuse of rhetoric. Our intellectual powers are activated through speech. Sophistic speech feeds irrational emotions and behavior. Socrates' speech activates the mind, making it possible to think clearly about public affairs. Sophistic speech polarizes us. Socratic speech overcomes polarization by talking to people one by one, asking them to say exactly what they think. Readers should ask themselves the same questions and be honest about what they think. Although Socrates uses simple language that anyone listening can understand, he is focused more on talking to members of the powerful elite because they will determine the future of the society. The emergence of a class of paid sophists who taught future leaders how to appeal to emotions and all sorts of manipulative techniques was a major factor in what took Athens down. Plato is showing his students that they have the power to educate or manipulate the voters in the Assembly and on juries. If they abuse this power, their cities will become less stable, and authoritarian leaders will gain power.

When I teach Plato's dialogues, I ask students to come with their own examples of the types of characters and arguments in the dialogues and explain why they think they are analogous. Then they explain why this kind of abuse of freedom is also leading to the decline of their societies. I have taught Plato this way to students from around the world and in colleges in Prague, Beijing, Bangladesh, and Indonesia. The students understand the problems and can recognize examples in their own countries. Today's students do not like polarization and do not want to lead a polarized nation in twenty years. I tell them that as college students it is up to them to stop the polarization and start talking to one another. Students should realize that their cultural situations, including the current polarization, are not "by nature" but are the result of human choices. Some of those choices were made long ago, some in the recent past, and some are being made right now. College students are old enough to be responsible for how they live and are just as accountable as their elders for the polarization in their countries. When they understand their responsibility to create a better world for their children and the consequences if they do not, they become more motivated to do what they can.

I tell students what Socrates told Glaucon and Adeimantus at the end of the *Republic*. In Book II, Glaucon and Adeimantus asked Socrates to convince them to love justice for its own sake. Socrates tries, but in Book VI Socrates speaks of how the most promising young people are corrupted by their elders to seek irrational goals. He asks Glaucon if there is any possibility that any of these young men would want to practice philosophy. Glaucon replies that there is no way at all (494c–495a). In Book VII, when Socrates is discussing dialectical training and how difficult it is, he tells Glaucon that he will not be able to understand what Socrates is talking about. He is telling Glaucon that Glaucon must subject himself to years of dialectical education before he can lead. Glaucon rejects Socrates' offer. In Books VIII and IX, Socrates discusses the types of irrational souls: the timocrat (lover of honor), the oligarch (lover of wealth), democrat (lover of the freedom to live as he pleases), and tyrant (love of absolute power). In Book X, Socrates appeals to the irrational fear of punishment after death to motivate Glaucon. He says, "each of us must neglect all other subjects and be most concerned to seek out and learn those that will enable him to distinguish the good life from the bad and always to make the best choice possible in every situation. . . . This is the way that a human being becomes happiest" (618b–619a).

This is not idealism. This is realism. If a city is to avoid falling into authoritarianism, the future leaders and as many citizens as possible need to be conscientious about their choices. It is unrealistic to think citizens and students, especially leaders and future leaders, do not need to love wisdom in order to prevent authoritarianism. That is what the Athenians thought. We know what happened to them.

Plato's *Ion:* Showing How the Patterns Apply to One Dialogue

Plato's *Ion* focuses on one aspect of the decline of Athenian culture. Ion is paid to recite Homer, whose works were the most respected texts for teaching people how to understand human life and how we ought to live. The dialogue shows how these "sacred" texts are being used by irrational members of the elite to achieve their irrational goals. Instead of reading Homer as trying to purge citizens of their irrational desires, by showing how irrational behavior leads to destruction, Homer is being read as promoting the irrational behavior it so vividly describes.

In *Republic II,* Glaucon and Adeimantus say that their elders claim that Homer celebrates and nurtures irrational emotions. There are many reasons to think that Plato does not think this is the message of Homer. The Athenians have forgotten that their poetic tradition uses purgation to educate the soul and motivate people to seek wisdom and justice. Greek mythology, Hesiod, tragedy, and Plato's dialogues describe people giving in to irrational passions and the great harm this does to everyone involved. The stories show people why they should reject irrational behavior and replace it with a passion for wisdom and justice. This not what the Athenians are learning from Homer or the other Greek poets. There are many things Socrates says to motivate readers to reject this literal reading of Homer. Citing two examples relevant to this essay, in the middle section of the *Republic,* Socrates says that he thought Homer had "the divine image in mind" when he wrote his work. In the *Ion,* Socrates says that Homer's work is "the best and most divine" (530c1).

Other dialogues also have characters who are "specialists" in Hesiod, Homer, and other texts that are trying to educate the soul in how to live. These characters misquote the texts for their own personal gain. Socrates also misquotes these texts, but my claim is that he is doing so to educate the souls of his interlocutors. When looked at in context, Socrates' misquotes have an important pedagogical motive. The *Ion* contains many examples. The dialogue begins right after Ion has won first prize for his recitation of Homer in front of a crowd at Epidaurus. The dialogue is divided into three parts. Each part reveals one of Ion's corrupt motives. The first part focuses on Ion's drive for fame, the second reveals his desire for wealth, and the third his desire for power. Ion clearly is a man living in the cave. The fact that he has just earned first prize in a contest among rhapsodes indicates that the Athenian audiences and judges honor recitations of Homer that embellish the words and trigger irrational emotions. Given that the festival is in Epidaurus, a center for healing the body and soul, Ion's victory indicates that the souls of the Athenians are unhealthy, although they do not think so.

In each section, Socrates is acting as the antithesis of Ion. In the first section, when Ion takes such pride in embellishing Homer, Socrates says of himself, "I say nothing but the truth, as you'd expect from an ordinary man" (532e). The first section also focuses on the most important question, whether the rhapsode has to have thought long and hard about what the poet intended to teach, "the rhapsodist must become an interpreter of the poet's thought to those who listen, and to do this well is quite impossible unless one knows just what the poet is saying" (530b). Socrates points out that the other poets also talk about the same themes, including "the relations of men good and bad, [and] . . . the relations of the gods to one another and to men" (531c). If Ion is focused on the substance of the artwork, he will be able to recite every poet who writes on these topics. Ion, however, loves Homer and only Homer. Socrates drives Ion into perplexity, "Then what can be the reason, Socrates, for my behavior?" (532c). Instead of admitting he does not know or that he is a failure, Ion says, "of this thing I am conscious, that I excel all men in speaking about Homer, . . . and that everybody else avers I do it well. . . . [S]ee what that means" (533c). This is the end of the first one-third of the dialogue.

In the next section, Socrates gives the kind of embellished, emotional speech that he said earlier he does not do. He advocates an anti-rational view of poetic inspiration as "a power divine. . . . [A] poet is a light and winged thing, and holy and never able to compose until he has become inspired, and is beside himself, and reason is no longer in him" (534a–b). There are many reasons to reject this as Socrates' final view. In the *Phaedrus*, Socrates discusses many types of poetic inspiration. The philosophical muse is the highest while other types of imitative poetry are at the sixth level. Most importantly, in the context of the *Ion*, after Socrates delivers this speech, Ion says, "Socrates, your words in some way touch my very soul" (535a). Clearly, Socrates has chosen his speech based on what he thinks will appeal to this interlocutor. Further, after Ion is moved, he tells Socrates what he really thinks, saying, "If I set them [audiences] weeping, I myself shall laugh when I get my money, but if they laugh, it is I who have to weep at losing it" (535e). Socrates then concludes that it is "divine possession" that moves Ion. Ion rejects this because he thinks he has a skill or a kind of knowledge (536d). If my way of reading Plato is correct, the second section is showing us exactly why we cannot detach poetic inspiration from reason. Artists or art critics have to explain why someone's inspiration is motivated by the love of wisdom and justice or corrupted by greed or the desire for fame and why. They have to explain the important lessons the poet is trying to teach us.

In the third section, Ion wants Socrates to tell him exactly what kind of knowledge or skill he has. When Ion claims to speak well on "every point" in Homer (536e), Socrates takes quotes from Homer literally, as trying to teach listeners a specific skill. Earlier, Socrates said the exact opposite, that the rhapsode has to "learn his thought, not just his verses . . . [N]o one would ever get to be a good rhapsode if he did not understand what is meant by the poet" (530c). Further, in the first section, Socrates says that the content of the poets is about good and evil, justice and injustice. Now, in the third section, Socrates misquotes and distorts Homer as if Homer were trying to teach audiences about a kind of knowledge or skill. This line of reasoning leads Ion to describe, again, his real motivations.

First, he claims that he teaches what it is "suitable" for a man, woman, slave, and other individuals to say. He thinks that the ultimate goal of having this skill is to be given positions of power, such as being appointed a general. Ion does not think a general needs to study human nature, justice and injustice in order to prevent war or prevent excesses in war. This, among other lessons, is what Socrates earlier implies that Homer is really trying to teach in the *Iliad*. Ion does not think a general needs to have the appropriate knowledge and skills so his troops can achieve their goals. All that is necessary and sufficient for being a good general is to generate emotion, so the troops will be willing to face danger. With Ion as the most popular Homeric rhapsode, it should be no surprise that the Athenians began to value power and conquest over justice and wisdom. Also, the kind of dialectical speech Socrates engages in throughout the dialogues, including the *Ion*, is what got him into trouble. It was not suitable for anyone to question authority figures and expose their ignorance and arrogance, as Socrates is doing throughout the dialogues. Socrates got killed for not saying what is "suitable." The goal of learning how to say what is suitable is power. Socrates' goal is truth. In a corrupt society, the love of wisdom and truth is threatening and punished.

Certainly, I realize that this description of the *Ion* is incomplete and general, but it shows how the dialogue follows patterns that occur in every dialogue I have studied carefully. Ion is on the low road, the world of the cave, which assumes people by nature are irrational and seek pleasure, wealth, power, and glory. Socrates is on the high road and tries to turn Ion around. All of Socrates' speech is driven by his mind, his idea of the good, and what he should say to Ion to try to turn him around. All of Ion's speech is driven by his imagination. He holds a mirror to the world, where it appears that everyone pursues irrational goals. He develops the skill of teaching people how to read Homer in ways that will justify and promote their irrational goals. The dialogue takes place at a specific location, the world of trust (*pistis*) and the characters employ various kinds of reasoning (*dianoia*). The dialogue is named after a character who makes a mistake in judgment about what a rhapsode is and should be doing to preserve a free and open society. Both Ion and Socrates are using rhetoric, speech designed to persuade listeners. Ion has the skill of stimulating irrational human emotions. Socrates uses speech to try to make Ion change.

Even if Socrates fails in relation to Ion, readers can learn what Ion did not seem to learn. Profound cultural texts that teach lessons on how to live should never be used to promote the glory, wealth, or political ambitions of those who quote from them. Citizens should be able to identify this kind of corruption and call it out, even if they lose status, money, or power for doing so. If citizens do not engage in this kind of critical self-examination and examination of others, if they do not teach each other to think critically, their free and open societies will become less stable and more authoritarian.

Teaching Plato Today

Apart from their major fields of study, college students around the world are old enough to be able to think critically. They need to examine everything they learned through habit, imitation, and custom and move beyond uncritical loyalty to their religion, their nation, their family, or any kind of group identification. After examining what they have been taught, they must make the transition from living by habit to living by the power of their minds. This transition can be initiated by any combination of experiences during college. Friends, coaches, professors, and mentors of all sorts will provide different models for how to live or what to avoid, forcing them to think for themselves.

One goal of this essay is to explain what I think today's college students can gain from reading and reflecting on Plato's dialogues. College students, especially those who have read Plato, should take the lead in modeling an examined life, knowing how quickly the freedom they enjoy can be lost. They should leave college knowing they know little about the serious questions in life, but they need to keep asking what is best, most just, and wisest in a situation. Circumstances change, so that what works at one time will not work at another time. They have to know they will have to change their minds in order to preserve the goal: maximizing human flourishing. Everything that makes life worth living is at stake: free scientific inquiry, free artistic expression, freedom to say what you think publicly and be held accountable by others so that citizens can collectively become wiser, freedom to elect their leaders, sit on juries and engage in public life, freedom to belong to the communities they like, based on religious or sectarian beliefs or personal interests and hobbies. Living in and inheriting a society that provides us the freedom to develop ourselves as human beings is the greatest gift we can nurture in each other and pass on to the next generation.

Works Cited

Alderman, Harold. "Dialectic as Philosophic Care." *Man and World,* vol. 6, May, 1973, pp. 206–19.
Baltzly, Dick. "Plato and the New Rhapsody." *Ancient Philosophy*, vol. 12, no. 1, Spring, 1992, pp. 29–52.
Bloom, Alan. "An Interpretation of Plato's *Ion*." *Interpretation,* 1970, pp. 43–62.
Carothers, Thomas, and Andrew O'Donohue, editors. *Democracies Divided: The Global Challenge of Political Polarization.* Brookings Institution, 2019.
Dorter, Kenneth. "The *Ion*: Plato's Characterization of Art." *Journal of Aesthetics and Art Criticism*, vol. 32, fall 1973, pp. 65–78.
Homer. *The Iliad.* Translated by E. V. Rieu. Penguin Classics, 1957.
Morris, T. F. "Plato's *Ion* on What Poetry is About." *Ancient Philosophy*, vol. 1, no. 2, fall, 1993, pp. 265–72.
Pappas, Nickolas. "*Ion*: The Problem of the Author." *Philosophy*, vol. 64, July, 1989, pp. 381–89.

Partee, Morriss Henry. "Inspiration in the Aesthetics of Plato." *Journal of Aesthetics and Art Criticism*, vol. 30, fall, 1971, pp. 87–95.

Plato. *Ion*. Translated by Cooper Lane. *The Collected Dialogues of Plato*, edited by Edith Hamilton and Huntington Cairns, Princeton UP, 1961, pp. 215–28.

———. *Letter VII*. Translated by Glenn R. Morrow. *Plato: Complete Works*, edited by John M. Cooper, Hackett, 1997, pp. 1646–67.

———. *Phaedrus*. Translated by Alexander Nehamas and Paul Woodruff. *Plato: Complete Works*, edited by John M. Cooper, Hackett, 1997, pp. 506–56.

———. *Republic*. Translated by G. M. A. Grube and revised by C. D. C. Reeve. *Plato: Complete Works*, edited by John M. Cooper and D. S. Hutchinson, Hackett, 1997, pp. 1177–1307.

Ranta, Jerrald. "The Drama of Plato's *Ion*." *Journal of Aesthetics and Art Criticism*, vol. 26, Winter, 1967, pp. 219–29.

Different Ways of Being Different, Different Ways Not to Be

Parmenides and the Critical Relativism of Alain Locke

Rose M. Cherubin

It is an honor and a privilege to be asked to contribute to a celebration of the work, and the person, of Tony Preus. Tony has for decades been the major moving and organizing force behind The Society for Ancient Greek Philosophy. That Society gave me and many others our start in presenting research, and a truly supportive community of scholars with whom we could share ideas. Under Tony's leadership, the Society's meetings have been an environment that has fostered and championed respectful inquiry and dialogue across diverse schools of thought and philosophical traditions. He supported and organized meetings that brought together the SAGP with groups focused on Islamic philosophy and science, African philosophy, and several Asian philosophical traditions, for a wonderful opportunity at cross-pollination. Tony Preus himself has been a model of this open-minded and open-hearted search for understanding; at many sessions he offered critical questions in response to the presentations, and the criticism was always deeply informed (his breadth of learning and insight are astounding), highly respectful, and brilliantly constructive. I offer this essay, based on a talk I gave at the SAGP meeting in 2017, in the hope that it will reflect at least some of my debt and the immense gratitude that Tony deserves.

Introduction: Parmenides' Opinions of Mortals

On one hand, the opinions of mortals frame Parmenides' poem. The poem calls upon us to acknowledge motion, multiplicity, light and night, male and female, mortal and immortal.[1] Then the part of the poem that seems to come latest (of what we have) describes what the goddess says are the opinions of mortals. In between, the opinions of mortals also furnish the terms of the goddess' speech about what-is and roads of inquiry, for this also invokes motion and multiplicity.

On another hand, the goddess says that mortals' opinions are untrustworthy, at odds with what inquiry requires, and at odds with themselves.

On another hand, she says that she is offering an account of mortals' opinions so that no mortals' opinions will overtake/outstrip her listener. This may mean, and many commentators—including Curd, Graham, Rossetti, and Palmer—understand this to mean that Parmenides intended the account of the opinions of mortals to be on some level accurate or useful in understanding the world.

On another hand, there is no evidence that any mortals with whom Parmenides could have been acquainted held the opinions the goddess attributes to mortals.

On yet another hand, there is something about what the goddess identifies as mortals' opinions that does reflect some fundamental structural features of opinions that actual mortals did (and do) hold.

On yet another hand, if there are acknowledgments of multiplicity and motion, how if at all does Zeno fit into this picture?

There is something about Parmenides' goddess's account of the opinions of mortals that has not, to my knowledge, seen much study, and that I think can shed some needed light and darkness on these difficulties. That is, I think that there may be a way to explain how the goddess's presentation of what she says are the opinions of mortals at B8.51–61 and B9:

- reflects actual mortals' opinions in fundamental respects;
- affords some level of predictive and descriptive success;
- has advantages over some common ways in which mortals understand their opinions—advantages with respect to the treatment of not-being, change, and difference; and
- is still deceptive, untrustworthy, and not reliably oriented toward *alētheia*—in ways to which Zeno points.

Problems of Change, Difference, and Multiplicity as Outlined in B8

Parmenides' goddess argues that on the road of inquiry she recommends, signs indicate that what-is is (i.e., one is to say and conceive that what-is is) ungenerated, unperishing, whole, all of one kind, unmoving, unended (or complete), not admitting of "was" or "will be," one, and continuous (B8.1–6). She associates multiplicity, difference, and change with not-being, and change in particular with coming-to-be and perishing. On the grounds that motion, change, difference, and multiplicity require that what-is *not be*, and/or that what-is-not *be*, the goddess holds they have no place—they contravene what the signs indicate—on the road of inquiry that she recommends.

I suggest that the Light-Night conceptual scheme that the goddess presents in B8.53–61 and B9 provides a way to represent mortals' opinions that at the surface level avoids invoking not-being when referring to change, multiplicity, and difference.

The Light-Night Scheme

Scope and Contours of the Light-Night Conceptual Scheme

In the goddess's detailing of the opinions of mortals, Light (*phaos*, B9.1) is fiery, bright, mild, and everything Night is not; Night (*nux*, B9.1) is dense (*pukinos*), dark, weighty, and everything Light is not (thus presumably cold, for example).[2] Curd (107ff.) characterizes Light and Night as enantiomorphic opposites, such that Light is what Night is not, Night is what Light is not, what is not Night is Light, and what is not Light is Night. This is accurate as far as it goes; but it seems to me not to be the whole story. Clearly, Parmenides has presented an exclusive opposition, but Night is not *simply* lack of Light or vice versa.[3] Each has its proper characteristics. Neither is obviously prior to the other, and both are required for perception and perceptible natural phenomena. Moreover, any cosmic completion or perfection (B19) seems to involve an arrangement of both Light and Night. Both of these points merit attention.

In the Light-Night conceptual scheme, objects will be differentiated by their respective concentrations and configurations of bits or regions of Light and Night. There are some rings of unmixed fire separated by bands of Night (B12), and other objects involve various blendings and arrangements of Light and Night (B9, B16, and by implication B18 if Theophrastus is correct).

Let us turn to the specification of the characteristics of Light and Night. If he had meant simply that one of Light and Night is the absence of the other and that its characteristics are simply absences of the characteristics of the other, Parmenides could have had the goddess list characteristics for only one. But he has her quite carefully specify characteristics of both.

Consider the brightness of Light: Certainly a lack of brightness happens to leave darkness. But the sensation of darkness is not simply an absence of the sensation of brightness, or a sensation of an absence of brightness (if that is possible); it has its own characteristics. And an absence of the sensation of darkness or a sensation of an absence of brightness is not simply the sensation of brightness; the sensation of brightness, and so brightness itself as able to produce this sensation, has its own characteristics. (If it seems more obvious that brightness is not merely absence of darkness, that may be because we are used to thinking that darkness is an absence of brightness but not vice versa. However, Parmenides does not give priority to either side in the extant fragments; he presents them as symmetrical.)

Similarly, cold is *what we have where* there is an absence of heat and heat is *what we have where* there is an absence of cold. But the sensation of cold is simply not a lack (or diminution or negation) of the sensation of heat or vice versa, and cold is not simply a lack of heat or vice versa. Indeed, when a source of heat is removed we may or may not feel cold; when a source of cold is removed we may or may not feel hot. Today we are used to saying that cold is the absence of heat. We do not say that heat is what we have where there is an absence of cold or of cold stuff (Night), as Parmenides' goddess would; and we do not say that heat "is" the absence of cold. Where we have asymmetry (cold "is" the absence of heat but heat "is not" the absence of cold), Parmenides' goddess has symmetry; Parmenides' goddess does not claim as we do that heat "is" the absence of cold (Light the absence of Night) or that cold "is" the absence of heat (Night the absence of Light).

We can see then that in the Light-Night framework any object of perception will need to be understood in terms of both Light and Night (this is also Theophrastus' interpretation). And in fact we seem to need both light and darkness in order to see anything; we seem to need both heat and cold to feel temperature; we seem to need both rarity and density in order to hear,[4] smell, or perceive motion; we need both heaviness and lightness or unresistance to feel weight or pressure. Parmenides shows an awareness of this: The fiery Sun is a torch but is *aidēlos*, unseen or causing invisibility at B10.3; Night is *adaē*, unknowing or unknown, at B8.59 and *aphantos*, obscure or made invisible, at B9.3. Either of Light or Night when on its own, or when present in a degree that overwhelms its opposite, prevents visibility; whereas both together in closer proportion (and certain kinds of arrangement?) promote visibility.

This means that in Parmenides' goddess's account of the opinions of mortals, no object, quality, or difference is to be understood entirely as an absence or a not-being of any other. Light and Night, and similarly hot and cold, wet and dry, male and female (which seem to differ at least in part in their proportions of Light and Night[5]), light and darkness, and so on are not pairs in which either side is the logical or necessary or conceptual negation of the other. They are opposites, and contraries, contingently or within arbitrarily specified contexts.

One reason for emphasizing this is to suggest that Aristotle's account of Parmenides' Light and Night is not just terminologically but structurally inaccurate. I suggest this not in order to enter the controversies on whether Aristotle was what we would think of as an accurate historian of inquiry but in order to develop an understanding of the possibilities that Parmenides' account offers that Aristotle's Parmenides—and some of Aristotle's own discussions of hot and cold—do not.[6] These possibilities are relevant, I think, for today's discussions about framing differences.

Aristotle assimilates Parmenides' Light and Night to fire and earth or hot and cold and does not refer to them as Light and Night (*Physics* 188a19–22; *Metaphysics* 984b3–6, 986b19–987a2; and *Parts of Animals* 648a5–649b1 and possibly by implication *Generation of Animals* 765a35–b4). More important for our discussion, at least some of the time Aristotle claims that Parmenides associated hot/fire/Light with being or what is, and cold/earth/Night with not-being or what is not (e.g., *Metaphysics* 986b29–987a2). That claim, I think, must be incorrect as an account of Parmenides' understandings of Light and Night.

Moreover, Theophrastus reports something that does not fit well with the idea that Parmenides associated Light with being and Night with not-being (or vice versa for that matter): Theophrastus reports that Parmenides says that a dead person or corpse (*nekros*) does not perceive light and heat and sound, but does perceive (*aisthanesthai*) cold, silence, and the other opposites [to what a living person perceives]; and that ὅλως δὲ πᾶν τὸ ὂν ἔχειν τινὰ γνῶσιν, entirely all of what is has some knowing (Theophrastus I.4). Against Aristotle's assertion about Night as what-is-not or not-being, note that Theophrastus' Parmenides says that corpses perceive something: cold, silence, probably darkness. If all of what-is has some knowing/awareness, then not only does Night register as a thing perceived or apprehended, but the Night component of compound objects such as corpses would also have (or contribute to) awareness.

What the Light-Night Conceptual Framework Addresses and What It Does Not Address

The Light-Night Framework and the Opinions of Mortals of Parmenides' Time and Place

We can now address two of the puzzles about Parmenides' goddesss's account of the opinions of mortals in B8.51–61 and B9 with which we began: First, why does she claim that mortals lay down this Light-Night framework when no mortals with whom Parmenides could have had contact are known to have said that what is is Light and Night? That is, what if any relationship does this Light-Night story have to the actual opinions of actual mortals whom Parmenides could have known? Second, how would becoming acquainted with the Light-Night framework ensure that the young man of the chariot will not be surpassed by any mortals' opinions? Addressing the first question will help us address the last.

I suggest that the poem points to two kinds of thing that might be called "opinions of mortals." The first is the belief that there are horses, chariots, humans, divinities, cities, roads, light, darkness, motion, and all of the features of the lived and observed world that are named in the proem. The second is the way we understand or interpret the first: When we think that what is includes horses, chariots, humans, divinities, and so on, what do we think that involves? What do we think is going on? What do we opine that what-is would have to be like, if there are to be such things?

I would like to suggest that the goddess refers to this second kind of opinion in B8.38–41, where she says that "all things have been named/ such as mortals have laid down trusting to be true/ coming to be and perishing, to be and not [to be]/ and changing place and exchanging bright colors." I suggest that the goddess is saying that mortals' standard understanding or interpretation of what is going on in the observable world involves coming-to-be and perishing, being and not being, and motion and change. This is incompatible with some of the requisites of inquiry: coming-to-be and perishing violate the strictures of *dikē*, for example. The account that the goddess gives of mortals' opinions in B8.51–61 and B9 is, I suggest, an alternative way of interpreting, understanding, and accounting for things like horses, chariots, motion, and so on—a way that does not advert to not-being or to any account of coming-to-be, perishing, or to motion that immediately invokes not-being. (The "immediately" is important.)

At the same time, it is also worth remarking that the goddess does not characterize the Light-Night framework as something that mortals have deduced or discovered through observation and reasoning. Rather, she says that Light and Night are opinions or judgments (*gnōmas*) that we have "laid down" or "laid up" (*abetment*) to specify forms (*morphias*), B8.53. *Katten* generally referred to laying up stores of something, depositing something (for future use), or laying something aside (*Greek-English Lexicon*, n.l. κατατίθημι II, esp. 1, 4, 6). It reflected a human choice, one that could be well-made and well-informed, worthy of trust, or otherwise.

Relation of the Light-Night Scheme to Its Characterization by the Goddess as Something That Will Not Be Surpassed by Other Mortals, but Is Still Not Trustworthy or Able to Give Alētheia (ἀλήθεια)

Thus the Light-Night framework will be an improvement over mortals' familiar conceptual frameworks for describing and accounting for what-is, if it is at least as successful in describing, explaining, and predicting observable phenomena as the more familiar frameworks, and if it does not invoke not-being in those descriptions, explanations, and predictions as quickly as the more familiar frameworks do. We should not expect the Light-Night framework to be in complete accord with the signs on the recommended road of inquiry; the goddess does say that the opinions of mortals are untrustworthy (we will see below how that plays out). If the Light-Night framework is to be unsurpassed by mortals' opinions, it needs only to be better, or less bad, for some valued purpose, than familiar accounts. And it is that.

For one thing, the Light-Night framework that the goddess articulates provides an underpinning to what mortals say is (in general, multiple things, some of which move, and some of which are available to sensation; specifically, things like sun, moon, earth, stars, water, animals, males, and females). It provides this underpinning in a way that does not require or even allow us to reduce the being of any one kind of thing, or any one kind of being, to the non-being of another. It enables us to express difference without immediate reference to not-being. It also enables us to explain change and movement by referring to persistent components or substrata.

There is an additional way in which the Light-Night framework might have seemed advantageous to a fifth-century Greek: Parmenides used it in presenting his innovative proposals and discoveries in astronomy and physiology. For example, B14 describes the moon as a "night-shining borrowed light wandering around the earth;" the source of the light being the sun in B15. Theophrastus and Aristotle understand B16's mention of "blending" (*krasis*) in the human body to refer to a mixing of Light and Night (Aristotle *Metaphysics* 1009b17–25; Theophrastus 1.3–1.4, pages 69 and 157–59). While the physiological proposals do not stand up well today, the account of the moon certainly does. That it fostered a sort of predictive success is evident when one considers the testimonia indicating that Parmenides figured out that the earth and moon were spherical, the notion of the moon shining by borrowed light having been a key step in that inference (see e.g., Rossetti 2016 and Graham).

In these ways, then, it seems to be an improvement (by the goddess's standards) over other ways in which mortals might understand difference, not-being-a-certain-way, motion, and change.

Despite these successes in certain contexts, the Light-Night framework does not overcome certain fundamental obstacles to inquiry that the goddess has noted for any account of what-is that involves multiplicity, difference, or change. It provides a way to avoid certain problems in some contexts (not by solving the problems but by moving them to other contexts). Zeno makes clear that these deficiencies are structural.

Consequences: Relationship to Zeno's Paradoxes

Unlike other ways to express or understand mortals' beliefs, the Light-Night scheme does not reduce all difference to not-being (of any kind). It allows for explanations of difference and change that do not require one to say that anything absolutely is-not, perishes into nothing, comes to be from nothing, et cetera.

However, inquiry requires that we suppose both distinctness-change-difference-multiplicity, and, incompatibly, the continuity, completeness, freedom from coming-to-be and perishing, and stable unitary identity of what-is that are enforced by *dikē*, *anankē*, and *moira*. Incompatibilities with *dikē*, *anankē*, and *moira* certainly would count as examples of the "deceptiveness" of mortals' opinions.

This is where Zeno comes in. Zeno's arguments show that even in the Light-Night framework, distinctness and change involve either saying that something is reducible to/constructible from nothing, or that Light and Night are interreducible (which either comes out to pretty much the same thing, or comes out to saying that they are not different), or that there are gaps (not-being, nothing) between things or process stages or objects (or levels of sound, or, perhaps, causal connections).

For example, consider the region of space described in Parmenides B12, where bands of unmixed fire alternate with bands of night. Zeno's paradoxes of multiplicity apply here. First, as there cannot be nothing in between the bands, they must either be continuous with one another (which is impossible: Light and Night are opposites) or else there must be something in between them, either a bit of Light or a bit of Night or both; and then the problem repeats itself. . . . Second, the extreme of each band must either have some magnitude or none at all. It could not have no magnitude, as then it would not add to/be part of the band; positive magnitude is not reducible to or constructible from nothing. But if it had positive magnitude, that would be unlimited (no end could be found); then the band would not be an object distinct from others, in the sense that we would not be able to determine where, or if, it began and ended (DK 29 B1, B2). The paradoxes would also apply to the bits of Light and Night in each object, and to compound distinct objects as wholes.

Brochard and Glazebrook both have noted that the paradoxes of motion take up the implications of supposing that time and space are each either indefinitely divisible or atomic. Again, the atoms could not have no magnitude; the indefinitely divisible thing will never reach the boundary of the next thing or the goal. These implications will work quite well in the Light-Night framework; the fact that Light is supposed to be unresistant means that objects can move through it unobstructed. There is no need, then, to assume that the distances over which things move have nothing, no being, in them; they could quite easily contain Light as Parmenides presents it (although the aforementioned problems of boundaries and differentiation still arise).

Either the falling millet seed makes no sound come to be, and a small number of seeds falling together make no sound, but a number of seeds above a certain threshold value does make a sound; or any arbitrarily small number or fraction of seeds makes a sound (DK 29 A29). In the first case, either there is a gap, a discontinuity, between making a sound and making no sound, and the difference between sounding and making no sound is inexplicable and unmeasurable; or the "gap" is nothing and there is no difference between making a sound and making no sound. But this will work equally well if we replace "making no sound" with "being silent," a quality of Night that is opposite to sound according to Theophrastus: the difference between sounding and silence is either inexplicable and unmeasurable or else there is no difference between sound and silence. In the second case, wherein any fraction of a seed makes a sound, let us say for contrast with the first case that there is no smallest part of a seed, and so no softest sound. In that case there is no gap between making a sound (moving air, for Aristotle) and not making a sound/being silent; they are continuous and so not distinct.

Thus Zeno can be understood as arguing that regardless of whether we claim that motion involves coming-to-be from nothing or perishing into nothing, and regardless of whether we claim that distinctions involve not-being-at-all, our talk and conceptions of motion and distinction result in contradictions. Zeno shows that mortals' opinions both rely on the assumptions that there is a distinction between being and not being, and between being-a-certain-way and being-a-different-and-opposite-way, while, at the same time, making those assumptions unintelligible, self-contradictory. He also shows that mortals' opinions assume a distinction between being and becoming but make that unintelligible as well.

Then the Light-Night framework fails to fulfill the requisites for inquiry; it contains incommensurabilities at the core of what enables predictive and descriptive success.

A "Non-Dualistic" Framework for Difference

If I may, I would like here to suggest that keeping both its flaws and its advantages in mind, we might benefit from exploring Parmenides' Light-Night framework as a preliminary working model for addressing differences today. That is, it is all too common to present differences—of race, class, gender, sex, culture, and so on—in a way that involves what Plumwood has called a "dualism." In Plumwood's formulation, a dualism is "an intense, established, and developed cultural expression of . . . a hierarchical relationship, constructing central cultural concepts and identities so as to make equality and mutuality literally unthinkable. Dualism is a relation of separation and domination . . . characterised by radical exclusion, distancing and opposition between orders construed as systematically higher and lower, as inferior and superior, ruler and ruled, centre and periphery" (447). Dualism "results from a . . . denied dependency on a subordinated other," such that "the denial and the relation of domination/subordination shapes the identity of both the relata" (448).

A dualism may exhibit some or all of a group of features that include what Plumwood calls "backgrounding" (making a dependency of the favored side on the other side seem inessential or inconsequential, sometimes by denying the dependency or its context, as in the case of a slaveholder's dependency on enslaved people or a public figure's dependence on the work of those in his/her private household), "radical exclusion" (in which a difference in one aspect is seen as definitive, and any shared features are denied or seen as minimally important), and "relational definition," in which one side of a duality is taken as a norm and "the underside of a dualistically conceived pair is defined in relation to the upperside as a lack, a negativity" (450). The example Plumwood gives is de Beauvoir's description of a situation in which "humanity is male and man defines woman not in herself but as relative to him" (for added complexities in Aristotle, see Bianchi Ch. 1).

Parmenides' presentation of the Light-Night framework challenges and provides an alternative to dualistic accounts of differences in three ways:

- the framework does not reduce one side to the not-being of the other, or to a negation; nor does it subordinate or present one of two interdependent sides as inferior and the other superior;
- it does not deny interdependence (at least, not the way the goddess formulates it);
- Parmenides' goddess's account does not deny the context of the interdependence, viz., it does not suggest that its dichotomy is unconditional, exhaustive, or valid across all contexts. It *points to* the context of the interdependence.

We have already seen that the Light-Night framework does not reduce either Light or Night to the not-being or privation of the other. The goddess presents neither side as subordinate. As Mourelatos has noted, she describes both sides in terms that connote desirability and terms that connote undesirability. For example, Night is both *pukinos*, a term that can connote an advantageous complexity, and *adaē*, a term that can connote a deleterious obscurity (Mourelatos 241–43). Even if Theophrastus is correct—he may not be—that the understanding that comes through Light is "better and purer" than that which comes through Night, still he notes that for Parmenides, no understanding is possible without both Light and Night (both in the understander and in the things understood).

What, though, of context? Parmenides' goddess draws our attention to two aspects of the context in which mortals accept Light and Night (or something that can be described through Light and Night). First, she notes that mortals *laid down* (*katethento*; *ethento*) these opinions through judgments.[7] This suggests that these opinions are not unavoidable; we make a choice, possibly an arbitrary or prejudiced or ignorant one, to lay them down. Second, she notes that we lay down these opinions/judgments to specify forms, outward aspects (*morphai*). Thus she indicates that we lay down these judgments to specify what we get from sensations, or how we conceive of or delineate what we get from sensations. She makes her listener and readers aware, that is, of the "universe of discourse" that we specify through these opinions. Thus she makes us aware, if we pay attention, that that universe of discourse might or might not be able to incorporate all that is, might or might not be conceivable in other ways, might or might not be limited by our customs, habits, preferences, prejudices, sensory limitations or failings, or mental or emotional blind spots.

One might contrast, against Parmenides' account, the early twentieth-century racial (white/non-white) dualisms that Alain Locke (1885–1954) identified as classifications produced in and for the sake of imperialist capitalism (*Race Contacts and Interracial Relations*).[8] In Locke's analysis, racial distinctions were often derived from what would make certain kinds of imperialistic worldview coherent and seemingly able to describe observations. One form some of these dualisms took was presenting the arts and learning of the colonizers as examples of intellectual activity and capability, and those of the colonized as either primitive (deficient) attempts, unthinking emotional expressions, or examples of intellectual passivity and incapacity. The complementaries of colonizer and colonized were presented in a way that made them seem like fullnesses and privations respectively, so that what could have been expressed positively as areas on a spectrum (e.g., development of written cultural forms vs. development of oral forms) became expressed as completeness vs. privation (literacy vs. illiteracy, civilization vs. savagery, mature vs. primitive). Locke describes a system in which context is submerged or denied, so that the injustice of the "laying down" of judgments to specify claimed forms is inarticulable and disguised either as neutral or as paternalistic benevolence.[9] Parmenides' goddess shows us context, so that we may rescue it and its sources from oblivion, that is, seek *alētheia*.

Insofar as they are "laid down" for unscrutinized reasons, mortals' opinions are for Parmenides not just, but even unjust, *adikos*: their origins, justifications, and explanations are obscure; their limitations and any exclusions they make (any aspects of what-is that a given group of mortals may rely on yet fail to see or not want to see) are unchallenged.[10] In this way the goddess's, and Parmenides', account of mortals' opinions can be a step toward seeking justice and *alētheia* from a starting point within mortals' flawed opinions. That is the only kind of starting point we have, after all. This is a way of starting a dialogue with our assumptions, a way of seeking what our conceptual framework would otherwise consign to oblivion. In this way it has promise, I think, as a way of challenging dualisms and articulating and examining differences[11] today, with the aims of justice and truth. It offers a way to call into scrutiny one's own presuppositions while still allowing fruitful investigation to continue.

Alain Locke also proposes guidelines and means for engaging in that dialogue, and I think that Parmenides offers support and illumination of these practices. Locke refers both to this stance and to the procedural guidelines as "critical relativism."

Critical Relativism

As far as I can tell, Locke first used the phrase "critical relativism" in 1950 in "The Need for a New Organon in Education." However, the "cultural relativism" for which he advocated in earlier work such as "Value," "Values and Imperatives," "Cultural Relativism and Ideological Peace," "Pluralism and Intellectual Democracy," and elsewhere is always explicitly critical. He decries relativism that is not critical, and especially relativism that is not self-critical, as "anarchy" ("A Functional View of Value Ultimates," "Pluralism and Ideological Peace") and as "chaotic" ("Pluralism and

Intellectual Democracy," "Functional View"). He also warns that versions of relativism that reduce to behaviorism, and versions that "abet bigotry" through unexamined assumptions of superiority or fitness of one framework or set of values ("Pluralism and Intellectual Democracy," "Pluralism and Ideological Peace"), are dogmatic and tyrannical, that they are absolutisms poorly disguised; these silence the very voices to which they claim to listen.[12] In what follows, I will use the phrase "critical relativism" to refer to all examples of relativism that Locke describes as "critical" and advocates for on that basis.

How is critical relativism supposed to work? Locke speaks of it as desirable in at least four kinds of undertaking—education ("Need for a New Organon"), political dialogue ("Pluralism and Intellectual Democracy," "Cultural Relativism," "Pluralism and Ideological Peace"), research in the natural and social sciences ("Value," "Cultural Relativism"), and research in philosophy ("Value," "Values and Imperatives," "Functional View," "Cultural Relativism"). This suggests that there are multiple registers in which critical relativism will function. It may involve different questions in each. At the same time, Locke suggests that ideally each will inform the others; I will, therefore, address the complex of these.

In "Cultural Relativism and Ideological Peace," Locke identifies three "working principles" of cultural relativism that he thinks will enable it to work as a "realistic instrument of social reorientation and cultural enlightenment," and also of a "more objective and scientific understanding of human cultures." These are:

1. "the principle of *cultural equivalence*," to orient inquiry into "functional equivalences" that will provide "objective but soundly neutral common denominators" among cultural beliefs and institutions that diverge in surface detail;

2. "the principle of *cultural reciprocity*," which would acknowledge interactions between and within elements of cultures and thus "invalidate" generalizations especially about purported superiorities and inferiorities in favor of comparing "limited, specific, and objectively verifiable [functional] superiorities or inferiorities;" and

3. "the principle of *limited cultural convertibility*," an acknowledgment of incommensurabilities among "elements" of different cultures especially insofar as "institutional forms" are

distinct from "values," such that even when one culture borrows from or is influenced by another, that import may take a different shape and have a different role in the borrower culture (total assimilation may be impossible or detrimental). (*Philosophy of Alain Locke* 73)

Locke elucidates these with six further principles of a method of critical relativism in "Need for a New Organon," of which I will cite only the first, second, and fourth as most relevant:

1. "implement an objective interpretation of values by referring them realistically to their social and cultural backgrounds" [and thus, I infer, to the conceptual frameworks and assumptions that underlie them];

2. "interpret values concretely as functional adaptations to these backgrounds, and thus make clear their historical and functional relativity. An objective criterion of functional sufficiency would thereby be set up as a pragmatic test of value adequacy or inadequacy;"

3. "confine . . . consideration of ideology to the prime function and real status of being the adjunct rationalization of values and value interests." (*Philosophy of Alain Locke* 273–74)

From these broad outlines, I propose, we can discern two moments of the practice of critical relativism: First, it involves dialogue between cultures or social groups. This dialogue involves an attempt by representatives of each group to understand the products and values of another group well enough to compare them with respect to function and well enough to demonstrate what they reflect—from the standpoint of their own background. Second, it calls for participants in these dialogues to study those products and values—their own as well as those of the others—in what Locke calls a "scientific" and "objective" manner. That is, critical relativism involves both dialogue between members or ideas or values of different cultures, and reflective dialogue within a culture regarding the values and products and posits of that culture.

Questions about this arise immediately. What could Locke mean by "objective"? How if at all does he think "objectivity" can be achieved? Complicating this question is the fact that Locke argues in "Value" that the goal of scientific objectivity, and the frameworks of axioms and hypotheses that are used in the sciences or in philosophy, themselves reflect normative choices and embody values. How then is the practice of cultural relativism to avoid the imperialism and injustice of operating under an uninvestigated set of values and directives? How is that practice to avoid implicitly posing some one set of values as superior, as an unquestioned invisible norm?

The key to answering these questions, I think, is in the senses in which Locke uses the term "objective." One sense in which he uses the term is to describe identifying (carving out) something as an object of scientific study or as a cultural "given," as in the call for an "objective comparison of basic human values" in "Pluralism and Intellectual Democracy" (*Philosophy of Alain Locke* 55, and cf. 59–60)[13] and the description of values that have become cultural touchstones to the extent that they are now not appreciated at all by members of the culture for which these values are touchstones ("Value," *Philosophy of Alain Locke* 123–24).[14] One finds further details and illustrations in the discussion of concrete examples of value change in "A Functional View of Value Ultimates" (*Philosophy of Alain Locke* 87–92).

Locke also uses the term "objective" in a second sense, namely to describe processes and approaches that employ intersubjectively verifiable means of testing,[15] and that involve trying to steer clear of subjective preferences and "freeing our minds from such hypostatizing [of our own values or traditions] and its provincial limitations and dogmatic bias" ("Pluralism and Intellectual Democracy" 59).

Importantly, Locke does not see this "freeing" as something that can be accomplished all at once, or completely and unconditionally. He argues in "Value" that: "Values are not simply fortuitous and gratuitous and should be eliminated by strict science, but are essential to cognitive process and compatible with any sort and degree of objectivity. Facts too are always reactions—upon prior facts—and are generated by their evaluation. . . ." (*Philosophy of Alain Locke* 119–20). The "freeing [of] our minds from provincial limitations and . . . bias" that Locke proposes is, I think, more Socratic than Cartesian. That is, Locke does not propose that we should (or can) get rid of or put aside, once and for all, all of our previous opinions, as Descartes does e.g., in *Discourse* Part Two (29, AT 13–14).[16] Rather, as we will see below, Locke proposes a continual examination and critical analysis of fundamental opinions and conceptions, one of whose features is to uncover and bring to scrutiny those ideas and ways of thinking that are so familiar, central, and ingrained that we may not realize that we use them, or may not see alternatives. Moreover, Locke does not understand an "objective" approach as one that is free from all normative or valuative assumptions, or even as one that is not dependent on any particular culture's epistemological frameworks.

Part of Locke's program for critical relativism is the progressive uncovering, acknowledging, and interrogating of these layers of normative-intertwined-with-descriptive assumptions. I suggest that the "objectivity" in this is not a static characteristic that we know (or can know) we have achieved but instead something like a commitment to a process. This would be a process of coming to acknowledge more and more of one's starting points, and of examining them from as many different perspectives as possible. To claim to have thrown off all of one's traditional or disciplinary assumptions, and to have freed oneself from the influence of feelings and desires, is in some respects the opposite of what Locke has in mind. For to claim such independence assumes that we already recognize all of our dependencies, and that we can still use language and seek truth without them—both of which assumptions Locke denies.

For example, he ends "Pluralism and Intellectual Peace" with an affirmation of this observation of Horace Kallen's: "The unities it [sc. a pluralist/relativist philosophy] validates . . . will be instrumental ones: its attitude toward problems will be tentative and experimental, it will dispute all finalities and doubt all foregone conclusions; its rule will be Nature's: *solvitur ambulando* [it will be solved in/by walking]" (*Philosophy of Alain Locke* 102). This recommendation that we treat claims and values (both culturally unique ones and shared "unities") as temporary, instrumental, and deserving of testing appears also in "Value." In the examination of values, Locke proposes:

> Logically we are to start with nothing but postulates. It may be legitimate to take them [sc. values] as methodological principles, but even then, they must be regarded as hypotheses to be assumed experimentally, until they have adequately approved and verified themselves by their applications to the actual problems which they concern . . . [T]he testing of a value-postulate always, in a sense, presupposes its truth, though not in any sense that makes this presupposition alone a sufficient reason for regarding it as absolutely true. . . . (*Philosophy of Alain Locke* 120–21)[17]

If the intertwining of valuations and estimations of what-is is multilayered, as Locke suggests, then this investigation and testing of hypotheses will also need to be multilayered. We will need investigate our value-hypotheses as we identify them now, then look at the axioms, definitions, and further assumptions that they seem to us to embody. We will also need to consider then whether, how, and why these suppositions might be appropriate to serve as bases of justice, right, goals, or laws. Reflection on comparisons with other cultures' or discourses' valuations (as we now understand them) will potentially reveal lacks in or incomensurabilities with our own, and we will need to investigate those. These will in turn suggest hypotheses about the bases for our values and our estimations of what is, and we will need to investigate those in turn, and so on, with no clear terminus.

Thus, for Locke, critical relativist investigations of values include investigations of truth, or truths, as what logics, sciences, and philosophy value. And these investigations will have two moments. The first is building: discovering cross-cultural commonalities and coming to non-arbitrary agreements on hypotheses to take up in action. This requires some sort of democracy (not necessarily national or political democracy). The second is investigating the terms we used to come to those agreements, trying to acknowledge where we are standing and what that might be missing, to uncover our own ignorance.

It may then reasonably be asked whether Locke's critical relativism also interrogates justice and/or democracy: does it ask about what they are, whether our understanding of them is accurate and adequate, whether they should be understood as goals or appropriate norms?[18] A substantial response would extend beyond the scope of this paper; but a short answer is that critical relativism takes the responsibility of that inquiry very seriously.

First, as noted above, critical relativism involves a commitment to treating claims and values as temporary, instrumental, and deserving of testing; this would include claims as to what justice and democracy might be and why they are to be taken as normative in investigations. Second, consider the principles of "cultural equivalence, "cultural reciprocity," "limited cultural convertibility," "implementing an objective interpretation of values by referring them realistically to their social and cultural backgrounds," and "interpret values concretely as functional adaptations to these backgrounds," and that "the testing of a value-postulate always, in a sense, presupposes its truth, though not in any sense that makes this presupposition alone a sufficient reason for regarding it as absolutely true," mentioned above. These present the guiding values as a preliminary conceptual framework that is to be investigated both in its theoretical underpinnings and in its consequences, and revised progressively depending on that investigation. Third, for Locke, justice and democracy, even the partial or imperfect versions we now have as we work toward more full realization, support the development of inquiry as their alternatives do not. Fourth, for Locke there are multiple kinds and dimensions of democracy to be investigated and realized, and arguably multiple kinds and dimensions of justice as well (for example, critical relativism points up areas of epistemic injustice).[19]

From this we can see that Locke is proposing a way to address questions that are I think crucial to seeing whether and how philosophical inquiry can be a part of a quest for justice. If philosophy is to be a part of the quest for justice, we will need to learn how to constitute resistance within philosophy to the norms and presuppositions that have operated systematically to exclude certain voices, problems, interests, and questions.

Some important and influential efforts to integrate philosophy in seeking and establishing justice have come up short with regard to inclusivity. Jürgen Habermas and Karl-Otto Apel hold that communicative interaction requires that a participant's motivation to accept a claim as true, right, or truthful is not based on a response to a threat or a promised reward but is what Habermas and Apel call "rational," that is, based on reasoning independent of concerns with personal benefit (Habermas 58–59; cf. Apel 258–59). This assumes that some commitment to be "rational" that some people have agreed to is all they (and we all) need in order to have a discourse that does not reduce to "might makes right," and that does not reduce all values to "might makes right." As Dussel, Cassin, and Simpson have shown, this is demonstrably inaccurate and pernicious: it effects exclusion via denial of the terms of the exclusion.[20] Locke, by contrast, is suspicious of any claim to have rejected all arbitrary assumptions, all potentially coerced and coercive conceptual frameworks, all values and priorities other than something unconditionally shared. And Locke offers us a set of guidelines for interrogating both the explicit and the internalized assumptions and frameworks through which we act and communicate. This interrogation is not a one-time activity, as in, for example, Descartes; instead it is ongoing, recursive, and potentially unending. It is always in motion, and always self-critical. Here we might examine Parmenides' framing of his text: In the first line of the poem he depicts the young man's (*kouros*) journey as ongoing (ἵπποι ταί με φέρουσιν, "the mares that carry me," B1.1); not only is the need for self-criticism at every turn implied, but the goddess even calls explicitly for reflective scrutiny of her own pronouncements (κρῖναι δὲ λόγῳ πολύδηριν ἔλεγχον/ ἐξ ἐμέθεν ῥηθέντα, "judge for yourself by means of reason/ an account [*logos*] a much-contesting refutation/ Out of what I said" (B7.5–6).

This has one more consequence that may be of interest: if my characterizations of the texts of Parmenides and Locke are correct, their radical character that highlights incompleteness, and that calls for resistance of the norms by which philosophy has constituted itself as a respectable product of European modernity, have been made invisible. Locke's guidelines help us to make ever more of what-is visible, by making visible the words and accounts (*logoi*) through which we identify what-is—very much along the lines of Parmenides' understanding of *alētheia*.

Notes

1. See e.g., Benardete, "'Night and Day, . . .'" Miller, "Ambiguity and Transport." That the passage we know as the beginning of the proem was the beginning of Parmenides' text is attested by Sextus, *Against the Mathematicians/ Pros Mathematikous* vii.111.

2. Mourelatos has also shown that each characteristic of Light is opposed, in different ways, to all characteristics of Night, and vice versa (245). I am using initial capitals for Parmenides' Light and Night to distinguish them from what were usually called "light" and "night." For example, what was usually called "night" was not generally thought to be "weighty" (*embrithes*, B8.59); what was usually called "light" was not necessarily thought of as "mild" (*ēpion*, B8.57).

3. Benardete (194) notes that "nonbeing disappears as soon as the goddess turns to Opinion." This is perhaps too strong: consider B8.57–58, where Light is described as a being (*on*) that is Laid down as wholly like itself and not at all like Night, that is, as not being like Night. Benardete Seems to be adverting to the fact that within the surviving fragments that seem to belong to the Section on the opinions of mortals, *mē* and *ou* do not appear modifying forms of *eon*. See also 205 and 220.

4. This was known as early as Homer, who has Odysseus stop up his men's ears with wax to avoid hearing the Sirens (*Odyssey* 12.173–77).

5. See Journée.

6. For an extensive analysis and critique of the implications of Aristotle's account of hot cold as he applies it to sexual difference and species difference, see

Bianchi. Parmenides' account shows that Aristotle's view was not, as is sometimes assumed, generally accepted and unchallenged by Greek-speaking inquirers.

7. μορφὰς γὰρ κατέθεντο δύο γνώμας ὀνομάζειν (B8.53); see also ἀντία δ' ἐκρίναντο δέμας καὶ σήματ' ἔθεντο/ χωρὶς ἀπ' ἀλλήλων (B8.55–56).

8. Locke is not alone today in this analysis, but it is worth noting that these lectures were given in 1916.

9. Cf. Memmi 126–33.

10. Mortals' opinions violate not only *dikē*, of course, but also *anankē* and *moira*.

11. By "differences" here I mean both differences or distinctions believed to obtain between things or kinds (e.g., between sexes in any given way of construing them) and differences among cultures or discourses or communities regarding distinctions (e.g., how each might define and identify sexes).

12. This presentation of anarchy and tyranny as potentially linked and as extremes opposed to a middle point of justice harks back at least to Aeschylus (see e.g., *Eumenides* 525–27 and 695–97) and to Plato (e.g., *Republic* 560e–569c). I have found no indication as to whether Locke had their work in mind in his references to anarchy and tyranny. It is possible, given that he studied ancient Greek language, literature, and philosophy extensively at Harvard and Oxford, and that he taught ancient Greek philosophy and literature at Howard. See e.g., Stewart 60, 64, 110, 124, 150, 301.

13. I am grateful to Christopher Di Teresi for emphasizing the importance of this.

14. Examples of this are literary works that are designated as "classics," then mainly read by those who are forced to do so in school, and appreciated by few readers.

15. He also occasionally uses "objective" to refer to the objects of study themselves, insofar as they are intersubjectively "pragmatically confirmed by common human experience" ("Pluralism and Intellectual Democracy," *Philosophy of Alain Locke* 56). Locke notes that this may differ from confirmation within scientific discourse, and he does not presume in favor of one or the other. Thus this "objective reality" sounds very much like Heraclitus' *xunos* (e.g., DK 22 B2, 80, 113, 114, 116) the world we claim to have in common by the fact of participating in discourse.

16. ". . . for all the opinions that I had up to then given credence, I could not do better than to undertake, once and for all, to remove/get rid of them, in order to replace them after that either with other, better ones, or even with the same ones, once I had adjusted them to the level of reason." My translation; the original is "pour toutes les opinions que j'avais reçues jusques alors en ma créance, je ne pouvais mieux faire que d'entreprendre, une bonne fois, de les en ôter, afin d'y en remettre par après, ou d'autres meilleures, ou bien les mêmes, lorsque je les aurais ajustées au niveau de la raison."

17. Cf. Barnes 33, 75, 79, 123.

18. I am indebted to an anonymous reader for SUNY Press for drawing my attention to this question.

19. On democracy, see Locke, "Creative Democracy," "Five Phases of Democracy," "Pluralism and Intellectual Democracy," "World View on Race and Democracy;" Barnes ch. 3; 268; on justice see the above plus Locke, "Negro Needs as Adult Education Opportunities" and Cherubin "Culture and the Kalos;" on both, see Locke, "Cultural Relativism and Ideological Peace," "Ethics of Culture," and "Negro in the Three Americas."

20. See e.g., Cassin, Dussel Part I, Ch. 3, and Simpson Ch. 3-5 (involving a proposal with much in common with Locke's vision of "critical relativism"); cf. Plumwood, and Peller 778, 796-800, 806-7, 847.

Works Cited

Aeschylus. *Aeschylus*. Translated by Herbert Weir Smyth, vol. 2, Loeb-Harvard UP, 1926.

Apel, Karl-Otto. "The A Priori of the Communication Community and the Foundation of Ethics: The Problem of a Rational Foundation of Ethics in the Scientific Age." *Towards a Transformation of Philosophy*. Translated by Glyn Adey and David Frisby, Routledge & Kegan Paul, 1980, pp. 225-300.

Aristotle. *Generation of Animals*. Translated by Arthur L. Peck, Loeb-Harvard UP, 1943. archive.org/stream/generationofanim00arisuoft#page/n5/mode/2up

———. *Metaphysica*, edited by Werner Jaeger, Scriptorum Classicorum Bibliotheca Oxoniensis. Clarendon, 1957.

———. *Parts of Animals*. Translated by Arthur L. Peck and Edward S. Forster, Loeb-Harvard UP, 1983.

———. *Physica*, edited by William D. Ross. Scriptorum Classicorum Bibliotheca Oxoniensis, Clarendon, 1950.

Barnes, Corey L. *Alain Locke on the Theoretical Foundations for a Just and Successful Peace*. African American Philosophy and the African Diaspora series, Palgrave Macmillan, 2023.

Benardete, Seth. "'Night and Day,' . . . : Parmenides." *Mètis* 13, no. 1, 1998, pp. 193-225.

Bianchi, Emanuela. *The Feminine Symptom: Aleatory Matter in the Aristotelian Cosmos*. Fordham UP, 2014.

Brochard, Victor. *Études de Philosophie Ancienne et de Philosophie Moderne*, edited by Victor Delbos, Vrin, 1926.

Carter, Jacoby Adeshei, and Leonard Harris, editors. *Philosophic Values and World Citizenship: Locke to Obama and Beyond*. Lexington Books, 2010.

Cassin, Barbara. " 'Parle si tu es un homme' Ou l'exclusion transcendantale." *Les Études Philosophiques*, vol. 2, 1988, pp. 145–55.

Cherubin, Rose. "Culture and the Kalos: Inquiry, Justice, and Value in Locke and Aristotle." Carter and Harris, pp. 7–20.

Curd, Patricia. *The Legacy of Parmenides: Eleatic Monism and Later Presocratic Thought*. Parmenides Publishing, 2004.

Descartes, René. *Discours de la Méthode/Discourse on the Method: A Bilingual Edition with an Interpretive Essay*, edited, translated, introduced, and indexed by George Heffernan, U of Notre Dame P, 1994. doi.org/10.2307/j.ctv1bvnf2j

Diels, Hermann, and Walther Kranz, editors. *Die Fragmente der Vorsokratiker, Griechisch und Deutsch*. 9th ed., Weidmann, 1952.

Dussel, Enrique D. *The Underside of Modernity: Apel, Ricœur, Rorty, Taylor, and the Philosophy of Liberation*. Translated by Eduardo Mendieta, Humanities Press, 1996.

Glazebrook, Trish. "Zeno against Mathematical Physics." *Journal of the History of Ideas*, vol. 62, no. 2, 2001, pp. 193–210.

Graham, Daniel W. *Science Before Socrates: Parmenides, Anaxagoras, and the New Astronomy*. Oxford UP, 2013.

Habermas, Jürgen. "Discourse Ethics: Notes on a Program of Philosophical Justification." *Moral Consciousness and Communicative Action*. Translated by Christian Lenhardt and Shierry Weber Nicholsen, MIT Press, 1990, pp. 43–115.

Homer. *The Odyssey*. Translated by Augustus T. Murray; revised by George E. Dimock, Loeb-Harvard UP, 1919–1995.

Journée, Gérard. "Lumière et Nuit, Féminin et Masculin chez Parménide d'Elée : Quelques Remarques." *Phronesis* 57, no. 4, 2012, pp. 289–318.

Liddell, Henry George, Robert Scott, Henry Stuart Jones, and Roderick McKenzie. *A Greek-English Lexicon*. Revised edition, Oxford UP, 1996.

Locke, Alain L. "Creative Democracy," edited by Christopher Buck and Betty J. Fisher. *World Order* 38, no. 3, 2006, pp. 40–41.

———. "Cultural Relativism and Ideological Peace." Locke, 1989, pp. 69–78.

———. "The Ethics of Culture." Locke, 1989. pp. 176–85.

———. "Five Phases of Democracy: Farewell Address at Talladega College," edited by Christopher Buck. *World Order* 36, no. 3, 2005, pp. 42–45.

———. "A Functional View of Value Ultimates." Locke, 1989, pp. 81–93.

———. "The Need for a New Organon in Education." Locke, 1989, pp. 263–76.

———. "The Negro in the Three Americas." *The Journal of Negro Education* 13, no. 1, 1944, pp. 7–18. doi.org/10.2307/2292916.

———. "Negro Needs as Adult Education Opportunities." Locke, 1989, pp. 254–61.

———. *The Philosophy of Alain Locke: Harlem Renaissance and Beyond*, edited by Leonard Harris, Temple UP, 1989.

———. "Pluralism and Intellectual Democracy." Locke, 1989, pp. 53–64.
———. "Pluralism and Ideological Peace." Locke, 1989, pp. 96–102.
———. *Race Contacts and Interracial Relations: Lectures on the Theory and Practice of Race*, edited by Jeffrey C. Stewart, Moorland-Spingarn Series, Howard UP, 1992.
———. "Value." Locke, 1989, pp. 109–26.
———. "Values and Imperatives." Locke, 1989, pp. 43–50.
———. *World View on Race and Democracy: A Study Guide in Human Group Relations*. American Library Association, 1943. hdl.handle.net/2027/pst.000050797394
Memmi, Albert. *The Colonizer and the Colonized*. 1974. Translated by Howard Greenfeld, with introductions by Jean-Paul Sartre and Nadine Gordimer, Earthscan Publications, 2003.
Miller, Mitchell. "Ambiguity and Transport: Some Reflections on the Proem to Parmenides' Poem." *Oxford Studies in Ancient Philosophy*, vol. 30, Oxford UP, 2006, pp. 1–47.
Mourelatos, Alexander P. D. *The Route of Parmenides*, revised and expanded edition, Parmenides Publishing, 2008.
Palmer, John Anderson. *Parmenides and Presocratic Philosophy*. Oxford UP, 2009.
Parmenides. *The Fragments of Parmenides*, edited by David Sider and Henry W. Johnstone, Bryn Mawr Greek Commentaries. Bryn Mawr College, 1986.
Peller, Gary. "Race Consciousness." *Duke Law Journal* vol. 39, no. 4, 1990, pp. 758–847. doi.org/10.2307/1372723
Plato. *Republic*, edited and translated by Christopher Emlyn-Jones and William Preddy, vol. 2, Loeb-Harvard UP, 2013.
Plumwood, Val. "The Politics of Reason: Towards a Feminist Logic." *Australasian Journal of Philosophy*, vol. 71, no. 4, 1993, pp. 436–62.
Rossetti, Livio. "*Pseudophaēs* e *pseudophanēs*. La luna secondo Parmenide." Setaioli, 2016, pp. 613–24.
———. *Un altro Parmenide: Luna, Antipodi, Sessualità, Logica*. Storia della Filosofia antica, vol. 2, Diogene, 2017.
Setaioli, Aldo, editor. *Apis Matina: Studi in onore di Carlo Santini*, EUT Edizioni Università di Trieste, 2016.
Sextus Empiricus. *Against the Mathematicians/Pros Mathematikous, Sextus Empiricus: Against the Logicians*. Translated by R. G. Bury, vol. 2, Loeb-Harvard UP, 1935.
Simpson, Lorenzo C. "Critical Interventions: Towards a Hermeneutical Rejoinder." *The Agon of Interpretations: Towards a Critical Intercultural Hermeneutics*, edited by Ming Xie, U of Toronto P, 2014, pp. 252–74.
Stewart, Jeffrey C. *The New Negro: The Life of Alain Locke*. Oxford UP, 2018.
Theophrastus. *Theophrastus and the Greek Physiological Psychology before Aristotle*, edited and translated by George Stratton., W. Brown, 1967. Originally published by G. Allen & Unwin, 1917.

The Art of Training the Black Horse
The "War within the Soul" and Socrates' Palinode

Meredith Trexler Drees

> Loosen the lead and gather him without coaxing;
> Be sincere in beckoning him by singing in the evening.
> Wild grass and cold springwater are the means to ensure friendship;
> Obedient gaze and raised eyebrows—such is his behavior.
> Even without attendance for a moment, the horse's nature excels;
> Resting at leisure, there is no need to make a snare.
> Led by his head to turn around, the horse returns home;
> A black horse with silver mane, his nature is not corrupted.[1]
>
> —Louis Komjathy

Plato's *Phaedrus* makes use of his famous theory of a divided soul, using the metaphor of the charioteer. In this metaphor, the soul is represented by a winged chariot, which is drawn by two horses. The part of the soul that, ideally, leads the others (reason) is represented as the charioteer. The white horse represents the love of honor (253d),[2] and the black horse represents the need to selfishly indulge in one's sexual desires and get one's way. In the Palinode, Socrates describes a seemingly pervasive case where the charioteer and white horse oppose the black horse, and the struggle to rein the black horse in inhibits the chariot's (soul's) ascent to the Forms.[3]

However, if a cooperative black horse is part of a harmoniously functioning soul (or chariot, in this case), it is a good question as to how exactly the charioteer is to guide the horses effectively, especially the black horse. Socrates does indicate that the black horse can be trained: The black horse will impede the chariot's ascent if the charioteer "has failed to train it well" (247b). This is interesting because, undoubtedly, the well-known vision of Beauty that is described in the Palinode—the one who takes the black horse "back on his haunches"—is not an act of training, and it is not an intentional attempt to control the horse on behalf of the charioteer. It is an experience that gives rise to a sort of awakening and insight, which *forces* the horse under control. Thus, the effects of this vision of Beauty are particularly applicable to the soul whose charioteer has *not* trained his black horse well.

In this essay I shall argue that it is possible to train the black horse of the *Phaedrus*, as it were, and I shall examine the question as to whether the aesthetic education that is described in Books II and III of the *Republic* is one way to accomplish such training.[4] The descriptions of the tripartite soul in the *Republic* and the *Phaedrus* indicate that Plato refers to the same soul, just through respectively different approaches. It is an interesting question as to whether a more thorough understanding of the "training of the black horse" will, in turn, shed light on the relationship between these two dialogues, specifically in the context of Plato's view of moral progress. With that in mind, I shall need to begin with a more thorough discussion of Plato's division of the soul.

The "War within the Soul"

According to Socrates, we often see cases when a person's appetites "force him to act contrary to reason, and he rails at himself with that within himself which is compelling him to do so" (*Republic* 440b). In the *Republic*, Plato's introduction of the tripartite soul is what seems to make cases like this—cases of *akrasia*—a possibility.[5] Plato's first description of the three parts of the soul—reason (*to logistikon*), spirit (*to thumoeides*), and appetite (*epithumetikon*)—comes in Book IV. As the motivational conflict argument for tripartition of the soul unfolds, we learn that there are three activities of the soul: one part desires physical gratification, one part gets angry and loves honor, and one part desires actively learning.[6] We are told that the result of these differing motivations can be a "civil war within the soul" (*tes psuches stasis*) (440e). Furthermore, one part of the soul is set apart from the others insofar as it has the capacity for calculation (*logismos*). This rational part of the soul's desires arise from calculation

(439d, 603, 604d). The appetite is unreasoning and non-rational (439d), and the spirited part gets angry without calculation (441c). Plato does describe the appetitive and spirited parts as having certain beliefs and as being able to be persuaded by argument (554d) and as having the ability to recognize a means to certain ends. This ability is characteristic of the appetite—the lover of money or profit.

My view is that Plato consistently holds that all desires are for things qua good—that every soul (and the whole soul) always pursues the good.[7] With an eye to Jessica Moss's work, I have argued elsewhere that while the objects of the lower parts of the soul may not always be good things, this does not necessarily mean that the motivations are independent of the good (Trexler Drees 5–23). Seeking the good but reaching only an appearance of it gives rise to desires for things that only appear but are not good. Hence, it is possible to pursue the good and, at the same time, be motivated toward bad things. While all three parts of the soul always pursue the good, only the rational part of the soul can grasp what is truly good as opposed to that which merely appears to be good. All parts of the soul are capable of desiring false appearances, but the lower parts, since they are confined to perception, are more apt to be confused about the good and may fail to pursue the *real* good.[8] These cases of conflict are the ones of particular interest to this project: specifically, cases where the lower parts are strong enough to overcome one's reasoned view of what is good overall may prompt a person to act against what reason has calculated as good. Again, on my view, all parts of the soul desire the good, but they sometimes mistake false appearances of good for true ones and, hence, pursue the wrong objects. Harmony within the soul is the goal of the virtuous life, just as harmony among constituents is the goal of the virtuous city. Just as civil war may occur when one part of the city is drawn out of order, civil war occurs in the soul when any one part is drawn to a merely apparent good.

Each part of the soul has a way of grasping the good, and all are versions of motivations toward it: the appetite grasps objects of physical gratification insofar as they are appearances of goodness, the spirited part grasps honorable things insofar as they are appearances of goodness, and the rational part grasps the good itself.[9] Since the whole soul always seeks things qua good, but its parts can be mistaken about the good, and hence, mistakenly pursue bad things, it would make sense for education, on Plato's view, to be aimed at training the soul to avoid mistaking appearances of goodness for the real good.

The three parts of the soul play different roles, grasp different things, and are developed at different times (441a). It is important to present the lower parts of the soul with goodness that they can grasp early on so that they do not, by merely experiencing appearances of goodness and becoming devoted to them due to the immediate gratification that they give, miss out on the potential to grasp a higher good. Thus, the beginning stages of recognition of the good will occur within the lower parts of the soul, and if one wants to appeal to these parts of the soul, it must be done through an appropriate medium—something aesthetic.[10]

Thus, education is aimed at training the soul to avoid mistaking appearances of the good for the real good, and this training begins in the lower part of the soul. This, in my view, is the thought behind the conversation that takes place in Books II and III of the *Republic*, where proper education of the guardians is discussed. If the guardians are "full of spirit right from birth," but reason comes later, their education must first involve things that appeal to the spirited part of the soul. Pleasant things appeal to the appetite and beautiful things appeal to the spirited part of the soul—they are *kalon*, and they motivate the attraction to noble and honorable things (442). Thus, education will begin with music and poetry, and "the start of someone's education determines what follows" (425c).

Aesthetic Education in The *Republic*

For Plato, grasping goodness is something that begins in the lower parts of the soul; that is, it begins in the parts of the soul that are limited to perception. As the discussion of appropriate education unfolds in Books II and III of the *Republic*, we see that it begins with proper exposure to media that the lower parts can grasp, for example poetry. As was evidenced by my arguments in the last section, moral education can only come to full fruition if an agent becomes able to distinguish what she has grasped through appetite and spirit from a higher good that is only understood by reason. In terms of being motivated toward the good, the best-case scenario for the lower parts of the soul is that they should be trained to track the higher value that reason calculates as good, and it would seem that this training is the goal of the aesthetic education that is described in Books II and III of the *Republic*.

At *Republic* 401d, Socrates explains that all artists must represent good characters in their work. They must pursue "what is fine and graceful" so that something of their works will lead young people to "friendship and harmony with the beauty of reason" (401d). Poetry can train a person to detect and accurately respond to discipline and order, and, eventually, to "become fine and good" (402). Since poetry is a medium through which the lower parts of the soul can grasp good character, it can be used as a means to introduce good things to a person who is in the beginning stages of moral education.[11] Thus, on Plato's view, experiencing poetry can have a positive transforming effect.

For Plato, poetry is "especially effective because it can make a person assume the identity of another" (Asmis 348). This imitative aspect of poetry, however, is something that may be used either to benefit or harm the soul, since poetry is something that both expresses and shapes character (397c, 398b, 400e). Some poetry misrepresents what is ethically appropriate, and when a person performs this kind of poetry, since imitation has the capacity to move and change a person, it can cause that person to embrace the wrong kind of behavior. The character development that takes place here both causes and is caused by behavior. That is, experiences of poetry can give rise to one's moral or immoral behavior, depending on the behavior of the characters in the poem they experience. Thus, according to Plato, poetry has ethical implications. This is the reason that Plato argues in favor of the censorship of poetry: if poetry comprises bad content and expresses bad characters, since the listeners and actors tend to develop in their own souls the characters in the poem, exposing the guardians to bad poetry is a recipe for the development of bad guardians. While it has often been thought that Books II and III of the *Republic* are not compatible with the (apparently) total exclusion of imitation in Book X, my view is that this exclusion is, in fact, only apparent. It is aesthetic education that helps to train our "horses" and free them from the "image makers" to whom Plato refers in the allegory of the Cave. Without aesthetic education, young people are unable to identify that which is allegorical, but once they have experienced such education, poetry may return to their city.[12]

Since the appetitive and spirited parts of the soul are cognitively limited to perception (and they accept evaluative appearances), and since the pleasure involved in poetry appeals to the lower parts of the soul (606d, 607), these parts of the soul will be most likely to accept the appearances/images that are presented in poetry. These appearances will be false at worst and reflective of (but removed from) the truth, at best. Therefore, these lower parts of the soul will accept (and pursue)[13] the worthless or the bad if it is imitated in poetry. This, then, is why Plato maintains that "if you admit the pleasure-giving Muse, whether in lyric or epic poetry, pleasure and pain will be kings in your city instead of law or the thing that everyone has always believed to be best, namely, reason" (607). As mentioned earlier, reason may also accept images given in poetry, and poetry will appeal to all parts of the soul. However, poetry is a medium that can reach the lower parts of the soul even through their limitations, while reason is not limited to perception. The right sort of poetry will help the soul find friendship with reason, but dangerous poetry, through its appeal to the lower parts of the soul, may facilitate pleasure's rule and conflict within the soul. As Gabriel Richardson Lear explains, "poetic image-making has a function, according to Socrates: It allows the rulers and others in authority to say something, for civic benefit, about the truth of the past . . . beautiful and good poetry is truthful in its pattern because it is an image of reality, and this is what it is *for*" (115).

Indeed, though Plato's discussion of poetry in Books II and III shows that poetry can have a positive transforming effect, it is also clear that Books II and III advocate the censorship of poetry: if poetry comprises bad content and expresses bad characters, since the listeners and actors tend to develop in their own souls the characters in the poem, guardians who are exposed to bad poetry are likely to develop bad characters. When poetry misrepresents what is ethically appropriate, and when a person performs this kind of poetry, since imitation has the capacity to move and change a person, it can cause her to embrace the wrong kind of behavior. As Socrates explains, poetry does in fact have the power—in the case of buffoonery, sex, anger, and desires, pleasures, and pains—to "nurture and water" the lower parts of the soul and establish "them as rulers in us when they ought to wither and be ruled" (606d). However, by being exposed to poetry that captures the nature of something true—while they cannot perceive it—the appetite and spirit can be trained to track the higher value that such poetry presents. Poetry that imitates appearances and involves ignorance will corrupt those who experience or perform it, but poetry that imitates things as they are can be used in moral education.

Good poetry is, as Elizabeth Asmis puts it, "carefully designed to confer a maximum of moral benefit by providing an experience that simulates that of a good person as closely as possible." This is the sort of poetry that can aid one in the recognition of reason—by training a person to develop a good character, something akin to reason, it allows for a person to see the kinship between reason and oneself (402). G. R. F. Ferrari explains that:

> The poet has a skill all on his own: not understanding, but capturing the appearance, the look and feel of human life. But just as an image is, or rather should be (in Plato's view), for the sake of its original, the art of image-making is destined to be the helpmate of that art that seeks truth. Poetry cannot, so to speak, be trusted on its own but as the ward of a philosophic guardian can put its talent to good use. (108)

Since reason is essential to the art that seeks truth, good poetry is the "helpmate of that art that seeks truth." Thus, while the ignorant sort of artist is the one who is banished from the city, the artist who implants "the image of good moral habit" in his poetry or music creates the art that potentially "returns from exile."

This is one way in which the lower parts of the soul can be trained to pursue the higher value that reason calculates as good: some experiences of beauty via art can be used in moral training; that is, these experiences can be used to promote the kind of training that Plato suggests should take place during the beginning stages of education in the *Republic*. This is an affective kind of training, and a kind of aesthetic education[14] whereby a person learns to feel appropriately toward appropriate things. Experiences of beauty via art have the capacity to influence a person's character, and they can, in turn, help give rise to appropriate behavior. However, there is another way in which aesthetic experiences gives rise to moral progress, on Plato's view. This other type of aesthetic experience (and moral progress), which I have argued does not involve training, but rather a kind of vision that provides increased moral understanding, is exemplified in the Palinode of Plato's *Phaedrus*.[15]

Training the Black Horse

In previous work I have argued that beauty plays two roles in Plato's general theory of moral progress:[16] (1) Some experiences of beauty via art can be used in moral training; that is, these experiences can be used to promote the kind of training that Plato suggests should take place during the beginning stages of education in the *Republic*. This is an affective kind of training, whereby a person learns to feel appropriately toward appropriate things. Experiences of beauty via art have the capacity to influence a person's character, and they can, in turn, help give rise to appropriate behavior. (2) An erotic experience of a beautiful person, as it is described in the *Symposium* and *Phaedrus*, is a more profound sort of experience. This kind of experience can be distinguished from (1) in that it adds a higher kind of cognitive component which is lacking in (1). In (1), cognition is involved (cognition is involved in all affection), but only as perception-based thought, which merely has access to appearances. Some erotic experiences of beautiful people, on the other hand, provide an insight into the nature of true value and a certain kind of vision. They lead to the knowledge of true Beauty and illuminate the value of the life lived by the lover of wisdom. Therefore, erotic experiences of beautiful people may promote increased moral understanding as opposed to affective training.

I have argued that this sort of moral growth takes place through the type of aesthetic experience described in both the *Symposium* and the *Phaedrus*. For my purposes here, I shall focus on the *Phaedrus*, particularly Plato's famous metaphor of the charioteer. Socrates explains:

> Let us liken the soul to the natural union of a team of winged horses and their charioteer. The gods have horses and charioteers that are themselves all good and come from good stock besides, while everyone else has a mixture. To begin with, our driver is in charge of a pair of horses; second, one of his horses is beautiful and good and from stock of the same sort, while the other is the opposite and has the opposite sort of bloodline. This means that chariot-driving in our case is inevitably a painfully difficult business. (246a)

From this passage, it is apparent that the souls of mortals are in a less-than-ideal state. Mortal souls are contrasted with the souls of the Gods, which comprise only "good stock." These chariots "move easily, since they are well-balanced and under control, but the other chariots barely make it" (247b). Their drivers face a "painfully difficult business," since one of their horses is a deaf, shaggy "crooked jumble of limbs" that is hardly in control and inherently disposed to indecency (253e).

Socrates explains that the black horse is naturally indisposed to serve the charioteer, and that dissension between the horses results in an increased potentiality for discord in the whole soul. This, in turn, presents a serious problem, since (ideally) the parts of the soul will find harmony in hierarchical order. The charioteer must guide the soul; that is, he must become a proficient steersman, and the direction of the chariot must be given by him, not by the horses (247d). That is to say, reason must control the desires of the lower parts of the soul.

The passage of particular interest to me can be found at 247b where Socrates says that the black horse will impede the chariot's ascent if the charioteer "has failed to train it well." As noted earlier, the vision of Beauty that is described in the Palinode that effectively takes the black horse "back on his haunches" is not an act of training, and it is not an intentional attempt to control the horse on behalf of the charioteer.[17]

Socrates explains that when the mortal soul encounters its beloved—when the charioteer looks in his eyes—the soul "fills with the goading of desire" (254a). The charioteer remains controlled, but the black horse "leaps violently forward" and tries to aggravate its yokemate and its charioteer (254a) in order to sway the chariot toward the beloved and "suggest to him the pleasures of sex" (254b). Yet, as they approach the boy, they are "struck by his face as if by a bolt of lightning" (254b). The charioteer then sees a vision of beauty, and, as a result of this vision, he is able to rein the horses in.

During this erotic experience of beauty, it is the black horse's response to the erotic experience that leads him off track. The black horse responds by directing *eros* merely toward the satisfaction sexual desires. On the other hand, the charioteer, who has looked "into the eye of love" (253e), also clearly possesses *eros*, but he (reason) does not share the black horse's desire. In fact, he thinks that the black horse desires something that is "dreadfully wrong" (254b). It is something contrary to that which is sought by reason that leads the black horse off track. Thus, *eros* can be directed toward whatever is desired, and the black horse, since it has an unreasonable desire, can direct *eros* off track. It would seem, then, that both the charioteer and the black horse express *eros*, but they direct their *eros* toward different objects of desire. This means that *eros* can be directed toward reasonable objects of desire or it can be falsely directed; it will be reasonable only as long as reasonable desires are followed rather than unreasonable ones. Hence, this particularly illuminates the importance of the charioteer's command of the horses.

It is noteworthy that when the charioteer "looks in the eye of love," (253e) he is able to pull the disobedient black horse back on its haunches, though it is quite unwilling. The charioteer finally falls violently on the reins, due to his vision of the Forms—this is not a deliberate act of control or leadership over the other two parts. Both before the vision of Beauty and after it the charioteer seeks control. However, after the vision, the charioteer has seen Beauty "where it stands on the sacred pedestal next to Self-control" (254b). It is this that makes the charioteer capable of mastering the black horse in this case.

Since the charioteer is the only one who has the potential to see the Forms (247d, 248a), while all of the parts of the soul glimpse the boy, only the charioteer recalls the Form of Beauty itself. The metaphor of the charioteer shows that the potential glimpse of the Forms that occurs during an erotic experience of beauty can give rise to order in the soul. The experience provides an insight into the nature of true value and a certain kind of vision, and moral progress results from the erotic experience of beauty that prompted the charioteer to guide his horses effectively. It is an experience that gives rise to a sort of awakening and insight, and importantly it is one that, at first, *forces* the horses under control. Thus, the effects of this vision of Beauty are particularly applicable to the soul whose charioteer has *not* trained his black horse well. However, one might wonder whether, if a person has already experienced the moral training of the *Republic*, will that person have a different kind of erotic experience of beauty, should they encounter someone such as the beautiful boy of the Palinode?

It is evident in both the *Symposium* and the *Phaedrus* that an erotic experience of beauty will not affect everyone in the same manner. Some people will not be moved from an image of beauty to "a vision of Beauty itself." Furthermore, some people will focus on the mere image, surrendering to pleasure and setting out "in the manner of a four-footed beast . . . wallowing in vice . . . without a trace of fear or shame" (251). Plato clearly distinguishes this "fallen prisoner of love" from the person "who has seen much in heaven" and who will be able to bear the burden of this "feathered force" of the erotic experience of beauty with dignity (252c). Hence, the erotic experience that beauty evokes gives rise to options; that is, one might be "raised aloft" or one might simply be a "fallen prisoner of love." Transcendence will not occur when the black horse succeeds in directing the chariot toward its unreasonable desire. This means that either the black horse must be trained to obey the charioteer, or the charioteer must have the capacity to recall a vision of Beauty such that the horse is forced to comply, as described at 254e.

The *Phaedrus*, like the *Symposium*, suggests that while some people will reach the level of the most blessed Mystery (250c) and a vision of Beauty itself, some will not reach the level of such a vision. In the *Phaedrus*, one can become a "fallen prisoner of love," and in the *Symposium*, we have seen that lovers who are attracted simply to bodily aspects of the beloved or who lack proper guidance, will not cultivate a desire to ascend to the level of understanding. Indeed, the vision of the beautiful itself will not be disclosed to everyone (*Symposium* 210a).

Furthermore, while Plato argues in the *Symposium* that all love is for the good, we have seen that there are inferior and superior kinds of eternal good that each of our soul's desire. Some people will reach only the lower Mysteries, but some people will come to understand the greater Mysteries. This is akin to an experience of poetry, which as I explained earlier, can be done well or poorly. Similarly, in the *Phaedrus*, when some people see "what we call beauty" down here, they will "surrender to pleasure, eager to make babies" (250e). However, other people will be lovers of wisdom, cultivating their talents in philosophy. Additionally, in the *Phaedrus*, as in the *Symposium*, Socrates speaks of a greater Mystery, "the Mystery that we may rightly call the most blessed of all" (250c).[18] This Mystery can be grasped only by the person who properly and appropriately "uses the reminders" of the things of the soul during its primordial vision (249c). This is the person who has been led correctly (252e). This person "is always at the highest, most perfect level of initiation, and he is the only one who is perfect as perfect can be," drawing closest to the divine (249d).

Thus, there are people who will transform as the result of an erotic experience of beauty, and there are people who will not. There is also a specific case in which the moral training of the *Republic* or the moral growth that may result from an erotic experience of beauty are not necessary: the Gods' souls are already in order, and they are in control of their desires, as opposed to mortals (247a, 246d–e). The Gods do not need assistance—they are already elevated.[19] Importantly, in the case of mortals, it is an erotic experience of a beautiful person that begins the process of nourishing the soul (248c). Thus, the mortal soul is particularly suited for the erotic experience of a beautiful person, whereas the souls of the gods—the ones that are already in proper hierarchical order—are already nourished by beauty. In the case of a mortal, it is an erotic experience of a beautiful person that potentially leads the soul to become more like the souls of the gods.[20]

I am suggesting that there is another similar case where a person has properly ordered their soul, as the result of the aesthetic training of the *Republic*. If this person encounters the beautiful beloved, they need not rein the black horse in. Presumably, if the person has undergone moral training, their appetitive part (their black horse) will not need to be violently brought under control (just as in the healthy city, no part will need "brought under control" and no violence is necessary). In the healthy soul, both "horses" will be trained to track the higher value that reason calculates as good. In this case, one might think that the person's soul is indeed closer to the soul of a God than that of the person whose soul is out of order. If this is correct, the person with the well-ordered soul would seemingly have a different sort of erotic experience of beauty than the person whose soul is in civil war or "untrained."

With my arguments from earlier sections in mind, one will recall that, for Plato, grasping goodness is something that begins in the lower parts of the soul; that is, it begins in the parts of the soul that are limited to perception. In the *Republic*, we see that it begins with proper exposure to aesthetic media. Moral education can come to full fruition only if an agent becomes able to distinguish what she has grasped through appetite and spirit from a higher good that is only understood by reason. In terms of being motivated toward the good, the best-case scenario for the lower parts of the soul is that they should be trained to track the higher value that reason calculates as good. This training is the goal of the aesthetic education described in Books II and III of the *Republic*, which just is role (1) that is played by beauty in Plato's general theory of moral progress. Role (2) is another sort of way in which beauty motivates moral progress, but this sort of motivation will not likely be necessary for the person who has successfully undergone (1). They may still have an erotic experience of beauty, but it will be a higher sort of experience than that which is possible for the soul that is still in "civil war."

I suggest that someone who has a properly ordered soul and has trained the lower parts to track the higher value that reason calculates as good will experience beauty differently than the way in which the lover in the metaphor experiences it. If one's "black horse" is trained to track the higher value that the "charioteer" calculates as good, Beauty will not need to "strike him like a bolt of lightning" (254b), or force order upon the soul, since the soul is already in order. The person with the well-ordered soul has a richer experience of beauty—something closer to the way in which the souls of Gods are continually nourished by it (246de). On this reading, the kind of experience of beauty described in the metaphor is something that delivers the unruly soul to the same place that a properly trained soul would naturally arrive.

Conclusion

I have argued that it is possible to train the black horse of the *Phaedrus* and that the aesthetic education described in Books II and III of the *Republic* is one way to accomplish such training. A thorough understanding of this kind of moral training seems to suggest a relationship between the process of moral progress the *Republic* and process of moral progress in the *Phaedrus* that is worth further exploration.

Revisiting the epigraph with which I began this essay, experiences of beauty via art, such as those described in the *Republic* are, to quote the poem, "the means to ensure friendship" between the untrained horse and, as Plato puts it, the "beauty of reason when it comes" (401d). Experiences of beauty via art may facilitate character development and, thus, the horse's "obedient gaze." The black horse, who has been trained in this way, when "led by his head," will turn around and return home.

Notes

1. I borrowed this poem from Louis Komjathy's *Taming the Wild Horse: An Annotated Translation and Study of The Daoist Horse Taming Pictures*. Columbia UP, 2017. The Daoist Horse Taming Pictures are a series of illustrated poems that use the analogy of horse training or taming the wild horse in order to present the idea of reining in sensory engagement and harnessing psychological patterns through meditation. The poems were likely written by Gao Daokuan. For more on the Horse Taming Poems, see chapter 1, "In Search of The Wild Horse." Reprinted with permission of Columbia University Press.

2. This horse may also represent the level of aspiration attained in the lesser Mysteries of the *Symposium*. See Ferrari for more information on this point (264).

3. I would like to thank Anne Mamary, Thomas Tuozzo, Philip Meckley, and Douglas Drabkin for their helpful feedback on this essay and for our discussions on these topics. I would also like to thank Bryan Martel, my research assistant at KWU, for his time and interest in this work, as well as our conversations on the research related to this essay.

4. A well-functioning soul (or a successfully operating chariot) involves mutual relationships, friendships, as it were, among the three parts. Socrates is speaking within the context of a particular case in which the black horse has gone astray when he references the possibility of training that horse at 247b. For my purposes here, in connection with the case that is described in the Palinode, I

am focusing on the training of the black horse, in particular. However, Socrates' remark does not exclude the white horse from also needing training.

  5. See Glen Lesses for more discussion of the view that, in the *Republic*, Plato tries to reconcile his acceptance of the possibility of *akrasia* with a Socratic account of motivation. Also, see Moss (35).

  6. These classes of motivation are explained thoroughly by Hendrik Lorenze in *The Brute Within*. I would note that, while each part has a respective motivation, this does not necessarily exclude, for example, the spirited part taking pleasure in honor or the calculative part finding the Beautiful beautiful.

  7. "Good-independent" readings insist that Plato's tripartition of the soul implies that only the rational part of the soul desires the good, while the desires of the non-rational parts of the soul in no way depend on apprehension of their objects as good. These desires, since they have no concern for good, may come into conflict with our rational desires, which are directed toward the good. *Akrasia* takes place in instances in which desires come into conflict, when a person acts in accordance with non-rational desires instead of rational desires. Proponents of good-dependence argue, however, that only a rational-part-ruling soul can understand in what goodness consists, and that souls that are ruled by the lower parts err on account of confused notions of the good. According to the good-dependence theorist, it is this kind of confused notion of the good that gives rise to (and accounts for) the sorts of *akratic* actions that Plato describes in the *Republic*. See Woods and Kahn. Furthermore, Irwin gives an account of good-independence, but he does allow for the spirit to be good-dependent, in part.

  8. Annas and Irwin discuss the way in which the rational part can be distinguished from the other two insofar as it has a capacity that they lack.

  9. It is important to note that the rational part is not exempt from failing in the pursuit of goodness. However, it is the only part that *can* grasp the real good. Thus, a rational-part-ruling soul is a person's best bet when it comes to making moral progress.

  10. I am referring to that which appeals to the lower parts of the soul, specifically the parts which are attracted to pleasure and beauty at first glance. This is not to say that the rational part is not attracted to beauty, especially in the case of something like Parmenides' poem. The thought here, however, is that since the beginning stages of good-recognition happen within lower parts of the soul, the good must be presented to them in a medium that they can grasp, and Plato gives the aesthetic media of poetry and music as examples.

  11. Socrates also emphasizes the role of music in moral education, and it seems that a progression (analogous to the one we have seen in the case of poetry) takes place in this case. However, I do not have room to give an analysis of Plato's discussions of music here.

  12. Reading Plato's work itself requires a poet's skill. Plato's metaphors, though they do not present literal facts, still teach us truths about our lives. This

is, in part, why this essay begins with poem epigraph, gesturing at Plato's use of *Muskie* and the truths we might learn about our lives of multiplicity from Plato's dialogues. My thanks to Anne Mamary for providing insights on this topic through our discussions of various iterations of this essay.

13. At 500d we are told that people imitate that toward which they feel wonder. We feel wonder when we experience poetry and, on Plato's view, this is why we imitate or pursue the content therein.

14. Aesthetic education refers to the education brought about by aesthetic experience, as Plato describes it. Education brings about moral progress, for Plato, and aesthetic education involves experiences of beauty that can be used in moral training.

15. See Trexler Drees (27–43).

16. See Trexler Drees (5–43).

17. One might suggest that a kind of training is implied here, by repeatedly forcing the horse under control. However, this position assumes that forcing is a type of training, and I'm not certain it necessarily qualifies as such. In fact, this view is inconsistent with the training that is described in the *Republic* and in the *Laws*. In the *Laws*, Book VII, training does not involve force, but rather play (794), and in the *Republic* it involves exercise for the body and "music and poetry for the soul" (*Republic* 376e). Plato's theory of education just is a kind of moral training, on my view.

18. "Beauty was radiant to see at the time when the souls . . . saw that blessed and spectacular vision and were ushered into the Mystery that we may rightly call the most blessed of all" (250c–d).

19. However, even the horses of the Gods must be nourished by their charioteers (247e). Yet, unlike humans, the Gods are wise enough to know what to feed the horses. See Griswold (93).

20. Related to this is Plato's description of the relationship between the lover and beloved later in the text. The proper relationship is such that the older one of the two makes the younger one *like a God*. Hence, since the "horses" and "charioteers" of the Gods willingly play their own hierarchical roles, one might suggest that this evidences the fact that the sort of philosophical friendship that Plato describes also occasions the well-ordered soul.

Works Cited

Annas, Julia. *An Introduction to Plato's* Republic. Oxford UP, 1981.

Asmis, Elizabeth. "Plato on Poetic Creativity." *The Cambridge Companion to Plato*, edited by Richard Kraut, Cambridge UP, 2006, pp. 338–64.

Ferrari, G. R. F. "Platonic Love." *The Cambridge Companion to Plato*, edited by Richard Kraut, Cambridge UP, 1992, pp. 248–71.

———. "Plato and Poetry." *The Cambridge History of Literary Criticism*, edited by George Alexander Kennedy, vol. 1, 1989, pp. 92–148.

Griswold, Charles. "The Palinode." *Self-Knowledge in Plato's Phaedrus*, Yale UP, 1986, pp. 92–148.

Irwin, Terrence. *Plato's Moral Theory*, Oxford UP, 1977.

———. *Plato's Ethics* Oxford UP, 1995.

Kahn, Charles. "Plato's Theory of Desire." *Reviews of Metaphysics*, vol. 41, 1987, pp. 77–103.

Komjathy, Louis. *Taming the Wild Horse: An Annotated Translation and Study of The Daoist Horse Taming Pictures*. Columbia UP, 2017.

Lear, Richardson Gabriel. "Plato on Learning to Love Beauty." *The Blackwell Guide to Plato's* Republic, edited by Gerasimos Santas, Blackwell, 2008, pp. 104–25.

Lesses, Glen. "Weakness, Reason, and The Divided Soul in Plato's Republic." *History of Philosophy Quarterly*, vol. 4, no. 2, 1987, pp. 147–61.

Lorenze, Hendrick. *The Brute Within*. Oxford UP, 2006.

Moss, Jessica. "Appearances and Calculations: Plato's Division of the Soul." *Oxford Studies in Ancient Philosophy*, edited by Brad Inwood, Oxford UP, 2008, pp. 35–68.

———. "Pleasure and Illusion in Plato" *Philosophy and Phenomenological Research*. vol. 72. no. 3, pp. 503–35.

Nicholson, Graeme. *Plato's* Phaedrus, Purdue UP, 1999.

Plato. Republic. Translated by G. M. A. Grube and C. D. C. Reeve, *Complete Works*, edited by John M. Cooper, Hackett, 1997, pp. 1177–1307.

Woods, Michael. "Plato's Division of the Soul." *Proceedings of the British Academy*. vol. 73, 1987, pp. 23–47.

"Riches without Envy"
Picturing the Words of *Philebus* 40a10[1]

Mateo Duque

In order to defend the view that the life of the mind is more worthy than the life of pleasure, Socrates in the *Philebus* at one point supports the controversial claim that there are false pleasures. In order to back this up, at 38e12–39c6, he uses a metaphor to discuss what we might call "mental representations": he says that our internal assertions are as if there was a scribe writing words in our souls like in a book and that after this there is a painter who paints images based on the scribe's words, in the soul as if on a canvas. In this essay:

1. I demonstrate that Plato is both describing and instantiating the aesthetic concept of ekphrasis, the transformation of one form of representation into another.

2. I show that Plato is complicating a view implied in the scribe and painter analogy: that we think primarily in words and *then* in images.

3. I argue that the act of interpretation is necessary to go from words to images, and I examine one particular ambiguous phrase to illustrate the need for interpretation.

At 40a–b, Socrates acknowledges that many of us have a hope for a future with vast wealth and the pleasures that come with it. Socrates says that this internal image is mostly true for good people and false for bad people. In order to interpret this idea properly, I argue that it depends on how we read the phrase "*chruson gignomenon aphthonon*" at 40a10, which I contend is a written riddle. 40a10 has traditionally been read as if the good person will come to have a lot of money; instead, I read it as the good person will come to have goods *without envy*—the literal meaning of *aphthonon*. People who are morally good will possess an abundance (not of material wealth but of spiritual goods, virtue) without having envy toward others. Not all words are univocal. When we read words like Plato's or a poet's, we can often draw several meanings from a single word or phrase. It seems that the words by themselves can lead to different pictures or images. This is especially true for this line in the *Philebus* where there is the more common picture of "a lot of money," but I want to urge that there is a rival image at play: "goods without envy."

The Scribe and Painter Analogy 38e1–39c6[2]

Near the beginning of the *Philebus*, Protarchus and Socrates agree that a life of *only* enjoyment, pleasure, and delight as well as a life of *only* thinking, knowing, and understanding are not sufficient on their own, but that the best life is one that is a mixture of the two. However, both Socrates and Protarchus want to see which life—whether the life of pleasure or the life of the mind—deserves the "second prize" (22c8). In order to defend the priority of the life of the intellect, Socrates introduces the concept of "false pleasures" at 36c7–8. Protarchus resists this idea. The gist of Protarchus' opposition is that, while judgments may be true or false, regardless of the object of one's pleasure, if one is enjoying and deriving pleasure from something, then there is no way that the pleasure itself can be false. We can, for example, take pleasure in a completely imaginary scenario, something that cannot and will never be the case, a pure fantasy (like in a dream, I become a dolphin), but the pleasure we get from this is still real.

In order to defend "false pleasures," at 38e12–13, Socrates, talking about making silent internal assertions, says, "it seems to me that our soul at that time in some way resembles a book."[3] This is a prelude to when he introduces the metaphor of the scribe: "When memory coincides with perception at the same time, these and the impressions concerned with them appear to me like some sort of writing in our souls with words. And whenever this very impression he writes is true, true opinions and true accounts [*doxa te alēthēs kai logoi*] of it happen to come about; but whenever the writer inside us writes [*par' hēmin grammateus graphē*] false things this sort comes about, the opposite of truth results" (39a1–7). Protarchus agrees and Socrates continues with the metaphor, introducing the painter: "Then a painter [*zōgraphon*], who after the scribe [*meta ton grammatistēn*], paints [*graphei*], from the words [*tōn legomenōn*], images [*eikonas*] of these things in the soul" (39b6–7).[4]

Ekphrasis

Ekphrasis is when one artistic medium (like painting) represents the work of another medium (like the words of a poet). One of the most famous examples of ekphrasis is Homer's description of the shield of Achilles (*Iliad* 18.478–608). Plato's metaphor in the *Philebus* describes the ekphrastic process in our soul whereby a painter converts the words of a scribe into an image. And yet Plato is himself a writer and must use literary images to present his points. Like Homer describing Achilles' shield, Plato conveys vivid representations in the metaphor of the scribe and painter inside of us. Lydia Goehr describes ekphrasis as effecting "intermedial and energetic movements of form and sensorial experience, in which words speak *poetically* or *musically* through *painting* in order . . . to recorporealize and rematerialize that which is or has been made absent. Many also note that what ekphrasis aims to do, it cannot actually or literally do. It can neither bring all corporeal senses into action nor render present or existent that which is absent or non-existent" (392; emphasis in original). What kind of scribe is inside us? Is she or he poetically gifted? Plato seems to imagine a police sketch artist who represents "just the facts, ma'am." In this way, description—denotative, referential, or otherwise—is separated from the less "exact" tasks of interpretation, evocation, evaluation, and justification (Goehr 394). However, as I will emphasize later, words are not univocal or neutral. The painter cannot simply "read off" the words of the scribe, the painter must also interpret what she or he sees in order to paint images.

The Implied Priority of Words over Images in Our Thinking

While the metaphor of the scribe and the painter goes by quickly in the *Philebus*, there is an implication of the view Socrates has presented: the priority of words over images in our thinking. In the analogy the priority is temporal—the painter paints *after* [*meta*] the writer. But, because the point is about our internal representations, the priority is also *logical*; according to this metaphor, words come prior to images in our reasoning. This is not merely an ancient debate. As Daniel Dennett attests (using modern terms) in "Current Issues of Philosophy of Mind": "A particularly active controversy within the area of internal representation concerns the nature of the supposed vehicles of representation: are they propositional (like sentences) or imagistic or analogical (like pictures or maps)" (258). The question of whether we think with images or words remains alive even today.

The *Philebus* gives a clear temporal and logical ordering, first words *then* images, but there are other places where Plato complicates this view.[5] There are two ways in which Plato confounds this clear view: (1) images (as shapes) help us to read, recognize, and understand words; (2) the use of captivating word-images in the dialogues.

In the *Philebus*, there is no mention of an intermediary who would read the text aloud to the painter as would most often be the case in the fifth and fourth centuries BCE ancient Greece (Nagy 417–31). Instead, it seems as if the painter reads the text himself and then paints an image. But this makes reading a necessary process in this metaphor for internal representations. The necessity of *reading* written words as opposed to hearing speech calls into question the immediacy and/or priority of words over images in thinking.

Let me give a few examples from the Platonic corpus where Plato discusses the cognitive work required to read and how recognizing shapes and images is actually *prior* to reading. At *Theaetetus* 163b–4c, Socrates marks a difference between merely hearing the high and low notes of a foreign language that one does not understand, as opposed to hearing speech in a language that one does know. Additionally, Socrates speaks of someone who sees the shapes and colors of the marks on the page versus someone who knows how to read and sees them as letters and words. Here, Socrates gestures toward a distinction between the bare sensation of the shapes and colors of written words (as an experience that someone illiterate may have of a text) as opposed to the knowing perception of someone after having learned the alphabet. It is only after being able to distinguish the letters and words as different from each other that someone can read. So, in reading, it is only by *first* recognizing shapes and colors *as* particular letters (or seeing images) that we can then understand them as words representing and referring to objects (grasping their linguistic meaning). Plato often brings up the experience of children learning how to read and learning how to recognize letters and understand syllables and then their combination (*Theaetetus* 206a–b; *Statesman* 277e; *Republic* 3.402a). Lastly, at *Theaetetus* 206e–208a, Socrates brings up the example of someone learning to read and write who is trying to write the name 'Theaetetus' but does not adequately know the difference between the letter theta (Θ) and the letter tau (T). This shows us someone who can visualize the image of Theaetetus and pick him out of a lineup but who is unable to read or write Theaetetus' name properly. Do we want to say that this person does not know Theaetetus?

It is also revealing that in the *Philebus* Plato has Socrates use two activities, writing and painting, that in other dialogues Socrates criticizes and denigrates. In fact, at *Phaedrus* 275d–e, Socrates compares writing to painting. He says that if someone were to question paintings they stay solemnly silent, and the same with written words: "if you question anything that has been said because you want to learn more, it continues to signify the same thing forever" (275d8–9, this and the following are from the Woodruff and Nehamas translation; cf. *Protagoras* 329a). Later in the *Phaedrus*, Socrates questions the belief that writing can have "great certainty and clarity [*kai megalēn tina en autō bebaiotēta ēgoumenos kai saphēneian*]" (277d8–9).[6] And in *Republic X*, Socrates lumps together painters with poets (as imitators) and says that both deal with appearances that are at a third remove from the truth (598a–9a), and they consort "with a part of us that is far from reason" (603a, this and the following are from the Grube/Reeve translation). Now, in the *Philebus*, Socrates uses writing and even takes written words to be prior to images for our internal representations. My objection is similar to Derrida's insight that in the *Phaedrus* Plato has Socrates use the very metaphor of writing (which he has been denigrating) to describe "knowing, living animate discourse, but as an *inscription* of truth in the soul, . . . the so-called living discourse [is] described by a 'metaphor' borrowed from the order of the very thing one is trying to exclude from it, the order of its simulacrum" (149).[7] This is the return of the repressed.

Furthermore, Plato often describes Socrates' speeches as themselves composed of images [*eikones*]. In the *Republic*, Socrates warns both Glaucon and Adeimantus that the account he is giving them cannot be the real thing but only an image, a representation, of what they are asking for. He says: "You won't be able to follow me any longer, Glaucon, even though there is no lack of eagerness on my part to lead you, for you would no longer be seeing an image [*eikona*] of what we're describing, but the truth itself" (*Republic* 7.533a1–3). And Socrates characterizes himself as a lover of images: "In any case, listen to my simile [*eikonos*], and you'll appreciate all the more how greedy for images [*glischrōs eikazō*] I am" (*Republic* 488a1–2). Although images are described as second best here, they do not seem to have the much more negative connotations that Socrates ascribes to them elsewhere—even in other parts of the *Republic*. They are necessary for understanding Socrates' argument of the *Republic*. This idea of Platonic and Socratic word-images [*eikones*] seems to undermine the strict distinction and hierarchy of words *over* images. In order to paint a picture, the painter inside of us must *interpret* the words of scribes because one can possibly imagine multiple images from even a single word. In order to illustrate this point, I will turn to a phrase riddled with ambiguity, 40a10, which can be read in at least two ways.

Multiple Images from One Word

After introducing the scribe and painter metaphor, Socrates continues his argument for "false pleasures." After Socrates brings up the painter inside us, Protarchus asks how and when the painter paints these internal images, and Socrates answers: "Whenever someone receives opinions and utterances [*doxazomena kai legomena*] from vision or some other senses at that time, and then views the images of those opinions and utterances [*tōn doxasthentōn kai lexthentōn*] inside himself" (39b9–c1). Those words and pictures that come to be in us are all really [*sphodra* 39e3–4] hopes [*elipides*] concerned with the future, and we are always filled with hopes throughout our whole lives (39e4–6). Socrates elaborates, giving a rather surprising and puzzling consequence: "But in fact there's also the painted images [*phantasmata ezōgraphēmena*]. And someone often sees himself coming to have **abundant money | riches without envy** [*chruson gignomenon aphthonon*] and many pleasures follow upon it. Moreover he looks upon [*kathora*] a painting of himself [*enezōgraphēmenon auton*] and enjoys it immensely [*eph' autō chaironta sphodra*]" (40a9–12; emphasis added). I will have much more to say about the phrase "*chruson gignomenon aphthonon*," but I want to show the final steps in Socrates' surprising reasoning. He says: "[I]n the case of good people [*agathois*] these pictures that are set up for them [*ta gramamena paratithesthai*] are for the most part true [*alēthē*], because they are beloved by the gods [*theophileis*], while

"Riches without Envy" | 89

in the case of bad people [*kakois*] it is the opposite [*tounantion*], again, for the most part" (40b2–4). Socrates gives a theological justification for his point. The hopes written and then painted in us will be for the most part true for good people, who are beloved by gods, and for the most part false for bad people.

In the final few moves of his argument, Socrates says: "Therefore bad people [*tois kakois*] have painted pleasures [*hēdonai . . . ezōgraphēmenai*] show up, no less than anyone else, but they are somehow false [*pseudeis de autai pou*]" (40b6–7). "Thus, the bad people [*oi ponēroi*] delight in false pleasures [*pseudesin . . . hēdonais*], but the good people [*oi d'agathoi tōn anthrōpōn*] in true ones [*alēthesin*]" (40c1–2). And here, Socrates concludes his argument for "false pleasures": "In fact, according to our argument now there are false pleasures [*pseudeis . . . hēdonai*] in the souls of humans, indeed imitating [*memimēmenai*] by caricatures [*geloiotera*] the true ones [*tas alētheis*], and likewise pains" (40c4–6). Socrates seems to use the gods as a guarantee for "just desserts." And yet, I want to argue that when interpreted correctly *chruson* here should not just mean material wealth, but something else—Plato is severely critical of mere pecuniary prosperity in many other places.[8] The scribe and painter analogy may give the impression that words are not simply transformed into images, but the act of interpretation is necessary to picture images from words. In order to prove this, I want to look at a phrase, "*chruson gignomenon aphthonon*," that is ambiguous and about which Plato encourages at least two interpretations (40a10).

Philebus 40a9–12 has been a thorn in many an interpreter's side; it is also not obvious how those lines fit with the ones that follow at 40b2–c6. The traditional reading of 40a10, "*chruson gignomenon aphthonon*," reads *aphthonon* as qualifying *chruson*: in a *quantitative* way as a "bounteous" or "plentiful" amount of gold (e.g., Gosling's "a vast sum of gold"; Hackforth's "great quantities of gold"; D. Frede's "enormous amount of gold"). But what if this line was not as straightforward as it first appears but is instead a kind of riddle? My contention is that 40a10 is actually a polysemous aphorism—almost Heraclitean—which the reader, before interpreting its true meaning, must first properly "'see" (the very first word of the *Philebus* is the imperative *hora*, "see"). The traditional reading of this line is the obvious, natural meaning of the words. In fact, "a lot of money" is what many people would say if asked what it is that they desire. This is the meaning that the "bad people" talked about later in 40b–c would see if they were to read Plato's words. This is the first possible way of reading the phrase.

There is another way of reading 40a10; one can translate *aphthonon* literally as a *qualitative* modification of *chruson*—as meaning "without envy"—and *chruson* not as "gold" but in a more poetic fashion as "anything dear" or "precious" (LSJ A.3). So, the new gloss on 401a10 would be: anything of value that comes to the one imagining this scenario is "not begrudgingly" or "without envy" (LSJ A.II.2).[9] Reading 40a10 in this way allows us to better understand the sequel, in which Socrates says that good people, who are beloved by the gods, have more true internal pictures, while bad people have false ones, and Philebus agrees (40b–c). Good people will "see" and imagine future hopes of riches without envy, and "riches" in the broadest sense possible, including goods of the soul, virtues.[10] Furthermore, the good person *would* get many pleasures from goods that are psychologically uplifting; for example, she might surreptitiously help others with this money. Thus, her self-image would be true. But beyond the pecuniary, the lines are about all valuable things that one may hope for, including psychological goods, corporeal goods (like health, and beauty), and even virtues. The last one is the most important. The real riches are virtues. This is the way that Socrates and the good, beloved-by-the-gods people would read these lines of Plato. Non-virtuous people will "see" the phrase and imagine unlimited *material* wealth; since they expect material gain, their hopes and future self-images will be wrong and false, especially because external goods, like money, are not always up to us, whereas virtue is.

There is an irony in the fact that although Plato is trying to depict psychological imaging, he is a writer, he is himself a scribe, who must work with words and so cannot just present images like a painter. Plato has just switched from talking about the writer in the soul to the painter in the soul, but his medium is still *logoi*. Even words on a page, which are meant to represent the picturing of a painting, must first be properly interpreted or "seen" before its untold and unenvied riches are revealed. We must know what images properly attach to the meaning of a word or phrase. With words there is often ambiguity and polysemy; they are not univocal, perspicuous, and ready to be imagined with no mediation, as Plato seems to imply with the scribe and painter metaphor. There can be multiple images associated with one word, and we must know which one to pick carefully. I will show some Platonic passages related to "envy" [*phthonos*] that give strong evidence to interpret *aphthonon* the way I do, as "without envy."

"Envy" [*Phthonos*] in Plato

Envy [*phthonos*] is an emotion that Plato discusses often throughout his corpus. At *Laws* 3.679b7–c2, the Athenian says: "Now the community in which neither wealth nor poverty exists will generally produce the finest characters because tendencies to violence and crime and feelings of jealousy and envy [*zēloi kai phthonoi*], simply do not arise" (Saunders translation).

The ideal society that would produce the best characters would contain no jealousy or envy because it would have neither rich nor poor. In the *Phaedrus* 247a7, Socrates says, envy "[*phthonos*] has no place in the gods' chorus." And at *Timaeus* 29d7–e2, Timaeus says: "Now why did he who framed this whole universe of becoming frame it? Let us state the reason why: He was good and one who is good can never become envious [*phthonos*] of anything. And so, being free of it [*toutou ektos*], he wanted everything to become as much like himself as was possible" (Zeyl translation). As we can see, the highest Platonic ethical standard, be it in a utopia or in the god that created the universe, is one without envy. Envy is such a mortal, all-too-human emotion; whereas, "becoming as like god as possible" might mean becoming someone without envy (*Theaetetus* 176b1). "The philosopher must, therefore, like the god whom he wishes to resemble, be rid of envy" (Brisson 211; cf. *Republic* 6.500b–c). A good person will not envy or begrudge others. For Plato, gods and good people do not have envy. But what is wrong with envy? Beatriz Bossi describes the plight of envious person well:

> Not only because [the envious person] ignores his unfair behavior towards others, but mainly because he is likely to judge improperly his own condition, as safe and sound with regard to the risk of self-deceit about his own character and temperament. In addition, the envious person . . . must have a biased way of perceiving what he himself deserves and lacks, in comparison with the way he perceives what others possess and deserve. . . . We should conclude that the envious does not judge properly, feels superior to his peers and ignores the real condition of his soul. (231)

The envious person embodies well Aesop's fable of the dog carrying meat or the image from the New Testament of someone more concerned with the splinter in others' eyes than with the beam in his own (Matthew 7:5).[11] The envious person, because he is so concerned with others (and their goods and their faults), fails to accurately and adequately assess himself, especially when it comes to the possibility of deceiving himself. He does not have a proper and right self-image. As Thomas Tuozzo writes, "[T]he malicious person himself lacks self-knowledge, for if that person in fact knew the goods he possessed, he would not allow his self-image to be influenced by a comparison with others" (511; quoted in Bossi 231n27).

The Athenian draws the contrast between the virtuous person *without envy* and the envious person in the *Laws* 5.731a2–b3, saying:

> Let every one of us be ambitious to gain excellence, but *without envy* [*aphthonōs*]. For a man of this character enlarges a city, since he strives hard himself and does not thwart the others by slander [*diabolais*]; but *the envious man* [*ho de phthoneros*], thinking that the slander [*diabolē*] of others is the best way to secure his own superiority, makes less effort himself to win true excellence, and disheartens his rivals by getting them unjustly blamed; whereby he causes the whole city to be ill-trained for competing in excellence, and renders it, for his part, less large in fair repute. (Bury translation with minor changes and emphasis added)

Here we can see that the person without envy is a great social and political asset, one who enriches a city because he goes after true virtue. But the envious person is petty and uses slander [*diabolē*] to harm and hurt others who are doing better than him. As a result, the envious makes a city poorer in spirit. Finally, Plato plays with etymology of *apthonos* to justify how the philosopher, being without envy, cannot inspire a movement of envy in others at *Republic* 500a3–7. Socrates asks, "Or do you think that someone being free from envy and gentle [**aphthonon te kai praon onta**] is harsh [*chalepainein*] to someone who is not difficult [*tō mē chalepō*] nor is envious [*phthonein*] of someone not envious [**mē phthonerō**]? I'll anticipate your answer and say that a few people may have such a harsh character, but not the majority"[12] (emphasis added). Someone who is without envy [*aphthonon*] does not have envy [*mē phthonerō*]. This helps to clarify how we are warranted in reading *aphthonon* as "without envy" in the *Philebus* passage 40a10, as I have argued. This is against the common sense of *aphthonon* as "abundant" or "unstinting." There is a different denotation to the same phrase, *aphthonon chruson*, depending on who sees it. The way that one reads the phrase and imagines it can give insight into the values, future hopes, and the kind of life and person someone is. The bad people think and see "a lot of money" and good people think and see "riches (in the broadest sense) without envy."

Conclusion

In this essay I have looked at Plato's metaphor of what we can call "internal representation" in the *Philebus*. Plato has Socrates analogize our thinking with an image of two craftspeople inside of us: there is a scribe who writes words on our souls as if in a book and a painter who paints images in our soul as if on a canvas. These words and images can be true or false. First, I demonstrated that Plato is both describing and utilizing the concept of ekphrasis with this analog. I complicated an implication from this analogy that we think first in words and *then* in images. I demonstrated that Plato is both describing and utilizing the concept of ekphrasis with this analogy. Finally, I suggested a more profitable way of interpreting the phrase "*chruson gignomenon aphthonon*" at 40a10. It has traditionally been read as if the good person will come to have a lot of money; instead, I read it as the good person will come to have goods *without envy*—the literal meaning of *aphthonon*. People who are morally good will possess an abundance without feeling envy.[13]

Notes

1. I would like to thank Tony Preus. I would also like to thank Colin Behrens, Matthieu Real, and Farhad Taraz. I would especially like to thank Jonathan Fine who helped me revise the final version of this essay.

2. For some of the literature on the *Philebus* specifically about 38e12–40c7 (about false pleasures; the scribe and the painter metaphor; and the gods rewarding good men and punishing bad men), see Austin; Bartlett; Campos; Carpenter; Delcomminette; Dybikowski; Dimas; Evans; Fletcher; Forte; Frede; Garner; Giménez Salinas; Hampton; Harte; Ionescu; Lisi; Lovibond; Marcos de Pinotti; McLaughlin; Migliori; Mooradian; Moss; Muniz; Ogihara; Parry; Penner; Reidy; Sommerville; Thein; Vogt; and Whiting.

3. This and the following quotes from the *Philebus* are my translation, in consultation with the Davidson, Frede, Gosling, Hackforth, Migliori, and Pradeau

translations. The analogy of thought as a silent internal conversation with oneself is in *Theaetetus* 189–90a and in *Sophist* 263a–4b.

4. I cannot take up an interesting proposal by Fletcher: "the scribe corresponds to the thing in the soul that makes judgments and the painter corresponds to the thing that takes pleasure; thus, the activities of writing and painting correspond to the activities of judging and taking pleasure, and the resulting writing statements and pictures correspond to judgments and pleasures respectively" (3).

5. I am not claiming that Plato is reversing his position in the *Philebus*; I want to show that he is presenting it as a problem.

6. My translation. On rereading in the *Phaedrus*, see Duque "(Re)reading without Writing?: A Performative Contradiction in Plato's *Phaedrus*" (2021 manuscript).

7. For writing in the soul in the *Phaedrus*, see 276a5–6, 278a3.

8. The following are examples of Plato's circumspection about money and its excesses. *Phaedrus* (289c1–3), Socrates' final prayer at the end of the dialogue: "As for gold, let me have as much as a moderate man could bear and carry with him." *Republic* 9.591d5–e5 reads:

> Will he also keep order and consonance in his acquisition of money, with that same end in view? Or, even though he isn't dazzled by the size of the majority into accepting their idea of blessed happiness, will he increase his wealth without limit and so have unlimited evils?
>
> Not in my view.
>
> Rather, he'll look to the constitution within him and guard against disturbing anything in it, either by too much money or too little. And, in this way, he'll direct both the increase and expenditure of his wealth, as far as he can.
>
> Hampton offers another: "in Book VIII of *The Republic*, in Plato's account of the oligarchic man who centers his life around the amassing of wealth. He controls his indulgence in bodily appetites not out of reason but out of fear of squandering his money (553b–559d; cf. *Phaedo* 68e–69a)" (59).

9. In an earlier version of this essay I argued that the good person would not make others envious. I realized this position goes too far because, like honor, it relies on other people and *their* psychological states. Good persons can rely only on what is completely up to them, their own virtue. Once we understand what kind of goods are involved, the idea that good things will come to good people is not so far-fetched and it relates to the idea in the *Apology* that a good person cannot be harmed (30c, 41c).

10. See also Aristotle's *Nichomachean Ethics* (1.8 1098b13–18).

11. The portrait I wish to draw here of the "envious person" is quite congruent with the account of the foolish person in Whiting, an excellent article on the *Philebus*.

12. My intervention for *Philebus* 40a10, "*chruson gignomenon aphthonon*," is in some ways similar to Justina Gregory and Susan B. Levin's intervention into *Symposium* 210d10 "*en philosophia aphthonō*." Although I did not know about this article until after I had written my essay. Another paper that touches upon *phthonos* in Plato and specifically in the context of the *Timaeus* is F. G. Hermann. I thank Jonathan Fine for both of these references.

13. I have written this essay in honor of someone who embodies and inspires living the life of "riches without envy": Tony Preus. I first met him in 2018 when I went to the Society of Ancient Greek Philosophy (SAGP) annual meeting in Newport News, Virginia, but I really got to know him between 2020 and 2022 while I was a postdoctoral fellow at Binghamton University, where he has been my mentor. Tony welcomed me to Binghamton at a difficult moment, during the height of the COVID pandemic. I want to thank him for his kindness and generosity of spirit. In the fall of 2022, I became an assistant professor of philosophy at Binghamton University, and I owe a lot to Tony.

Works Cited

Austin, Emily A. "Fools and Malicious Pleasure in Plato's *Philebus*." *History of Philosophy Quarterly*, vol. 29, no. 2, 2012, pp. 125–39.
Bartlett, Robert C. "Plato's Critique of Hedonism in the *Philebus*." *American Political Science Review*, vol. 102, no. 1, 2008, pp. 141–51.
Bossi, Beatriz. "On Mild Envy and Self-Deceit (*Phlb.* 47d–50e)." Renaut and Candiotto, pp. 220–37.
Brisson, Luc. "The Notion of φθόνος in Plato." Renaut and Candiotto, pp. 201–19.
Bywater, Ingram, editor. *Aristotelis: Ethica Nicomachea*. Cambridge UP, 2010.
Campos, Daniel. "La verdad del placer en el *Filebo*." Dillon and Brisson, pp. 243–49.
Carone, Gabriela Roxana. "Hedonism and the Pleasureless Life in Plato's *Philebus*." *Phronesis*, vol. 45, no. 4, 2000, pp. 257–83.
Carpenter, Amber Danielle. "Hedonistic Persons. The Good Man Argument in Plato's *Philebus*." *British Journal for the History of Philosophy*, vol. 14, no. 1, 2006, pp. 5–26.
Cooper, John, and D. S. Hutchinson, editors. *Plato: Complete Works*. Hackett. 1997.
Davidson, Donald. *Plato's* Philebus. Routledge, 2012.
Delcomminette, Sylvain. "False Pleasures, Appearance and Imagination in the *Philebus*." *Phronesis*, vol. 48, no. 3, 2003, pp. 215–37.

Dennett, D. C. "Current Issues in the Philosophy of Mind." *American Philosophical Quarterly*, vol. 15, no. 4, 1978, pp. 249–61.
Derrida, Jacques. "Plato's Pharmacy." *Dissemination*, edited by Barbara Johnson, U of Chicago P, 1981, pp. 61–171.
Dillon, John, and Luc Brisson, editors. *Plato's Philebus: Selected Papers from the Eighth Symposium Platonicum*. Academia Verlag, 2010.
Dimas, Panos. "Two Ways in Which Pleasures Can Be False: *Philebus* 36c–42c." *Plato's Philebus: A Philosophical Discussion*, edited by Panos Dimas, Russell E. Jones, and Gabriel R. Lear, Oxford UP, 2019, pp. 124–40.
Dybikowski, James. "False Pleasure and the *Philebus*." *Phronesis*, vol. 15, no. 1–2, 1970, pp. 147–65.
Evans, Matthew. "Plato on the Possibility of Hedonic Mistakes." *Oxford Studies in Ancient Philosophy* vol. 35, 2008, pp. 89–124.
Fletcher, Emily. "Pleasure, Judgment and the Function of the Painter-Scribe Analogy." *Archiv für Geschichte der Philosophie*, vol. 104, no. 2, 2022, pp. 199–238.
Forte, Joseph. "Explaining Hope in Plato's *Philebus*." *International Philosophical Quarterly*, vol. 56, no. 3, 2016, pp. 283–95.
Frede, Dorothea. "Rumpelstiltskin's Pleasures: True and False Pleasures in Plato's *Philebus*." *Phronesis*, vol. 30, no. 2, 1985, pp. 151–80.
Garner, John V. *The Emerging Good in Plato's* Philebus. Northwestern UP, 2017.
Giménez Salinas, José Antonio. "Creencia, estado afectivo y verdad: placeres de expectativa en el *Filebo* de Platón." *Anales del Seminario de Historia de la Filosofía*, vol. 33, no. 2, 2016, pp. 395–418.
Goehr, Lydia. "How to Do More with Words. Two Views of (Musical) Ekphrasis." *The British Journal of Aesthetics*, vol. 50, no. 4, 2010, pp. 389–410.
Gregory, Justina, and Susan B. Levin. "Φιλοσοφία Ἄφθονος (Plato, *Symposium* 210d)." *The Classical Quarterly*, vol. 48, no. 2, 1998, pp. 404–10. www.jstor.org/stable/639831
Hackforth, Reginald, editor. *Plato's Examination of Pleasure: A Translation of the Philebus, with an Introduction and Commentary*. Cambridge UP, 2011.
Hampton, Cynthia M. *Pleasure, Knowledge, and Being: An Analysis of Plato's Philebus*. SUNY Press, 1990.
Harte, Verity. "The *Philebus* on Pleasure: The Good, the Bad and the False." *Proceedings of the Aristotelian Society*, vol. 104, no. 1, 2004, pp. 113–30.
Herrmann, F. G. "φθόνος in the World of Plato's *Timaeus*." *Envy, Spite and Jealousy: The Rivalrous Emotions in Ancient Greece*, edited by Konstan, David and N. Keith Rutter. Edinburgh UP, 2003, pp. 53–84.
Ionescu, Cristina. *On the Good Life: Thinking Through the Intermediaries in Plato's Philebus*. SUNY Press, 2019.
Lisi, Francisco L. "Ley, placer e intelecto en el *Filebo*." Dillon and Brisson, pp. 179–87.

Lovibond, Sabina. "True and False Pleasures." *Proceedings of the Aristotelian Society*, vol. 90, 1989, pp. 213–30.
Marcos de Pinotti, Graciela E. "Placer y phantasía en *Filebo* 36c3–40e5." Dillon and Brisson, pp. 188–93.
McLaughlin, Andrew. "A Note on False Pleasures in the *Philebus*." *The Philosophical Quarterly*, vol. 19, no. 74, 1969, pp. 57–61.
Migliori, Maurizio. *L'uomo fra piacere, intelligenza e bene: commentario storico-filosofico al "Filebo" di Platone*. Vita e pensiero, 1993.
Mooradian, Norman. "Converting Protarchus: Relativism and False Pleasures of Anticipation in Plato's *Philebus*." *Ancient Philosophy*, vol. 16, no. 1, 1996, pp. 93–112.
Moss, Jessica. "Pictures and Passions in the *Timaeus* and *Philebus*." *Plato and the Divided Self*, edited by Rachel Barney, Tad Brennan, and Charles Brittain, Cambridge UP, 2012, pp. 259–80.
Muniz, Fernando. "Propositional Pleasures in Plato's *Philebus*." *Journal of Ancient Philosophy*, vol. 8, no. 1, 2014, pp. 49–75.
Nagy, Gregory. "Performance and text in ancient Greece." The Center for Hellenic Studies, 2009. chs.harvard.edu/curated-article/gregory-nagy-performance-and-text-in-ancient-greece
Ogihara, Satoshi. "False Pleasures: *Philebus* 36c–40e." Dillon and Brisson, pp. 291–309.
Parry, Richard. "Truth, Falsity, and Pleasures in *Philebus* and *Republic* 9." Dillon and Brisson, pp. 221–26.
Penner, Terry. "False Anticipatory Pleasures: *Philebus* 36a3–41a6." *Phronesis*, vol. 15, no. 1–2, 1970, pp. 166–78.
Plato. *Laws*. Translated by R. G. Bury. Loeb-Harvard, 1926.
———. *Laws*. Translated by Trevor J. Saunders. Cooper and Hutchinson, pp. 1318–616.
———. *Phaedrus*. Translated by Paul Woodruff and Alexander Nehamas. Cooper and Hutchinson, pp. 506–56.
———. *Philebus*. Translated by Dorothea Frede. Hackett, 1993.
———. *Philebus*. Translated with Notes and Commentary by J. C. R. Gosling, Oxford UP, 1975.
———. *Republic*. Translated by G. M. A Grube, and revised by C. D. C. Reeve. Cooper and Hutchinson, pp. 971–1223.
———. *Timaeus*. Translated by Donald J. Zeyl. Cooper and Hutchinson, pp. 1224–91.
———. *Philèbe*. Translated by Jean-François Pradeau, Flammarion, 2002.
Reidy, David A. "False Pleasures and Plato's *Philebus*." *The Journal of Value Inquiry*, vol. 32, no. 3, 1998, pp. 343–56.
Renault, Olivier, and Laura Candiotto, editors. *Emotions in Plato*. Brill, 2020.
Sommerville, Brooks A. "Attitudinal Pleasure in Plato's *Philebus*." *Phronesis*, vol. 64, no. 3, 2019, pp. 247–76.

Thein, Karel. "Imagination, Self-Awareness, and Modal Thought at *Philebus* 39–40." *Oxford Studies in Ancient Philosophy*, vol. 42, 2012, pp. 109–49.

Tuozzo, Thomas. "The General Account of Pleasure in Plato's *Philebus*." *Journal of the History of Philosophy*, vol. 34, no. 4, 1996, pp. 495–513.

Vogt, Katja Maria. "Imagining Good Future States." *Selfhood and the Soul: Essays on Ancient Thought and Literature in Honour of Christopher Gill*. Oxford UP, 2017, pp. 33–48.

Whiting, Jennifer. "Fools' Pleasures in Plato's *Philebus*." *Strategies of Argument: Essays in Ancient Ethics, Epistemology, and Logic*. Oxford UP, 2014, pp. 21–59.

Karl Marx and the Riddle of the *Nicomachean Ethics* 5.5

Howard Engelskirchen

What is life but activity?

—Karl Marx, *Economic and Philosophic Manuscripts*

The Riddle

In *Nicomachean Ethics* 5.5, Aristotle acknowledged defeat. He asked why goods in the market exchange on the basis of equality—one house for five beds in his example—and admitted he was unable to provide a fully persuasive reason for the phenomenon. In order to exchange on the basis of equality there had to be some property all such goods shared that rendered them commensurable. Conscious of the vast natural diversity of things offered for sale or purchase, he concluded, "in truth it is impossible that things differing so much should become commensurate" (1133b18-19). But, he added, "with reference to demand they may become so sufficiently." In *Aristotle's Economics*, Scott Meikle has analyzed this and other of Aristotle's offered solutions and shown why none succeed. I will not revisit these questions. Instead, I want to show how Karl Marx not only offered a solution to the question Aristotle posed but also show that he did so on terms agreeable to, if not drawn from, Aristotle's thought. The solution remained nonetheless unavailable to Aristotle, Marx explained, because ancient Greek society was based on slave labor. Since understanding the product of labor as a commodity depends, as we shall see, on grasping the equality of all different kinds of labor, under the circumstances, the concept needed "could not be deciphered" (*Capital I* 152).

MONEY AND THE RIDDLE OF MEASUREMENT

To situate the problem, I notice Aristotle's reference in *Nichomachean Ethics* 5.5 to money as, "as it were," a middle term (1133a20; Ostwald translation). Money, he argued, serves as a unit of measure, but he himself explained that in order to measure, the thing measuring must share the feature being measured—"the measure of spatial magnitude is a spatial magnitude" (*Metaphysics* Iota, 1053a24–25). We can use a yardstick to measure length because it is long. If it is the value of things in exchange that we're measuring, then we need to find something that allows us to draw the things measured under the aspect of value. Money offers no escape from the problem of commensurability; it too must share the property that renders commodities commensurable.

FROM THE POWER OF ABSTRACTION TO A VECTOR COMPOSITE OF LABORS

Marx initiated his own search for measure with a methodological suggestion used by Aristotle before him. In exploring the meaning of substance, Aristotle asks in *Metaphysics* Zeta 3 what would be left if we stripped away all the empirical features of an object distinguishing it—the three spatial dimensions, color, weight, and other natural qualities and properties. What we're left with, he observed, would be undifferentiated matter, and Aristotle rejects this for the role of substance, because, undifferentiated, it lacks the distinctive features of being a "this thing," separate and distinguishable.

But Marx, who made the "power of abstraction" altogether fundamental to his methodological approach,[1] thought something like, "hold on a minute—there might be something to pursue here." If we start with objects exchanged in the market and abstract from all their material, physical, useful, or other natural properties, we're left with the fact that all these things are products of labor. As such, they share a *social* property that reflects the mutual relations to one another of laboring people engaged in different activities of labor. We're often referred to the idea of the classical economists that "labor is value." But the very problem Aristotle engaged was establishing a ratio between the distinct labors of the farmer and the builder and a shoemaker, and these activities pursue different ends, making them, for Aristotle, "no more commensurable by nature than the things themselves" (Meikle, *Aristotle's Economics* 184). There must be abstraction from labor's specificities.

But then to what will we prescind? Aristotle measured motion by time (*Physics* 219b1–4), and from its beginnings, consistent with this, classical political economy measured the activity of labor by its duration. But for Marx this was not a matter of totaling the specific labor of the builder or shoemaker or the farmer in isolation or as a simple aggregate. Instead, he noticed the interrelation of commodity labors, each with the other, and realized that they were, in their aggregate, *social* labor in its market totality. Thus, Marx introduced the concept of homogeneous human labor to capture this emphasis by referring to the totality of labor gathered by the market as one huge mass of labor time expended. By treating these labors as one without regard to their particularities, we find an undifferentiated mass of human labor time, portions of which can then be allocated to any product offered for sale. That is, the value of each product will be measured not by the duration of actual labor expended on it but by the discrete portion of the homogeneous mass of total labor time appropriate to it—it is not, say, the half-day spent by a shoemaker on a pair of shoes that measures but instead a distribution of overall social labor time expressing a product's "*social weight*," where social weight, he explains, is a consequence of (1) "the total amount of labour time society has at its joint disposal" and (2) "the relative absorption by the different products" of the appropriate share of each in this overall amount (*Capital III* 1022).

In sum, for Marx the distribution of homogeneous human labor among the objects of exchange is "as if different individuals had amalgamated their labour time and allocated different portions of this labour time at their joint disposal to the various use values" (*Contribution to the Critique* 274). The power of abstraction has allowed us to access a social property common to all goods offered for market exchange.

This is new. Classical political economy took labor measured by time as the basis for regulating market exchange, but by focusing on the *social* connection of each commodity to all others and by abstracting to time as the measure of *social* activity, Marx was able to move conceptually beyond the individual laborer's work to social labor as a causally potent mix of mutually related activities. With each commodity bearing a discrete portion of the amalgamated and undifferentiated whole of labor time, labor of one kind can be compared with labor of another—both are reduced to the single dimension of a specific quantity of the same social mass. The concept of homogeneous human labor becomes a vector-like composite of all different labor activities brought as products to market.[2] As bearers in common of a shared property they are equal; homogeneous human labor accounts for their commensurability.

Crystals of This Social Substance

Marx's reference to homogeneous human labor as the property common to objects exchanged in the market occurs at the very beginning of *Capital I* where he explains value as "crystals of this social substance": "they are merely congealed quantities of homogeneous human labour, i.e., of human labour power expended without regard to the form of its expenditure. All these things now tell us is that human labour-power has been expended to produce them, human labour is accumulated in them. As crystals of this social substance, which is common to them all, they are values" (*Capital I*, 128). For Aristotle, we think we understand when what we take to be the cause of a fact is an explanation for the fact such that it is not possible for the explanation to be otherwise (*Posterior Analytics I*, 71b9–12). By specifying homogeneous human labor as a common property rendering commodities each commensurable, we will want to know how and why homogeneous human labor comes into being.

How Homogeneous Human Labor Comes to Be

Early in *Capital I* Marx offers an answer. In section two of the book's first chapter he explains that the commodity as a product of labor is produced independently as a use value not useful to its producer as a result of a spontaneously evolved division of labor. That is, as participants in the division of labor, producers do not labor to meet their own needs but instead sell what they've produced in order to obtain things required for their well-being and further productive activities. Homogeneous human labor then emerges as the gathered result of "mutually independent acts of labour" confronting one another in market exchange: "Only the products of mutually independent acts of labour, performed in isolation, can confront each other as commodities" (*Capital I* 132).

    This extends also to free working people who alienate their capacity to labor in order to obtain a wage. Workers do this because they are separated from the raw materials and tools of labor that would make it possible for them to produce for themselves. With nothing to offer but their ability to work, they are slotted into a market exchange economy as separate individuals who independently produce their labor power as a commodity and alienate it in order to appropriate the things they require for their survival.

How the Entity Commodity-Producing Labor Is Constituted

In *Capital as a Social Kind*, I offered a real definition of value and also of capital in terms of what the French political economist Charles Bettelheim called the "double separation" that characterizes capitalist production (Bettelheim 77). As we've just seen, generalized commodity production is the result of an intersection of separations: (1) of the separation of entities that produce in isolation from one another, and (2) of the separation of the working person from the tools and raw materials they would otherwise need to survive on their own. Although in that analysis I explained also the importance of conceptually grasping the constituent elements of capital both on the one hand as this material structure of separations and on the other as the activity of labor (Marx, *Grudrisse* 832: "the same relation from opposite poles"; and see Engelskirchen 82, 100), my own emphasis privileged understanding the material structure. I now ask whether attention to Aristotle's study of substance as the key to understanding other features of being (*Met.*, Theta 1; 1045b28–29) can enrich not only our understanding of Marx's investigation of "this social substance" but also his analysis of the "two sides of the same coin" activity/structure relationship of the whole.

Compare, for example, the much-discussed passage of *Metaphysics*, Eta 6 (1045a20–25). Aristotle writes: "Clearly, then, if people proceed thus in their usual manner of definitions and speech, they cannot explain or solve this difficulty [the problem of unity]. But if, as we say, one element is matter and another is form, and one is potentially and the other actually, the question will no longer be thought a difficulty. . . . [A]s has been said, the proximate matter and form are one and the same thing, the one potentially, the other actually." Explicitly coupling homogeneous human labor and the structure of separation that characterizes Marx's analysis of production based on value locates conceptually the entity that accounts for the product of labor as a commodity: call it the social form of "commodity-producing labor." "Commodity-producing labor" would be constituted by (1) proximate matter and (2) form—proximate matter as the structure of separations to which I've referred and homogeneous human labor as the labor activity that infuses the entity's proximate matter with form. Together these constituent elements may be characterized as one thing grasped from two different perspectives: social labor as a structure of potentiality or capacity, or, alternatively, social labor considered from the perspective of actualizing activity (*Grundrisse* 832).

Notice also that the separations to which I've referred would be characterized, in Aristotelian terms, as instances of the privation of form (*Met.* Delta 22 1022b22–1023a6). Illness, for example, is the privation of health. That is, if there is to be any production at all, the separation of workers from the means of production must be overcome. So, too, if the products of independent labor are to be distributed to meet society's aggregate needs, the isolation of independent instances of production must be overcome. Thus, the twin separations characterizing commodity-producing labor are surmounted in two ways. First, in labor activity as it actually occurs, goods produced are presupposed as bearers of homogeneous human labor (presupposed because production is for sale, not the producer's own use). Second, market participants alienate what they produce in order to appropriate what they need according to the quantity of homogeneous human labor at their disposal. As Marx often reminds, commodity-producing labor depends on alienating in order to appropriate.

In sum, it is the activity of labor considered as homogeneous human labor that overcomes the privations of separation. The Aristotelian "what it is" of commodity-producing labor, its inner nature, is homogeneous human labor, and it is not surprising that Marx called one of the two "best points of my book" the critical examination of the labor that accounts for value (*Selected Correspondence* 192).[3] It is value that will determine the ratio in which one commodity will exchange for another in the market.

Homogeneous Human Labor as the Middle Term

Homogeneous Human Labor as Activity, as Embodied Activity, and as a Relation of Products

Before proceeding, let me clarify labels associated with distinct forms taken by the social relation of homogeneous human labor in a market economy. The core meaning of the term refers to the actual activities of laboring persons in production grasped, as we have seen, as an organizing principle of their separated private labors. As such it takes proximate matter—"mutually independent acts of labor, performed in isolation"—and gives this the form of activity performed in anticipation of sale. The structure of separation provides potentiality; homogeneous human labor provides form by aggregating conjoined instances of private labor in order to organize the whole as market ready social labor.

The term "value" refers to homogeneous human labor activity "crystalized" in products of labor. Marx's reference to "crystals" (*Capital I* 128) means that the activity of living labor as substance has become fixed in a thing the way a cabinet maker's work is embodied in the finished cabinet.

"Exchange value" is the term applied to the value relation of one commodity to another in the market. The social relation among persons I've specified just above as homogeneous human labor is here "concealed beneath the material shell" of a relation of things (*Capital I* 167).

Notice that exchange value emerges necessarily. To say social labor is embodied in the product of labor as value is meaningless unless we have a way to manifest this. Twenty yards of linen can tell the world it is twenty yards of linen; it cannot say how much twenty yards of linen are worth. It cannot, for example, offer stopwatch records showing the hours actually spent producing it. Those hours were clocked as concrete private labor. It is the distribution of social labor necessary to meet the aggregate of social needs that must be given expression. The linen does this by relating itself to all other commodities with which it could be exchanged as an equivalent. In the event, the physical body of another commodity, disregarded in locating the meaning of value, now steps to the fore to say "that linen is worth just what in my natural physicality I am—well, my physicality is *not* that value, but it *represents* that value; because the linen and I are equivalents, you can use me to get an idea of it." The money commodity does this by offering a measure in terms of ounces or pounds of whatever it is, say gold or silver. And because every commodity has an exchange value relationship with money—has a price—the linen succeeds in relating itself to each other commodity in the market.

In sum, homogeneous human labor takes the form of (1) a social relation of *activity* in production; (2) this *activity embodied* in the form of "crystals of this social substance"—"value"; and (3) value expressed as *a relation* of one product to another in exchange—"exchange value."

The term "capital" can be added to the list. Marx calls capital "the ultimate development of the value relation" (*Grundrisse* 704), and he emphasizes that it must be explained as a social relationship, which, as we have seen, consists in the "one and the same thing" fused interpenetration of proximate matter (potential) and form (activity). But capital also gets referred to as a thing, and, as such, capital is just an accumulation of values. It is distinct from simple value in that it has, as we shall see momentarily, the capacity to increase itself. Aristotle distinguished "economics"—the simple exchange of a commodity for money and the money again for a commodity, C-M-C—and "chrematistics," the exchange of money for a commodity in order to obtain more money, M-C-M' (where M' represents the original M invested plus an added increment) (*Politics* I.8–10; Marx, *Capital I* 253–54). The point here is that, although market relations in ancient Greece were significant, C-M-C is not self-sustaining and, as such, commodity-producing labor in this simple form was always subordinate to a goal of agricultural self-sufficiency significantly reliant on servile labor. Neither was capital then self-sustaining, but it bore the potential to become so in the course of its maturation over time. For now, it is enough to appreciate that capital, like value, is given expression by crystals of homogeneous human labor.

And the phrase "commodity-producing labor" can be specified as well. This refers to any historically specific form of the production of commodities for market sufficiently developed to display both the regular and stable use of money and the circulation of goods. Thus, it includes both the C-M-C and the M-C-M' social labor forms. Commodity-producing labor is the substantial entity formed by the hylomorphic unity of a structure of separation and the activities of homogeneous of human labor.

The Middle Term as the Most Appropriate Explanatory Factor

In science, for Aristotle, the key to explaining the reason for a fact is given by the middle term of a demonstrative syllogism. The middle term locates the explanatory factor that makes it possible to understand the reason one thing belongs to another. According to Aryeh Kosman's reading, *apodeixis*—scientific understanding—can be understood according to its root meaning in Greek—as a "showing forth" or as *"revealing or uncovering."* ("Understanding" 378). Scientific understanding reveals the nature of the phenomenon under investigation. Thus, to explain why the planets do not twinkle, Aristotle shows that being near is a characteristic of planets (all planets are near), and non-twinkling belongs to being near (what is near does not twinkle); therefore, non-twinkling characterizes planets. The demonstration reveals that the planets do not twinkle because they are near. "Being near" is the middle term (*Posterior Analytics I*, 78a30–b2).

Also, some pages earlier at *Posterior Analytics I*, 73a34–b5 Aristotle wrote: "One thing belongs to another in itself both if it belongs to it in what it is . . . and also if the things it belongs to themselves belong in the account which makes clear what it is." Aristotle's examples are geometrical; I paraphrase Mary Louise Gill's explanation in the context of a discussion of *Metaphysics*, Zeta 4 where we read, "the essence of each thing is what it is said to be in virtue of itself" (1029b14). In "Aristotle's Metaphysics Reconsidered," Gill comments that the essence of something is limited to the properties of that thing which must be mentioned in the account of what it is *per se*. This can be either because (1) the predicate must be mentioned in the account of what the subject is, or (2) the subject must be mentioned in the account of what the predicate is. Thus "being near" as an essential predicate of planets must be mentioned in the account of what a planet is. Further, a property of "being near" is not-twinkling and thus "being near" must be mentioned in the account of what non-twinkling is. Because "being near" must be mentioned both in an account of what a planet is *and* in the account of what non-twinkling is, "being near" is the middle term between the planets and the property of not-twinkling that they manifest.

Homogeneous human labor is the explanatory factor that explains both the product of labor as a commodity and the entity commodity-producing labor of which the commodity is a manifestation. If we ask why a product of commodity-producing labor sold in the market is commensurable, we can explain that homogeneous human labor belongs to all such products, that commensurability is a property of all homogeneous human labor, and therefore, commensurability is a property of all products of labor sold in the market.

But we will want to ask also why products of labor sold in the market come to possess homogeneous human labor as a property of them. In fact, Marx treats them as *defined* by the exchange value form of homogeneous human labor—the commodity has a price, he writes, but it *is* exchange value (*Grundrisse* 190; *Contribution to the Critique* 308). Thus, although the commodity can be characterized as both a use value and an exchange value, as a use value it functions in exchange only as a material bearer of exchange value. It is not use value but exchange value that is able to reveal what the product of labor does in exchange. Thus, it is homogeneous human labor in this form that is fully explanatory of the commodity's commensurability.

Notice also that homogeneous human labor is the specific form of activity that realizes the social labor potential of commodity-producing labor; it reveals what commodity-producing labor is. And because to be a commodity is to be a product of commodity-producing labor, then to be a commodity is to be *enformed* necessarily by homogeneous human labor; homogeneous human labor makes the products of commodity-producing labor what they are. Again, because commensurability is necessarily predicated of homogeneous human labor and homogenous human labor is necessarily predicated of commodity-producing labor, then commensurability is necessarily predicated of commodities as products of commodity-producing labor (*Posterior Analytics I*, 75a6–7). Homogeneous human labor is the middle term.

Material Forms Adequate to the Concept of Capital

An important consequence of the foregoing is that if homogeneous human labor is taken to be the organizing form of commodity-producing labor and thus an activity able to overcome structures of separation in the cycles of production and exchange, then, as the inner nature of this form of social production, it will drive development of it in virtually all respects. Interested readers can follow two provocative examples—one with respect to the evolution of the forms of capital and the other with respect to the forms of labor. Homogeneous human labor is characterized by abstraction from all-natural particularity or feature of use. It is in all respects homogeneous and indifferent to specificities of either person or product. It is impersonal and each instance is equal to any other instance in the right proportion. This is illustrated in a text familiarly referred to as the "Fragment on Machines" (*Grundrisse* 690–712): Marx compares capital's expression as "fixed capital"—buildings, machinery, and the like—to "circulating capital"—money and goods circulating in the market. He asks, which of these is "the *most adequate form of capital* as such." While machinery appears as the most adequate form of fixed capital, "it does not correspond to the concept of capital, which, as value, is indifferent to every specific form of use value" (*Grundrisse* 694). Circulating capital is in this respect more fully adequate to the concept of capital because, like the homogeneous human labor that it is, it is indifferent to use and ultimately has only its realization in money as its goal.

Labor as Adequate to the Concept of Capital

Similarly, in the evolution of labor itself, labor becomes more and more indifferent to the actual tasks undertaken. Guild or craft labor presupposed training and devotion to a craft; the mass of modern labor mainly reflects the abstract features of homogeneous human labor and is indifferent to any particular specificity. The evolution of machinery tends to reduce every task to simple and repetitive motions anyone can perform: "labor loses all characteristics of art," its particular skill becomes "irrelevant," and it becomes "purely mechanical activity, hence indifferent to its particular form" (*Grundrisse* 295–97). Machinery "does not in any way relate to the individual worker as his instrument; but rather he himself exists as an animated individual punctuation mark, as its living accessory" (*Grundrisse* 470). Capital is indifferent to the task of meeting human need because its inner nature, the impetus and goal of its activity, is determined by amassing crystals of this social substance, homogeneous human labor. The abstract nature of homogeneous human labor shapes our world.

The Inversion of Value as Self-Moving Substance

I referred above to the distinction Aristotle made between economics and what he called chrematistics. We contrast the simple circulation of value such as occurred in the ancient world with the mature cycle of capital, intimations of which were already present 2,500 years ago. But, as I've emphasized, these were in no way dominant. Nonetheless, in M-C-M', we get a result Aristotle condemned: money itself becomes the object of exchange. Of course, M-C-M' is the cycle of circulation that drives the modern world; it is this Marx calls "the General Formula for Capital" (*Capital* 248). He writes: "The simple circulation of commodities—selling in order to buy—is a means to a final goal which lies outside circulation, namely the appropriation of use values, the satisfaction of needs. As against this, the circulation of money as capital is an end in itself, for the valorization of value takes place only within this constantly renewed movement" (253). And he adds, the "limitless" movement of M-C-M' explains value as having the capacity to increase itself and to do so because of what it is. A consequence is that "[v]alue is here the subject," and, indeed, "the dominant subject of this process" (253). More: "in the circulation M-C-M, value suddenly presents itself as a *self-moving substance*" (255–56; emphasis added).

If we reflect a minute, we realize an inversion has taken place. Value, remember, is characterized as "crystals of this social substance." "This social substance" begins as the gathered relationship of the distinct labors of working people aggregated so as to render their separate labor activities homogeneous. The concept's referent is the real *activities* of persons. But crystals of this social substance are embodied in things, and, as such, Marx underscores the relation of things in exchange is now "nothing but the definite social relation between men themselves which assumes here, for them, the fantastic form of a relation between things" (*Capital* 165). And by seeing a relation of things rather than a relation of persons we assume that value is an intrinsic property of the things we see rather than a mutual relation of laboring persons to one another. This is what Marx calls "commodity fetishism." Thus, instead of "social substance" reflecting, as in Aristotle, natural human sociality and a development of what it is to be human through a social and political life over which individuals associated together have control (Meikle, "Metaphysics of Substance," 305), value as social substance embodied becomes "the rule of things over man, of dead labour over the living" (*Capital I* 990). Instead of controlling their social lives, individuals find the imperatives of value escape communal control; market behaviors have their source in the will and consciousness of individuals, but these individuals "find out that the same division of labour which turns them into independent private producers also makes the social process of production and the relations of individual producers to each other within that process independent of the producers themselves" (*Capital I* 202).

Conclusion: The Trajectory of *Nichomachean Ethics* 5.5

From the Centrality of Activity to an Ontology of Things

The young Marx gave expression to an Aristotelian engagement with the centrality of activity in the sentence that serves as the epigraph to this chapter: "What is life but activity?" (*Early Writings* 327). That this emphasis was enduring for him is reflected in the so-called "Rough Draft" of *Capital* where he envisioned a time when the rich individuality of each person would manifest in labor that "appears no longer as labour, but as the full development of activity itself" (*Grundrisse* 325). We can thus imagine that he would resolve the tension between ability (*dunamis*) and the priority of activity (*energeia*) presented in today's readings of the *Metaphysics* by arguing that the activity of being just is "The absolute working out of [an individual's] creative potentialities . . . [making] the development of all human powers as such the end itself . . . where he does not reproduce himself in one specificity, but produces his totality, . . . Strives not to remain something he has become, but is in the absolute movement of becoming" (*Grundrisse* 488). Aryeh Kosman, whose work has been pivotal in bringing the priority of activity to the fore, would, if I understand correctly, disagree. In part his reading appeals to *Metaphysics* Lambda where the prime mover can only ever be unqualifiedly active with never an admixture of potential: "for that which is potentially may possibly not be" (1071b19). It follows, as Aristotle explains, that for the prime mover there must necessarily be "a principle, whose very substance is actuality" (1071b18–20). *Imago dei,* then (and Kosman imagines a lovely dialogue with the deity on the point, *Activity* 85): the substance of our mortal being will be best understood as activity as well. Yet, he later adds, startlingly, "with regard to the activity that Aristotle identifies with substance, a Megarian would, as it were, be correct" (*Activity* 178).[4]

It is certainly possible to agree that the substance of being is activity while rejecting the appeal to Megara. Set that issue aside, then; we can nonetheless still engage the hugely provocative question Kosman raises on the last pages of *The Activity of Being*: "As historians of western philosophy," he asks, "[w]hat has happened in our reading of Aristotle to lead us away from the centrality of activity?" Why is it that the focus has been on "an ontology of things" at the expense of "an ontology of instances of being actively expressing their essential nature" (253).

Indeed. And the inversion reviewed in the section immediately above suggests an answer. Powers of individuals actively laboring find expression only as relations of things. The gathered exercise of human capacities at work finds expression only in a gathering of things in the marketplace. The social relation of persons to, and as participants in, society's labor finds expression only in the price tag that tells how much this or that thing is worth. Dead labor rules living; things rule the human person. Rather than a rich and infinitely diverse manifestation of the singularly particular abilities and expressive powers of associated individuals, only the abstract commensurability of things gets expressed. With respect to the ontology of things, Kosman's question reflects the far-reaching upshot of commodity fetishism.

Forms of Association; Forms of Exchange

One other aspect of the riddle of the *Nicomachean Ethics* 5.5 remains. Aristotle argues that the community is held together by exchange so that the very association of citizens with one another depends on exchange. That dependence then measures just how serious is the riddle of commensurability, "for neither would there have been association if there were not exchange, nor exchange if there were not equality, nor equality if there were not commensurability" (1033b15–17).

Yet we might ask the following: having situated commensurability as the product of a form of association materially characterized by a structure of separation coupled as "one and the same thing" with the homogeneous human labor that expresses, organizes, and reproduces it, suppose we ask whether the forms of exchange we take for granted might not themselves rather depend on the forms of association in place? Like Aristotle, Marx envisioned social life under the common control of associated individuals (Meikle, "Substance"). But *Capital* showed this could not be founded on the privations (read "illnesses") of commodity-producing labor. Barring crises, with each cycle of production and circulation, capital's constitutive separations can be overcome by market exchange. Still, in the event, not only things but also the abstractions of homogeneous human labor rule individuals and their activities (*Grundrisse* 164); moreover, a dynamic that escapes their conscious control accounts for market behaviors. Confronted with the global reality of market relations triumphally dominant, we can readily imagine Marx's meditations on the riddle of the *Nicomachean Ethics*, 5.5 suggesting a sketch for the entire trajectory of his project. Forms of exchange depend on forms of association, not the reverse, and it is the privation of a structure of separation piled on separation that must be overcome by our rich and freely developed association with one another (Marx and Engels, *German Ideology* 80).

Notes

1. "[I]n the analysis of economic forms neither microscopes nor chemical reagents are of assistance. The power of abstraction must replace both" (*Capital* 90; see Engelskirchen 56–59).

2. This homogeneous mass distributed as value is also called by Marx "abstract labor," and in the appropriate context this emphasis can be helpful. But

I want to emphasize the causal efficacy of homogeneous human labor, and the term "abstract labor" has carried suggestions that its reference is merely conceptual, a reference to a general idea of labor applicable to all times and all places. That is not Marx's meaning. Think of the random motions of the molecules of a gas; the causal forces given expression by those independent motions taken in the aggregate, their average kinetic energy, is what we call temperature. The price of coffee is here and now one thing, there and then another, but over time a composite of forces imposes itself as a center around which particular instances of price oscillate (*Grundrisse* 137).

3. In a letter to his close friend Frederick Engels (August 24, 1867) written on publication of the first edition of *Capital* in 1867, Marx wrote that "The best points in my book are: 1) the two-fold character of labour, according to whether it is expressed in use value or exchange value," and "2) the treatment of surplus value independently of its particular forms as profit, interest, ground rent, etc." Marx made the point in *Capital* itself: "I was the first to point out and examine this twofold nature of labor contained in commodities" (*Capital I* 132).

4. The Megarian denied that I have the ability to speak French unless I'm actually speaking it. Aristotle rejected such views, explaining that then "that which is not happening will be incapable of happening" and that "these views do away with movement and becoming" (*Met.* Theta 3, 1047a12–14). As Professor Gill points out in "Aristotle's Hylomorphism Reconceived" (see also "Critique of Aryeh Kosman"), for living beings taken as the paradigmatic model of substance, *Metaphysics* Theta may be understood to modify the core meaning of *dunamis* (ability, potential, capacity) ("Hylomorphism" 8). In such cases *dunamis* provides the impetus for activity that "enhances, maintains, and renews . . . the organism as the actual thing that it is" (16).

Kosman wants to understand the priority of *energeia* on the model of sight and seeing: exercise of the ability to see just is seeing. Comparably, "there is nothing that we would describe as having the ability to be a human being that is not actively being so" (*Activity* 178). Fair enough, but the demur is not with the insight that the substance of a living being is fully present in its activity of actively being what it is; the concern is with effacing the here and now dynamic quality of a living being's substance. A human actively being human, for example, embodies, not always manifest, a homeostatic capacity to respond to an everchanging world in a way a Megarian would not embrace. Like any creature, humans are ultimately constrained by the real possibilities embodied and encoded in us. Yet we also have no full idea—in response to change in the world around us and in us—what the potentialities to be discovered within those possibilities are. Or so I think Marx argued: for an individual actively being human the activity of being just is "the absolute movement of becoming" (488).

Works Cited

Aristotle. *The Complete Works of Aristotle*. Translated by Jonathan Barnes, Princeton UP, 1984.

———. *Nicomachean Ethics*. Translated by Martin Ostwald, Bobbs-Merrill, 1962.

Bettelheim, Charles. *Economic Calculation and Forms of Property*. Monthly Review Press, 1975.

Engelskirchen, Howard. *Capital as a Social Kind: Definitions and Transformations in the Critique of Political Economy*. Routledge, 2011.

Gill, Mary Louise. "Aristotle's Hylomorphism Reconceived." *Proceedings of the Aristotelian Society*, vol. 121, no. 2, July 2021, pp. 183–201.

———. "Critique of Aryeh Kosman, *The Activity of Being: An Essay on Aristotle's Ontology*." *European Journal of Philosophy*, vol. 26, no. 2, 2018, pp. 854–59.

———. "Aristotle's *Metaphysics* Reconsidered." *Journal of the History of Philosophy*, vol. 43, 2005, pp. 223–51.

Kosman, Aryeh. *The Activity of Being: An Essay on Aristotle's Ontology*. Harvard UP, 2013.

———. "Understanding, Explanation, and Insight in Aristotle's *Posterior Analytics*." *Exegesis and Argument: Studies in Greek Philosophy Presented to Gregory Vlastos. Phronesis* (Supplementary volume), edited by Gregory Vlastos, Edward N. Lee, Alexander P. D. Mourelatos, and Richard Rorty, Assen, van Gorcum, 1973, pp. 374–92.

Marx, Karl. *Economic and Philosophical Manuscripts of 1844*. Karl Marx: Early Writings. Translated by Gregor Benton, Penguin, 1992, pp. 279–400.

———. *Capital I*, Penguin, 1990.

———. *Capital III*, Penguin, 1991.

———. *A Contribution to the Critique of Political Economy*. Marx Engels Collected Works, vol. 29, International Publishers, 1987, pp. 257–417.

———. *Grundrisse: Foundations of the Critique of Political Economy (Rough Draft)*. Penguin, 1973.

———. and Friedrich Engels. *The German Ideology*. Marx Engels Collected Works, vol. 5. Translated by Clemens Dutt et al., International Publishers, 1976.

———. *Selected Correspondence*. Progress Publishers, Moscow, 1955.

Meikle, Scott. *Aristotle's Economic Thought*. Clarendon, 1995.

———. "History of Philosophy: The Metaphysics of Substance in Marx." *Cambridge Companion to Marx*, edited by Terrell Carver, Cambridge UP, 1991, pp. 296–313.

The Tragedy of Natural Philosophy

Myrna Gabbe

Plato's *Phaedo* is as much a dialogue on the immortality of the soul as it is on happiness and hope. In Plato's recounting of Socrates' last day, we are met with a man whose joy in life is not curtailed by its impending end. As Plato tells it, Socrates lived his last day as he always did: eager to philosophize, even on the most pressing of topics, the immortality of the soul. The focus of this essay is the first argument for the soul's immortality in a sequence of four: the so-called Cyclical Argument (CA). This argument purports to demonstrate that the soul goes to Hades when one dies and returns from Hades when one is born on appeal to widely accepted principles of change. The essay's aim is to show that Plato articulates these principles at the outset of the dialogue to establish them as the objects of the dialogue's critique. The principles, I show, had a central place in ancient Greek cultural and intellectual heritage, underwriting theories of the cosmos, the virtues, and the soul. I argue that Plato wants to unseat their reign because they commit their adoptees to untenable philosophical conclusions and tragic outlooks on life and death.[1]

The Cyclical Argument gets under way after Cebes expresses his concern that most people would be unconvinced by Socrates' claim that the soul is immortal. Cebes explains:

> The matter of the soul causes people to have strong doubts and to worry that once separated from the body it no longer exists anywhere, but is destroyed and perishes on the day when the human being dies, immediately as it is being separated

from the body, and that as it comes out it is dissipated like breath or smoke, flies away in all directions, and isn't anything anywhere. For if it really *did* exist somewhere alone by itself, gathered together and separated from these evils you just described, then there would be much hope and a noble hope at that, Socrates, that what you say is true. But this very point doubtless requires no little reassurance and proof, that the soul exists when the human being has died, and has some power and wisdom.[2] (69e7–70b4)

The theory here described understands dying as the separating of the body and the soul, and postulates that as the soul is released from the body, the two parts begin to disintegrate. The process is thought to end when the body and soul are reduced to their elemental constituents and each bit finds its way to its source: earth to earth, water to water, aither to aither. Cebes tells us that the worry that this theory is true is the worry that when we die, our souls will not be anything existing anywhere. He remarks that more than reassurance is needed to give people hope in life after death.

What Cebes wants by way of "proof" is an argument demonstrating the immortality of the soul. Generally speaking, the Athenians would have turned to the mystery cults, as Cicero reports, to learn "the beginnings of life" and gain "the power not only to live happily, but also to die with better hope" (xiv, 36). And that, initially, is what Plato does as well. He has Socrates introduce the Cyclical Argument with a reference to the mysteries and the doctrine of reincarnation at their core:

Let's see whether or not it turns out that when people have died their souls exist in Hades. Now there is an ancient saying which comes to mind, that souls exist there when they have come from here, and that they come back here and come to be from dead people. If this is so—that living people come to be again from those who have died—surely our souls would exist there? For, I take it, the souls would not come to be again, if they did not exist. (70c4–d2)

Most scholars believe that the doctrine of reincarnation described above belongs to the Orphic tradition; that Plato endorses Orphic beliefs; and that the Cyclical Argument translates this Orphic doctrine into philosophical language, giving it rational grounds. The Orphic eschatological tradition teaches that reincarnation allows individuals the chance for redemption by means of the mysteries and other purificatory rites and ordinances (Athanassakis and Wolkow xiv). If a person has not properly purified their soul during life, their soul goes to the afterworld to be purified through punishment, after which it transmigrates into a body for another chance at redemption. The redeemed avoid punishment altogether, making their way to Elysium, where they enjoy a blessed, eternal existence. The irredeemable, by contrast, are sent to the underworld where they are punished eternally for their crimes. It is clear that Plato is deeply influenced by the Orphic tradition. After he has Socrates deliver his third argument for the immortality of the soul—an argument that aims to show that souls are not likely subject to dissolution, as the many worry—Socrates explains reincarnation as the product of pollution. By indulging the pleasures of the body, the soul pollutes itself, preventing the individual from being content in life and escaping pure and free in death (81b1–c1). Souls laden with the corporeal are forced to wander the earth in punishment until they reincarnate as an animal or human befitting their prior way of life (81d6–82b8). Plato returns to this theme of punishment and redemption at the end of the dialogue, where Socrates is made to describe in plodding detail the regions of the afterlife and the punishments for having lived an unphilosophical life (107d6–114c8). That Plato begins and ends the arguments for the soul's immortality with allusions to the mysteries indicates his commitment to their general tenets.

The Cyclical Argument purports to demonstrate that the soul goes to Hades when one dies and come from Hades when one is born by establishing that coming to be and dying are ordinary processes, subject to general principles of change. Just as these principles ensure that change is cyclical, so also do they ensure that life comes from death and death from life. The CA runs on the establishment of the following three principles.

1. "Everything that has a coming-to-be . . . comes to be in this way: the opposites from nowhere other than their opposites" (70d9–e2).

2. "Between the pairs of opposites" there are "two processes of coming-to-be" (71a12–b2).

3. The processes of coming-to-be "always balance the other by . . . going round in a circle" (72a12–b1).

Principle [1] establishes that whenever a subject acquires some property, it comes to be from its opposite. Plato later makes clear that the subject of the properties transform, not the properties themselves (103b6). Plato has Socrates give a number of examples to prove the universality of the principle: the beautiful comes to be from the ugly, the just from the unjust, the larger from the smaller, to give a few. In the case at hand, the opposing properties are being alive and being dead, which we are to understand as being embodied and disembodied respectively. The soul is the subject of the change. It becomes alive by acquiring its body and dies by losing its body.

Principle [2] establishes a mechanistic link between the opposing properties: some physical process that the subject admitting the opposite property endures. It thus establishes that there are two physical processes between any pair of opposing states. Just as between the large and small there is increasing and decreasing, so also between being alive and being dead is there uniting and separating. Perishing is the process through which the soul comes to be separate from the body; generation is the process through which the soul comes to be united with the body. Socrates is thus made to conclude that the soul could not be subject of these two opposing properties unless it persisted through life and death.

In order for the individual to die after having come to life and come to life again after having died, there must be a connection between the two processes. Without a physical connection whereby the process changes its course and turns direction, it will end at the termini opposite from which it started. Thus, Plato has Socrates posit Principle [3], which establishes that the processes of becoming go around in reciprocal exchange. Socrates is made to defend this premise by arguing that if the processes did not bend back on themselves, all that could sleep would eventually be asleep, all that could combine would eventually be one, and all that could die would eventually be dead.

Scholars disagree on almost every aspect of the Cyclical Argument. They disagree on its objective, its relationship with the following Recollection Argument, and on Plato's estimation of its success, to give some examples. Barnes, for instance, denies that the CA is meant to prove the immortality of the soul (401): a reading that Gallop vociferously rejects (207–09). Long and Sedley take the argument not so much as a defense of the "soul's immortality *ab initio* than attempts to provide formal corroboration of an existing religious tradition" (xxvi). Bonitz (303–06) and Archer-Hind (10, 71) believe that the CA and Recollection Argument should be read as a single argument for the immortality of the soul. Barnes thinks that the CA is meant to stand alone (400). And whereas Barnes insists that "Plato intended us to take the Argument seriously" (399), Bluck (20) and Gallop (217–20) find indication that Plato takes the argument to be weak. Still, a good deal of the scholarly discussion focuses on Plato's establishment of Principle [1], which Plato has Socrates illustrate and defend with confounding examples.

Principle [1] establishes that the termini of all change are polar opposite properties in order to bring the transition between life and death under the governance of universal principles of change. Thus the first set of examples Plato has Socrates marshal in its defense are opposites of this sort: the beautiful comes to be from the ugly and the just from the unjust. But, as many scholars note, these examples do not establish Principal [1], for the beautiful does not always come to be from ugly and the just does not always come to be from the unjust.[3] The remaining examples Plato has Socrates provide are comparatives: the larger, stronger, faster come to be from the smaller, weaker, slower; conversely, the smaller, weaker, slower come to be from the larger, stronger, faster. But as Bostock explains, these examples "do not illustrate the principle about opposites because the properties concerned are not in any sense opposite properties" (50).[4]

Was Plato simply confused about which kinds of opposites align best with Principle [1]? Were the principles of change articulated in the CA "part of the heritage of unquestioned assumptions into which Plato was born," as Bluck claims (21)? Or did Plato have Socrates present the argument with contradictions and confusions to alert his readers to the incoherence of the principles?

It is hard to imagine Plato failing to recognize that the oppositional pairs provided are poor examples to illustrate Principle [1]. On Plato's view, the just cannot corrupt their souls any more than can the truly unjust find their way to moral perfection. As we saw, there are permanent dwelling places for those at the moral extremes in the eschatological myth that Plato has Socrates recount at the dialogue's end. The just are released from their bodies to dwell in some region on the surface of the earth (114b6–c8), while the irredeemable are sent to Tartarus with no hope for escape (113e1–6). Change from these genuinely opposing states is not, in Plato's view, possible.

And there are other peculiarities of the argument's presentation that raise suspicion. Take this claim, for instance, that anticipates the Cyclical Argument: "If this is so—that living people *come to be again* from those who have died—surely our souls would exist there? For, I take it, the souls *would not come to be again*, if they did not exist" (70c8–d2, my emphasis). This passage trades in ambiguity and obfuscation. We can make sense of it only if we take Plato to employ two senses of coming-to-be. In the first line, we are to understand that people come to be from having not been before, thanks to a process by which their souls become embodied. But in the last line, it is claimed that souls come to be only because they already exist. So, here, souls do not come to be alive in the way that people come to be; they come to be alive by leaving Hades and entering the world of the living. Thus, Socrates is made to employ a second sense of coming-to-be that involves not coming to be at all.

Plato has Socrates speak of death in similarly perplexing ways. Consider this restatement of the Cyclical Argument: "It has already been shown . . . that everything living comes to be from what is dead. For if the soul exists before as well, and if, when it enters upon living and comes to be, it must do so from nowhere other than from death and from being dead, surely it must exist also when it has died, simply because it has to come to be again" (77c6–d4). When Plato has Socrates describe the soul as existing "when it has died," he means that the soul survives being disembodied. But given that the argument is premised on the grounds that being alive is the opposite of being dead and opposites come to be from one another, it is curious that Plato should have Socrates describe the soul as both alive (existing) and dead (disembodied) in the same breath. Doing so only calls attention to the fact that the argument's conclusion undermines Principle [1]. Life does not, for Plato, come from its opposite. Life comes from life.

It is telling that the theory articulated by Cebes at the outset of the argument conforms much better to these principles than Plato's own. This is because the theory's account of being alive and being dead treats the two as genuine opposites with genuinely opposing processes. Coming-to-be involves the gathering of the elements that constitute the body and the soul and the uniting of these two aspects of the individual; dying involves the separation of the body and soul and the dissolution of their elemental constituents. These processes can go on in eternal exchange, without postulating a soul that resists the principles. But many deny that Plato rejects the argument elsewhere in the dialogue. As Barnes says, "we have as much reason for supposing that Plato himself was seriously committed to it as for supposing that he was seriously committed to any of the other arguments in the *Phaedo*" (399). Yet if we look closely at how these principles were employed by the natural scientists, we see that Plato not only had reasons to reject the principles but that he challenges them in his refutation of natural science.

The principle that properties come to be from their opposites is often associated with Heraclitus.[5] This is both because Heraclitus emphasizes the oppositional character of nature and also because Plato adopts Heraclitean flux in the *Timaeus* to characterize the behavior of the receptacle: the material source of elemental bodies. But it is not clear that Heraclitean flux conforms to the principles of the CA argument. As Hackforth notes, Heraclitus is "regarded . . . as establishing the *unity* or *identity* of opposites" (his emphasis) and "Socrates does not contend for the unity of 'living' and 'dead'" (63). On the face of it, Anaximander's and Empedocles' cosmological theories exemplify the principles of the CA better than Heraclitus's.

According to the testimonia, Anaximander taught that the cosmos was engendered from the *apeiron*: the unbounded or unlimited *archê* of the cosmos. There is some question as to the nature of the *apeiron*, but according to Aristotle, Anaximander conceived it much like other natural scientists conceived their *archê*: as an imperishable and divine material substance (*Ph* III 4, 203b13–15). Earlier in the *Physics*, Aristotle reports Anaximander to hold that oppositional properties like the hot and cold emerge from the *apeiron* through a process of separation (*Ph* I 4, 187a20–21). These oppositional properties are thought to give rise to all manners of natural processes, including but not limited to the generation of the cosmos and the first beings.[6]

For the purposes of this essay, most relevant is Simplicius' testimony, which preserves the only direct quote from Anaximander, in bold below:

> Of those who say it is one, in motion and unlimited, Anaximander, son of Praxiades of Miletus, was a follower and student of Thales. He said that the *archê* and element of existing things was the unlimited, being the first to give this name to the *archê*. He says this is not water, nor any of the other so-called elements, but some other unlimited nature, from which are generated all the heavens and the *cosmoi* in them. The source of generation for extant things is that into which destruction occurs, according to what is necessary/proper. **For they pay penalty and retribution to each other (*allêlois*) for injustices according to the ordering of time**, as he says in a poetic fashion. (*Physics*, 24, 13)[7]

We might think that the *apeiron* is that out of and into which the generation and destruction of extant things occur. But, as Gregory points out, the *allêlois* (dative plural) indicates that extant things are made to pay a penalty and retribution *to each other* for the destruction that they cause by coming to be (69). Thus, "extant things" are believed to refer to the oppositional properties, which come to be out of, and perish into, the other.

The conventional view is that the phrase "ordering of time" refers to the revolution of the sun around the earth. The sun accounts for the daily reciprocal changes from hot to cold and light and dark, as well as the yearly seasonal changes from hot to cold and dry to wet.[8] For Anaximander, then, the oppositional nature of the generated powers guarantees continual ordered change. We have, then, a cosmological story that adheres closely to the principles of the CA. Opposites come to be from opposites via opposite processes in reciprocal exchange.

What is particularly interesting about Simplicius' testimonia is the moral valence that Anaximander is said to attach to generation and destruction. According to Simplicius, Anaximander treats generation as a just penalty and retribution for unjust destruction. It is just that cold comes to be from hot because hot must pay the penalty for having annihilated cold; in turn, it is just that hot comes to be from cold because cold must pay the penalty for having annihilated hot.[9] This attachment of moral value to ordinary generation and destruction is notable because Plato has Socrates connect moral and physical changes in the CA by bringing the two under a single causal account: just as being alive comes from being dead, so too does the just come from the unjust. That Plato has Socrates do so (at the expense of the argument's coherence, no less) suggests that he wants the reader to make the connection between the principles laid out in the CA and the theories of Anaximander and other like-minded thinkers. It also suggests that he wants his reader to associate the CA with Anaximander's muddled conception of justice.

Gregory imagines that Anaximander means to project a positive moral outlook with his theory of natural justice. According to Gregory, Anaximander's cosmos is invariantly just because at any given moment the opposing pairs of productive powers have equal strength and equal global distribution (67). But aside from the optimism driving it, Plato would have found little in it to commend. In Anaximander's theory, justice always involves injustice because it is conceived principally in terms of penalties and retributions, a conception informed by the theory that opposites come to be from opposites. So, even if Gregory is right that justice is stable and invariant when viewed from the cosmic perspective, Anaximander nonetheless imagines this balance to emerge from the continual retribution of crimes committed against each other. The cosmos for him is just because no crime goes unpaid. By contrast, Plato does not conceive justice as a righting of a wrong. In the *Republic*, justice is treated as a virtue the city or soul has when each of its parts are doing their own proper work. And in the *Phaedo*, Plato insists that neither the form of the just nor the justness in us admits the opposite, a situation that cannot be avoided, if cosmic justice requires injustice (102d). Moreover, on Anaximander's theory, justice is won from injustice *by the same act* as that which was deemed unjust (i.e., destruction of the opposite property that previously destroyed it). That means that it is always destined to fail, a pessimistic worldview, if there ever was one. And yet the then current beliefs that glory and flourishing requires war and justice is maintained by conflict, struggle, and payment, conform to this conception. In the *Phaedo*, Plato argues against the common notion that virtue arises from and is maintained by vice (68c5–69a4). His examples are bravery and temperance. The common view, we learn, is that bravery and temperance are achieved when young men learn to fear dishonor more than death and deprive themselves of some pleasures for the enjoyment of others. Plato has Socrates challenge this understanding of virtue by showing that not only does it make virtue come out of vice (for bravery is born from fear and cowardice), virtue requires viciousness. For on this conception, temperance is maintained by the enslavement of the soul to pleasure. Plato rejects the notion that virtue involves the exchange of "pleasures for pleasures, pains for pains and fear for fear" (68a7–8), arguing that purification through philosophy is the only means by which people can rid themselves of the vice that all but guarantees an unpleasant death (69b8–d2).

To be clear: Plato does not explicitly associate Anaximander with the common conception of the virtues. At this point, however, my interest is merely to show that a variety of theories were adapted to the principles of the CA and that Plato would have believed those theories incoherent. The situation is more clear with Empedocles. Trépanier convincingly argues that Plato knew Empedocles' poetry well and featured several Empedoclean themes in the *Phaedo*, including the notion of philosophy as purification (18). But for our purposes, what is most salient is that Empedocles' cosmos is strictly governed by the principles of the CA and that Plato directs his objection to natural science toward Empedocles.

According to the orthodox reading of the fragments, Empedocles' cosmos continually transforms from one termini to its opposite, then back around again.[10] The material principles of Empedocles' cosmos are six immortal entities: earth, water, aither, fire, love, and strife (17/109).[11] Love brings together the elements; strife separates them apart. The roots—as the principles are sometimes called—"never cease from constantly alternating" through the waxing and waning influence of love and strife (25/17.6). When love is triumphant, and strife retreats to the limits of the cosmos (32/36), the roots are filled with desire for one another and unite by blending (26/21.8). Conversely, when strife is triumphant, and love retreats, the elements separate out. The structured cosmos—the cosmos as we know it—arises midway between the opposing termini: both when love acquires a commanding presence among the many, and, in turn, when strife acquires a commanding presence in the one. During this golden age of mortal flourishing, love and strife are balanced and intermingled throughout the cosmos and its beings. For strife is necessary for the existence of discreet beings, as much as love is necessary for the bonds that holds the parts of creatures together. Humans reincarnate into other humans and animals during this period (111/117). But, as Inwood argues, humans are not, for Empedocles, immortal because they are compounds and compounds are subject to generation and destruction (55). Indeed, the golden age is terminal, destined to collapse when either love or strife becomes dominant.

Empedocles' cosmology is very different from Anaximander's. But because his theory is informed by the same assumptions of becoming, it is subject to the same kinds of perversions. Consider that in Empedocles' theory there is no clear distinction between good and bad states. Take the termini of cosmic change, for instance. Although the two ends are engendered by, and manifest opposing states, they are both desirable. When love dominates, the roots compose a perfect unity, "a rounded sphere, rejoicing in its joyous solitude" (33/27.4). When hostility reigns, the elements are revealed to be just what they are, immortal and divine (26/21.8). As Inwood explains: "the pure existence of separate elements . . . is the ultimate purification from our mortal life" (48). And yet it is a state where the power of strife is manifest through and through. It might be objected that love and strife are, for Empedocles, mere physical powers and, thereby, only metaphorically good or bad. But Empedocles does not detach moral value from these roots altogether, for our possession of love and strife is what accounts for our ability to both love and hate (17/109). Consider also that in Empedocles' theory ideal states are won by conflict and suffering and are destined to fail. Take for instance the coming to be and destruction of the golden age of mortal beings. When love is ascendant, the increasing desire for unity gives way to limbs without torsos and heads without necks. Eventually, the parts will be fitted together in a unity that is, in Empedocles' words, "a wonder to behold" (61/35.17). But, tragically, this period will not last forever. For the very love that created such a world will also eventually destroy it. The same is true for the reign of strife. When strife is ascendant, mortals first make their presence as limbs without torsos and heads without necks. Eventually, strife will have the power to break the bonds of unity just enough for the creation of discreet beings. But this state too will come to an end. The very hostility that created these beings will also be their destruction.

Plato's critique of natural science appears between the penultimate and final argument for the immortality of the soul. To prove that the soul is not just long-lasting (Empedocles' view) but immortal (95c4–7), Plato has Socrates challenge the natural scientists' understanding of generation and corruption. His interest is to pave the way for his theory of forms. Socrates is made to critique the natural scientists by demonstrating the incoherence of their mechanistic treatment of addition and division, concepts which feature in their theories of generation and corruption.

Plato does not mention Empedocles in his refutation of natural science, but his audience would have recognized his reference to Empedocles in the account of natural science provided at the outset of the refutation. Plato has Socrates explain that he was once taken by questions such as, "Is it when the hot and the cold start to decompose . . . that living things grow into a unity? Is it because of blood that we think, or air, or fire?" (96b2–4). According to Aristotle, Empedocles believes milk is produced from the decomposition of blood (*GA* IV 8 777a4–11).[12] And according to Theophrastus, Empedocles believes blood is the seat of intellection (A86 = *De Sensibus* 1–2, 7–24). This is why Inwood lists this passage from the *Phaedo* as testimonia (A76) for Empedocles' views. Moreover, Plato's audience would have seen how Socrates' refutation of the natural scientists' treatment of addition and division undermines Empedocles' (and also Anaximander's) theory of generation and destruction. The critical passage appears at 96e. After introducing a series of what seems to be incontestable claims—claims such as "ten [is] more numerous than eight on account of their being two added to it, and that two cubits [is] larger than one on account of its exceeding the other because of a half" (96e1–3)—Plato has Socrates say:

That I'm no doubt a long way indeed from thinking that I know the cause of any of these. I don't allow myself to say even that, when somebody adds one to one, either the one it was added to has become two, or the one that was added and the one it was added to became two, on account of the addition of the first to the second. For I find it astonishing that when each of them was apart from the other, each turned out to be one, and they weren't two at that time, but when they came near each other, this supposedly became a cause of their coming to be two, namely the union that consisted in being put near each other. No, nor can I still persuade myself that if somebody divides one, this, the division, has now become a cause of its coming to be two. For then there comes to be a cause of coming to be two that is opposite of the earlier cause. Back then, you see, it was because they were brought together into proximity with each other, and one was added to the other, but now it is because they are brought apart, and one is separated from the other. No, and I can no longer persuade myself that by using this approach I know why one comes to be, nor, in short, why anything else comes to be or perishes, or is. Instead I throw together on impulse my own different kind of approach, and I don't adopt this one at all. (96e6–97b7)

We are here told that the natural scientists treat addition and division as physical processes: the former resulting when things are "put near each other," the latter when they are "separated from the other." It bears emphasis that both Anaximander and Empedocles thought that multiplicity was created through separation and, presumably, that bringing multiplicities near made them one. In any case, with Empedocles there can be no doubt.

Plato has Socrates provide two arguments against the natural scientists' treatment of addition and division. The first argument runs on the tacit assumption that all mechanical processes involve a subject. For the argument demonstrates that no subject becomes two, when one is added to one. Plato provides two possible subjects of addition: the one (be it the one to which the other is added or the one added) and the two together. Plato does not tell us why he thinks neither can serve as subject, but it is easy enough to surmise. We are to see that the one cannot increase in number or change its form by addition. The oneness of a thing remains even when it belongs to a plurality. Conversely, the two together cannot be the subject of addition because they did not exist at the beginning of the process. The second argument focuses on the processes by showing that this account of addition and division makes a single process the cause of opposite results. Plato has Socrates use division as his example. By division two things become one, when each is considered on its own or when each is separated far enough, but by division one thing is made two when each is considered as a part of a plurality or when the parts are separated only a little. The argument works for addition as well. Bringing two things together that were far apart can make each of the things that were formerly considered one a plurality, but bringing them together a lot can make a plurality a unity.

The confusion described in the second argument whereby a single process gives way to opposite results has various manifestations in Anaximander's and Empedocles' cosmologies. On Anaximander's theory, every generative act is both just and unjust. The coming of night (darkness) is unjust because its arrival entails the destruction of day (light). But the coming of night is also requital for the injustice day committed when day annihilated night. Similarly, on Empedocles' theory, love is responsible both for the creation and destruction of the golden age of mortals, just as strife. Moreover, both love and strife are capable of bringing about unities and multiplicities. Strife makes a plurality out of a unity by introducing hostility into the one. But it also makes each root a separate unity, just what it is, when the roots exist apart as a plurality. Love does the same. Bringing together disparate things turn a plurality into a unity, if the things are brought very close to each other. But love can also make things that were once a unity (just what each is) into a plurality by bringing them together just near enough.

In this essay I have argued that the principles of the CA were well established in Greek thought, that a variety of theories were adapted to them, and that they were associated with positions that Plato found untenable. I argued further that Plato attacks these principles in his criticism of natural science, directing his argument toward Empedocles, who explicitly hangs his cosmology on them. What remains to be explained is why Plato would present the CA as a philosophical justification of the mysteries, when he accepts the doctrines of reincarnation and liberation at their core. Why even associate the principles of the CA with the mysteries? The reason, I believe, is that the rites were also adapted to the principles. According to Burkert, the mystery experience "is patterned by antithesis, by moving between the extremes of terror and happiness, darkness and light" (93).

The initiates walked long distances, were deprived of food, water, and light, and were humiliated and mocked on their journey.[13] Because the mysteries were revealed at the end of their trials, the revelations were coupled with relief and joy. Plato rejects the idea that a vacillation between extreme emotions can lead to happiness in this life and hope for the next. In the prelude to the arguments, Plato has Phaedo report that he, like the others, felt "an unusual mixture blended together from both the pleasure and the pain . . . that his life was just about to end" (59a5–7). They felt pain when they reflected on their loss, but pleasure when reminded that Socrates was going to a better place. Weeping at one moment, laughing the next, their emotions dragged them from one opposite to the other in reciprocal exchange. The tragedy, we are to see, is not Socrates' impending death. The tragedy is that Phaedo and the others reportedly took no pleasure in philosophizing on that last day they shared with Socrates (59a3). Socrates, by contrast, was serene, happy, and hopeful.

Notes

1. An earlier version of this essay was presented at the annual meeting for the Society of Ancient Greek Philosophy at Fordham University. Under Tony Preus's leadership, the meetings of SAGP provided a friendly and open venue for scholars to exchange work and ideas. The importance of such a venue cannot be overstated. By ensuring that friends could reunite in their shared love of the ancients, Tony helped us to realize our versions of a philosophical life. Thus, I dedicate this essay on living and dying with happiness and hope to him.

2. All translations of the *Phaedo* are provided by Long and Sedley. Compare to 80d9–10.

3. See, for instance, Barnes (405) and Hackforth (49).

4. To use Bostock's example, if one grows a foot to become larger from being smaller, one does not acquire a state that is in opposition to that of the former. Being six feet is not in opposition to being five feet. See also Hackforth (63–64).

5. See, for instance, Hackforth (63–64) and Burnet (11).

6. See Gregory (104–5) for a discussion of the testimonia on the generation of the productive opposites from the *apeiron*.

7. Translation provided by Gregory (68).

8. See Gregory (73–76) and Vlastos (168–74).

9. For the intriguing argument that Anaximander was influenced by legislative prose, see Sassi (81–93).

10. For recent defenses of the orthodox reading of Empedocles' poem see Inwood (44–55) and Trépanier (184f).

11. Translations and reference numbers are provided by Inwood.
12. See Coles for the argument that Empedocles and Diogenes are the originators of the view that milk and semen are putrefactions (σύντηγματα) (55–57).
13. See Bowden for a vivid reconstruction of the rites (26–48).

Works Cited

Archer-Hind, Richard D. *The* Phaedo *of Plato*. London: Macmillan, 1894.
Athanassakis, Apostolos, and Benjamin Wolkow. *The Orphic Hymns. Translation, Introduction, and Notes*. John Hopkins UP, 2013.
Barnes, Jonathan. "Critical Notice of Gallop: Plato's *Phaedo*." *Canadian Journal of Philosophy*, vol. 8, no. 2, 1978, pp. 397–419. Bonitz, Hermann. *Platonische Studien*. Berlin: Franz Vahlen, 1875.
Bostock, David. *Plato's* Phaedo. Clarendon, 1986.
Bowden, Hugh. *Mystery Cults of the Ancient World*. Princeton UP, 2010.
Burkert, Walter. *Ancient Mystery Cults*. Harvard UP, 1989.
Burnet, John. *Plato's* Phaedo. Clarendon, 2011.
Cicero. *De Re Publica, De Legibus*. Translated by Clinton W. Keyes, Loeb, 1928.
Coles, Andrew. "Biomedical Models of Reproduction in the Fifth Century BC and Aristotle's Generation of Animals." *Phronesis*, vol. 40, no. 1, 1995, pp. 48–88.
Empedocles. *The Poem of Empedocles*. Revised edition. Translated by Brad Inwood, U of Toronto P, 2001.
Gallop, David. "Plato's Cyclical Argument Recycled." *Phronesis*, vol. 27, no. 3, 1982, pp. 207–22.
Gregory, Andrew. *Anaximander: A Re-assessment*. Bloomsbury Academic, 2016.
Hackforth, Reginald. *Plato's* Phaedo. Cambridge UP, 1955.
Plato. *Meno and Phaedo*. Translated by A. Long and D. Sedley, Cambridge UP, 2010.
———. Plato. *Phaedo*. Translated by R. S. Bluck, Routledge, 1955.
Sassi, Maria Michela. *The Beginnings of Philosophy in Greece*. Princeton UP, 2018.
Trépanier, Simon. *Empedocles. An Interpretation*. Routledge, 2004.
Vlastos, Gregory. "Equality and Justice in Early Greek Cosmogonies." *Classical Philology* vol. 42, no. 3, 1947, pp. 156–78.

"Turn the Brightness Outward"
Muthos and *Paideia* in Pindar and Plato

Hyun Höchsmann

Pindar sets the frame of reference of his *epinikia* (victory odes) by drawing upon myths and maxims, establishing the parallels between the events of victory and divine or heroic achievements, and enhancing the individual consciousness beyond a transient moment of celebration. Pindar does not commemorate the victors as individuals but transforms them into the representatives of the highest *arete* (excellence/virtue).[1] In endowing individual achievements with an enduring purpose and meaning in the context of shared traditions and knowledge, Pindar's *epinikia* point to the sphere of possible transcendence of regional dissidence and strife.

The present reading of Pindar's correlation of myths and victors for the poetic task of the paideutic function of the *epinikia* builds on Werner Jaeger's study of *arete* in Pindar's *epinikia*. As emphasized in Jaeger's study of Greek *paideia* (education/learning), Pindar transforms the victors to "true models of *areta*": "*Areta* is not only the root of all Pindar's faith, but the guiding structural principle of his poetry" (214). Pindar's victory odes seek to instruct through praise. His incorporation of myths and maxims emphasizes the connection between the particular and the universal, and between *arete* and truth. Pindar's *epinikia* establish the groundwork for the task of poetry articulated in the educational program of Plato's *Republic*. Pindar's distinction between the traditional narrations of myth and his interpretations of myths as *logos* (Olympian 7.21, Nemean 1.34) bring Pindar closer to Plato's view of myths and supplies a defense of his odes against Plato's criticism of the poets in the *Republic* 2.363–67. In *Pythian* 3 (written for Hieron, tyrant of Syracuse) Pindar affirms the vigor of moral capacity to surmount adversities to "turn the brightness outward" (τὰ καλὰ τρέψαντες ἔξω, *Pythian* 3.83).[2]

Pindar's *Epinikia* and the Transformation of the Individual to the Universal

To situate Pindar's *epinikia*, the emergence of epinician poetry can be traced to ca. 520 BCE with the commissioning of odes to be performed by a chorus in honor of the returning athletic victors (Morris 19–48). Epinician poetry brought the victor's fame back to the community. This idea was already in Homer: "it was only by rejoining his fellows that the warriors can receive their acknowledgement and honor" (Crotty 109–10).[3] Epinician poetry consolidated the Homeric commemorative tradition in formal performances of the poems in the wider context of the *polis*. Building on the Homeric recognition of confirming individual identity within the community by conferring honor, Pindar's odes are the epitome of the new epinician poetry.

Pindar's fifteen victory odes for Sicilian victors include his most renowned poems, including the first two *Olympians* and the first three *Pythians*. The majority of the Sicilian odes date from ca. 476 to 466 BCE and were composed to celebrate the victories of the powerful tyrants of Sicily, Hieron of Syracuse, and Theron of Akragas or their families or athletes at the games. The Sicilian tyrants amply demonstrated their wealth and power in competing at the games and by commissioning Pindar and Bacchylides to commemorate their victories.

The conventional epinician form in Simonides was transformed by Pindar to the religious hymn. As Jean-Pierre Vernant has elucidated in *Myth and Thought among the Greeks*: "[T]he essential issue resides in the dual nature of games. Both spectacle and religious festival—a national spectacle . . . which joins and opposes the diverse cities in a great public competition. Each city is engaged in a struggle in which the victor represents his community more than he does himself. Religious festival too: the contests are sacred ceremonies" (344). Presenting distinct events (Apollo's reception, the victor's homecoming, the ode's reception) simultaneously, in *Pythian* 5.60–76 Pindar integrates the incommensurable particular events into the universal.

ὁ δ' ἀρχαγέτας ἔδωκ' Ἀπόλλων
θῆρας αἰνῷ φόβῳ,
ὄφρα μὴ ταμίᾳ Κυράνας ἀτελὴς γένοιτο μαντεύμασιν.
Ὅ καὶ βαρειᾶν νόσων
ἀκέσματ' ἄνδρεσσι καὶ γυναιξὶ νέμει,
πόρεν τε κίθαριν, δίδωσί τε Μοῖσαν οἷς ἂν ἐθέλῃ,
ἀπόλεμον ἀγαγὼν
ἐς πραπίδας εὐνομίαν,
μυχόν τ' ἀμφέπει
μαντήϊον· τῷ καὶ Λακεδαίμονι
ἐν Ἄργει τε καὶ ζαθέᾳ Πύλῳ
ἔνασσεν ἀλκάεντας Ἡρακλέος
ἐκγόνους Αἰγιμιοῦ τε. τὸ δ' ἐμὸν γαρύειν
ἀπὸ Σπάρτας ἐπήρατον κλέος·
ὅθεν γεγενναμένοι
ἵκοντο Θήρανδε φῶτες Αἰγεῖδαι,
ἐμοὶ πατέρες, οὐ θεῶν ἄτερ, ἀλλὰ μοῖρά τις ἄγεν·

[And Apollo, the first leader, gave the beasts over to flight and terror, so that his oracles to the guardian of Cyrene would not go unfulfilled.

It is Apollo who dispenses remedies to men and women for grievous diseases,

and who bestowed on us the cithara, and gives the Muses' inspiration to whomever he will, bringing peaceful concord into the mind, and who possesses the oracular shrine; wherefore

he settled the mighty descendants of Heracles and Aegimius in Lacedaemon

and in Argos and in sacred Pylos. But it is my part to sing of the lovely glory that comes

from Sparta, where the Aegeidae were born, and from there went to Thera, my ancestors, not without the gods; they were led by a certain fate.]

As Jacob Burkhardt has emphasized, in *Pythian* 4.53–56, Pindar's "choral lyricism" is imbued with social and political significance (*History* 223).

μὲν πολυχρύσῳ ποτ' ἐν δώματι
Φοῖβος ἀμνάσει θέμισσιν

Πύθιον ναὸν καταβάντα χρόνῳ
ὑστέρῳ, νάεσσι πολεῖς ἀγαγὲν Νείλοιο πρὸς πῖον τέμενος
Κρονίδα.'

[And when at a later time he enters the temple at Pytho,
within his house filled with gold
Phoebus will admonish him through oracles
to convey many people in ships
to the fertile domain of Kronos' son on the Nile.]

Plato's Criticism of Poetry

In the *Republic* (2.363–67), Plato criticizes the poets (including Homer, Hesiod, Archilochus, Pindar, Simonides, and Aeschylus) for implicit endorsement of justice for the reputation, honor, and awards it brings (Naddaf 329–49). In the *Gorgias*, poetry is linked with "conscious" deception. But had Plato left the matters there, he would have merely mitigated the severity of Heraclitus' (B 42) and Xenophanes' (B 11) castigation of Homer and Hesiod. Readily acknowledging Homer as "the most poetic of poets and the first of tragedians," Plato explains that "we must know the truth" and "we can admit no poetry into our city save only hymns to the gods and the praises of good men" (*Republic* 606e–607a). The initial exclusion of Homer and the poets from the *kallipolis* (ideal city) have overshadowed Plato's emphatic subsequent invitation welcoming the poets in the *Republic* (10.607c–e):

> Then may she not justly return from this exile after she has pleaded her defence, whether in lyric or other measure?
> And we would allow her advocates who are not poets but lovers of poetry to plead her cause in prose without meter, show that she is not only delightful but beneficial to orderly government and all the life of man. And we shall listen benevolently, for it will be clear gain for us if can be shown that she bestows not only pleasure but benefit.

Pindar's *epinikia* aim at what Plato requires of poetry: via hymns to the gods and praises for noble or heroic deeds, strive for moral enhancement toward *arete*.

The present hypothesis is that Pindar's *epinikia* present a response to Plato's readiness to welcome Homer and the poets to the *kallipolis* and invitation to demonstrate the wisdom and moral efficacy of poetry.[4] Given Plato's criticism of encomiastic discourse in *Lysis*, *Apology*, and *Symposium*, at first sight, there appears to be an unbridgeable gulf between Pindar's odes and Platonic *paidea*. However, a closer reading reveals an elective affinity between Pindar and Plato on poetry and *paidea*.

Plato's Criticism of Encomiastic Discourse

While Socrates is not as critical as Euripides, who castigates the athletes as useless to the city in time of war,[5] in the *Apology*, Socrates is unimpressed with athletic praise and declares that the difference between "any of you who has won a race at the Olympic games with a pair of horses or a four-in-hand" and himself is that "he makes you seem to be happy, whereas I make you happy in reality" (36d). In the *Lysis*, Ctesippus, in what almost reads as a parody of the epinician convention, makes fun of Hippothales for inflicting on his acquaintances interminable victory odes (ἐγκώμιον, 205d) he has composed in his pursuit of Lysis, elevating "his ancestors, wealth, chariot victories in the Isthmian games, relation to Heracles, and so on" (Moore 526). Socrates wades in with incontrovertible logic, urging Hippothales to desist the encomiastic urge: this kind of encomiastic bombast is mere self-flattery (as the purported high status of the object of pursuit, Lysis, increases the esteem for himself as the pursuer) and will be of no avail since overblown praise of the beloved will only make his suit more arduous (205b–206a).[6]

Is there something categorically wrong with praise? If truth is what we are after, we cannot praise without knowing the subject of the praise. This is how Socrates' speech differs from all the encomia of *eros* in the *Symposium* (198d–199c): Socrates seeks the knowledge of *eros* before singing its praises. Socrates begins his speech by complementing Agathon on his "admirable" procedure of differentiating his speech (195a) from the previous speeches and beginning with the nature of *eros* (199c–d). Engaging Agathon and the celebrants of *eros* in the quest for the origin and the nature of *eros*, Socrates' exploration supersedes Agathon's praise of *eros* as the emblem of radiant beauty. With the spontaneous and unsolicited encomium of Socrates by Alcibiades, who bursts onto the scene with unrestrained exuberance of a Dionysian reveler, Plato gives a resplendent demonstration of how the best kind of praise comes from true understanding.

How might then Pindar reply to Socrates' critique of encomiastic discourse in the *Apology, Lysis and in the Symposium*? What are Pindar's aims in his *epinikia*? Not flattery motivated by desire to entice, but *paidea*. Pindar's frame of reference is the shared tradition and knowledge in myths and maxims at the foundations of communal aspiration toward *paidea*. The elevation of formal epinician poetic discourse gives the fineness of enduring form beyond the fleeting random praises in ordinary linguistic encounters or "the spontaneous overflow of powerful emotions."

Snell's illuminating discussion of Pindar's conception of poetic task to "Turn the brightness outward" (71–89), presents a further possible Pindaric response: The poet instructs through praise. The poet's songs spread knowledge further through the community and into the future; therefore, poems excel other materials and forms of praise and commemoration, the statue, which is confined to a specific place.

> οὐκ ἀνδριαντοποιός εἰμ᾽, ὥστ᾽ ἐλινύσοντα ἐργάζεσθαι
> ἀγάλματ᾽ ἐπ᾽ αὐτᾶς βαθμίδος
> ἑσταότ᾽: ἀλλ᾽ ἐπὶ πάσας ὁλκάδος ἔν τ᾽ ἀκάτῳ, γλυκεῖ᾽ ἀοιδά,
> στεῖχ ἀπ᾽ Αἰγίνας . . .

> [I am not a sculptor, to make statues that stand motionless on the same pedestal. Sweet song, go on every merchant-ship and rowboat that leaves Aegina. . . .] (*Nemean* 5.1–3)

Pindar's *epinikia* aim at commemorating *arete*, not only for the individual alone but also for educating the *polis* (Morris 37). The myths in Pindar's *epinikia* "with the purifying agency of the epic," help to draw a parallel between the events on earth and divine or heroic actions; as a result, the aspirations of mortals are endowed with a purpose and meaning. Maxims show the connection between the particular and the universal, stimulating the mind to a further search for the enduring values and approaches to truth (Snell 82–94).

Pindar's *Epinikia* as *Logos alathes*

Pindar appears to have been the first to contrast *muthos* to *logos* with respect to traditional stories about the gods.[7] In the first Olympian ode (composed in 476 BCE) 1.28–29, *muthoi* and *pseudea* (lies) are used synonymously to contrast the ignoble stories about the gods with his own *logos alathes* (true *logos*, reason, language of truth, or historic truth).

ἦ θαυματὰ πολλά, καί πού τι καὶ βρο τῶν φάτις
ὑπὲρ τὸν ἀλαθῆ λόγον
δεδαιδαλμένοι ψεύδεσι ποικίλοις ἐξαπα τῶν τι μῦθοι

[Yes wonders are many, but then too, I think, in men's talk
stories are embellished beyond the true account
and deceive by means of elaborate lies.]

In *Nemean* 7.20–25, *muthoi* and *pseudea* are used synonymously with respect to the pleasantness of Homer's narrative and contrasted with *alētheia*.

ἐγὼ δὲ πλέον' ἔλπομαι
λόγον Ὀδυσσέος ἢ πάθαν διὰ τὸν ἁδυεπῆ γενέσθ' Ὅμηρον·
ἐπεὶ ψεύδεσί οἱ ποτανᾷ τε μαχανᾷ
σεμνὸν ἔπεστί τι· σοφία δὲ κλέπτει παράγοισα μύθοις· τυφλὸν
  δ' ἔχει
ἦτορ ὅμιλος ἀνδρῶν ὁ πλεῖστος. εἰ γὰρ ἦν
ἓ τὰν ἀλάθειαν ἰδέμεν . . .

[And I expect that the story of Odysseus came to exceed his
  experiences,
through the sweet songs of Homer,
since there is a certain solemnity in his lies and winged art-
  fulness, and poetic skill deceives, seducing us with stories,
  and the heart of the mass of men is blind. For if they had
  been able to see the truth . . .]

In *Olympian* 7.20–23[8] and Nemean 1.31–34,[9] Pindar refers his account of traditional stories as *logos*. In Pindar's elevated discourse, his *epinikia* strives for *logos alathes*, signaling the shift from *muthos* to *logos* in early Greek thought and literature.

Pindar and Plato on the Parallelism between the Divine and the Mortal

What is achieved by the victor celebrated in Pindar's *epinikia*? "An instance of man coming close to the divine," replies Vernant. Vernant continues:

"Victory consecrates the victor. . . . It suffuses his person with sacred prestige. In the form of ritual scenario that is the contest, the triumph of the athlete, as seen in Pindar evokes and extends the exploit accomplished by the hero and the gods; it raises man to the level of the divine" (345). Pindar's *Nemean* 6.1–8 relates directly to the parallelism between the divine and the human existence in the *Theaetetus* and the *Timaeus*.

> ἓν ἀνδρῶν, ἓν θεῶν γένος: ἐκ μιᾶς δὲ πνέομεν
> ματρὸς ἀμφότεροι: διείργει δὲ πᾶσα κεκριμένα
> δύναμις, ὡς τὸ μὲν οὐδέν, ὁ δὲ χάλκεος ἀσφαλὲς αἰὲν ἕδος
> μένει οὐρανός. ἀλλά τι προσφέρομεν ἔμπαν ἢ μέγαν
> νόον ἤτοι φύσιν ἀθανάτοις,
> καίπερ ἐφαμερίαν οὐκ εἰδότες οὐδὲ μετὰ νύκτας ἄμμε πότμος
> οἵαν τιν᾽ ἔγραψε δραμεῖν ποτὶ στάθμαν.

[There is one race of men, one race of gods; and from a single mother we both draw our breath. But all allotted power divides us: man is nothing, but for the gods the bronze sky endures as a secure home forever. Nevertheless, we bear some resemblance to the immortals, either in greatness of mind or in nature, although we do not know, by day or by night, towards what goal fortune has written that we should run.]

Pindar's view of mortals as having "some resemblance to the immortals, either in greatness of mind or in nature," is further developed by Plato. In the *Theaetetus* 176a–b, Socrates explains that as reason is the divine element in human beings, in the activity of reason we can ascend to the level of the gods, "becoming like a god (*homoiosis theoi*) insofar as it is possible" for a mortal. In the *Timaeus* the gulf between the gods and mortals is bridged by the activity of reason. Plato explains that when the soul attains goodness through reason and the result is *eudaimonia* (happiness, well-being, flourishing), there is an approximation to the divine: "If a man perseveres in pursuing learning and wisdom, he will certainly be led to immortal and divine thoughts reaching truth and will attain immortality to the full extent it is possible for human nature" (*Timaeus* 90b–c).[10]

Myth in Pindar and Plato

A Pindar scholar has observed that "Myth is the shaky ladder by which man climbs into eternity" (Newman 169–89).[11] (Or perhaps a Wittgensteinian ladder that is to be kicked off once we have climbed upon it?) The ladder metaphor, less shaky, is continued by Deborah Steiner in *Crown of Song: Metaphor in Pindar*: metaphor in Pindar creates "a special ground where poets encounter their divine counterparts" and "a ladder which the poet and his subjects may travel" (154). "Myth, like metaphor, contributes to the construction of the particular world in which Pindar sets his victors, where poet and athlete mix freely with gods and heroes, and cross the everyday boundaries of space and time" (137). Steiner emphasizes the poetry's participation in "a Platonic world of fundamental being" (151). On this plateau of elevated Pindaric language, it might be said that, mixing metaphors, myth in Pindar's odes is the Archimedean fulcrum on which the multitude of phenomena might be lifted.

In *Myth and Philosophy from the Presocratics to Plato* Kathryn Morgan has pointed out that the term *muthos* is used three times in Pindaric epinician poetry and that Pindar's use of *muthos* can have both negative and positive connotation (19). In *Nemean* 7.23, *sophia* deceives by leading people astray with *muthoi*. The primary reference is not poetic tales (the *muthoi* are speeches of Odysseus as he schemes to obtain the arms of Achilles). In *Pythian* 4.298 *mythesasthai* (to speak, to tell) is used in a positive context, in relation to the poet's own art. In response to Gerard Naddaf's assessment that there is an ambiguity in Pindar regarding the separation between *muthos* and *logos*, it could be pointed out that, as in Plato's myths, the content and aim of Pindaric myths determine its relation to truth (Introduction to Brisson vii–ix).

The vital constituent element of Pindar's epinician form is the myth presented in a series of succinctly visualized scenes intended to link the high moment of the present to the lofty past and to hold forth a glimpse of temporality beyond the transitory moment of victory. Pindar integrates stories from the epic tradition or the local oral tradition by focusing on the episode most appropriate for the ceremony for which he was composing and then by expressly connecting the person, the family, and the city or divinity to be celebrated. Pindar's incorporation of myths brings a strong epic element into his odes (Burkhardt, *History* 223–24). Myth for Pindar is "the evocation of a universally valid but partially apprehended order," with which the temporal is briefly and tangentially united (Newman 172). Pindar's myths set forth mortal *arete* as the proximity to the divine and emulation of achievements of the gods. As Snell has elucidated, Pindar's evocation of myths gives to the transient present a reality beyond the coincidence of the past and the present.

It is being acknowledged with increasing readiness in recent scholarship that myths form an integral part of the exposition of Plato's philosophy.[12] The central place of the transmigration of the soul in Plato's ethics is emphasized by Luc Brisson in "Myths in Plato's Ethics": myths have "a fundamental and permanent" importance in revealing "the emergence of a tendency to orient ethics towards physics . . . by resituating man within his place on the scale of all living things" (63–76). Pindar has a moral purpose in linking the present reality with the mythic narrative: he emphasizes the dangers of excessive pride in achievement. Pindar's recasting of traditional myths for didactic purposes amplifies their broader paideutic significance and is aligned with Plato's convictions regarding the myths in the educational program of the *Republic*. One of the most significant philosophical expansions of Pindar's myths in Plato is the genealogy of *eros* in the *Symposium* 203 b–c.[13] Pindar's myth of the birth of *eros* from Poros and Penia is transformed by Socrates to blow away the prevailing views of all the encomia of *eros* as a god and establishing that *eros* is not a god but a *daimon*, an intermediary between the gods and mortals.

Agones among Pindarists

The terrain of ἀγῶνες (contests, competition) among the competing Pindarists concerning the function of Pindaric recourse to myth in the *epinikia* is laid out by Peter W. Rose in "The Myth of Pindar's First *Nemean*: Sportsmen, Poetry, and Paideia."[14] In direct opposition to Jaeger's reading of *arete* as the foundation of Pindar's *epinikia* (214),[15] the polemical stance spearheaded by Wolfgang Schadewaldt subsequently followed by E. Bundy and the ensuing adherents has argued that Pindar's *epinikia* follow primarily the convention of the epinician genre. It is always some particular commissioned occasion that determines the selection and the adaptations of myths for the given specific context, the overarching aim being exclusively encomiastic.[16] Notwithstanding Hermann Fränkel's incisive criticism of the inadequacies in Schadewaldt's approach to the place of myth in Pindar's *epinikia* ("Wege" 355), substantial research has focused on the centrality of the connection of particular myths to the encomiastic intent, emphasizing the details of the myths to the details of the victor's circumstances.[17]

The argument that the correspondence between myth and the victor pertains exclusively to the victor as an individual seeking praise and to his particular social and political circumstances does not take into account the significance of the intersection between the private and the public sphere in the panhellenic world of Pindar. *Agones* are both individual and communal. In response to the claim of Bundy and others that the only significant aim of Pindar is to praise the victor, Peter W. Rose emphasizes that the task of Pindaric *epinikia* extends beyond the confines of individual domain and encompasses "the panhellenic paideia, the poet's presentation of mythic paradeigmata" (pattern or example) imbued with the ideals of enduring importance for Greek society.

The argument that the main aim of Pindaric myths is the relation of the details of the myth to the details of the victor's circumstances within in the confines of the encomiastic convention overlooks the broader function of myths in the Greek world. The function of myths in reinforcing social norms of behavior in most societies is widely acknowledged (Kirk 20–22).[18] Furthermore, it is fundamental to Pindar's encomiastic aim that the odes aspire toward a wider significance to Greek society beyond conferring honour and renown to the victor and the limited range of individual circumstances. Pindar transposes the victor's achievement to the context of the sphere of the ideals as embodied in the myths. As Burkhardt has emphasized, in the content and mode of composition of his victory odes, Pindar deliberately refrains from depicting the individual agonistic victory, which would have made for "insufferable monotony," but draws upon the myths, thereby "incorporating a vigorous epic element into his odes" (*History* 223–24).

Pindar's universalism is not a poetic conception of remote ideal unity but reflects the political and social realities and mercantile transactions of the panhellenic world of his time: "A much-studied feature of Greek society has been the set of institutions by which individuals, who . . . maintained contact with Greeks in distant cities. Proxeny, ritualized friendship (*xenia*), intermarriage, kinship diplomacy, isopoliteia (exchange of citizenship between communities), commercially motivated maritime interconnectivity—all these institutions and practices mitigated polis-particularism and found expression in long-distance reciprocity between . . . persons, families, and whole communities" (Hornblower and Morgan 6). As Jaeger has clarified, the communal celebrations on the occasions of the victories at the games of Olympia and Pytho, Nemea, and the Corinthian Isthmus transcend the regional dissidence, rivalry, and strife "in the universal admiration of its triumphs" (205). In the re-interpretation of myths and interweaving of the individual actions with myths and history, in Pindar's odes the ideals and values upheld in the Panhellenic tradition are confirmed "suddenly in astonishing new moral and religious vigour" (186).

Poetry as *Paideia* in Pindar's *Epinikia*

The ideal of *kalokagathia* (beautiful and good) changed in the fifth century BCE and "the extension of the *agon* into a competition in every area of life brought individual personality a new prominence" (Burkhardt, *Greeks* 241). The cult of individuality prevailed, as amply demonstrated by Empedocles, who wore purple and announced that he is a god who descended to earth and Gorgias who wore a golden diadem and a Delphic crown as well. In contrast to the inflation of individuality, Pindar's epinician odes point out the limitations of mortals and the harm of *hubris*.

Recalling Aristotle's complaint in the *Metaphysics* (2.995a 7–8) that there are people who will take the arguments of a speaker, including a philosopher, seriously only if a poet can be cited as a "witness" in support of them,[19] we will not go as far as Wittgenstein who declared that "*Philosophie dürfte man eigentlich nur dichten*" (Philosophy can only properly be written as poetry—*Vermischte Bemerkungen* 483)[20] but emphasize that the inseparable connection between poetry and *paideia* is the guiding insight for Plato's discussion of the task of poetry in the *kallipolis*. For Plato the task of *paideia* is not only the education of the individual but also formation of the foundation of political life to check the rise of tyranny. For this reason, Plato sought to educate Dion in Syracuse, as explained in the *Seventh Letter*.

Pindar's consistently "moralizing" treatment of inherited mythology, what Wilhelm Nestle termed "*Ethisierung des Mythos*" (ethicization of myths), is aligned with Xenophanes' criticism of the depiction of disreputable conduct of the gods in Homer and Hesiod (153–80).[21] In Pindar's time there was an extensive criticism of didactic efficacy of myth in the political, social, and ethical arena. *Nemean 7*, in conformity with the epinician exclusion of ethically problematic myths, presents a "moralized" version. Pindar wrote the first, second, third *Pythian*, and first *Olympian* for Hieron. The four *epinikia* for Hieron celebrated not only the athletic victory but above all the virtues of the figure of the Sicilian dynasty and military conquests. Pindar modeled a positive portrait of Hieron through a combination of the occasion of praise and mythological topoi. Pindar contrasts the "great wrongdoers" who, abusing the privileged position granted them by the gods, stained themselves with ὕβρις (hubris, pride) with Hieron as a wise ruler who is aware of the limits imposed by divine support and benevolence and, therefore, far from the Persian model of royalty. Precautions against hubris may be prudent given that victory fosters a propensity toward self-assertion.

Pindar's interpretation of myth is at the foundation of poetry Plato envisages in the educational program of the *Republic*. Pindar and Plato are aligned in their commitment to the task of the education of those who hold political power. Jaeger observes that Pindar regarded the education of the kings was the highest and the most important task of the poet and "like Plato, he hoped to influence them for good" (221). Pindar and Plato are in unison regarding the capacity of poetry to engage the world in a formative and transformative activity. Pindar's and Plato's emphasis on the significance of the moral and political function of poetry continues to reverberate in the present from Dylan Thomas to Seamus Heaney. Thomas wrote: "A good poem helps to change the shape and significance of the universe, helps to extend everyone's knowledge of himself and the world around him" (192–93). Referring to the task of poetry in society, Seamus Heaney has emphasized "the idea of poetry's answer" to the crisis in the individual and in the world: "[R]esponsible poetry, and the idea of poetry's answer, its responsibility, being given in its own language rather than in the language of the world that provokes it, that too, has been one of my constant themes" (1). Behind "defences and justifications" of the value of poetry, Heaney finds Plato "calling into question whatever special prerogatives or useful influences poetry would claim for itself within the polis." Heaney affirms that "Plato's world of ideal forms also provides the court of appeal to which poetic imagination seeks to redress whatever is wrong or exacerbating in the prevailing conditions" (1).

In the concluding lines of *Pythian* 8.95–98, Pindar's last ode written in 448 BCE, the ephemeral mortal existence is illuminated by "the brightness given by Zeus":

ἐπάμεροι· τί δέ τις; τί δ' οὔ τις; σκιᾶς ὄναρ
ἄνθρωπος. Ἀλλ' ὅταν αἴγλα διόσδοτος ἔλθῃ,
λαμπρὸν φέγγος ἔπεστιν ἀνδρῶν καὶ μείλιχος αἰών·

[Creatures of a day. What is anyone? What is anyone not?
A dream of a shadow is man.
But when the brightness given by Zeus comes, a shining light
  is on man, and a gentle lifetime.]

Notes

1. See Jaeger's clarification of the Doric conception of *arete* (205-22).
2. Translations of Pindar are adapted from the Loeb edition of Pindar, the Perseus Digital Library, Snell and Lattimore. Snell and Lattimore render "καλὰ" in Pythian 3.83 as "brightness."
3. See also, Ober and Hedrick (37).
4. See Havelock for the view that early Greek philosophy arose in opposition to the tradition of oral poetic performance as *paideia* (44-67).
5. Euripides, *Autolykos*, fr. 282, Hornblower and Morgan (8).
6. For Plato's criticism of encomiastic discourse, see Nightingale (112-30). Demos, on the other hand, argues that Plato is not antagonistic toward the lyric praise. Pender discusses Plato's recourse to lyric in the *Phaedrus*.
7. Naddaf's Introduction to Brisson, *Plato the Myth Maker* (viii). See also, Hornblower and Morgan (22); Richardson (383-401).
8. ἐθελήσω τοῖσιν ἐξ ἀρχᾶς ἀπὸ Τλαπολέμου
ξυνὸν ἀγγέλλων διορθῶσαι λόγον,
Ἡρακλέος εὐρυσθενεῖ γέννᾳ.

I am eager, by announcing for those from the beginning from Tlapolemos, to set up/erect a common *logos* (account), for the lineage of Herakles broad in strength.

9. οὐκ ἔραμαι πολὺν ἐν μεγάρῳ πλοῦτον κατακρύψαις ἔχειν, ἀλλ᾽ ἐόντων εὖ τε παθεῖν καὶ ἀκοῦσαι φίλοις ἐξαρκέων. κοιναὶ γὰρ ἔρχοντ᾽ ἐλπίδες πολυπόνων ἀνδρῶν. Ἐγὼ δ᾽ Ἡρακλέος ἀντέχομαι προφρόνως, ἐν κορυφαῖς ἀρετᾶν μεγάλαις ἀρχαῖον ὀτρύνων λόγον . . .

I take no pleasure in keeping great wealth hidden away in my hall, but in using what I have to be successful and to win a good name by helping my friends. For the hopes of men who toil much come to all alike. But as for me, I cling to the theme of Herakles gladly, rousing an ancient *logos* from among the great heights of his excellence. . . .

10. See Calvo and Brisson; Sedley (327-39).
11. The following discussion builds on Newman's essay.
12. I am grateful to Luc Brisson for his stimulating ideas on philosophical significance of myths. Brisson and F. W. Meyerstein; Brisson, *Introduction à la Philosophie du Mythe*.
13. "Penia (Poverty), scheming to make a child for herself from Poros (Resource), lies down next to him and she begot Eros. On account of this Eros was born as a follower and servant of Aphrodite, having been conceived during the celebration of her birth, and in his nature, he is a lover of the beautiful (since Aphrodite is also beautiful). So, being a son of Poros and Penia, Eros was established in such a fortune."

14. The following overview of the polemical debate among Pindarists regarding the place and the function of myth in Pindar is a summary of Peter W. Rose's balanced assessment (145–75).

15. See below the concluding section, "Poetry as *Paideia* in Pindar's *Epinikia*" for Jaeger's discussion of *arete* in Pindar.

16. Schadewaldt (259–353); Bundy (1–34; 35–92).

17. Young (70). See also Thummer, Koehnken, and Currie.

18. See also, Lévi-Strauss (29).

19. See Halliwell (94–112).

20. Wittgenstein's remark hearkens back to the dawn of philosophy in India, China, and Greece, when philosophy was written as poetry: *Rig Veda*, *Dao De Jing*, and the writings of the pre-Socratic philosophers are in the form of verse.

21. See also, Maslov (49–77), Havelock, and Rose. Xenophanes DK 21 B I. 21–24, 10, 1; Heraclitus DK 22 B 40, 42, 56, 57, 104, 106.

Works Cited

Brisson, Luc. *Introduction à la Philosophie du Mythe*, Volume I: *Sauver les mythes*. Librairie Philosophique, J. Vrin, 1996.

———. *How Philosophy Saved the Myths*. Translated by Catherine Tihanyi, U of Chicago P, 2004.

———. *Plato the Myth Maker*. Translated by Gerad Naddaf, U of Chicago P, 2000.

———. "Myths in Plato's Ethics." *Lecturae Platonis*, vol. 4, edited by Maurizio Migliori, L. M. Napolitano Valditara, and Davide Del Forno, Academia Verlag, 2004, pp. 63–76.

Brisson, Luc, and F. W. Meyerstein. *Inventing the Universe*. SUNY Press, 1995.

Bundy, Elroy L. "Studia Pindarica." *University of California Publications in Classical Philology*, vol. 18, no. 1-2, 1962, pp. 1–34, 35–92.

Burkhardt, Jacob. *History of Greek Culture*. Dover, 2003.

———. *The Greeks and Greek Civilization*. St. Martin's, 1999.

Calvo, Tomas, and Luc Brisson, eds. *Interpreting the* Timaeus—Critias. *Proceedings of the IV Symposium Platonicum, Selected papers*. Academia Verlag, 1997.

Crotty, Kevin. *Song and Action: The Victory Odes of Pindar*. Johns Hopkins UP, 1982.

Currie, Bruno. *Pindar and the Cult of Heroes*. Oxford UP, 2005.

Demos, Marian. *Lyric Quotation in Plato*. Rowman & Littlefield, 1999.

Diels, Hermann, and Walther Kranz. *Die Fragmente Der Vorsokratiker*. Weidmannische Buchhandlung, 1912.

Fränkel, Hermann. "Wege und Formen Fruehgriechischen Denkens." Verlag C. H. Beck, 1968.

———. "Man's 'Ephemeros' Nature According to Pindar and Others." *Transactions and Proceedings of the American Philological Association*, vol. 77, 1946, pp. 131–45.

Halliwell, Stephen. "The Subjection of *Mythos* to *Logos*: Plato's Citations of the Poets." *The Classical Quarterly*, vol. 50, no. 1, 2000, pp. 94–112.

Havelock, Eric A. "Pre-Literacy and the pre-Socratics." *Bulletin of the Institute of Classical Studies*, vol. 13, no. 1, 1966, pp. 44–67.

Heaney, Seamus. *The Redress of Poetry*. Farrar, Straus, and Giroux, 1996.

Hornblower, Simon. "'Dolphins in the Sea' (Isthmian 9. 7): Pindar and the Aeginetans." *Pindar's Poetry, Patrons, and Festivals: From Archaic Greece to the Roman Empire*, edited by Simon Hornblower and Catherine Morgan, Oxford UP, 2007, pp. 287–308.

Jaeger, Werner. *Paideia*, vol. I. Translated by G. Highet, Oxford UP, 1939.

Kirk, Geoffrey Stephen. *Myth: Its Meaning and Functions in Ancient and Other Cultures*. U of California P, 1970.

Koehnken, Adolf. *Die Funktion des Mythos bei Pindar*. De Gruyter, 1971.

Lévi-Strauss, Claude. "The Story of Asdiwal." *The Structural Study of Myth and Totemism*, edited by E. Leach, Routledge, 1967.

Maslov, Boris. "From (Theogonic) Mythos to (Poetic) Logos: Reading Pindar's Genealogical Metaphors after Freidenberg." *Journal of Ancient Near Eastern Religions*, vol. 12, 2012, pp. 49–77.

Moore, Christopher. "Pindar's Charioteer in Plato's *Phaedrus* (227B9–10)." *The Classical Quarterly*, vol. 64, no. 2, 2014, pp. 525–32.

Morgan, Kathryn. *Myth and Philosophy from the Presocratics to Plato*. Cambridge UP, 2000.

Morris, Ian. "The Strong Principle of Equality and the Archaic Origins of Greek Democracy." *Demokratia—A Conversation on Democracies, Ancient and Modern*, edited by Josiah Ober and Charles Hedrick, Princeton UP, 1996, pp. 19–48.

Naddaf, Gerard. "The Role of the Poet in Plato's Ideal Cities of Callipolis and Magnesia." *Kriterion*, vol. 48, no. 116, 2007, pp. 329–49.

Nestle, Wilhelm. *Vom Mythos zum Logos: Die Selbstentfaltung des Griechischen Denkens von Homer bis auf die Sophistik und Sokrates*. A. Kröner, 1940.

Newman, John K. "Pindar and Callimachus." *Illinois Classical Studies*, vol. 10, no. 2, 1985, pp. 169–89.

Nightingale, Andrea Nelson, "The Folly of Praise: Plato's Critique of Encomiastic Discourse in the *Lysis* and *Symposium*." *The Classical Quarterly*, vol. 43, no. 1, 1993, pp. 112–30.

Ober, Josiah, and Charles Hedrick, eds. *Demokratia—A Conversation on Democracies, Ancient and Modern*. Princeton UP, 1996.

Pender, Elizabeth E. "Sappho and Anacreon in Plato's *Phaedrus*." *Leeds International Classical Studies*, vol. 6, no. 4, 2007, pp. 1–57.

Pindar. *Nemean Odes, Isthmian Odes, Fragments*. Edited and translated by William H. Race, Loeb-Harvard UP, 1997.
———. *The Odes of Pindar*. Translated by Richmond Lattimore, U of Chicago P, 1947.
———. *Olympian Odes, Pythian Odes*. Edited and translated by William H. Race, Loeb-Harvard UP, 1997.
Plato. *Platonis Opera*, edited by John Burnet, Clarendon,1902.
Radt, Stephan L. "Thummer, E. 'Pindar: Die Isthmischen Gedichte.'" *Mnemosyne*, vol. 25, no. 2, 1972, pp. 194–200.
Richardson, Nicholas James. "Pindar and Later Literary Criticism in Antiquity." *Papers of the Leeds Latin Seminar*, vol. 5, 1985, pp. 383–401.
Rose, Peter W. "The Myth of Pindar's First Nemean: Sportsmen, Poetry, and Paideia." *Harvard Studies in Classical Philology*, 1974, pp. 145–75.
Schadewaldt, Wolfgang. "Der Aufbau des Pindarischen Epinikion." *Der Aufbau Pindarischen Epinikion*. De Gruyter, 2015.
Sedley, David. "'Becoming Like God' in the *Timaeus* and Aristotle." *Interpreting the Timaeus—Critias. Proceedings of the IV Symposium Platonicum. Selected Papers*, edited by Tomas Calvo and Luc Brisson, Academia Verlag, 1997, pp. 327–39.
Sigelman, Asya C. *Pindar's Poetics of Immortality*. Cambridge UP, 2016.
Silk, Michael. "Pindar Meets Plato: Theory, Language, Value and the Classics." *Texts, Ideas and the Classics: Scholarship, Theory and Classical Literature*, edited by S. J. Harrison, Oxford UP, 2001, pp. 26–45.
Snell, Bruno. *The Discovery of the Mind: The Greek Origins of European Thought*. Translated by Thomas G. Rosenmeyer, Blackwell, 1953.
Steiner, Dorah. *Crown of Song: Metaphor in Pindar*. Oxford UP, 1986.
Thomas, Dylan. "On Poetry." *Quite Early One Morning*. New Directions, 1954.
Thummer, Erich. *Pindar: Die Isthmischen Gedichte: Analyse der Pindarischen Epinikien. Text und Übersetzung der Isthmischen Gedichte*, vol. 1. Universitätsverlag C. Winter, 1968.
Vernant, Jean-Pierre. *Mythe et Pensée Chez les Grecs*. 1965. *Myth and Thought among the Greeks*. Translated by Janet Lloyd and Jeff Fort, MIT, 2006.
Wittgenstein, Ludwig. *Culture and Value*. Translated by Peter Winch, U of Chicago P, 1984.
———. *Vermischte Bemerkungen in Werkausgabe in 8 Bänden, Band 8*, edited by Georg Henrik von Wright and Heikki Nyman, Suhrkamp, 1984, pp. 445–575.
Young, David. "Pindaric Criticism." *Minnesota Review*, vol. 4, 1964, pp. 584–641. Reprinted and revised in *Wege der Forschung, Band 134: Pindaros und Bakchylides*, edited by W. M. Calder and J. Stern, Wissenschaftliche Buchgesellschaft, 1970.

Don't Be a Drag, Just Be a Queen

Anne J. Mamary

If you are squeamish, don't prod the beach rubble.

—Sappho, Fragment 145

Ostensibly a ten-book-long dialogue on justice, Plato's *Politeia* (or *Republic*) pours the idea of justice into every aspect of Socrates' interlocutors' lives. The night-long journey winds a long conceptual way home to Athens from Socrates and Glaucon's visit to the festival for the Thracian goddess Bendis. Although walking on dry land, the two men are delayed in conversation with Cephalus and his guests as they return from the port at Piraeus. The journey home is fraught with personal and political delays as the band is blown this way and that as if navigating a stormy sea. As Homer's Odysseus was held hostage, survived shipwreck, and circumnavigated many a life-threatening obstacle, Plato's Socrates urges his friends to reconsider the very heart of their cultural assumptions about justice and education, about power and class, and about gender. As Penelope waited for Odysseus to return as he tossed about from sea to island to rocky shore, Socrates tells his friends that there is a "female drama" (451c) and both encourages them to reweave their masculinist assumptions and to return to Athens and to him, Plato's Penelope, transfigured.

Already in the *Republic*'s opening words, Plato prepares his hearers and readers for a journey into something at once ancient and new. When Socrates says, "I went down (*kateben*) . . . to Piraeus" (327a), he conjures Homer's Odysseus, who also says "I went [down] inside (*kateben*) the house of Hades to ask about the journey home" to Ithaka and Penelope (23.252–53). Eva Brann notes that *"he Peraie* [means] the 'beyond land'" and so suggests reading the opening lines of the *Republic*: "'I descended yesterday to the land beyond the river, together with Glaucon, the son of Ariston . . .'" (118). Brann's reading points to John Bremer's observation that Piraeus was once an island, the opening words of the dialogue already pointing to the waves to come (19). Intercepted on their way home, Socrates and Glaucon are about to embark on a conversation that will lead to "the beyond"—beyond convention, beyond ordinary experience—as did Odysseus' homeward way.[1]

Bremer suggests that Plato's opening word, the aorist *kateben*, invites the translation "down went I," which unsettles both who the I might be and to where the journey both "down" and "home" leads (18). Homer's opening words have a similar effect. "Tell me . . . O Muse. . . ." at the start of *The Odyssey* surely introduces Odysseus as a "complicated man" (1.1–2), but the Muse is invoked to tell the tale of his attempted return home from the sack of Troy, as Plato's *Politeia* is framed by the ongoing Peloponnesian war and Glaucon's role in Athens. They require *mêtis*: cunning and craft. Odysseus is a man of *mêtis*, yet in both dialogue and epic, Socrates' weaving and unweaving and reweaving of his interlocutors' ideas of justice (*dikaiosyne*) and Penelope's weaving and unweaving and reweaving of Laertes' shroud and her reputation (*kleos*) both show their cunning and bring to the fore a female craft, a female *mêtis* (Levaniouk 262).

Waylaid on their return to Athens, Socrates and Glaucon (and we readers) are returning to the city of Metis' daughter, Athena. Not only does Metis, the Oceanid, reinforce the idea that we are embarking on a water journey, despite walking on dry land, but she is also the goddess of cunning, wisdom, and craft. Her daughter is the deity of war, yes, but also of wisdom and weaving. Like her mother, Athena is crafty, and Barbara Clayton describes how Athena gives Penelope *mêtis* in both senses of the word. Her cleverness and her "weaving . . . saved and transformed her and her city (25). Olga Levaniouk notes "weaving's multi-layered self-referentiality" (261), while Clayton writes that in *Homer's* Odyssey "weaving is the device itself" (21). In both Plato's and Homer's tales, the reader is drawn in to be a cunning artful interpreter of texts and our own lives, "form and content . . . never separated" (Bremer 26).

As Athena is "a weaver of words" (Clayton 24), Socrates' opening words and Odysseus' tale set the stage for a descent into the "beyond"

Don't Be a Drag, Just Be a Queen | 151

and a journey of homecoming, rewoven.² Socrates and Glaucon repair to Cephalus' house for the promise of a feast and a torchlit race on horseback, which turns out to be a feast of conversation on justice in the soul and in the city. Socrates and Glaucon have just been to the festival of the newly introduced goddess, Bendis, "a Thracian stranger identified with Hecate, the guardian deity of the underworld" (Brann 118). Socrates declares the festival for Bendis at Piraeus well ordered, and, in his praise, makes the strange somehow familiar (*Republic* 327a). In the nightlong relay of the conversation about justice, he makes home—the familiar—strange, using conventional names for virtues yet recomposing their meaning almost beyond recognition. They are sailing into the "beyond" as Plato's Socrates weaves and unweaves their senses of justice and their senses of themselves as affluent men and what it would mean to live together in a good *polis*. As they journey into the composition of the citizen (*polites*) and (also in) the community (*polis*), they are considering the very weave of their lives, of their *politeia* (Sallis 313).

Embarking on their voyage, Cephalus—Head—is strangely disembodied as he describes the freedom from the madness of the passions and desires old age brings (329d).³ Defining justice as honesty and repaying debts, Cephalus puts justice squarely in the category of business dealings. Polemarchus—War Leader—defines justice as helping friends and harming enemies (332d). He does not yet recognize that harming another also has consequences for his own well-being, for the composition of his own soul and his community. Thrasymachus—Fierce Fighter—then leaps, snarling, into the conversation and defines justice first as "the advantage of the stronger" (338c) and then as a proposition for weaklings, who lack the fortitude to practice injustice with impunity. Though he does not commit himself exactly, Glaucon points out that most people have a gentler version of Thrasymachus' view only because they lack the manly wherewithal to carry it off. So, justice becomes a contract entered only grudgingly neither to commit nor to suffer injustice (359a).

We see in Cephalus a quenched *erōs*, in Polemarchus a rash *andreia* (courage/manliness), in Thrasymachus a tyrannical *epithumia* (appetitiveness), in Glaucon a hot-headed *thymos* (spiritedness), and in Adeimantus a self-centered *sophrosyne* (excellence of character, moderation/temperance). Cephalus' lack of *erōs* is not only of the tyrannical kind but also of the philosophical sort, madly desirous of wisdom, friendship, *dikaiosyne*, and the Good. As Howland notes, "Plato is clearly aware of the double-edged nature of *eros*. Like *sophrosyne* (which Adeimantus mistakes only for individual happiness), *eros* and *epithumia* are native to the whole of the soul and the whole of the *polis*" (*Odyssey* 152).

When Socrates proposes that justice is the harmony of *epithumia*, *thymos*, and *andreiea*—woven together by an erotically wise *sophrosyne*—whether in an individual or a society, he uses the same words as do his interlocutors, but he reweaves their meanings, making the familiar strange so that the men scarcely recognize them (427e–428a, 430d–e). The little company collectively appears to have the "right" virtues for justice, yet their conventional view of justice as unpleasant political compromise speaks to a lack—a lack of power to practice injustice and to exact vengeance. Socrates starts his discussion of the origins of human polities also with a recognition of lack—a recognition that no person is self-sufficient. In his description of the healthy city, he illustrates both *sophrosyne* and justice as he describes a small community of interdependent people exchanging their crafts. This community is guided by the moderation of natural desires, following the weave of the night sky or the "pattern of it laid up in heaven" (592b). Having modest but sufficient shelter, clothing, and food, "they will feast with their children, drinking of their wine, thereto, garlanded and singing hymns to the gods in pleasant fellowship, not begetting offspring beyond their means lest they fall into poverty or war. . . . [A]nd so, living in peace and health, they will probably die in old age and hand on a like life to their offspring" (372b, c–d).

Already Glaucon balks. He wants a definition and defense of justice but is not ready to go as far as living a sustainable, modest life, accusing Socrates of "founding a city of pigs" (372d). As Marina McCoy notes, Glaucon's phrase is actually "city of sows," and his word choice suggests female genitalia (151). His insult for this healthy city both insults women (and pigs!) and also points to his overblown and swollen sense of himself by class, citizenship, and gender. Glaucon claims to want an unconventional definition of justice and recognizes that to embrace Socrates would require so thorough a change in society's fabric that he would not recognize his own *polis*, just as Athena made the familiar so strange that Odysseus did not recognize Ithaka on his homecoming (13.187–200).

Glaucon clings to such luxuries as are customary, saying people "must recline on couches, . . . dine from tables and have made dishes and sweetmeats as are now in use" (372d–e). Socrates recognizes that Glaucon wants to discuss "the origin of a luxurious [or fevered] city, . . . [swollen with] relishes and myrrh and incense and girls and cakes . . ." (372e, 373a).

With their fevered appetites, people will also want to eat meat, which will require taking neighboring land by force "to have enough for pasture and ploughing, . . . [having] abandon[ed] themselves to the unlimited acquisition of wealth, disregarding the limit set by our natural wants" (373d). Here in the choices determined by unbridled acquisitiveness, in overtaxing the earth, in the (unmentioned) exploitation of slaves, male and female, and laborers who mine for metals and tend the farms, in the exclusion or marginalization of free women from humanity, is the origin of war (373e).

As soon as the fevered or luxurious city presents itself, Socrates begins trying to heal it. In the *Odyssey*, "braided Dawn" brought Odysseus and his men to the "beautiful, dreadful goddess Circe," who "was weaving as she sang, an intricate, enchanting piece of work," which especially caught Polites' (whose name means citizen) attention (10.145, 136, 221–23). Upon inviting them into her home, she fed them and gave them a drugged wine "to make them totally forget their home" before transforming them "to pigs in body and voice and hair, . . . [after which] they squealed at their imprisonment" (10.236–42). "Circe with her braided hair" is unable to transform "Odysseus, the man who can adapt to anything" (10.311, 330–31).[4]

While Glaucon squeals at what seems to him the healthy city's imprisonment—that being turned into a sow (into a girl!) is the worst of insults—Socrates attempts to convince him that being unwoven and rewoven into that very "sow," that inquisitive, cunning, healthy woman, living neither in luxury nor poverty, is the best of all possible lives. As Jacob Howland notes, "in a reversal of Homer, . . . Socrates is cast [as Plato's braided-haired] Circe," trying to unweave in the night "the heroic manliness" Glaucon and the rest have woven (or had woven for them) in the daytime of their lives (*Glaucon* 63, 65). Even though Glaucon is soon seemingly willing to forgo "a little Corinthian maid [and] . . . delights of Attic pastry,"[5] the customary luxuries soon return, as Adeimantus protests that the guardians will not be happy (405a, 419a).

Glaucon's description of justice as bitter compromise, too, reveals this common view of *andreia* as one of constant vigilance against attack, of vengefulness, and of scheming against others. Justice becomes a kind of cowardice, a kind of emasculation. The men think of justice as a drag, while Plato pushes them to be "drag queens," as he has Socrates try to help them reweave this bleak world of compromised men without another kind of courage, the *sophrosyne* needed for "the courage of a citizen" (*andreia*). He is helping them to have the good sense and courage to compose a new fabric of their lives on the most intimate level of gender and sexuality (430c).

In *Plato through Homer*, Zdravko Planinc traces the waves Odysseus faced as he attempted his return to Ithaka and Penelope as they reappear in Plato's men's journeys. As Homer brings to life Odysseus' adventures, Plato's language embodies the very issues his characters discuss, as Bremer, Clayton, and Levaniouk suggested. Sometimes Plato uses male erotic language, both in content and imagery. For example, the shepherd who finds Gyges' ring plays out a male drama, climbing a social ladder on which only men could set foot, the queen being one of his prizes (359a–360b). The erotic language of the *Phaedrus* is often overtly masculine, with its image of the soul sprouting wings and issuing forth streams of particles (251b–d).

Plato nearly swamps the discussion as Socrates reminds them that there is also a female drama played out in three waves that come crashing down on the men and threaten to wash them ashore to examine the beach rubble that Socrates makes of their conventional masculine and class assumptions (451c). Socrates challenges gendered assumptions with female erotic imagery in waves that send ripples forward and backward along the diameter of the *Republic*, ripples that frame the dialogue in female strength, creativity, thoughtfulness, and *daimonic* power. The waves flow back to the opening festival of Bendis. They surge ahead through an echo of Nausicaa's rescue of the shipwrecked Odysseus to wash ashore in Penelope's test of Odysseus and Socrates' of Glaucon and his friends.

While Brann suggests that Calliope is the Muse of Kallipolis (153), Planinc suggests that Kallipolis is more like Calypso's *polis*, where Odysseus was held captive (*Plato* 20). Planinc argues that the *Republic*'s company faces a Platonic version of Odysseus' challenges on their nightlong conceptual journey. Odysseus faced three waves, the first two nearly killing him and the third giving him a glimpse of a good society and a way home. Similarly, Glaucon and company's first two waves threaten to derail their discussion of justice. The third gives a glimpse of the Good, which, Planinc suggests, leads from Kallipolis through the *erōs* of the *Phaedrus* to a homecoming in the *Laws*, just as Odysseus escapes Calypso's island to find safety in the land of the Phaeacians, who deliver him home to Ithaka through the *erōs* of his marriage bed with Penelope (*Plato* 20).

Readers meet Homer's "Calypso with her braided curls . . . singing and weaving with a shuttle made of gold" in the cave on the island where she forced Odysseus to stay in spite of his desire to sail for home (5.58,

5.61–62, 5.13–14). Perhaps Odysseus feels something of what Penelope undergoes at the hands of the suitors, when he has the rare experience of his bodily integrity being snatched from his own hands. Yet "Calypso, Queen of goddesses," (5.242) also gives another model for sexuality when she refuses to keep on hurting the man she loves, saying "Stop grieving, please. You need not waste your life. I am quite ready now to send you off" (5.160–61). She encourages him to use his cunning and craft to make a raft and swears "by the waters of the Styx below" that she will not make any more pain for him, even though she knows he will face terrible difficulties on his journey (5.162–63, 5.185). Plato's Kallipolis may well be Calypso's *polis*, in the sense that the men find attempts to heal their fevered city a kind of captivity.

Socrates may also be Plato's Calypso when he tries to give the same message to the men as she did to Odysseus: love requires more than one's own personal fulfillment; it also requires attention to the good and well-being of the one loved. Calypso let Odysseus go, knowing he would face fierce waves. Socrates tries to liberate his friends, knowing the three waves of the female drama might well be too much for them. Socrates' first wave is his insistence that for the guardian and philosopher classes, women and men should take gymnastics training together naked (452a–b). Considering the strict gender segregation in Plato's time and the near isolation and total disenfranchisement of citizen-class women, Socrates frames the suggestion as something ridiculous that could be expected to end the discussion in chaos. But Glaucon, perhaps at once tragically and comedically, embraces Socrates' proposal as a way of taking what he wants without detection. This may say more about Glaucon's unhealthy sense of the erotic than it does about his egalitarian view of women. He is all too happy to (re)turn women's sexuality into a commodity for his own pleasure, even though he agreed to forgo the "Corinthian maids" sacred to Aphrodite.

Plato's language reveals the men's masculinist *erōs*. James Arieti points out that most translations of *The Republic* hide the explicit sexual references in the Greek text in the discussion of coeducation at 452a–c (236). He calls to the fore Plato's

> double entendres in the words *hoplon* ["arms"] and *ocheseis* ["bestriding"], even though *skomma* ["jibes"] . . . 'generally implies scurrility.' *Hoplon* may also mean 'penis.' . . . The noun *ochesis* is cognate with *ocheuo*, which has a variety of sexual

uses. . . . In the *Republic* (586a) it is used of men behaving like beasts. When one recalls that the guardians have been compared to horses (413d, 375a), the pun becomes less subtle. (244)

Plato's men are not yet freed from what Gene Fendt calls "an eros too tyrannical to allow clear thought on many topics" (173). That is, when Socrates-Circe tries to heal the company's fevered *erōs* by transforming them into sows, in what I find to be an example of Plato's wicked sense of humor, he-she shows that "Glaucon lacks the philosopher's pure, powerful *erōs*" (Howland, *Glaucon* 11).

After the *Odyssey*'s first wave, which left Odysseus clinging to his shattered raft, the human-turned-goddess, Ino, gave Odysseus a veil of immortality and advised him to abandon his foundering raft to swim ashore. Refusing, Odysseus faced Poseidon's Earthquake and a second wave, which destroyed the rudderless, mastless raft to which he was clinging. As he swam to shore, he survived only because Athena calmed the water, allowing him to be carried on the third wave sent by Zeus to a glimpse of Phaeacia (5.314–87). When "Dawn with dazzling braids brought day," Odysseus was able to cross the river to the beyond—to the land of Phaecians, who were noted for their wisdom (5.390, 5.451–64). Socrates and Glaucon, too, clinging to their rudderless *polis*, face a second wave, the community of wives and children, with its apparent program of eugenics. As Planinc puts it:

> The eugenics program confuses psychic and somatic matters, as did the first wave, and it makes as much a mockery of true wisdom as the first wave did of true courage. But Glaucon does not find it laughable. He finds it compelling. His *eros* and his belief that geometrical thinking is wisdom both prevent him from understanding that the second wave destroys the city in speech as completely as Poseidon's second great wave destroyed Odysseus's raft. The eugenics program fails, as it must, and the city breaks up (545e–47b). (*Political* 282)

On one level Plato's proposals are serious. On another, his own characters mistake them for serious. The comedy is that they do not find themselves laughable but rather bend these potentially revolutionary proposals to their own advantage, not seeing them as a critique of the conventions of marriage that led to their own births. According to Sarah

Pomeroy, marriage in Plato's Athens was an economic agreement between a young teenager's father and her bridegroom, a grown man (63–64). In the "exchange of virgins among men," to borrow an idea from Luce Irigaray, there is no erotic necessity (56). This relationship between men in which women are exchanged was designed to preserve the wealth of the groom's family by ensuring "legitimate" heirs (Pomeroy 60). Wealthier families sometimes employed wet nurses. So, there is a sense in which what Socrates describes is not so far out of the common way, yet he turns that common way on its head.

In regard to equal opportunities for education for women and men, Plato does offer something quite radical. Socrates suggests that gender differences are as contingent to understanding and enacting justice as hair or baldness are to one's skill as a cobbler (454a–c). So, it is immoderate social convention and the requirements of motherhood rather than sex that keeps women from following their talents and which ignores the real craft and cunning required for child-rearing. In Socrates' proposed healthy city, the city of artisans, and in Athens, too, women of the artisan class had neither the luxury nor the misfortune of being cloistered. The serious part of the first two waves is in their invitation to rethink both the male and female dramas (along with and co-constituting class dramas), and, in so doing, to rethink appetite, courage, and wisdom and the justice to be found in their moderation and harmony.

Perhaps women and men are not essentially different, as Plato suggests, or maybe it is more accurate to say that Plato finds gender to be as specific as one's other mysterious human gifts, multiple, not dual. But those differences, whether entirely culturally formed or given by nature, ought not to be an excuse for the tyranny of one over the other. Joanne Waugh argues that Plato was serious about opportunity for women and a concomitant rethinking of a kind of masculine drama implicit in "the traditional connection between *Sophia*, public discourse and citizenship . . ." (211, 217). She argues that Plato wrote dialogues in part to offer an alternative model of public discourse to the conventional one "embodied in flesh [of naked male bodies] and stone [of the architecture of Athens] and not just in words" (213). More specifically, she continues "that philosophy does not require the body, stance, and voice of a *kaloskagoathos* [of the conventional Athenian beautiful and good man] is suggested by a statue of Socrates where he is represented as a Silenus—the ancient rustic god of the dance of the wine press" (217). Instead, he recomposes the conventional notion of the beautiful and the good man, wresting it from the naked body of the male citizen in its context of imposing Athenian public architecture, which act as a ring of invisibility behind which to hide injustice. His Socrates always has his bare feet planted on the earth as he journeys to "the beyond."

What if Plato is suggesting a liberation of female *erōs* in his wave imagery rather than a public (read male) appropriation of it? The first wave is not potentially disastrous for the *polis* because it encourages women to participate in music and gymnastics education. It rather reveals something dangerous in Glaucon's view of women (and young men, also) as objects for consumption. Glaucon is ridiculous in his continued immoderation. The second wave could move the characters to think of all people in the community as having common interests, of all children as "ours" and equally worthy of loving attention, rather than as male or state property. Socrates' alternative is not to banish but to rethink, to re-embody, *erōs*. The men are stuck in Calypso's *polis*, because they have not yet learned from her how to empower the beloved, even when it breaks her own heart.

If Plato is writing a philosophy driven by erotic necessity, and if he is writing the second wave as comedic, he is writing at the same time a space for women to participate in a philosophical *erōs*. So, when Glaucon agrees that he is "careful to breed from the best (*ton ariston*)" (459a), he is, perhaps unwittingly, participating in a laugh at his own expense. He, with his brothers Adeimantus and Plato, are sons of Ariston, sons of the best. But, as the three brothers demonstrate, excellence, Ariston, is not simply a function of parentage.[6] Rather than affirming a sense of entitlement that breeds greed, including a greedy *erōs*, Socrates throws his version of Calypso's golden shuttle back and forth to weave the company's way back to the healthy city and the virtues interwoven with *sophrosyne*.

Like the "sows" in the healthy city, the guardians are "sober and brave . . . [having] neither superfluity . . . nor any lack. [They desire golden souls rather than] the acquisition of mortal gold" (416e). As Arieti observes, "Adeimantus will overcome his materialistic view of happiness later . . . [465–66]," as his *sophrosyne* is recomposed (235). The men have moments of understanding that the "city of sows," really is the healthy and just city. As M. D. Usher puts it, "Plato's City for Pigs—with all the humor, irony, earnestness, observation, speculation, indeed aspiration that went into its construction—is a model city, imaginatively and practically designed to be sustainable over the long term" (109). As Odysseus glimpsed Phaecia as the waves tossed him about, Admeinatus catches a glimpse of a just *politeia* when he says wistfully that if he and his company had learned about justice not as a bitter compromise but as a golden weave of citizen and *polis*, "we should not now be guarding against one another's injustice, but each would be his own best guardian, for fear lest by working injustices he should dwell in communion with the greatest of evils" (367a).

The shipwreck that landed Odysseus on Calypso's island also started in a wave of failed *sophrosyne*. After hearing and surviving the sirens' song while tied to his mast, the rest of Odysseus' crew drowned after stealing the sun god's sacred cattle. In a reversal of roles, Calypso unraveled Odysseus' identity and sexuality after she rescued him from the shipwreck Zeus brought upon them after his men ate Helios' cattle (12.390–418). As Plato's audience, we might recall Glaucon's fevered insistence that people will want to eat meat, thus leading to war to seize enough land for grazing cattle. The overtones of Odysseus' captivity on Calypso's island might help Socrates' friends to think about what a typical Athenian masculine *erōs* does to women (and to men). Yet Calypso rescued Odysseus from the raging sea and "loved and cared for [him]," also giving a glimpse of the possibility of a more egalitarian *erōs*.

As Socrates and Glaucon tried to right the "raft" tossed about in Plato's first two waves, Socrates says: "I have hardly escaped the first and second waves, and you seem not to be aware that you are now bringing upon me the third, which is the greatest and heaviest . . ." (472a). Socrates' proposed third wave, that justice requires that "philosophers become kings" (473d)—or queens!—points, too, in the direction of healing of the company's fevered *erōs*. Plato shows the gender injustice that has historically made women weaker and men stronger and then reweaves what was coded feminine as strength as the company sails on in search of justice. Realizing how much he is asking of his company (and of Plato's readers), Socrates acknowledges that the third wave "is likely to wash us away on billows of laughter and scorn" (473c). To avoid drowning, even in a wave of laughter (Fendt 379), Socrates' men must realize that there is no weaker and stronger except that the unjust is weaker than the just, a realization that strips their very souls naked.

Arriving in Phaiacia, Odysseus was also stripped naked in every sense of the word. He ascended from sleep after coming ashore, and "grasping a leafy branch he broke it off to cover up his manly private parts" to meet Nausicaa as he emerged unclothed from the forest" (6.128–29). When she clothed him and led him to her parents, the wise King Alkinous and the wiser Queen Arete, his identity was unknown (7.53). He had no reputation behind which to hide, no title, no armed men at his back. Although Nausicaa worried about being seen with a man and sent Odysseus to her mother to protect her reputation, she was at the same time protecting her bodily integrity as a woman. She was the one who made the wise decisions that eventually guided Odysseus' return home. There is no erotic conquest, no motivating sense of personal gain. She helped him, one human being concerned with the welfare of another. She performed a female version of the drama of Gyges' ring and embodied Plato's third wave, and his insistence that justice might be made manifest when philosophers become queens or when kings become philosophers (473). Without being present, Nausicaa guided the drama, sending the as-yet-unknown Odysseus to the "extremely clever and perceptive" Queen Arete, not to seduce her and use her for his personal rise to power, but to seek her wise council and aid (*Odyssey* 7.73).

Although Odysseus revealed his identity, it was not his name or his physical prowess that aided his homeward journey. The queen and her daughter were both passionate and thoughtful. It was their superior strength in this regard that persuaded the king to intervene on Odysseus' behalf. When he returned to Ithaca, Odysseus' physical strength, likewise, did not make him "the stronger." The "strength" of slaying the suitors was not really strength at all. Penelope's weaving and unweaving, though, held them off, preserved her physical integrity, and put the choice about her own body literally into her own hands (Clayton 23). Precisely because of her *métis*, rather than accident of birth or marriage, Penelope is the "perfect king"—or queen (Levaniouk 259).

Perhaps Kallipolis could be Calliope's city, if the interlocutors could realize that it is the cure for the fevered city, not an embrace of that fever. Brann writes that "evidently it was Pythagoras who first appropriated the oldest of the Muses, Calliope, for philosophy. Socrates gives her . . . the same office in the *Phaedrus*, where . . . Calliope cares for those who compose 'human stories' (259d)" (153). When Calypso respected Odysseus enough to free him from her cave, and Penelope wove, unwove, and rewove a shroud for not-yet-dead Laertes, readers might hear overtones of prisoners escaping from another cave, this one of Plato's imagination. Composing and re-weaving his companions' habitual understanding of their lives, Socrates says of the "image makers" in the cave who value affluence, power, and a tyrannical *erōs*, that "he would feel with Homer and greatly prefer . . . to be serf of another landless man, and endure anything rather than . . . live that life" and "be king over all the [living] dead" (516d–e, 386c).

Returning home, finally, Odysseus is changed. His familiar home is changed, and his familiar combative practice becomes, at least in part, strange. As Grace LaFrentz writes:

> Penelope has used the variations of *mêtis* accessible to her (primarily craftiness and trickery through weaving) in order to protect herself and her home. . . . Odysseus' heroism remains complicated and ambiguous, and we should certainly question the way that he uses *mêtis* to restore masculine order. His ultimate strength and success, however, lie in his unique ability to understand that the warrior code is not the only way. It can at times be supplemented, or even replaced, by alternate modes of thinking and acting—modes that may even be coded as feminine. (23)

Plato, too, is trying to be sure heroic manliness does not triumph for Glaucon, as Socrates-Circe tries to turn him into the "sow" of the ordinary citizen. In Penelope's final test of him, Odysseus proves his identity when he knows she could not have moved their marriage bed, because it was built around Athena's eternal olive tree. Penelope is sure her husband is home (23.179–209).

Glaucon, however, fails Socrates' "bed test," when "he finds Socrates' account of the three couches baffling and . . . ends up playing the part of one of the less sympathetic comic characters: the rejected suitor" (Planinc, *Plato* 122). He misunderstands Socrates-Calliope's story of human life, *erōs*, and homecoming to mean he, Glaucon, is somehow superior rather than understanding that he must see his life woven around Athena's eternal wisdom. While the dialogue, from the very start, leads its characters and readers to "the beyond," Glaucon stays firmly in the imperfect mundane. Planinc argues that Glaucon "produced an account of the just soul that is a true image of a true image of an imperfect original: . . . [Instead of taking the journey] "toward a vision of the good 'beyond being,'" . . . Glaucon flatly dismisses it as 'daimonic hyperbole' (509b–c)" (*Plato* 123). In the *Republic*'s closing myth of Er, Plato's Odysseus is perhaps even more changed than Homer's as he embraces the life of the healthy city. Drawing the last lot in the world of "the Spinners" (7.198; *Republic* 620d–e),

Plato's Odysseus' soul "flung away ambition, [and] went about for a long time in quest of the life of an ordinary citizen who minded his own business. . . . and upon seeing it said that it would have done the same had it drawn the first lot, and chose it gladly" (620c–d). As the story-telling Calliope, Plato's Socrates, with the *mêtis* of cunning and craft, weaves the possibility for Glaucon and company, too, to make different choices with their individual lives and for their *polis*.

Penelope's weaving and cleverness, Circe's transformative powers, Calypso's reweaving of *erōs* as liberatory practice, and Calliope's philosophical storytelling all show the possibility of recomposing *polites* and *polis*—the *Politeia*. They show that the *mêtis* of weaving is not only honored but available to all regardless of sex, whether philosopher-queen, drag queen, or ordinary citizen. As Penelope unwove at night what she had woven during the day, Socrates' night-long journey unweaves and recomposes the ordinary rules of his Athens, "weaving [both] fabric and strategies" (Levaniouk 262). Socrates tries to guide his men's homecoming to the city of Metis' daughter, rewoven, not to Penelope, but to Socrates, Plato's Penelope—and also Circe, Calypso, and Calliope—who has been waiting for and exhorting them all along.

Notes

1. I am grateful to Nick Pappas for his encouragement, wit, and problem-solving skills and to Howard Engelskirchen for his insightful suggestions for revisions to my chapter's introduction. My thanks, especially, to Meredith Trexler Drees for her help with this chapter and for being such a great editing partner through thick and thin.

2. At the end of Book X, Er also descends to the underworld and ascends again not having drunk from the River of Forgetfulness (Lethe—unconcealing) (621b). His tale serves as a guide to another land beyond the river where justice will always be pursued with *sophrosyne* so "we may be dear to ourselves and to the gods . . ." (621c).

3. For a discussion of Plato's characters in historical context, see Howland, *Glaucon* (35–37).

4. See Levaniok's "Odysseus and the Boar" for an interesting discussion of Odysseus being called a pig, both as an insult and a compliment (166–89).

5. In a personal conversation, Dr. Preus reminded me that Attic pastries were often phallic in shape. The men seem to think of other people's sexuality as theirs for the taking.

6. John Sallis connects the noble "lie" of the metals to the community of wives and children. We are all born of the earth, all siblings to each other. People are also born with their own unique capacities and interests (375–76). The "lie" in the myth of the metals and the second wave's eugenics program is trying "to control by law all mating—that is, by trying to treat 'erotic necessities' as though they were 'geometrical necessities'" (378).

Works Cited

Arieti, James A. *Interpreting Plato: The Dialogues as Drama*. Rowman & Littlefield, 1991.

Bernard, Mary. *Sappho: A New Translation*. U of California P, 1958.

Brann, Eva. *The Music of the Republic: Essays on Socrates' Conversations and Plato's Writings*. Paul Dry, 2004.

Bremer, John. *On Plato's Polity*. Institute of Philosophy, 1984.

Clayton, Barbara. *A Penelopean Poetics: Reweaving the Feminine in Homer's Odyssey*. Lexington, 2004.

Fendt, Gene. *Love Song for the Life of the Mind: An Essay on the Purpose of Comedy*. Catholic UP of America, 2007.

Homer. *The Odyssey*. Translated by Emily Wilson, Norton, 2018.

Howland, Jacob. *Glaucon's Fate: History, Myth, and Character in Plato's Republic*. Paul Dry, 2018.

———. The Republic: *The Odyssey of Philosophy*. Twayne, 1993.

Irigaray, Luce. *Thinking the Difference: For a Peaceful Revolution*. Translated by Karin Montin, Athlone, 1994.

LaFrentz, Grace. "Weaving a Way to *Nostos*: Odysseus and Feminine *Métis* in the *Odyssey*." *Vanderbilt Undergraduate Research Journal*, vol. 11, April 2021, pp. 18–28. ejournals.library.vanderbilt.edu/index.php/vurj/issue/view/234

Levaniouk, Olga. *Eve of the Festival: Myth-Making in* Odyssey 19. Harvard UP, 2011.

McCoy, Marina. "The City of Sows and Sexual Differentiation in the *Republic*." *Plato's Animals: Gadflies, Horses, Swans, and Other Philosophical Beasts*, edited by Jeremy Bell and Michael Naas, Indiana UP, 2015, pp. 149–60.

Planinc, Zdravko. *Plato through Homer: Poetry and Philosophy in the Cosmological Dialogues*. U of Missouri P, 2003.

———. *Plato's Political Philosophy: Prudence in the* Republic *and* Laws. U of Missouri P, 1991.

Plato. *Phaedrus*. Translated by Alexander Nehamas and Paul Woodruff. *Plato: Complete Works*, edited by John M. Cooper, Hackett, 1997, pp. 506–56.

———. *Republic*. Translated by Paul Shorey, vols. 6 and 7, Loeb-Harvard UP, 2006.

Pomeroy, Sarah B. *Goddesses, Whores, Wives, and Slaves: Women in Classical Antiquity*. Schocken, 1975.

Sallis, John. *Being and Logos: Reading the Platonic Dialogues*. 3rd ed., Indiana UP, 1996.
Usher, M. D. *Plato's Pigs and Other Ruminations: Ancient Guides to Living with Nature*. Cambridge UP, 2020.
Waugh, Joanne. "Women, Citizenship, Democracy: The Challenge of the *Republic*." *Platonic Political Philosophy and Contemporary Democratic Theory*, vol. 1, edited by K. J. Boudouris, International Center for Greek Philosophy and Culture, 1997, pp. 210–23.

Plato on Hate and the Limits of Morality

Phillip Mitsis

> A kind Providence has placed in our breasts a hatred of the unjust and cruel, in order that we may preserve ourselves from cruelty and injustice. They who bear cruelty are accomplices in it. The pretended gentleness which excludes that charitable rancour, produces an indifference which is half an approbation. They never will love where they ought to love, who do not hate where they ought to hate.
>
> —Edmund Burke, *Letters on a Regicide Peace*, to the Earl Fitzwilliam

Plato's views on hatred are rarely remarked upon and certainly never receive anything like the scholarly attention lavished on his views about love, its conventional opposite.[1] This is odd, since hate, along with its benefits, is coupled with love at several key junctures in Platonic texts, and they are lauded together as mutually supporting mechanisms in education, virtue, knowledge, the state, religion, and so forth.[2] Moreover, ringing endorsements of the importance and value of hate are typically found in the context of arguments that usually are taken to represent not just a particular interlocutor's claims but also Plato's own.[3] Given that such claims for hate are apt to seem worryingly anomalous to most contemporary ears, I think it behooves us, rather than just ignoring them, to look more closely at why Plato seems so convinced about hate's importance for our lives, especially since that conviction is an integral part of his philosophy.

Obviously, the general topic of Platonic hatred is far too complex and unwieldy for a short essay, and one must be selective, so I will be focusing on just one strand of Platonic argument. I will not, for instance, be taking on the Socratic-style question, "what exactly is Platonic hatred?" or hate's relation to Socrates' injunctions against harming others, that is, by hating someone do you harm them or at least wish to harm them? Nor will I be taking up the kinds of questions that were to exercise Aristotle in the *Rhetoric* about the relation of hatred to anger and revenge or to particular psychic functions. All these are no doubt ultimately relevant, but I want to first try to isolate a feature of Platonic hatred independently of these latter worries and that might be characterized as unalloyed or pure,[4] and absolutely crucial in setting moral boundaries.

By way of an initial example, it might be helpful to begin with a passage from the *Laws,* where the Athenian defends the value of drinking parties for education and explains how choral song and dancing at divine festivals help to properly shape the young:

> . . . but it is the virtue that first develops in children that I am calling education, when pleasure and love (*philia*) and pain and hatred (*misos*) develop correctly in souls not yet able to grasp an account (*logon*), and when they do grasp the account they agree with it (*sumphōnēsōsi*) because they have been correctly trained by appropriate habits; this concordance is the whole of virtue, while the part of it that is correctly nurtured concerning pleasures and pains, so as to hate (*misein*) what should be hated straightaway from beginning to end, and love (*stergein*) what should be loved, by carving (*apotemnōn*) this very thing off in your account and naming it education, in my view you would be naming it correctly. (*Laws* 2, 653b1–c3)[5]

Pleasure and pain, on the one hand, and love and hate, on the other, serve as rudders for the correct (*orthōs*) training of one's habits.[6] Moreover, before we are able to grasp a rational account (*logon*), our loves and hatreds must be trained (*eithesthai*) to harmonize (*sumphōnein*, cf. 634e, 689d, 696c) with it.[7] Virtue as a whole, it is claimed, arises, develops, and becomes settled through the concordance of our grasp of the *logos* with our correctly educated loves and hatreds. This point about love and hatred is taken up immediately by the Athenian again in a difficult passage (654c4–d4) where three divergent psychological types are described. How these three are related and precisely the criteria that make for the best one are not exactly transparent and remain a matter of dispute,[8] but one sufficiently clear upshot of the Athenian's comparison is the importance in choral training of instilling appropriate habits and attitudes with regard to pleasures and pains and loves and hatreds, and of those in turn jibing with correct beliefs about the good and ugly:

> Now suppose that what he considers beautiful (*kala*) really is beautiful and what he considers ugly (*aischra*) really is ugly, and he treats them as such. Do we hold him to be better educated in choral dance and music than a person who is able to comply in particular cases with what is thought to be beautiful, using his body and his voice, but who fails to take delight in beautiful things and fails to hate their opposites? Or is the better educated person the one who gets it right in his pleasures and pains, embracing (*aspazomenos*) what is beautiful and detesting (*duscherainōn*)⁹ what is not, even if he is not quite able to get it right in voice and body or to grasp it in his thought?" (*Laws* 654c4–d4, translation modified)

These claims about the critical importance of loving and hating the right things, both ethical and aesthetical, are further taken up in *Laws* 3 where the argument is broadened in scope to include the entire citizenry of a *polis*, whose members display the height of ignorance if they fail to love what they believe to be good and hate what they believe bad:

> [The greatest ignorance (*amathia*)] is when someone hates (*misēi*) that which they nevertheless believe to be good and noble, and loves and embraces (*aspazētai*) that which they know to be unjust and evil. This disharmony (*diaphōnian*) between rational belief and pleasure and pain is, I maintain, the height of ignorance, and "the greatest," because it is of the greater part (*plēthous*) of the soul; for what is in this (i.e., the soul) pained and experiencing pleasure is just like the *demos* or greater part (*plēthos*) of a *polis*. And whenever the soul opposes knowledge, or opinion, or *logos*, which are the natural ruling principles, that I call ignorance (*anoian*, lit. lack of reason), which is the same as that of the *polis* when the *plēthos* refuses to obey their rulers and the laws; or, moreover, as that of one man, when fair reasonings are in his soul yet do nothing further, but rather the opposite of these. All these cases I term the most entirely discordant ignorance both for the *polis* and for each individual citizen. (*Laws* 689a4–c2)

Thus, loving and hating the right things in accordance with *logos* is a hallmark both of a properly educated individual and of an entire citizen body, while loving and hating the wrong things in opposition to it is the height of individual and communal ignorance. As for ignorance (*anoia*) itself, throughout the Platonic corpus we hear both loudly and often that it is something to be hated. And when conjoined with power, it not only is both *echthra* (hateful) and *aischra* (ugly), but *blabera* (harmful, damaging) as well *(Philebus* 49c1–2). Staying again with the *Laws* for the moment, in the Athenian's rather outdated but perhaps still pregnant image, we learn further that Justice herself is similarly indignant at falsehood, which is the complicit accomplice of ignorance: Justice is said, and rightly, to be the virgin daughter of Shame (*Aidous*), and falsehood by its nature is detested (*nemēseton*) by both Shame and Justice (*Laws* 943e).

If we turn to the central epistemological arguments in the *Republic*, the scope and intensity of these assertions about the importance and naturalness of hating ignorance and falsehood becomes striking. At the beginning of Book VI, for example, after the grand separation of the world of appearance from that of forms and the arguments about the nature of truth and knowledge, we see the outcome of such an education though love and hate[10] as Socrates begins to delineate the characteristics of the fully formed philosopher, chief among them being a single-minded preoccupation with truth and a corresponding hatred of falsity:

> Let this, indeed, be agreed by us concerning the natures of philosophers, that they always love learning (*mathēmata*), at least that which reveals to them being (*ousias*) that is always being, and is not wandering around between generation and destruction. "Let it be agreed." And indeed, said I, of the whole of it (*ousia*) they willingly let go neither a smaller nor greater nor more honored nor less honored part, as we narrated earlier concerning lovers and lovers of honor. "What you say is correct," he said. Consider further, then, whether it is necessary for those who are going to be such as these we were describing to have in addition this thing. "Which thing?" Absence of deceit (*apseudeian*) and a willingness to accept falsity in no way whatsoever, but to hate it, and to love (*stergein*) the truth. (*Republic* 485b10–c3; cf. 490b10–c1; for the gods, 382c5)

What follows next is a long description of the characteristics of philosophers that equip them to rule, replete with a remarkable combination of superlatives, black-and-white contrasts between philosophers "who seek integrity and wholeness in all things human and divine" (*Republic* 486a3–4) and the rest of us mortals, and a palpable contempt for ordinary human life that is either rapturously exalted or merely creepy, depending on one's predilections. One of the things that leaps to the fore is the intensity and narrowness of these philosophers' focus to the exclusion—or hatred—of everything else, a characteristic to which we shall have occasion to return.[11] But one worrying conclusion is that philosophers, who do not always have much time to contemplate the Forms, will perhaps spend the majority of their lives hating everything else that they must confront in a world of ignorance that wanders between generation and destruction.

First, though, one last preliminary that suggests an intriguing, though overlooked, opportunity for Platonic *homoiosis theōn*, at least to the extent that the hatreds required for mortal virtue are brilliantly displayed and exercised at the level of the divine. Plato's gods hate injustice, falsehood, the ugly, and, in the *Euthyphro*, the unholy, regardless of whether they themselves in unison or something independent of them serves as holiness's normative ground, and famously, whether or not Euthyphro can come up with a *paradeigma* for identifying all the instances of unholiness that the gods hate or, at least, should hate. In the *Symposium*, even if it mostly serves as a display of Agathon's clever wordplay, Love, the youngest of the gods, even hates old age and refuses to go anywhere near it (*Symposium* 195b2). By the same token, with respect to those who raise doubts about the traditional stories of the gods, the Athenian wonders how we can help ourselves from hating them and finding them hard to bear (*chalepōs pherein*, *Laws* 887c10–d2), as the paradigm of Socrates in the *Euthyphro* and *Apology* bears out.

In short, hatred permeates Plato's world from the individual, to the state, to the divine, and, rather than viewing it as some terrible flaw to be ameliorated or even ineffectually lamented over, Plato seems to embrace and elevate it, putting hatred on an equal footing with love in shaping his particular philosophical vision. Now, it is true, of course, that we do not have the equivalent of a malevolent *Symposium* that takes up in detail questions of hate with a corresponding learned priestess, let's call her *Misoponēria*, initiating Socrates into hatred's particular mysteries. A *scala odiorum* moving from the hatred of the annoying little laugh of a particular *despectum/am/um* to the form of absolute ugliness itself-in-itself could certainly have been an enlightening treat, but alas we are stuck instead with the *Parmenides*, which does not even mention a form of hatred.[12] Thus, one might reasonably wonder whether the instances of hate that have been adduced so far are less a product of considered theorizing than the unthinking result of the kind of typical cultural tic we sometimes find in Plato, on par, for example, with his inability to think his way beyond the *polis*. It is a pity, of course, that no Epicurean or Stoic was on the scene yet to rouse him from his parochial slumbers, since none of his interlocutors seems to raise any problematic queries about the value of well-placed hatred in the dialogues. We do get a tiny bit of chatter in Diogenes Laertius about Diogenes the Cynic continually skewering conventional pieties and, often amusingly, Platonic ones, but there is no real sense that Plato took any notice of Diogenes in his own writings—that is, no Socrates saying explicitly, "I am not a citizen of the *kosmos* but only of Athens or "I do not treat friends and enemies alike" as Diogenes claims to have done (cf. Diogenes Laertius 6.2.68). So I think we are in danger of being left with the potentially disappointing conclusion that perhaps Plato, with respect to love and hate, should just line up in the *Polarity and Analogy* queue behind Parmenides, who thought that males are formed on the right side of the womb, females on the left, and immediately in front of Aristotle, who claims that men are hotter and dryer than women (Preus 425).

Of course, we would like to think that somehow, even behind that impenetrable mask, Plato would not leave anything that seems both so endemic and ripe for examination as hatred untouched, however much we may worry that Platonic hatred might be little more than a kind of trailing cultural ligger at love's banquet. Yet, even if it is true that explicit large-scale Platonic examinations and justifications of it are lacking, I would argue that we still need to pay far more attention to the presence of hate in Plato's arguments and for a variety of reasons. So let me take a step in this direction by trying to tease out a few potential motivations for Plato's striking affirmations of hatred just in the few texts that we have looked at so far.

One initial hurdle in coming to terms with Platonic hatred may seem numbingly obvious but should probably still be addressed. Plato has a range of words that he uses in these contexts besides *misos* and even on this briefest of tours, we have seen *duscheraino, nemesao, echthra, apechthomai*—there are, of course, more—which have a range of meanings, many of which may not strike our ears in a way quite so straightforwardly morally problematic as "hate"—so, for example, "abhor," "feel disgust at," "despise," "to be indignant with," "loathe," "enmity," and so forth. The word "hate," as noun, verb, and adjective has begun to take on a singular problematic tonality—at least for speakers of American English—even if their senses are not always strictly individuated from these other hostile attitudes that somehow manage to seem less immediately off-putting to contemporary sensitivities. "Hate" has increasingly become a singular term of art for something whose status seems beyond moral defense: "hate crimes," "hate speech," and so forth, while we might have to ponder a bit to decide what we are to make of "enmity speech" or "loathe crimes." To be sure, I still might be able to respond to a friend who comes back from a fabulous trip while I have been languishing on my staycation with a sigh of "I hate you," but it is clear that this is in a very particular context that, at least as yet, remains socially permissible. Not so for typical public expressions of "hate."

So one worry is whether "*misos*" has anything like the h-word valence it mostly has now taken on in English, and though I think it is unlikely, care must still be exercised as discussions move between linguistic worlds. The fact that there is a wide semantic range of words in English related to "hate," just as there is for Greek "*misos*," presents further occasions for caution, no doubt, but I will not try to make even a preliminary move on the Rubik's Cube of lining up all the possible correspondences and mismatches on both sides of this particular Greek/English divide. It is not even clear to me that this would be possible, but I hope it is not really necessary for our more limited purposes, so I am going to go forward assuming that there is some recognizable core meaning of "hate" that overlaps with "*misos*," At the same time, Plato appears to be fairly flexible in sprinkling his various hate words in opposition to *philein*, which suggests he at least sees in their variety a sufficient kinship to oppose them to *philein*, but also to *stergein*, both of which, however, are not entirely without their own set of ambiguities and problems. I do not think Plato's use is so flexible, though, that we should begin to translate *misos* as "dislike," which is becoming a trend with some translators of both Plato and Aristotle—perhaps because they are uncomfortable with giving the impression that their heroes might be spouting anything that could give off an odious aura of hate speech. But in any case, perhaps like one of Plato's divers, we can take a plunge into these linguistic waters and still hope to come up with a plausible approximation of our original question—why is Plato so keen on hate?

One might have hoped that in some of the extended discussions employing *philia* and *misos* in the *Lysis* or *Gorgias*, for instance, or in the exchanges with Polemarchus in the *Republic*, we could find Plato being a mite more self-conscious about the seemingly natural and inherited polarity of love and hate in Greek thought and his further claim that we love the good and hate the bad. This latter assumption, of course, gets pretty good workouts in a host of arguments trading on opaque belief contexts. In the *Lysis*, for instance, Socrates is able to tie Menexenus up in a bewilderment of questions about whether we would love the good if there were no contrasting bad (*Lysis* 220c1 ff.) and how this affects our perceptions of friends and enemies. It is tough for his young interlocutors not to get lost in this particular maze, of course, but the basic assumed structures of love and hate and their relation to good and evil serve only as a kind of safe house from within which Socrates can generate his puzzles. No explicit justifications of the presumed benefits of hating the bad are to be had.

So I think it might help to return to Burke and to the second of his observations in the epigraph: "The pretended gentleness which excludes that charitable rancour, produces an indifference which is half an approbation." Burke may have been writing in the wake of the Platonic tradition, but he also had Christ looking over his shoulder, which requires a short, but I hope not unhelpful, digression. There is a long and storied tradition of interpretations of Luke 14:26, an echinate verse that is still giving exegetes fits.[13] Christ is speaking: "If anyone comes to me and does not hate (*misei*) his own father and mother and wife and children and brothers and sisters and even his own soul, he is not able to be my follower" (my translation). Some inventive Biblical scholars try to retranslate Jesus' *misei* as "dislike" or "turn away from," but it seems the God of love incarnate himself enjoins hatred not just against the elderly but against one's whole family circle, including oneself, and this seems serious. Indeed, we might be inclined to ask, where is Hierocles when we need him to turn this family circle argument in a more beatitudinous direction? Yet, without going into all the controversies of Christology in Luke, there is at least one strain of scholarship that, however plausible, is at least useful for our question. It argues that Luke tries to elevate Christ's divine status by having him act in the manner of Yahweh in the Pentateuch. Yahweh, one remembers, has an extensive repertoire of what would qualify at the human level as hate speech, hate crimes, and so forth, much of which not only parallels what we find in Plato—for example, hating injustice, iniquity—but also surpasses him by hating feasts aimed at rivals, the prideful, and even Esau before he was born (*Romans* 9:13). Moreover, Yahweh does not just hate the sin, but as Plato also seems to sometimes recommend, hates the sinners, whom he considers his enemies and acts accordingly, often even more than accordingly, for example, the flood, Sodom and Gomorrah, the first born of the Egyptians, and Canaanites. In this particular verse, goes the argument, Luke wants us to see Christ with his Father hat on, and by making this demand of his followers, Christ signals that all the sinners around him are worthy of hate (i.e., those who are not his followers), and most important, especially those sinners who might be the nearest and dearest to the prospective follower, hence most distracting and hard to quit. Indeed, potential followers must hate even their own souls in order to be able to follow Christ. It seems, therefore, that it is only by hating what is most cherished in one's sinning self and other sinners that one can draw a line sharp enough between Christ and everything else that is wicked in comparison. In order to give Him the kind of selective attention He demands, we must block out any possible attraction to something else, and that is what hate is good for. Love, on the other hand, is not great with borders. Elsewhere in Luke's account, Christ puts on a less fearsome and more humane face, and a mysterious dialectic of good cop/bad cop ensues, in turn terrifying and enchanting the reader in need of salvation. But a cop able to wield a big hate stick is needed to set categorical zero-tolerance limits when it comes to who can get into the club in the first place.

A move from Yahweh to the *Republic*'s philosophers and their upbringing might be a bit of an intertextual leap, but apart from the fact that Plato also likes to play good cop/bad cop with his readers, there is perhaps a useful intimation of a way forward with this general notion of hate carving off and individuating a moral domain in a way that allowing any benign regard for the opposition is incapable of, as is maintaining even neutral attitudes—Burke's "indifferences that are half approbation." They all allow for the blurring the boundaries. We can perhaps begin to see some adumbrations of this, for example, in passages like *Laws* 656b. In the course of a discussion about legislation for the proper kinds of movements and rhythms for choral dance, the Athenian describes the harm he thinks is done to someone if they are not really hating what is wicked, but merely blaming it in a puerile and unserious way, which has the effect of engendering hypocrisy, self-deception, and eventually leads to one becoming like what one fails to hate:

> Is it not probable or even inevitable that the result will be exactly the same as whenever someone, living among the

wicked habits of bad men, does not hate (*misei*) but accepts and even delights in (*chairēi*) them, yet blames (*psegēi*) them merely in a spirit of play, as if being in a dream about one's own wickedness? Then, to be sure, inevitably the person so delighted becomes similar (*homoiousthai*) to whatever they delight in, even though ashamed to praise it. Yet what greater good or evil would we say befalls us so inevitably?

Acquiescing to evil or taking secret delight in the wickedness of others sustains a dream world in which we fail to hate our own wickedness and inevitably we get dragged down into evil ourselves by a kind of *homoiosis kakōn*. The general notion at work here is little news in Plato, of course, and is part of why we are not allowed to take delight in tragic conflicts in the theater. But here, more particularly, Plato seems to raise the possibility that hate, and perhaps by extension self-hate, can become an important tool for self-criticism and moral awareness, and as we find out later in the argument, critical for correctly framing laws and eliciting obedience (cf. *Laws* 660 ff).[14] In a structural move familiar, for instance, to Aristotle's account of friendship, seeing wickedness in others and hating it might help us to become dissimilar to own current wickedness and thus begin to move us toward the good, rather than to the evil that inevitably ensues from incorrect *homoiosis*. Tepid tolerance is, therefore, also dangerous and can lead, also apparently inevitably, to taking actual rather than merely self-deceptive delight in our own wickedness.[15] Thus, claims about accepting and loving our flaws and those of others would no doubt be met by Plato with a hostile porcupine stare, as would the notion that when drawing boundaries with the young we should never label anyone good or bad. For Plato, moral limits require the beneficial and healing ministrations of hatred properly aimed both at ourselves and others, and that is not the job of acceptance or of love.

Unfortunately, hate and love as a team cannot invariably provide success stories, and there is another feature of hate that sometimes one catches a glimpse of in Plato that bears comment in this context. In a famous passage in *Laws* 9, for instance, the Athenian makes the argument that it is better to exact the death penalty from the morally uncurable both for their own sakes and for everyone's around them, since it will provide the double benefit of serving as a warning and also ridding the state of evil. But with respect to those who are salvageable, whether they have committed a large or small crime, the city must ensure they never voluntarily dare to do so again (or at least very much less) and by every means necessary: ". . . either by actions or words, or pleasures or pains, or honors or disgrace, or monetary fines or gifts, and in general everything by whatever means one will make them hate injustice, but love—or at any rate not hate—the nature of true justice, which is exactly the function (*ergon*) of the best laws" (*Laws* 862d4–10). It can be dangerous, of course, to put much stock in a passing remark, but this passage does seem to flirt with the notion that hatred is more ingrained, as well as easier and more effective to wield, than love. Although all the impressive incentives the Athenian lists may not be able to reform someone to the extent of making them love justice, they can at least induce them to hate injustice and not hate justice. Here the Athenian seems to at least give a nod to the kind of views espoused by Thucydides and a long line of thinkers who have a darker view of human nature, namely that we find it more congenial and natural to hate than to love, though, of course, Plato remains careful overall to try to link these tendencies to the right things.

Presumably, the backsliders in this passage were not trained entirely correctly in their initial experiences of love and hate, but it is interesting that the Athenian thinks corrections work more reliably in the particular direction of hate. By the same token, in our opening passage from *Laws* 2 there was the suggestion that hate may be more immediate and lasting: ". . . so as to hate (*misein*) what should be hated straightaway from beginning to end, and love (*stergein*) what should be loved . . ." Again, not to put too heavy a burden on small turns of phrase, but hating is described as being both more immediate and enduring. Taking these hints from these two passages and putting them together, they cohere enough, I think, to make a plausible Platonic point. Although hate and love team up in education, hatred's tendencies in the final analysis are better suited for controlling individuals in society who cannot be induced to love the nature of true justice. They can be brought to not hate it and to be obedient to the laws, but they are not the sort that we meet on their way to becoming philosophers in the *Republic*. Even with careful attempts from youth to instill the proper loves and hatreds, not everyone can become a philosopher capable of loving the nature of true justice. Accordingly, it appears that hatred may be ultimately more effective in drawing the limits that help prevent us from being morally incurable. Indeed, the overall moral of the passages seems to be a banausic consequentialist conclusion that money (etc.) cannot buy non-philosophers love, but it can induce them to hate what they should hate, at least enough to keep them out of jail or worse, thus transforming them into something more useful to themselves and others.

In closing, I would like to call attention to an argument made by David Konstan in his discussion of the history of forgiveness. He argues that the notion is absent from Classical antiquity, and in tracing its development, points first to its initial emergence in Kant and then how this omnipresent demand on our current moral sensitivities really begins to pick up steam in the nineteenth century (152). It is plausible to suppose, I think, that changing views of forgiveness went hand in hand with the fortunes of hate, since Kant is in many ways responsible as well for killing the notion of hate having moral uses.[16] Often today, public expressions of forgiveness are typically linked to a rejection of hate,[17] mainly, of course, of the kind of wrong hatred that generated a crime. But along with forgiveness go avowals that one does not hate the perpetrator and a sense that all hate is to be rejected tout court.

In the face of this, it seems today as if philosophers, both ancient and modern, have mostly abrogated any desire to critically examine such Platonic questions, having left them to the psychologists, in much the same manner an earlier generation of philosophers had done with philosophical questions about death. Over the past several decades, with some nudges from Epicurus, it dawned on philosophers, however, that they might not be immortal and writings on death have subsequently burgeoned. Accordingly, perhaps similarly reflecting on Plato's arguments might lead to the pressing issues involving hate that are surrounding us to begin to garner philosophical attention. This is not to argue, of course, that we should adopt whole-cloth Plato's arguments about hate and moral limits, but I think moral philosophy loses out if philosophers fail to take on Plato's more troubling questions about hatred and, by extension, worries about how those nurtured in the soil of placid relativities and universal empathies will be able to react when moral questions become more pressing and complex.[18]

Notes

1. There are many discussions of Plato's critique of misology (*Phaedo* 88c ff.), of course, including those arguing that Socrates comes uncomfortably close to being a misologist himself (cf. Miller, *ad loc*); but I will be focusing on

what I take to be explicit Platonic views about the positive psychological, moral, political, aesthetic, and epistemological value of correctly hating the right things.

2. Gregory Vlastos, for example, mentions hate only once in all of his writings and in a way that interestingly reflects Burke's claim. He suggests that, unlike Plato, the "historical" Socrates he has isolated in the dialogues suffers from a failure of love that is also apparently tied to hate. "If men's souls are to be saved, they must be saved his [Socrates'] way. And when he sees they cannot, he watches them go down the road to perdition with regret but without anguish. Jesus wept for Jerusalem. Socrates warns Athens, scolds, exhorts it, condemns it. But he has no tears for it. One wonders if Plato, who raged against Athens, did not love it more in his rage and hate than ever did Socrates in his sad and good-tempered rebukes. One feels there is a last zone of frigidity in the soul of the great erotic; had he loved his fellows more, he could hardly have laid on them the burdens of his 'despotic logic,' impossible to be borne" (513).

3. I remain agnostic about the reliability of such inferences, but those who take the passages discussed to reflect "Plato's view of love" must perforce take aboard the corresponding views of hate as Plato's own as well.

4. See note 11; this feature is reflected in the extent to which Platonic hatred is aimed at "evil" and "falsehood" conceptually.

5. At *Republic* 401d4–402a3, there is an earlier iteration of this argument in almost the exact same language, though with the addition of a notion found in Aristotle of *oikeiotēs*. Cf. note 9.

6. That love and hate are central features of human psychology from the very outset seems to be taken for granted by the Athenian Stranger. Cf. *Laws* 792a, where infants show what they love and hate to their nurses by crying and screaming.

7. Some scholars have argued that love and hate are subordinated under the respective categories of pleasure and pain, but it is not clear in the ensuing arguments that hate is necessarily a pain. Indeed, elsewhere in Plato, love is treated as a possible pain (cf. *Philebus* 47e1 ff). I think it more likely that loving and hating the right things is pleasurable, and the converse painful.

8. Sauvé Meyer, *ad loc.*, for a clear account of the problem and a plausible resolution.

9. "*duscherainō*" is a common variant of *miseō* in these contexts and in the active voice has the sense of "detest," "find odious," "be unable to bear," etc. Cf. *Nicomachean Ethics* 91179b26 ". . . a character akin (*oikeion*) to virtue must exist in the student in advance, loving (*stergon*) the *kalon* and detesting (*duscherainon*) the ugly (*aischra*)."

10. Earlier at *Republic* 401d4–402a3 is an earlier iteration of our opening text from the *Laws* in almost the exact same language, though with the addition of a notion, found in Aristotle, of *oikeiotēs*. Cf. note 9 above.

11. A focus that is grounded linguistically and metaphysically. Cf. *Republic* 485b10–c1, where it is argued that it is impossible for the same nature to be *philosophon* and *philopseudē*.

12. Such a philosophical ladder is largely meant to be hermeneutical. The question of whether Plato countenances negative forms has generated a large scholarly discussion; for opposite conclusions, see Nails and Thesleff. My own view tends toward Nails's, with the caveat that although Plato may in principle be committed to negative forms by his general arguments for positive ones, it seems not to have been a particular concern of his.

13. Jongkind and Williams, editors. See, for instance, Clement, *Stromata* 1.12, which turns this into a more limited lesson on the evils of the flesh.

14. Compare, for instance *Theaetetus* 168a: ". . . but in real argument he must be in earnest and must set his interlocutor on his feet, pointing out to him those slips only which are due to himself and his previous associations. For if you act in this way, those who debate with you will cast the blame for their confusion and perplexity upon themselves, not upon you; they will run after you and love you, and they will hate themselves and run away from themselves, taking refuge in philosophy, that they may escape from their former selves by becoming different."

15. *Republic* 535e2 ff. offers a parallel argument about the budding philosopher who lazily accepts involuntary falsehood (*to akousion pseudos*) and is thus polluted by ignorance (*amathia*) like a pig.

16. Though interestingly, in his "Lectures on Pedagogy," 9.482,489, 494 (cf. MS 6.420,429, 449), Kant allows the use of "contempt" as an appropriate *moral* punishment for children who have lied, although this seems to conflict with his general mandates for mutual respect.

17. It seems one of the sole areas of pushback is whether Nazis can be forgiven (and hence not hated). Most of these arguments are framed from within particular religious mandates in Judaism, but they do raise questions about violating a moral boundary when one forgives and claims to still love as human beings those who have perpetrated genocide. Cf. the work of Jean Améry and V. Jankélévitch, though the latter argues more narrowly that one cannot forgive someone who does not ask for forgiveness, whereas Plato, of course, in the passages we have seen, is not worried about such displays of autonomy on the part of malefactors, which speaks to Konstan's larger point. Simone de Beauvoir (250 ff) argued that hate directed at Nazis can help to rehabilitate them by forcing them to feel the diminishment of their dignity as a consciousness.

18. It is a pleasure to offer this essay to Tony Preus, who for twenty years was my closest ancient philosophy neighbor in upstate New York, then mentor at the SAGP, but above all, a model of a scholar of utter integrity who never blurs an ancient text to make a flashy ephemeral point and who has worked tirelessly to keep all of us and what we study afloat regardless of critical and methodological differences. I would like to thank Nick Pappas, David Konstan, Iakovos Vasiliou,

Gabe Shapiro, Jessica Moss, David Murphy, Claudia Yau, Richard Kraut, Elizabeth Asmis, Gabriel Richardson Lear, Max DuBoff, Brad Inwood, and audiences at NYU, the University of Chicago, and Yale for helpful comments.

Works Cited

Améry, Jean. *Jenseits von Schuld und Sühne: Bewältigungsversuche eines Überwältigten.* Klett-Cotta, 1966.
Burke, Edmund. *The Works of the Right Honorable Edmund Burke,* vol. 5, Eastburn, NY: Eastburn, Kirk, & Co., 1813.
De Beauvoir, Simone. *Philosophical Writings,* edited by Margaret A. Simmons and Sylvie Le Bon de Beauvoir, U of Illinois P, 2004.
Diogenes Laertius, *Lives of Eminent Philosophers,* edited by T. Dorandi, Cambridge UP, 2013.
Jankélévitch, Vladimir. *Le pardon.* Flammarion, 1967.
Jongkind, Dirk, and Peter J. Williams, editors. *The Greek New Testament,* Crossway, 2017.
Kant, Immanuel. "Lectures on Pedagogy" (1803). In *Anthropology, History, and Education.* Cambridge UP, 2007.
Konstan, David. *Before Forgiveness: The Origins of a Moral Idea.* Cambridge UP, 2010.
Miller, Thomas. "Socrates' Warning against Misology (Plato, *Phaedo* 88c–91c)," *Phronesis,* vol. 60, no. 2, 2015, pp. 145–79.
Nails, Deborah. "Two Dogmas of Platonism." *Proceedings of the Boston Area Colloquium in Ancient Philosophy,* Gary Michael Gurtler and William Wians, editors, vol. 28, 2012, pp. 77–101.
Plato, *Respublica,* edited by S. R. Slings, Oxford UP, 2003.
Preus, Anthony. "Aristotle on Sick and Healthy Souls," *The Monist,* vol. 69, no. 3, 1986, pp. 416–33.
Sauvé Meyer, Susan. *Plato Laws 1&2.* Oxford UP, 2015.
Thesleff, Holger. *Studies in Plato's Two-Level Model. Societas Scientiarum Fennica,* 1999.
Vlastos, Gregory. "The Paradox of Socrates." *Queen's Quarterly,* vol. 64, 1957, pp. 496–516.

Neither an "Exact Grasp" Nor a "Complete Falsehood"

The Truth Status and Rhetorical Function of the Tripartite Model of City and Soul in the *Republic*

Mark Moes

Miller on the Theoretical Inadequacy of the Tripartite Model of the Soul in the *Republic* and on the More Adequate Grasp of the Soul in the *Philebus*

Certain passages in the *Republic* (especially 435cd and 504ac) present Socrates as calling into question the theoretical adequacy of the tripartite model of the soul. Mitchell Miller has argued that the Platonic Socrates presents a much superior analysis of the well-ordered embodied human soul and its powers in the *Philebus*' account of the Form of a good human life, and that Plato uses Socrates' expressions of hesitancy about the adequacy of the tripartite model in *Republic* to alert his more astute readers both to the limitations of the tripartite soul model and to the need for the more adequate account like the one Socrates gives in the *Philebus* ("Exact Grasp").

According to Miller, Socrates' mention of an "exact grasp" of the nature of the soul at *Republic* 435cd needs to be read in connection with Socrates' distinction of the kinds of knowledge in *Philebus* 55c–59d, the only sustained text in all the dialogues that addresses the theme of exactness (*akriveia*). In that text Socrates places on a continuum from less exactness to more exactness four kinds of knowledge: the least exact is craft knowledge that relies on experience and practice (e.g., tuning in music), more exact is craft knowledge that applies mathematics extensively (e.g., building houses), yet more exact is pure mathematics as studied by philosophers (e.g., pure arithmetic and geometry), and the most exact is dialectical knowledge of Forms. It seems that Plato has Socrates fault the *Republic*'s model of the embodied soul as lacking exactness because he envisages the account in *Philebus* 55–59 as supplanting tripartition in a way that brings out the eidetic and mathematical order guiding the activity of the healthy soul.

The description of types of knowledge in *Philebus* 55–59 has striking parallels with the description in *Republic* Book VII of the five mathematical disciplines that prepare one for the dialectical study of the Forms. Both mention transitions from applied mathematics to pure mathematics to dialectic. The same immanence of abstract structures implied by the turn from pure arithmetic and geometry to their applications in astronomy and harmonics in *Republic* VII shows up again in the movement (in the opposite direction) along the continuum from applied to pure mathematics in the *Philebus*. Both underscore the immanence of abstract structures in the sensible world. Socrates implies in both that however immanent the mathematicals and Forms may be in the sensibles, the learner who has not yet reached understanding of mathematicals and Forms retains an attitude of *pistis*, an attitude based on the presumption that sense perceptible material realities are the only realities. He also insists that without the educational work of mathematics the learner will depend in the wrong way on sensory images in his or her conceiving of the Forms; he or she will conceive them as too much like spatio-temporal things. Socrates himself is portrayed in the *Parmenides* as in his youth needing to be brought to realize that Forms both are radically unlike sensibles in being free of spatial or temporal determinations and are somehow causally prior to all that instantiates them.

But the tripartite model not only lacks "exactness" but also relies upon this mistake of conceiving soul parts as if they were sensible things. When it comes time to use the city as a model for the embodied soul, Socrates projects into the individual soul *three agent-like individuals* as the "parts" that bear the three Forms of motivation within it. The calculative part is then conceived as falling into "civil war" with the appetitive part, and the spirited part as "allying" itself with either of the other parts. All three parts are supposed to exhibit their own desires, passions, beliefs, and degrees of understanding. This leaves the model open to the objection that each soul part, as an agent-like individual, will have to be analyzed as having three more parts within itself, leading to a theoretically destructive infinite regress of parts. Socrates decides to perform this projection anyway, for reasons we shall discuss below, and to postpone consideration of Forms in their difference from, and priority to, their participants.

Nevertheless, Socrates in the *Republic* does *point to* a better way of conceiving of the soul and its Forms, one that does not project agent-like parts into the soul, when he offers his simile between musical notes and the three "parts" of the soul at 443cd. Socrates' simile is striking because of the way in which it indirectly acknowledges the artificiality and deficiency of tripartition, holding open the possibility that the tripartite model of the soul in Books II–IV (and Books VIII–X) may misrepresent the soul's true structure. The simile's recourse to the one-many structure of a musical mode resonates with the division of the forms of pleasure and knowledge in the *Philebus*. The "incorporeal order that rules harmoniously over soul-and-body" yielded by the dialectical division of the intermediate forms of human life at *Philebus* 64b, as defining the normative order for the life of the human animal, has strong analogies to the Form of pitch, placing the powers of the human soul as limits (or "notes") on a continuum (or "scale") of somatic-psychological powers chosen for their *harmonious combinability*. Just as a musical performer draws from eight harmonious tones, distributed over an octave, in singing or playing a melody in excellent fashion, so the good person orchestrates his or her own powers—combines and organizes his or her expressions or actualizations—in such a way as to embody unity, proportion, truth, and beauty.

Socrates' model of the soul in the *Philebus* identifies an "octave" or "harmonic mode" of eight intermediate forms of human activity that can be harmoniously combined into a good life. These are placed on a continuum or scale at whose bottom end are placed "notes" concerned more with the nourishment of the body than with nourishment of the intellect, and at whose higher end are placed "notes" concerned more with nourishment of the intellect than with nourishment of the body. The "notes," starting at the bottom of the scale, are (1) healthy bodily pleasures, (2) anticipatory pleasures associated with temperance, (3) pleasures associated with the virtues that regulate various passions, (4) pleasures of perception of smells, colors, shapes, and tones, (5) empirical skills (like tuning in music), (6) arts that apply mathematics (building), (7) pure mathematics, and (8) reason and understanding in dialectic.

Blossner on the Theoretical Inadequacy but Rhetorical Appropriateness of the Tripartite Model of the City and Soul in the *Republic*

Norbert Blossner's insightful paper in the *Cambridge Companion to Plato's Republic* complements Miller's work by providing further reasons for thinking that Socrates knowingly employs a theoretically inadequate tripartite model of city and soul (345–85). Blossner mentions several theoretical problems with the model in addition to the objection that the parts of the tripartite soul are agent-like individuals. For example, he points out that it does not follow that if two things are just, each must have as many parts as the other, and the same kinds of parts. Second, he remarks that the behavior of an individual is not identical with that of its soul parts in the way that the behavior of a city is identical with that of its members, since the individual rules his or her soul polity, hands over the rule of his or her soul to a particular part and supervises the organization of his inner self. Third, he points out "ruling" in a just city, conceived in Book I as a craft that *serves* clients, is quite a different matter from "ruling" in the five different souls, where a dominant soul part has a coercive mastery over other parts with which it is in conflict. Blossner rightly suggests that these limitations of the model can hardly fail to have been noticed by Socrates or Plato.

In addition to highlighting such problems, Blossner goes some way toward showing why Plato depicts Socrates as knowingly employing a deficient psychological model. For one thing, the model plays an important role in the overall rhetorical argument that justice pays and the tyrant is unhappy, an argument constructed for non-philosophical interlocutors. For another, the model shows how all five personality types conceived in accordance with the model precisely *fail* to embody in their lives the unity, proportion, truth, and beauty embodied by the soul orchestrating its own powers in the way Socrates lays out in the *Philebus*, by bringing to light the debilitating effects of various kinds of *conflict* in city and soul.[1] Each arrangement of elements in city and soul is specified in terms of a division into *competing* factions or soul parts and of the *dominance* of one social group or soul part over another;[2] little or no provision is made in the scheme for coalitions of forces.[3] The model yields various pictures of cities bedeviled by factional politics and of souls cursed with conflicting aims and needs. Such a model is apt to cast light upon some human political and psychological *ills* rooted in intrapsychic conflicts and in misguided conceptions of happiness in a way that makes sense to Socrates' interlocutors.

How Plato's Use of Mimetic Irony and Dialogue Structure Explains His Depiction of Socrates' Use of the Tripartite Soul Model in the *Republic*

We can gain some understanding of the rhetorical work that Socrates attempts to accomplish within the dialogue by means of the model, and that Plato, as author of the dialogue, attempts to accomplish in relation to his readers by means of it, if we consider briefly Mitchell Miller's views about the rhetorical aim and the compositional structure of the Platonic dialogue. According to Miller, the rhetorical aim is to overcome obstacles in readers or auditors to the task of aspiring to the truth about the highest goods—ignorance of their own ignorance, hostility to philosophy, a tendency to assent to propositions without real understanding, and limited capacity for insight. Plato's dialogues, in Miller's view, anticipate these obstacles and respond to them by employing *mimetic irony* within a four-part compositional structure that runs as follows:[4] (1) in a first stage the guide elicits an opinion from the interlocutor or solicits his agreement to some problematic suggestion or thesis; (2) in a second stage, the guide pretends to have a great deal of sympathy for the thesis while at the same time showing its problematic character; (3) just when the interlocutor is reduced to *aporia* (puzzlement), the guide introduces a "reorienting insight" which sets the issues at hand in a new light and is capable of providing the basis for resolving the *aporia*; (4) in the fourth and final part of the dialogue, the *exegesis* part, the guide returns to the problematic thesis of the first stage and reassesses it with the aid of the reorienting insight, or at least with the reorienting insight in the background. In this section, oriented to the interlocutor's insight (or lack of it), the guide often seems to be *testing* his interlocutors to see whether and how well they employ the reorienting insight. Plato constructs the final part of the dialogue in such a way that the testing challenges readers/auditors to apply the reorienting insight to the issue at hand for themselves.[5]

Stages 1 and 2: Tripartition as a Problematic Thesis in Books II–V

Keeping this compositional structure in mind, we can begin to understand why Socrates introduces the tripartite model in the first place—as a *problematic* thesis about the soul. Recall that even the contractarianism that Glaucon articulated in his devil's advocate's defense of Thrasymachus presupposed that communities derive benefit from the just behavior of their members. Socrates' initial crucial and suggestive move in Book II is to transfer this intuition from the context of the city to that of the soul, by conceiving of the soul as a "community" of soul parts along the lines of a civic community. This move gives the thesis that justice pays off for just persons most of its plausibility in the first place. Projecting into the soul three agent-like parts corresponding to three classes of citizen of the *feverish* city, Socrates brings to light a model of the *feverish* soul in pursuit of external goods, of the soul of the "prudent autonomous individual" who manifests Thrasymachean selfishness.[6] Socrates' strategy in these maneuvers is to attempt to enable his interlocutors and auditors to achieve *insight into themselves*—into the (deficient) self-conceptions and conceptions of justice that they hold—an achievement that constitutes a *self-scrutiny*, a *self-diagnosis* of themselves as trapped within a culture of possessive individualism. Plato's plan, on another level, is that this will help those of his *readers or auditors who identify with Glaucon and Adeimantus* to gain a like self-knowledge.[7] Such an explanation seems consonant with Plato's putting into Socrates' mouth the words: "If we claim to have found the just man, the just city, and what the justice is that is in them, I don't suppose that we'll seem to be telling a complete falsehood" (444a).

It is not difficult for twenty-first-century readers to take the tripartite soul as a model containing partial truths about human psychology. Sexuality, bodily appetite in general, and aggression, when properly and rationally governed, disciplined, and educated, can serve the person and the group. As sources of energy that are, for better or for worse, not under automatic rational control, the pleasure- and status-seeking drives function, in accordance with Socrates' image in the *Phaedrus*, as more or less unruly horses needed to drive the chariot man. Though the horses sometimes need stern discipline and a degree of force, they can serve no purpose at all if they are harmed or killed.[8] Yet, even if reason and will had complete *control* over drives and emotions, the latter might still be misused in the making of bad choices. In the *Republic* Plato's Socrates recognizes this when in Books V–VII he attempts to show that the *rational part* of the feverish soul needs to be transformed by a better *noesis* of the Good (imaged in the cosmic "generosity" of the Sun) before the evils flowing from human action can be removed from personal or political life. Then, too, we have Socrates' remark in Book X that the soul in its true nature (another passage resonating with the *Philebus*) may not be divided into three parts (in our terms, had the evolutionary process run more smoothly, we would not have a triune brain with built-in conflicts, and would not need divine help in the form of rescue but only in the form of encouragement and exhortation and the like).[9]

Even if the tripartite account is not an adequate account of the truly good and just soul it might be appropriate and timely and fitting to the conversational context in which Socrates finds himself with his interlocutors, as well as to the larger conversational context in which Plato stands in relation to his audience. Plausibly, the militarist ideal of justice and goodness worked out in terms of the tripartite city and soul represents aspects of late fifth- and early fourth-century Spartan and Athenian culture that *rivals* the Socratic/Platonic way of thinking but *captures the interest* of the interlocutors. Socrates wants to mime certain views of his interlocutors, and Plato certain views of his readers, so that they might be held up for examination and scrutiny, and in the best case called into question by those interlocutors and readers, so that they might gain self-knowledge of their own ignorance of the true good. In Plato's depiction, neither Glaucon nor Adeimantus ever actually comes around to seeing the serious problems with the city-soul analogy as a means for discovering justice. Each is unimpressed by the fact that the putatively "just" soul is modeled upon a city which is a violent aggressor against its neighbors. Plato depicts them as presuming to know from the outset what justice really is, as accepting the conventional (contractarian) notion of justice as *self-restraint in one's actions toward others in pursuit of self-interest in respect of external goods*.

Stages 3 and 4: Reorientation and Return to the Original Questions about Justice in Books 8–9

These deficient conceptions of just city and soul continue to dominate the discourse of the *Republic* in Books II–V. But after the introduction of the trope of the philosopher-ruler in the middle of Book V and until the end of Book VII, the tripartite city and soul suddenly disappear! The conversation begins to focus upon the Forms and the Good and upon the content of the mathematical studies propaedeutic to dialectic. In this middle section, which in Miller's terms is the *reorientation* section, Socrates not only calls for a reconsideration of the nature of the virtues (hinting again that the Book IV account is inadequate) but also offers, in the Divided Line, a non-tripartite division of the powers of the soul (that ought to be compared and contrasted with the division of pleasure and knowledge in the *Philebus*). Indeed, in the Divided Line *logos* we find a model of the powers of the just soul in their relationship very different from the model of the tripartite soul. Socrates introduces, with the help of collection and division of the truth-seeking powers of the soul (the Divided Line), a new view of the soul's nature and powers based on the notion that the soul is capable of noetic and philosophical insight into the generosity of the Good. The new view of the soul requires the re-envisioning of a new just city as an image of the dispositions of a philosophical and just soul (perhaps sketched in the final division of statesmanship in the *Statesman*, and perhaps in the *Laws*). From the standpoint of the new and higher view Socrates attempts to display the half-truths and misconceptions of Glaucon's view. The whole *Republic* juxtaposes the *conventional politieia* of Books II–IV, its moral psychology, and its attempt to manage human badness by force (by means of more or less totalitarian "social engineering"), with the *philosophic politeia* of Books V–VII, its different moral psychology, and its method of inquiry into the Good.

Having disappeared from the central section of the *Republic*, the tripartite soul is brought back into play at the beginning of Book VIII. This coincides with a transition from the *reorientation* stage of the conversation to the *exegesis* stage—the stage in which Socrates returns to the original question about whether justice pays—but now *with the reorienting conception of philosophy as inquiry into, and imitation of, the true Good in the background*, and with the intent of testing the interlocutors for any insight they might have gained from the reorientation. At 543cd Socrates, apparently referring to the discussion of philosophy and of philosophic rule as a "digression," says to Glaucon: "Since we have completed this discussion, let's recall the *point at which we began the digression that brought us here* [pothen deuro exetrapometha, 'the part of the discussion from which we "turned aside" to come to where we are now'], so that we can continue on the same path where we left off." To which Glaucon replies: "That isn't difficult, for, much the same as now you were talking as if you had completed the description of the city. You said that you would class both the city you described and the man who is like it as good, even though, it seems, you had a still finer city and man to tell us about. But, in any case, you said that if this city was the right one, the others were faulty." The dialogue here indicates that even Glaucon is aware, however dimly, of a radical discontinuity between the pre-philosophic city of Books II–V (described at 427d as the city of Adeimantus, so dark and cave-like that an "adequate light" is needed in order to explore its justice and injustice), and the corresponding kind of soul modeled upon it, and the "still finer city and man" of Books V–VII. When Glaucon says "if this city was the right one," he is clearly referring to the tripartite pre-philosophic city, and when he mentions "the others" he is clearly referring to the tripartite timocracy, oligarchy, democracy, and tyranny. The fact that he still supposes the tripartite city is possibly the right one indicates that he is not grasping Socrates' suggestion.

Socrates' leading suggestions at the exegesis stage of the conversation (as in all four stages) are addressed to the interlocutor on one level *but addressed by Plato to the reader/auditor* on another. When, as often happens in the exegesis stage, the interlocutor has *not* grasped the reorienting conceptions or the ways in which they serve to refute the errors of the first two stages, the guide reverts to pre-reorientation modes of discourse. In Books VIII–IX, as has often been pointed out, Socrates suddenly begins to speak again in terms of the tripartite city and soul. It is as if Socrates is going back down into the Cave of the sick *polis* of Books II–IV, having briefly emerged out of the Cave during the discussion of Philosophy and the Good, needing now to revert to employing the language of the dim-witted Cave dwellers in order to be understood. All this suggests that Plato wants to associate the decline of regimes with the dis-unified state of the soul in the pre-philosophical *polis* and wants the parable of the decline to *further expose the deficiencies of the divided tri-partite soul*, at least to his best readers if not to Glaucon and Adeimantus.

To his pre-philosophic interlocutors, Socrates characterizes the parable of decline only as the first of three demonstrations that (a) justice "pays" and (b) the tyrant is miserable. On the surface, it seems that he is endorsing the aristocratic regime but bemoaning the inevitability of its decline. A significant problem with this reading, though, is that it invites the question whether any "good" regime would inevitably degenerate into an inferior one. Can any regime that "inevitably" falls apart have truly been the best regime? But when Socrates faults the Promethean breeding program as the thing that triggers the decline of the aristocracy into worse forms, he seems to be trying to show Glaucon and the others, in a way that will not anger them or violate their trust, something they do not yet understand. It is that a city whose structure as depicted the way it is in Books II–V, a city with citizens whose moral psychology mirrors that structure, is *bound to decline toward tyranny* unless it is rescued, in the sense of being completely reoriented, by philosophy. If Glaucon does not grasp this, Plato wants his best readers to grasp it. The idea is that human rulers who do not recognize their insufficiency and their ignorance of the Good are tempted to claim an omnipotence that is not their due, and inevitably decline toward tyranny. More radically, he wants them to grasp that the highest kind of "ruling," the practice of the true art of politics or statesmanship, is, as Socrates said in the *Gorgias*, the practice of philosophy as Socrates practiced it, a *craft* that serves its clients (compare the continuum of crafts in the *Statesman*). It is true that Socrates explicitly characterizes the parable of decline as but the first of three demonstrations that justice pays and that the tyrant is miserable. But presumably Socrates, aware that Glaucon has only half understood the digression on philosophy, and that he does not altogether comprehend Socrates' implicit condemnation of the aristocratic regime and soul, knows that he can at least achieve the limited goal of carrying on in the language of the Cave with the promised demonstration that justice pays and that Thrasymachean nihilism leads to misery.[10]

Not one of the leading factions or ruling parts in the five polities declining toward tyranny "rules" by reason understood as inquiry into the true nature of the human good. Recall that in Book IV Socrates said that the *logistikon* (thinking part) "rules" in the aristocratic soul without defining what kind of rational work this ruling consisted in, indeed suggesting that it did little more than calculate about the maximization of external goods. In Books V–VII, then, while apparently abandoning the tripartite model, he examined the notion of "philosophical" rule, and, by implication, made suggestions about the true work of reason.[11] If Books VIII–X constitute a *critical return to*, and *exegetical examination of*, the structure of the pre-philosophical city, it makes sense to suppose that Socrates there employs the language of the Cave in such a way as to express the importance of philosophical inquiry into goodness, recasting the *logistikon* as itself passionate for truth (for "true" pleasure) and goodness (the "best" pleasures), with the result that the other interests atrophy in the face of its over-riding interest.[12]

Only rule based upon philosophical inquiry aims at the well-being of the entire city or person in its true constitution, ensuring a beneficial outcome for groups or parts by *eliminating conflict* among them. Only such rule acts not by force but by pursuit of *common goods*. A key implication of the parable of the decline of polities is that only the philosopher's conception of happiness is just and unselfish, because the goods sought by the aristocrat, timocrat, oligarch, democrat, and tyrant are not common goods but rather zero-sum goods that can be gained only at another's expense. Striving for individualistic bourgeois success in the "aristocratic" way cuts one off from service to—and community with—others. Striving for prestige requires the inferiority of others. Striving for unlimited wealth impoverishes others. Striving for uninhibited negative freedom to satisfy moods and disordered desires deprives others of their negative and positive freedoms. Striving for tyrannical power deprives the citizen body of all freedoms. But knowledge and the other goods internal to rational crafts can be shared without being lessened because they constitute a common good; under normal circumstances such goods are even increased by being shared. Socrates began in Book II by promising to show some selfish individuals that justice pays and injustice harms the individual agent. But now in Book IX he ends by showing that the truest goods are *common* goods achievable only in community with others and that the pursuit of untrue goods brings harm at once to the individuals pursuing them and to the others with whom they come into conflict in pursuing them.

The Tripartite Soul "Not a Complete Falsehood": Two Senses of Truth and Falsehood

We can make better sense of Socrates' claim that the Tripartite Soul is "not a complete falsehood" if we distinguish between two senses of Truth and Falsehood. We have argued that Socrates uses the model as a teaching tool in his conversation with Glaucon and Adeimantus, as a piece of truth-conducive philosophical rhetoric designed to lead them to *self-scrutiny* and to deeper insight *into the deficiencies of their political and moral conceptions and practices*. The model falls short of "that which *is*" and misleadingly makes out the parts of the soul to be "autonomous" agent-like individuals. Nevertheless, despite these deficiencies, this model of the whole person helps to bring to light flawed conceptions of political justice and of the virtues exercised by "autonomous" individuals. The autonomy of the parts mirrors the autonomy of the persons. Socrates uses the model not only to scrutinize the failings of the "aristocratic" kind of person whose "justice" is *self-restraint in his or her actions toward others in pursuit of his or her own interests in respect of external goods*, but also to reveal the flawed conceptions of happiness guiding the lives of the other four types of persons. Plato uses the model in a similar way *vis a vis* his audience. If we distinguish two senses of truth, we can now see why the doctrine of the tripartite soul is true in one sense (not a "complete falsehood") and false in another (not an "exact grasp"). In an epistemological sense, truth is the adequation of thought to actual reality, even when this reality is not "ideal." In another, ontological sense, truth is the beautiful existence of a thing that is manifesting the normative order of its true and ideal Form. An idea has *epistemological* truth when it is an *adequate representation or sign* of an extra-mental reality (in this case of a set of prevalent flawed political and moral practices, and a flawed conception of moral psychology); a thing has *ontological* truth when it is an *adequate realization of* the idea or Form it exemplifies (often an idea or Form in the mind of its maker). The tripartite soul doctrine is "not a complete falsehood" because it has some degree of epistemological truth, some degree of verisimilitude. It brings to light an array of related types of sick and selfish political and moral practice, based upon mistaken conceptions of the human good, useful for eliciting diagnostic self-scrutiny in Glaucon and Adeimantus. But it is a model of types of soul that lack ontological truth (are *ontologically* false) because they are out of accord with the normative order of the Form of human life, because they are not true to type in respect of human goodness. The more exact grasp of the normative order of the good human life that Socrates works up in the *Philebus*, on the other hand, is both an epistemologically true and illuminating model of the normative order governing the healthy human soul *and* a norm of a human life that has ontological truth in being a beautiful and good life of its kind.

Notes

1. Ferrari notes (165–76, 189) well that the tripartite soul in Book IV is a soul in mental conflict, that its *logistikon* neither has its own goal (say, truth or moral goodness) nor considers anything other than external advantage (or whatever goal is given it through socialization), and that it may be in control without working toward a good end. He well says that the tripartite soul described at the end of Book IV cannot be the ideally just soul, in part because it is based around its spirited part and in part because its *logistikon* is not up to serving as an alternative base.

2. In Books VIII and IX the ascendancy of a particular class or soul part is linked to the dominance of a particular kind of striving or desire.

3. David Loomis writes: "In the city made in speech, the postulated luxury required that the city maintain itself in a state of war (373e). This in turn gave rise to the guardian class, whose breeding and training occupies the rulers

(374b–76b). So, too, in the soul, the unruliness of the appetites evokes and sustains a conflict in the soul which requires the alliance of the calculated and spirited parts in order to maintain order" (92).

4. For a discussion of how this structure is relevant to reading the *Phaedrus* and Book X of the *Republic*, see Moes (1–21).

5. For a longer discussion, see Miller (xxiii–xxxiii).

6. See note 3.

7. In a private communication to me, Miller suggested that I might read the just city and soul of Book IV "as a 'mean' (appropriate, timely, fitting) between the vicious types of city and citizen that its forceful subordination of spiritedness and appetites to reason overcomes and the soul of the philosopher that is transformed by the vision of the Good," and that I might read the tripartition "as allowing the basic conflict of the soul, and city, to become visible, *even as it is held in check*, in the cautious and self-protective possessive personality of a Glaucon on his best but ungenerous behavior [emphasis mine]." Miller's suggestion is that the tripartition model not only diagnoses the root conflict in the soul and city but also serves to encourage Glaucon and the others, who remain untransformed by the vision of the Good, to work at least for a kind of continence that falls short of true virtue.

8. The imperfect integration of reason with the drives and emotions has been illustrated by a much-cited work of brain science (MacLean). See also Kamtekar (167–202) and Burnyeat (1–23).

9. See Pendergast, especially the chapter entitled "The Problem of Evil" and the subsection of that chapter entitled "Concupiscence and Aggression."

10. In the second and third parts of that demonstration, in both of which the tripartite soul continues to be deployed—the arguments that the just life is more *pleasant* than the unjust life—Socrates presents some of the implications of the digression on philosophy without leaving the framework of the tripartite soul. He attempts to show, in a way understandable to non-philosophical interlocutors still speaking the "language of the Cave" and interested more in pleasure as they understand it than in knowledge, just what is wrong with the conceptions of happiness and the Good that characterize the leading factions of the five tripartite polities and the ruling parts of the five tripartite souls.

11. Ferrari notes that the *logistikon* has radically changed in nature in the second and third arguments against the tyrannical life in Books VIII and IX, having morphed from a mere deliberative supervisor of the other elements in the interest of the individual's success in relation to external goods into a drive to discover truth, truth about the best pleasures (165). Ferrari takes this development to show that Plato's "full picture of the human soul emerges only gradually in the *Republic*," leaving open the possibility that a suitably re-described tripartite soul might be endorsed by Plato (165). But in this he misses the full significance of the *reorientation* and *exegesis* sections of the conversation.

12. It can be argued that Book X constitutes a second stage of the exegesis section of the *Republic*, in which Socrates returns not to the original question about whether justice pays and the tyrant is miserable but to the question concerning the importance of mimetic drama to the inquiry into goodness.

Works Cited

Blossner, Norbert. "The City-Soul Analogy." *The Cambridge Companion to Plato's Republic*, edited by G. R. F. Ferrari, Cambridge UP, 2007, pp. 45–85.

Burnyeat, Myles. "The Truth of Tripartition." *Proceedings of the Aristotelian Society*, vol. 106, 2006, pp. 1–23.

Ferrari, G. R. F. "The Three-Part Soul." *The Cambridge Companion to Plato's Republic*, edited by G. R. F. Ferrari, Cambridge UP, 2007, pp. 165–201.

Kamtekar, Rachana. "Speaking with the Same Voice as Reason: Personification in Plato's Psychology." *Oxford Studies in Ancient Philosophy*, vol. 31, Winter 2006.

Loomis, David Eugene. "The Philosophical *Praxis* of Rhetoric in Plato's *Republic*." University of Notre Dame, PhD dissertation, 1979.

MacLean, Paul. *A Triune Concept of the Brain*. U of Toronto P, 1973.

Miller, Mitchell. "Introduction: Problems of Interpretation." *The Philosopher in Plato's Statesman*. Parmenides, 2004, pp. xxiii–xxxiii.

———. "A More 'Exact Grasp' of the Soul? Tripartition in *Republic* IV and Dialectic in the *Philebus*," *Truth: Studies of a Robust Presence*, edited by Kurt Pritzl, Studies in Philosophy and the History of Philosophy, Catholic U of America P, 2009, pp. 40–101.

Moes, Mark. "Dialectical Rhetoric and Socrates' Treatment of Mimetic Poetry in the *Ion* and in Book 10 of the *Republic*." *Philosophy Study*, vol. 1, no. 1, June 2011, pp. 1–21.

Pendergast, Richard. *Cosmos*. Fordham UP, 1973.

The Unity of Being

Parviz Morewedge[1]

Through a history-of-ideas approach, this essay highlights several East Asian perspectives in order to facilitate a non-Eurocentric approach to a meta-History of the West.[2] Often, such a history takes for granted a narrative starting with ancient Hebraic studies and moving teleologically through Attic Greek, Christian, Roman (secular and Holy) to Western Euro-American philosophies. The archaic approach of this study shifts the present memory of our perception of the past; it recovers the modern Oxford-Harvard hijacking of Greece from its Egypto-Irenic origin as it sees the Greek corpus through the eyes of scholars in the Middle East and North Africa.[3] With an emphasis on the logic of archaic-Shi'a doctrines and philosophical features of Hinduism and Zoroastrianism (beginning in sixth-century BCE Persia), this essay shows that the archaic Indo-European age is philosophically valuable in its own right even as it facilitated later conversations. The essay also provides logically distinct alternatives to the Western monotheistic approach as it clarifies the nature of philosophical analysis through the influences of some philosophers of the archaic age for whom logic, poetry, mathematics, and philosophy are integrated. Perhaps the essay's distinguishing mark is constructing a language for ουσία (*ousia*—substance, essence, true being) that highlights the Indic and Muslim senses of mysticism conceived as a unity of being by contrast with the underlying dualism of formal monotheistic theologies. Plotinus's vocabulary of a reed being cut from its root—from its source—shows this same longing for reunification as the analogy of the daughter, who, recognizing the absolute love for, of, and with the father, wants no otherness, no alienation (623).[4]

The Zoroastrian-Indic Connection: The Cosmic Dance of the Normative and the Experiential

Although scholars disagree on the specific time of Zoroastrianism, all agree that the Achaemenid Empire (550–330 BCE) adopted Zoroastrianism and that Zoroastrianism is connected with ancient Hinduism. There is a close resemblance between the vocabulary of ancient Indic sacred texts, the *Rig Vedas*, and the Zoroastrian *Avesta*. Likewise, there are similarities between the Hindu and Zoroastrian connections of the cosmos and ουσία with ethics and social justice in the human world. In the original Hinduism, Devas were the personification of cosmic passions and did not exist as a specific entity outside of the iconic mythological significations. Undermining the unity of all being, the Magi (the priestly caste), intentionally misinterpreted the Devas as evil forces in order to create fear and collect sacrifices, such as crops and cattle from farmers, formally in the name of the Devas but actually for themselves. *Avesta*—the major Zoroastrian scared writings—include explicit calls to end the injustice of sacrificing crops and cattle, which are for the human farmers to consume and not to appease "evil" forces that do not exist. Zoroaster—like Moses, Jesus, and Muhammad—was a reformer whose practical theology sought social justice for the common humanity.

    A notable feature of the archaic age—with the exception of the ascetic Manicheans and some Gnostics—is a positive regard for both the material aspect of the transcendental phenomena and for a pragmatic/normative dimension of human life (this is also true of the archaic-Shi'a perspective). In this vein, the so-called Devas are not specific actual deities, but general-universal icons of human passions, and Evil is depicted not as a substance but as the privation of life force. In contrast to the fixed rituals of monotheistic orthodoxy, Hindu worshippers vary their dances based on their reception of a universal passion. Often depicted as the Hindu God of destruction, Shiva performs a cosmic dance, which symbolizes the archetypal dialectics of various "life games" of destruction and rejuvenation of the cosmos and the cycle of birth and death. It is remarkable that the archaic Indic creed synthesizes the personal-particular with the divine-like universal rather than positing an alienation of human-particular from divine-universal.

In the Zoroastrian phase, as the Divine or Wise Lord (*Ahurā Mazdā*)) needs humanity to achieve its goal of providing the best possible world, a human will and the Divine plan are de-alienated. While the nineteenth-century Friedrich Nietzsche advocated that one needs to "kill God in order to be free" (84), the Zoroastrian implies the immanent status of *Ahurā Mazdā* that logically distinguishes it from the traditional monotheistic sense of the Divine. While Sunni Islam—following The Book of Job—does not postulate normative Goodness to Divine action, Shi'a Islam, by contrast, insists that Justice is a necessary aspect of the Divine. Indirectly, the welfare of humanity is embedded in the theology of the Divine.

The multi-dimensionality of the richness of humanity's material experience is another, though connected, way of seeing the unity of being in Persian, Hindu, and Zoroastrian wisdom traditions. The Iranian philosopher-scientist ibn Sīnā remarks on potentials of sexuality enacted in a desire for pleasure as a symbolic act signifying the sacredness of love and family, and as a pragmatic contribution to the sustainability of human race. Similarly, in Zoroastrianism, humanity is an instrument of the Divine actualization of the good world. Consequently, the will of the individual and the will of the divine will merge as a will-to-power/life-force that fights the privation of the joy of life.

These archaic Shi'a and Zoroastrian conceptions are metaphysically removed from the transcendent (in the sense of Immanuel Kant's noumena or *Ding an sich*) of the monotheistic sense of "the ultimate being." This monotheism implies free will; partakes of the divine predicates—for example, omnipotence—responsibility for genesis and persistence; and is the final cause of the rest of the universe. Moreover, God is the ultimate source of all norms and morality as expressed in the sacred scriptures. Finally, the Divine is more intimate with, and closer to, creatures than they are to themselves.

The primary Islamic philosophical use of virtue agrees with its Greek (ἀρετή, areté) and Zoroastrian (*āshā*) equivalents, signifying virtue as the perfection of an entity. Evil, again, is not a separate entity but is, instead, conceptualized as a lack of self-realization—as a privation or lack of unity. For example, wisdom is the excellence or virtue of human beings, and sensing courage is the virtue for the faculty of will. This rendering is opposed to the later ascetic view of virtue that implies a denial of bodily pleasures such as lust. According to Zoroastrian ethics, cardinal virtues include good universal wisdom (λόγος, *logos*) (*guftār-i nīk*), good thought (*pendār-i nīik*), and good action (*kirdār-i nīik*). The exercise of virtue is central to this creed. The Wise Lord (*Ahurā Mazdā*) needs human beings to actualize its will to power, which is to perfect the virtues of humanity through positive tasks such as rearing a family and the productive use of animals.[5]

As previously mentioned, Evil (*ahrīman*) is in the privation (*adam*) of virtue by a "lie" (*dūrūg*, the root of the English word "drugs"), such as the Magi's' sacrifice of domestic animals supposedly to appease the Deva's Virtue, which is actually the subversion of the proper community's need for animal husbandry. According to Henry Corbin, Zoroastrian influences are also evident in the Iranian and Shīʿī ethical theories. In the Shīʿī "jural" code of ethics, moral virtue is found not in the utility of the product of an act but in the "good intention" (*nīyat-i khair*) of the agent (91–96).

The Muslim vision of this political model depended on the Platonic notion of the king as a philosopher who is aware of the moral axioms suited to a healthy polity (*Republic* 473d). Muslims envision a prophet-statesman as the philosopher-king endowed with a prophetic sacred intelligence (*'aql qudsī*). The twentieth-century Shi'ism of Ruhollah Khomeini's Jurist-Imam connection (*vilayet-i fakih*) echoes Plato's model (*Republic* 608b–609c). Muslim philosopher Abu Nasr al-Fārābī (870–950), sought an essential unity among apparent diversities, e.g., religion and philosophy, Plato and Aristotle, theoretical thought and political context of humanity. In this vein he finds in philosophy reasons to achieve happiness, but the instrumentality of religion is needed to obtain virtue.

Following Plato's critiques of alternative forms of polity to his ideal city, al-Fārābī identified corrupt cities as the ignorant city (*al-madīna al-jāhilīya*), the dissolute city (*al-madīna al-fāsiqa*), the turncoat city (*al-madīna al-mubaddala*), and the straying city (*al-madīna al-ḍālla*). Al-Fārābī's Greek heritage is already visible on the most basic conceptual level. A society, on his account, is an association of human beings collaborating "[i]n order to preserve [themselves] and to attain [their] highest perfections." Without collaboration, he insists, "man cannot attain the perfection, for the sake of which his inborn nature [*fitra*] has been given to him" (*Perfect State* V, 15, 1:229). In function of their size, associations can or cannot furnish the basis for a "perfect [*kamil*] society." Thus, the smallest unit suited to harbor a perfect society is a city (*madina*). Smaller associations, such as villages, quarters, streets, and houses are *per se* imperfect; larger ones, like nations and the "union of all the societies in the inhabitable world," by contrast, are perfect. That is, the virtuous world (*al-ma'mūra al-fāḍila*) will exist only when all its constituent nations collaborate to achieve happiness (*Perfect State* V, 15, 2:229–31).

On ουσία and Time: From Zoroastrian to Medieval Thought

Medieval investigators were aware of the non-Greek, pre-monotheistic dimensions of Zoroastrian traditions.[6] According to al-Fārābī," the colloquial meanings of the Arabic *jawhar* (substance), of Persian derivation, were "gem," denoting something of particular value, and "ore," denoting that which constitutes the core of a particular kind of being. In philosophical parlance, *jawhar* became the standard translation of Aristotle's ουσία, which denotes the essence of being. This idea of substance or ουσία provides the basis for attributing being to other sorts of things—a fact that al-Fārābī readily interpreted as a systematic account of the colloquial meaning of *jawhar* (al-Fārābī, *Letters* 1.13.62–73, 97–105). The Arabic '*araḍ* (accident) was standardly used for the Greek συμβεβηκός (*symbebēkos*), denoting the accidental features that exist by virtue of substances. Although widespread agreement seems to have prevailed about the general meaning of the terms, a wide variety of views were put forth on the more specific question of what sort of thing the substance (and its accidents) is.

In the Greek context, Aristotle famously gives two slightly different accounts of ουσία. The essence of being, mentioned above, is one. A second account is in *Categories* 5, where substance is "that which is not said of a subject and which is not in a subject" (2a10–17). Although Shi'a philosophers accepted such a view of substance, they never accepted a notion of an infinite actual entity such as the Aristotelian unmoved mover. At best, they considered such a concept as the beholder of the λόγος in the best of all possible worlds—void of any free will or consciousness. Muslim philosopher Mir Damad (1561–1631/2) proferred an interesting solution to the cosmogony problem of how first substances—peculiar entities that persist in a temporal duration—are generated somehow from an atemporal entity such as the God of Monotheism or the Necessary Existent of ibn Sīnā by involving static universals. He postulated three categories that delineate different references to time:

1. meta-time/a-temporality (*Sarmad*) that applies to God or The Necessary Existent—entities to which temporality is not applicable due to their essence.

2. Eternity (*dah*r) that applies to universals that are not subject to change and are the formal dimensions of the changeable.

3. Temporality (*zaman*) that applies to particulars that are subject to change.

For Mir Damad, God generates the universals that in their realm of eternity, "being an existent" does not apply to them, as they are designable in light of God's. He follows ibn Sīnā and Tusi in asserting that "will" cannot be applied to a Diety or The Necessary Existent that are not subject to change (3–5).

There is a confusion among some recent scholars of Islamic philosophy between the use of being ("being-qua-being") and being (as an existent or first substance). In the Archaic-Shi'a tradition, the ultimate being (the God of monotheism) is neither a being nor a substance. As scholar of Scholasticism Étienne Gilson points out, in monotheism, God is the cause of the world—including matter; to that end, neither cosmologies of co-eternity nor emanation can be compatible with monotheism (3, 58). In sum, the difference between the archaic-Shi'a tradition and the subsequent medieval period is logically very clear. For example, the ultimate being of the archaic-Shi'a era is neither the Aristotelian substance (ουσία) nor the transcendent God of monotheism. The two life-games/constructs are logically incompatible. That is, in contrast with the Aristotelian and transcendent monotheistic traditions, the archaic-Shi'a posits no creation out of nothing, no divine will, no divinely revealed meta-nature source of norms, no independence from—and alienation with—human beings.

The Mediating Spirit

"The Spirit" (*penuma, ruha, rūḥ, nafas*), primarily mediates between the body and the soul. In its religious usage, spirit appears either as an icon such as God's breath or as a name for some of God's creatures, such as spirits and *jinns* who mediate between the heavenly Divine and humanity. A number of philosopher-mystics of the School of Unity of Being (*waḥdat al-wujūd*) attempt to forge a union with the Divine by a vision of spiritual embodiment of humanity and by a depiction of bodies such as the sun, the moon, and shrines of saints, as epiphanies of heavenly spirits. Such an agenda is a mystical extension of the first principles of religion (*uṣūl al-dīn*), which secure through God an absolute unity (*tawḥīd*) with the entire cosmos, including internal-spiritual dimensions (*bāṭin*). In this light, humanity strives by "spiritualization" to achieve—at least in a phenomenological perspective—a de-alienating intimacy (*uns*) with the heavens; the heavens are taken to be the primordial ground of being as well as their ultimate final cause.

The inclusion of "spirit" (*rūḥ*) in sense perception was documented by Abū Ḥāmid al-Ghazālī in *Mishkāt al-anwār* (*The Niche of Lights*), his treatise on the Qurʾānic sūrah on light. Al-Ghazālī outlines five senses of light as spirit. The first is the sensate spirit (*al-rūḥ al-ḥisās*), the experience of the five senses appearing first in the animal level of life. The second level is the imaginal spirit (al-rūḥ al-khiyālī), which concerns imagination by recall, an ability that develops in human beings at a later age and is available only to those animals with complex learning ability. In spite of its inspiring aims, the imaginal spirit originates from clay and its result is discernible to measure, shape, and discrete quantitative explanation. However, imagination organizes knowledge and is a beginning of rational knowledge.[7]

The third kind of spirit is the rational spirit (*al-rūḥ al-ʿaqlī*), the human ability to receive meanings (*maʿānī*), which surpasses both sensation and imagination and enables the quality of abstraction. The fourth kind is the reflective spirit (*al-rūḥ al-fikrī*), which exhibits deduction and abstract reasoning. Finally, the fifth level is the prophetic-sacred spirit (*al-rūḥ al-qudsī al-nabawī*), which is reserved for the prophets and for some 280 Spirit friends of God who intuit knowledge of the unseen world as well as meta-axioms of cosmology.[8] Similarly, the Book of Job 12:10 reads: "In His [God's] hand is the life-force [*nephesh*] of every living thing and the spirit [*ruāḥ*] of every human being." The Hebrew *ruāḥ* ("spirit") is related to *nephesh* ("breath") as the Qurʾānic Arabic "spirit" (*rūḥ*) is related to "breath" (*nafas*) (Morewedge, "Spirit" 278).

Henry Corbin elaborates that *"jism"* refers to an inert body and *"jasad"* to the physical remains of a person who has been endowed with the heavenly originated spirit. In the Muslim world, one regards a *jasad* not as a complex of Epicurean atoms that merely returns to nature, but as a sober reminder of a specific spiritual entity that has left the body and persists somewhere in the heavens (99–101).

In this vein, the attitude of religious Muslims parallels the perspective of Plotinus, who, according to Porphyry's account, envisions the body as a musician's instrument that is left behind after the release of the souls-spirits from the body to return to its primordial origin (Gerson).

In Islam, "spirit" thus has many senses, including "breath" in the divine creation of human beings; certain heavenly creatures, sometimes *jinns*, who function as mediators between heaven and earth; and, finally, "spirituality," the mystic's way to achieve union with the ultimate being.

The Muslim concept of spirit is not confined to religious contexts. The Islamic sciences of optics and medicine also make use of "spirit" (*rūḥ*). In *The Animal Spirit Doctrine and the Origins of Neurophysiology*, C. U. M. Smith, Eugenio Frixione, Stanley Finger, and William Clower offer three major examples of Muslim contributions to the medical sciences: Ḥunayn ibn Isḥāq, *Art of Medicine* (c. 850); al-Majūsī, *Complete Book of Medical Art* (980); and ibn Sīnā, *Canon of Medicine* (1025). Ibn Isḥāq, who is known to the West by his Latinized name, Johannitius, states that the optic nerve is a complex composite with a hollow shape. He assigns "hardness" to the motor nerves and softness to the sensory nerves, in which he placed the animal spirit (*rūḥ ḥayawānī*). This spirit originated from the vital spirit arising from its seat in the heart, resulting in movement, imagination, and reflection. These functions resemble the faculties of the animal soul, which include the genesis of the estimative internal sense (*wahm*).

An impressive account of Muslims' use of spirit in medicine is found in ibn Sīnā's *Kitāb al-qānūn fī al-ṭibb* (*Canon of Medicine*). In this work, as well as in his *Poems on Medicine*, the physician-philosopher extends the medical works of Galen of Alexandria (130–200) into a comprehensive theoretical account of the nature of theory and praxis of medicine that includes a set of treatments for various types of illnesses. A noteworthy dimension of this treatise is an empirical and behaviorist methodology, where accounts of medical remedies do not have any references to religion or to dominant normative modes of behavior, or any nonphysical references to spirituality or any specific mode of life. The physician determines treatment for the patient through the method of observing human behavior. The notion of spirit is explained as a vital force that acts as the link between the body, soul, and spirit. It is the role of the vital force to maintain a perfect equilibrium within the elements of the body, and between the elements of the body and the environment. There are three aspects or spirits to the vital force: the natural spirit, the animal spirit, and the vital spirit. In fact, it is reasonable to describe his system of medicine as depicting human beings as a complex set of functions, where spirit is merely one of the natural constituents of a unified human being without any reference to its supposedly otherworldly origin.

Monistic Mysticism: οὐσία and Light

As Zaehner writes in *Hindu and Muslim Mysticism*, a number of Muslim authors, especially Tusi, successfully crafted their version of Islam, via Mysticism, to preserve the essential de-alienation dimensions of Hinduism, as the two following logical distinctions illuminate. First, there are distinctions between and among formal religion, philosophical theology, and Monistic Mysticism. With respect to cosmogony (formal religion), God creates the world supposedly out of nothing. In philosophical theology (à la Aristotle's *Physics*), God and the World are co-eternal. In mysticism, The One begat the rest of the cosmos, and the human soul, through a process of self-realization, returns to unite with the One (119–20). Second, Islamic monistic mysticism may be clarified by the following parameters:

- Unity of being—the case of light

  ◊ All entities are essentially connected. Persons are viewed as modes, like waves of a sea; essentially the ultimate being and human being have the same designation. A useful analogy is Islam's illumination doctrine where bodies are expressed as particles of light and mental phenomena as illumination. God, or the ultimate being, is expressed as light of light (*nur-i a la nur*).

- A mediator figure

  ◊ If human beings are finite and God/nature/the One is transcendent and indefinite, then one needs a mediator figure—a link between the human and the ultimate being. According to ibn Sīnā, we have three different senses of the mediator figure:

    — Religion—the angel Gabriel brings the message from God to Muhammad in the cave.

    — Philosophy—the active intelligence is the intelligence of the moon (the last heavenly entity) from which fire-earth, air-water emanate.

    — Mysticism—the mystical sage (like Shams for Rumi)[9]

  ◊ Persian carpets and paintings embody these ideas. Their birds resemble the intelligence which flies to the heavens, while the four-footed animals symbolize bodies. The tree represents the tree of life.

- The way of salvation—love and intoxication

Obviously if a mystic begins by him/herself as an ego-type of a normal person and seeks a union with God, he or she must go through a path of self-realization, in two phases: states (*ahwal*) and stations (*maqamat*). A station is a position that a person achieves by performing certain tasks, such as overcoming his particular obsession with vanity. This is achieved by following the directions of the master. A state is an attitude, which happens to a person who changes her world perspective; for example, after becoming a parent or at the death of a parent, one goes through a significant change. The world is no longer the same. The aim of the mystical master is to make a person ready to move to the final phase of the mystical trip.

It is only through the intoxication of love that people become free.[10] Mystical development moves from the phase of Alienation to the phase of Love to the phase of Union. In Religion, mystical development is a harmony between persons and God by persons following God's commands. Taking a philosophical path, a person becomes divine-like when he or she is involved with certain tasks such as mathematics, love, and logic, but not with purely sensual activities like eating (without a Eucharist or fasting dimension) and sex (without a love dimension).

Regardless of whether a person starts from a religious or a philosophical perspective (and the two are not easily separated), a person engaged in Mysticism in Hindu, Zoroastrian, and Shi'a traditions goes through several phases in order to embody the divine perspective. In contrast to most monotheistic traditions, in which religious rituals are formal and strict and permit no variation—with the possible exception of a pause for meditation and inner prayer—in Hindu tradition, dances in honor of Shiva (the paradigm for both destruction/re-generation) have a twofold significance. They are both a universal tribute to the archetype of the λόγος of the twofold dialectics of destruction-rejuvenation and also the agent's own intentional embodiment of the universal archetype. In this mode there can be no alienation separating the personal and the external dimension of experience.

This intimacy of personal and the divine is also a prominent feature of Zoroastrian theology. In this tenor, the wise Lord recruits humanity to achieve its noble deed.

Investigations include a twofold dimension. The first is the archaic period's pre-monotheistic monism with a de-alienating essential connection between human beings and the divine. The second uses icons such as the "light motif" (e.g., "sperm," "fire [*Aqni*]," "inner light," "illumination" (*nur* in the Arabic)," "Mithra," and "λόγος," as well as "water") (Widengren 88, 91; Rudolph 336). For example, in the search for a monistic depiction of Cosmos, Zoroastrians use two isomorphic senses of "light." The idea of light as particles depicts the material dimension of the world, and light in the sense of inner illumination depicts the intentional aspect.[11] In addition, as used later by Plato, the Sun as the genesis of light served as a symbolic icon of the ἀρχή (*arché*—first principle) of existence and the mirror of the purity of the Good (*Dasein* in later Existentialist thought) (*Republic* 507b–509c).

A salient feature of Shi'a theology is Tusi's depiction of self-realization only in the intentional-*Dasein* dimension, leaving out—for the first time in Islamic mystical texts—reference to the external station (*maqam*). Remarkable similarities are observable in the doctrines of Tusi, a follower of ibn Sīnā, and the Spinoza-Leibniz expression of European rationalism. Let us note Spinoza's celebrated analogy that persons are not to be viewed as independent substances, but inter-dependent, analogous to waves (mode) of the same sea (substance), expressing variation of a totality (142). In Islamic unity-of-being (*al-wahdat al-wujud*) mysticism, there is only one entity—the One; all others are reflections of the One. In this vein, al-Ghazālī delineates the common assertion on deity, which is there is exactly one God, and the mystics' awareness "that there is none in existence save God" (*Niche* 16). For those who are aware of the secrets of the mystical way—phases of self-realization that are an ascent toward a recognition of unity—existence is "the Divine Blaze," like the burning bush revealed to Moses (Damad 36, 80, 120). The Sufi's position is that the world is a mere blazing of the Divine—like each part of the sea is a mode of the same sea. Following the Platonic tradition, love is a cognitive epistemic vector that leads to a self-realization of unity of the self with the eternal one—as a fire returns to the Sun and a drop of rain returns to the sea.

Muslim monists take the apparent mind-body duality as a preliminary illusion that one overcomes by further reflections.[12] Centuries later and a continent away, Leibniz's celebrated "best of all possible worlds" theodicy reflects Tusi's assertion of a unity between scientific and religious perspectives, ideas he inherited from another Shi'a theologian, Nasir

Khusraw. In sum, the spirit of unity in the tripartite Zoroastrian visions of the good in language—thought-intention-will—and actions facilitated another version of unity for the post-archaic age. It may be labeled as a unified perspectives of various aspects of the religious (breath as the icon), philosophical theology. Science (brain as the icon) and mysticism (heart as the icon) proffer an integrated unity for the subsequent Shi'a tradition and its later inheritors.

Notes

1. To Professor Anthony Preus, a friend of over forty years and a collaborator for organizing conferences for over thirty.

2. Because of space limitations, this essay does not fully reflect my career-long analysis of the syntactical approach to ontology, cosmology, and theology proffered by ibn Sīnā and expanded by Nasir al-Din al-Tusi. These works correlate to and influenced the axiomatic methods of Spinoza and Leibniz, as well as later twentieth-century Western logicians such as Rudolf Carnap (see Morewedge, "Philosophical Analysis").

3. See also Martin Bernal, *Black Athena: The Afroasiatic Roots of Classical Civilization*. In his three-volume series, Bernal argues that modern European thinkers, starting in the eighteenth century, removed archaic and Classical Greece from its Mediterranean cultural context.

4. Several recent scholars have already suggested the links among these traditions. For example, in *Mysticism, Sacred and Profane: An Inquiry into Some Varieties of Praeternatual Experience*, Robert Charles Zaehner delineates two senses of mysticism: religious-isolationist-separative-dualistic (depicting monotheism) and nature-integrating-secular (depicting the archaic age). In *Hindu and Muslim Mysticism*, Zaehner contrasts the Indic and the Muslim (unity-of-being) sense of mysticism with the underlying dualism of formal monotheistic theologies.

This unity is the opposite of the I-Thou model of monotheism that postulates a covenant between humanity (e.g., Noah and Ibrahim) and God. Henry Austryn Wolfson, in *The Philosophy of Spinoza: Unfolding the Latent Process of His Reasoning*, observed that the affinity of Gottfried Wilhelm Leibniz to the Near Eastern heritage was partially based on his familiarity with the works of Baruch Spinoza (1632–1677), who was influenced by the Spanish-Jewish philosopher Moses Maimonides (1138–1204). Maimonides's notion of philosophy, in turn, was based on his study of Muslim philosophers', including ibn Sīnā's (980–1037), work on Aristotle's corpus.

5. Zoroastrianism was an important source for Friedrich Nietzsche's ethics of the "will to power."

6. A paradigm case is Abu Rayham al-Biruni's analyses of the Indic notion of time and a purely experimental approach to physics, over the Greek perspective of time and what he takes to be the Aristotelian-ibn Sīnān tradition of classification of physics as a branch of philosophy (see Morewedge, "Al-Biruni"). Known to the West as a philosophical poet, Omar Khayyām questions the Greek mathematics underlying the synthetic a priori presumption of Euclid's fifth postulate (see Vahabzadeh).

7. Although officially al-Ghazali opposed philosophers' careless treatment of theological doctrines, his mystical writings contain careful, logical philosophical analyses. Al-Ghazālī's vision of imagination was later refined by German philosopher Immanuel Kant (1802), who assigns the role of imagination to instantiate understanding by forming the concept of number.

8. This use of "spirit" for the mental faculty is adopted by later philosophers such as ʿAzīz al-Dīn al-Nasafī in his *Kitāb-i insān-i kāmil* (*The Universal Perfect Being*).

9. For a detailed analysis of ibn Sīnā's scientific method used in this text, see Parviz Morewedge's "Logic of Proofs in Science and Philosophy."

10. Love in Plato's *Symposium* is also a mediator figure and leads people to the Beautiful (202e).

11. Henry Corbin traces the similarities in the Hindu and Shiʿa iconography such as the light and water motifs in *Spiritual Body and Celestial Earth: From Mazdean Iran to Shīʿite Iran*. In a similar vein, Mary Boyce's *A History of Zoroastrianism: Zoroastrianism under the Achaemenians* uses the primary sacred texts such as the *Avesta* and the *Rig Vedas* to identify an Indo-Iranian tradition. A useful parameter for differentiation between this monistic tradition and the later dualistic monotheism is the notion of salvation by de-alienation. Incidentally, for Hegel. Marx, Freud, and Heidegger, alienation indeed is the major issue of humanity. To that end, the ethics of self-realization is used to de-alienate the self from the ground of being, that is, the God of Monotheism and the One of the mystics.

12. A doctrine that Tusi shares with Leibniz is the impossibility of the notion of a material substance because it is incompatible with Euclidean Geometry.

Works Cited

al-Fārābī, Abu Nasr. *The Book of Letters (Kitāb al-ḥurūf)*. Medieval Islamic Philosophical Writings, edited by Muhammad Ali Khalidi, Cambridge UP, 2005, pp. 1–26.

———. *The Perfect State (Mabādiʾ ārāʾ ahl al-madīnat al-fāḍilah)*. 1985. Translated by Richard Walzer, Clarendon, 1998.

al-Ghazālī, Abū Ḥāmid. *The Niche of Lights (Mishkāt al-anwār)*. Translated by David Buchman, Brigham Young UP, 1998.

al-Nasafī, Azīz al-Dīn. *Kitāb al-insān al-kāmil (The Book of the Perfect Human Being)*, edited by Marijan Molé, Chāpkhāna-yi Taban, 1962.
Aristotle. Categories. *The Complete Works of Aristotle: The Revised Oxford Translation*, vol. 1, edited by Jonathan Barnes, Princeton UP, 1984, pp. 1–24.
Avicenna. *The Canon of Medicine (al-Qanun fiʿl-tibb)*, adapted by Laleh Bakhtiar, five volumes. Translated by Peymen Adeli Sardo, Kazi, 1999–2014.
———. *Poem on Medicine: A Textbook on Traditional Medicine*, adapted by Laleh Bakhtiar, Kazi, 2013.
Badawi, Abdurrahman. "New Philosophical Texts, Lost in Greek and Preserved in Arabic Translations." *Islamic Philosophical Theology*, edited by Parviz Morewedge, SUNY Press, 1979, pp. 3–13.
Bernal, Martin. *Black Athena: The Afroasiatic Roots of Classical Civilization*. Princeton UP, 1987.
Boyce, Mary. *A History of Zoroastrianism, Zoroastrianism under the Achaemenians*, vol. 2. 1982. Brill, 2015.
Corbin, Henry. *Spiritual Body and Celestial Earth: From Mazdean Iran to Shīʿite Iran*. Translated by Nancy Pearson, Princeton UP, 1977.
Damad, Mir. *Kitab al-Qabasat (Book of Embers)*, edited by Mehdi Mohaghegh, Toshihiko Izutsu, A. Musavi Bihbanhani, and Ibrahim Dibaji, McGill U, Institute of Islamic Studies, 1977.
Gerson, Lloyd. "Plotinus," *The Stanford Encyclopedia of Philosophy*, edited by Edward N. Zalta, 2018. plato.stanford.edu/archives/fall2018/entries/plotinus
Gilson, Étienne. *Being and Some Philosophers*. Pontifical Institute for Medieval Studies, 1952.
Gruner, Cameron O. *A Treatise on the Canon of Medicine of Avicenna*. Luzac, 1930.
Khomeini, Ruhollah. *Islamic Government: Governance of the Jurist*. 1970. Translated by Hamid Algar, Manor Books, 2002.
Leibniz, Gottfried Willhelm. *Theodicy: Essays on the Goodness of God, the Freedom of Men, and the Origin of Evil*. Translated by E. M. Huggard, Lector House, 2019.
Morewedge, Parviz. "Al Biruni," *Oxford Encyclopedia of Philosophy, Science and Technology in Islam*, edited by Ibrahim Kalin, vol. 1, Oxford UP, 2014, pp. 102–06.
———. "The Analysis of 'Substance' in Tusi's Logic and in the ibn Sinian Tradition." *Essays in Islamic Philosophy and Science*, edited by George Fadlo Hourani, SUNY Press, 1975, pp. 158–88.
———. "Logic of Proofs in Science and Philosophy," *Oxford Encyclopedia of Philosophy, Science and Technology in Islam*, edited by Ibrahim Kalin, vol. 1, Oxford UP, 2014, pp. 486–90.
———. "Philosophical Analysis and Ibn Sīnā's 'Essence-Existence' Distinction," *Journal of the American Oriental Society*, vol. 92, no. 3, American Oriental Society, 1972, pp. 425–35.

———. "The Spirit," *Oxford Encyclopedia of Philosophy, Science, and Technology in Islam*, edited by Ibrahum Kalin, vol. 1, Oxford UP, 2014, pp. 278–83.

Nietzsche, Friedrich. *Thus Spoke Zarathustra: A Book for All and None*. 1954. Translated by Walter Kaufmann. Modern Library, 1995.

Oakes, Jeffrey. "Polynomials and Equations in Arabic Algebra." *Archive for History of Exact Sciences* vol. 63, no. 2, 2009, pp. 169–203.

Plato. *Lysis, Symposium, Gorgias*. Plato in Twelve Volumes, vol. 3. Translated by W. R. M. Lamb, Loeb-Harvard UP, 1925, pp. 73–246.

———. *Republic*. Plato in Twelve Volumes, vols. 5–6. Translated by Paul Shorey, Loeb-Harvard UP, 1969.

Plotinus. *The Enneads*. Translated by Stephen MacKenna, 3rd ed., Oxford UP, 1962.

Rudolph, Kurt. *Gnosis. The Nature & History of Gnosticism*. 1983. Translated by P. W. Coxon, K. H. Kuhn, and R. McLachlan Wilson, Harper, 1987.

Smith, C. U. M., Eugenio Frixione, Stanley Finger, and William Clower. *The Animal Spirit Doctrine and the Origin of Neurophysiology*. Oxford UP, 2012.

Spinoza, Benedict de. *Ethics: Proved in Geometrical Order*, edited by Matthew J. Kisner, Translated by Michael Silverthorne, Cambridge UP, 2018.

Vahabzadeh, Bijan. "Khayyam, Omar xv, as Mathematician." *Encyclopaedia Iranica*, last modified 10 Sept, 2014. www.iranicaonline.org/articles/khayyam-omar-mathematician

Widengren, Geo. *Mani and Manichaeism*. Translated by Charles Kessler, Holt, Rinehart, and Winston, 1965.

Wolfson, Henry Austryn. *The Philosophy of Spinoza: Unfolding the Latent Process of His Reasoning*. 1934. Harvard UP, 2013.

Zaehner, Robert Charles. *Hindu and Muslim Mysticism*. 1960. Bloomsbury, 2016.

———. *Mysticism, Sacred and Profane: An Inquiry into Some Varieties of Praeternatual Experience*. 1957. Oxford UP, 1969.

The Double Meaning of Strife in Hesiod

Joyce M. Mullan

Introduction: Historical Precedents

Many scholars in recent years have honed in on the specifically Greek concept of *Agon* as contest or struggle and its role in preserving democracy. Hannah Arendt in her *Human Condition* started a cottage industry of agonistic democratic theorists. More recently, *Law and Agonistic Politics*, and in particular in that work, Andreas Kalyvas's "The Democratic Narcissus: The Agonism of the Ancients Compared to That of the Post-Moderns," continues the trend. I have learned a most productive analysis of the value of strife as struggle can be found already in Hesiod. After an earlier purely destructive depiction of *Agon*, Hesiod revisits and revises the idea to defend a more productive use of Strife. This will be quite influential in the domestic and international thought and politics of Ancient Greece.

As a reminder, religion and philosophy share with one another an attempt to explain the apparently unexplainable. In the archaic age of Greece, many stories were handed down about gods and humans, and it is almost universally believed they were under the spell of a kind of animism. Namely, they attributed spiritual qualities to what many now explain in terms of natural often material laws. More importantly, poets especially personified many aspects of both nature and human nature. The Presocratic philosophers, also, beginning the transition from myth to science, explained nature in terms of matter and change. Empedocles spoke of four natural elements, earth, air, fire, and water, that were brought together and scattered apart by forces of love and strife.

Early Greeks, indeed, commonly explained phenomena in terms of pairs, and in some of the pre-Socratic philosophers—particularly Heraclitus—in terms of the unity of opposites. Of course, the Presocratics also built upon, and significantly departed from, the early poets, who were also often of a philosophical bent. We can trace the origins of Empedocles' ideas from earlier thinkers, among them Pindar, Homer, Theognis, and Hesiod. The focus of this essay is the double legacy of Strife in Hesiod's *Works and Days*. Following Hesiod, I argue there are two kinds of strife or contest, one good and one evil. One is constructive and supportive of excellence (*Arête*) and the Common Good, the other destructive, hegemonic, and annihilating

Hesiod did write of Strife earlier in his account of the creation of the gods and world in his *Theogony*, and many scholars have noted the ambiguity.[1] In his *Theogony*, Strife is personified (together with many other values) as female. The main topic of this essay is not the misogyny of Hesiod, though other scholars have noticed it, especially in his portrayal of Pandora as a "beautiful evil" ("*Kalos Kakos*"), or his views marriage and wives. He writes: "[H]e had made the beautiful evil to be the price for the blessing, . . . [f]or from her is the race of women and female kind: of her is the deadly race and tribe of women who live amongst mortal men to their great trouble" (585–92). Sadly, misogyny was widespread at the time, despite the fact that many goddesses, including Eris were respected, or even revered in the case of Athena. Even so, much scholarship on sexual asymmetry in ancient societies notes the disparity of power and value assigned to the sexes, a nearly universal fact.[2] Accusations of deception and guile were also found against many other oppressed groups, not just women. Divide-and-conquer tactics on the part of rulers were just as destructive to an honest viewing and equitable treatment of them. Hesiod himself prefigures this, characterizing Strife or Eris as hateful or loathsome. Thus, "loathsome Strife bore painful Toil and Forgetfulness and Hunger and tearful Pains and Combats and Battles and Murders and Slaughters, and Strifes and Lies and Tales and Disputes, and Lawlessness and Recklessness, much like one another, and Oath, who indeed brings most woe upon human beings on the earth, whenever someone willingly swears a false oath" (*Theogony* 224–32).

The *Theogony*, according to Hesiod's own account, was awarded a laurel by the Muses to whom he sang in the opening of the later *Works and Days,* for speaking the truth. More important, Hesiod seems to imply that the Muses tell some poets half-truths (and he suggests that is what they told Homer, too). They can also speak the truth. That is, they can speak both truth and lies, as Katherine Olstein has argued (295–312). Whatever the truth, he does seem to have a pedagogic and ethical purpose in recounting the story, as he will also exhort and remonstrate his own brother, Perses, in *Works and Days*. Robert C. Bartlett argued that Hesiod followed the Muses in mixing truth with lies, as well (179). In the *Theogony*, Hesiod recounts the origin story of the gods as a series of stages, later repeated in his five ages of man in *Works and Days*. Thus, it is a story of punishments and rivalry, justice and injustice, either for excessive competitiveness or to prevent competition.

Zeus, himself, who otherwise is continuously portrayed as Zeus-father, tries to prevent his wife Metis from giving birth to their daughter (Athena) who might rival him in strength and wisdom. Little by little, though Zeus is not uniformly depicted as steadfast and righteous, he is eventually thought to be the guarantor of justice among humans. F. Solmsen, argued that Zeus' reign was morally better than the reigns he superseded. Zeus is also characterized as a long-range thinker who punishes recklessness and suggests that excessive competitiveness ever ends thus (515). Zeus' treatment of Prometheus could be thought of as punishment for his *hubris*, not respecting limits (*Péras*), in giving fire to humans.

There is a positive story about the goddess Strife, famously portrayed in the lead-up to Homer's *Iliad*, in the *Kypria*, fragment 1, that gives a divine rationale for the existence of Strife.

> There was a time when the myriad tribes of men
> wandering pressed down on the thick chest of the broad earth—
> And when Zeus saw this, he pitied her and in his complex
>   thoughts
> He planned to lighten the all-nourishing earth of human beings
> By fanning the great strife of the Trojan War,
> So that he might lighten the weight by death. And then in Troy
> The heroes were dying, and the will of Zeus was being fulfilled.

Hesiod refers to this in his *Works and Days*, as well, writing:

> Cronos' son Zeus made a better and more just third race,
> the divine generation of heroic men who are called
> *hemitheoi*, the earlier generation on the boundless earth.
> And then evil war and dread conflict wiped them out,

some of them under seven-gated Thebes, the Cadmean land,
where they struggled over the flocks of Oedipus,
and leading others in ships for booty across the sea
at Troy, for the sake of well-tressed Helen. (93–106)

In the earlier poem from the Trojan War cycle, the *Kypria/Cypria* (attributed to Stasinus), the rationale of Zeus and Themis is that the earth is straining from the overpopulation of humans, and, in a Malthusian move, the goddess Eris is employed to bring about the division that will start the Trojan War. She plays a crucial role in the Judgement of Paris. At the wedding feast of Peleus and Thetis, the uninvited Eris starts a beauty contest among Aphrodite, Hera, and Athena by throwing a golden apple among the guests labeled "to the most beautiful." When Paris, the prince shepherd, is given the chance to judge among the goddesses, he is swayed (or bribed) by the promise of Aphrodite of the love of the most beautiful woman in the world, namely Helen, of the face and apparently tresses that "launched a thousand ships" (Marlowe 12.81–87). In this version of things, Eris is thus employed for a higher purpose. She unwittingly begat the Trojan War. John Wilson argues for the importance of Strife in general and, following Euripides' view, the Judgment of Paris in particular as the real causes of the Trojan War and all the evils of succeeding generations (7).

The Double Lesson on Strife

What lessons or morals, then, is Hesiod trying to impart in his *Works and Days* and what or whom does he praise and what or whom does he blame? The most striking thing is, of course, his apparent reversal or modification of his earlier account of strife. Hesiod does not speak of Strife here as a goddess, but as twins:

> So, there was not just one birth of Strife, after all, but upon the earth there are two Strifes. One of these a man would praise once he got to know it, but the other is blameworthy; and they have thoroughly opposed spirits. For the one fosters evil war and conflict-cruel one, no mortal loves that one, but it is only by necessity that they honor the oppressive Strife, by the plans of the immortals. But the other one gloomy Night bore first; and Cronus' high-throned son, who dwells in the

aether, set it in the roots of the earth, and it is much better for men. It rouses even the helpless man to work. For a man who is not working but who looks at some other man, a rich one who is hastening to plow and plant and set his house in order, he envies him, one neighbor envying his neighbor who is hastening toward wealth; and this Strife is good for mortals. And potter is angry with potter, and builder with builder, beggar begrudges beggar, and poet poet. (11–12)

We will also have the echo of the value of competition and work much later in Adam Smith's theory of Capitalism in his *An Inquiry into the Wealth of Great Nations*: we do not get our daily bread from any altruistic deeds of a baker but from, ideally, free market competition to make the best product at the best price, which would not come about without rival producers (Book I, chapter 2).

As many commentators have pointed out, Hesiod's *Works and Days* has two stories to tell. Thomas Rosenmeyer says that "the passage on the two *Erides* sets the tone" (257–85). Prefiguring Aristotle's *Nichomachean Ethics*, addressed to his son Nicomachus, and *Cicero*'s *de Officias* to his son (Marcus Tullius also), Hesiod is addressing his brother Perses, with whom, however, he seems to have been involved in a lawsuit concerning the inheritance of their father's property. Yet, as Bartlett has also argued, "Hesiod speaks of justice and its human and divine supports in such a way as to go well beyond what would be of benefit to his brother" (177). He seems to be pointing beyond his brother to what will benefit and keep together entire communities, as well as addressing kings or judges.

Like later philosophers, he exhorts his brother to do good and not evil. Here, Hesiod urges Perses to avoid evil strife and pursue good strife, to which he also refers as the feelings of rivalry and competitiveness that motivate one to work for one's own achievements. Seth Benardete, noted, though, that "The *Works and Days* begins with an admission of a mistake; he now realizes that the goddess Strife is not merely the mother of Bloodshed and Lies, but also of rivalry and competition without which there would be no progress in the arts" (4). Though competition in work or trade rivals is good, evil strife is bad. Given the fact that the world is a product of divine will, however, humans are at times required to pay homage even to litigious strife, as P. C. B. Forbes claimed in his essay on the brothers (83). Forbes, concludes, however, that Hesiod progresses in *Works and Days* from litigant to teacher (87). In order to illustrate the effects of both, Hesiod vividly illustrates the story of Prometheus and Pandora and the Hawk and the Nightingale on the one side, and the value of working for what one has on the other.

Hesiod had told the story of Prometheus in his earlier *Theogony* and repeats it here. Pandora was not given to Prometheus himself—he was far too crafty to accept a gift from the gods—but she was given to Epimetheus (after thought) as a beautiful evil. She is given a box, told not to open it (we all know how that worked out), and lets loose all the evils of the world, except hope (or anticipation, as Glenn W. Most, in his new Loeb translation, has it). In his "Pandora and the Good *Eris* in Hesiod," Jonathan P. Zarecki makes much of the connection between labor and the possession of a wife. He argues that Pandora is not a beautiful evil but that she is good strife disguised as a burden. The idea is that good things (or a beautiful wife) are something for which you must strive. Hence Pandora and the good *Eris* become equivalent beings (5–29). The lesson appears to be that Pandora is punishment for the hubris of Prometheus and the punishment is the "gift" of Pandora. Jenny Strauss Clay has a different view. For her, it is more the Olympian perspective of the anxiety felt about the potential threat humans represent to immortals. Or alternatively, "the sending of Pandora and her jar would constitute part of Zeus' final dispensation, simultaneously ridding Olympus of noxious forces and foisting them on mankind" (125). Tellingly, Pandora is viewed, ultimately, as the bearer of both good and evil things (Olstein 312).

Hesiod then seems to shift the focus away from semi-mythological figures Prometheus and Pandora by speaking of the more plausible ages or stages of human development, which parallel to some degree the story of Genesis in the Bible. Frederick J. Teggart makes much of the comparison both with Genesis and the *Odyssey* in his "The Argument of Hesiod's *Works and Days*." In the beginning, human mortals enjoyed a carefree existence living off the fruits of the land. They did not toil or labor. The Second Age is one where humans seem still in their adolescence; they are at odds with each other, and they do not honor the gods. They end up in the Iron age, in which people must toil for their living. This age is one where people give honor to the doers of evil and is the very age in which Hesiod is living.

The story of the "Hawk and the Nightingale" that follows also has a mixed legacy. In Hesiod's account, the powerful Hawk who clutches the poor innocent Nightingale in its claws is one of the first illustrations of "might makes right," a tale that kings know well, as Hesiod says. Hesiod does not leave it at that, however, and exhorts his brother to honor Justice, for "outrageousness or *hubris* is an evil in a worthless mortal and even a fine man cannot bear her easily" (215). For those who give straight judgments to foreigners and fellow citizens alike and do not turn aside from justice, their city prospers (225). For them, peace is on earth, and Zeus never marks them out for painful war. Hesiod does not analyze the concept of *hubris* or "taking more than one's share" very explicitly. Nonetheless, it seems evident that he thinks injustice consists of *hubris*. . . . In a just city, on the other side, there is abundance (225–37).

Indeed, Hesiod castigated his brother for not accepting an equal share of their father's estate and blamed him for going to (bribe-taking) judges to get more. This provides an important clue for how he distinguished between evil strife and good. In "The Ambiguity of *Eris* in the *Works and Days*," Michael Gagarin argued that Hesiod is ambiguous because life is ambiguous. He does not offer neat dichotomies because, as he says, life is complicated and messy. Good and Evil Strife, for Hesiod, thus both consist in competitiveness and rivalry. One is characterized as excessive, the other productive. The one wants what the other has, the other works to get the same for him or herself.[3]

It is important to see, as well, that Hesiod's archaic conception of work will be at odds with later classical Greek ideas concerning good strife/*agon*/the contest. Now, the idea of strife as contest or striving is not a matter of the labor involved in trying to survive but more of an aristocratic struggle for excellence.[4]

Evil Strife

In the *Theogony* and *Works and Days*, Hesiod spells out the evil consequences of Strife for humans. Strife is a goddess who gives birth to many other human miseries. Further, the relation between Zeus and Prometheus can be characterized by a negative rivalry, resulting in bad consequences for humans; the parallels to the biblical story of the fallen angel Satan are equally evident, as well. Prometheus gives the destructive and constructive knowledge of fire to humans. Satan encourages Adam and Eve to eat from the tree of the Knowledge of good and evil. Even before this, however, the story of the *Theogony* is, as mentioned earlier, a struggle between older gods not to be superseded by their progeny, as well as the efforts on the part of their offspring not to be contained or eliminated. So, Hesiod recounts, Sky "became indignant at the defiant manhood of

Obriareus, Cottus, and Gyges, and bound them with a mighty bond" (617). When the battle commenced between the Titans and Olympians, "there was no resolution for their grievous strife, nor an end for either side, but the outcome of the war was evenly balanced" (635). When Sky "pressed down" and Earth was "pressed down" so great a sound was produced as the "gods ran together in strife" (687). This passage has been explained as a metaphor for the sexual union of the earth and sky, yet one might use another, more violent, word for it, as it resulted in more war and strife. When Zeus finally becomes ascendant—after overthrowing his own father, Cronos, who tried to consume him—he then metes out penalties for gods and men who quarrel with, and bring strife against, each other (782).

A lot of the *Theogony* is taken up with generation of gods, but also with war and destruction. Zeus becomes the final arbiter and giver to everyone of what they deserve at the end of the *Theogony*. Scholars still debate what to make of Zeus-father as described by Hesiod. Raising the lowly and putting down the proud, even so, he was not described as unequivocally just. This explains why Plato later said in his *Republic* that children should either not be taught anything at all about the gods, or only that they are good (380c). Bartlett, for his part, speaks of the defective way Zeus treats humans, just or unjust (204). In Hesiod's Iron age, however, evil things were mixed with good things. Perhaps Hesiod speaks this way because he wanted to qualify his earlier remarks about Zeus and his treatment of humans. For example, in *Works and Days*, Hesiod enjoins Perses not to let *Eris*, who rejoices in evil, keep him from work (28). Hesiod further exhorts his brother to avoid the day that commemorates Eris' giving birth to *horkos* or oath, since false oaths generate further strifes (804). This might appear strange, as the very occasion for which Hesiod constructs this narrative is the quarrel or strife between himself and his own brother—a quarrel he started provoked by his brother's apparent greed.

Good Strife: Erga/work

The idea of work, as good strife, is not discussed in a consistent way in Hesiod, either. As Bartlett explained, work is described as a harsh punishment meant to supply grievous woes to mortals (91) yet also a great boon from which all prosperity arises (308). The envy that spurs us to outdo our neighbors and better our condition (23, 312) is also the "ill sounding and horrible companion of all wretched beings that delight in evil (195–96)" (Bartlett 180).

Yet, when he speaks of the value of work as good strife, Hesiod compares staying away from work as evil strife when it causes you to "gawk" at the quarrels of others and listen to the assembly. Mixed messages abound here, too. But remember, the value of being a good citizen at this time was being a good loyal subject to whomever was in power. In Pericles's "Funeral Oration," centuries later, in praising democracy, we look down on those who mind (only) their own business, and we admire those who go to the assembly and pay attention to what is going on (2.37ff). Hesiod criticizes those who do not mind their own business. Even so, Pericles (perhaps with Hesiod and Homer in mind) says that we are such an exceptional people that we mind our own business very well as well as the business of the city. Hesiod enjoins building up your own reserves first. Then you can pay attention to everyone else (25). He then blames his brother, who, after they divided up their father's estate, came back for more and was able to get kings (who are often described, pejoratively, as gift eaters) to pass crooked judgments. Straight judgments, however, come from Zeus. He implies that his brother should have accepted the initial division of their father's estate and then made more of it himself. This is not totally at odds with Thucydides' Pericles either, for he says that it is no shame to be born poor, it is only a shame to do nothing about it.

Gods, in any case, kept the means of survival hidden from humans. Zeus passed along his punishment of Prometheus to us, but it is not a total evil. Pandora seems to be the punishment for Prometheus' transgression, but laboring to support herself and the children, she brings a mixed blessing. Olstein sees Justice as the prominent theme, writing: "The evils from Pandora's jar and the several ages of unjust men destroyed by Zeus represent individual and generational mortality. Nevertheless through Dike—Harmonious work and Bios attained in the Just City, a new Golden Age—men may hope to recapture their immortality" (295). Whereas Pandora is an unmitigated evil, having only the likeness of a modest maiden, later, Justice as the daughter of Zeus, is the real thing. Culture, then, is the product of harmonious Justice, not strife (296). Pandora is a "bane to men working for their bread" (56), and individual and generational mortality are the evil bane Pandora wrought, which is learned only in retrospect (301). Females can be good, too, as justice is, which brings harmony to cities and makes them prosper (as in the aftermath of the Hawk and Nightingale story). In the Silver age, when men have lost a sense of shame or righteous indignation (*Aidos* and *Nemesis*), evil is associated with not revering and paying homage to the gods (304).

Hesiod does speak disparagingly of toil and labor, yet he recognizes the value of work, too. He therefore urged Perses, "you of divine stock," to

> [k]eep working and always bear in mind our behest so that Famine will hate you And well-garlanded Demeter will love you and fill your granary with the means of life. For Famine, is ever the companion of the man who does not work, gods and men feel resentment against that man, whoever lives without working, in his temper is like stingless drones that consume the labor of the bees, eating it without working. . . . If you work you will be dearer by far to immortals and mortals: for they very much hate those who do not work. Work is not a disgrace, but not working is. (298–311)

As other scholars have noted, this passage—and especially its last line—was much discussed by later Socratics. Work is important because it is the means of recovering our livelihood or living (*Bios*), which, as Olstein argues, Demeter personifies (309).

In the classical period of Plato and Aristotle, manual labor, even the artistic craftsmanship of sculptors and architects, however, will be looked down on, partly because a lot of the work was done by slaves. This view of labor was not shared by Hesiod.[5] In later classical views of Hesiod, much attention was paid to the value of work, as well as the kinds of work that should be praised. In "Work and the Socratics," Wolfsdorf says Hesiod's encomium on work was much discussed and Socrates himself weighed in on the topic. He was even accused of misreading Hesiod, in thinking he praised all work, including disgraceful work, if it was for gain or profit and criticized all idleness. Xenophon argued instead that Socrates drew on the poets for salutary wisdom. The topic gets complicated, though, when philosophers began to criticize those who work with their hands, or those in business to make a lot of profit, and negatively compare them to those who would rather be beggars who are rich in wisdom (1–5).[6]

Legacy of the "Good" and "Bad" Strife

As noted earlier, the agonism and devotion to *Arête* (that is, excellence or virtuosity) of the aristocratic age, in pre-classical Greece, was not identical to Hesiod's conception of work, as Debra Hawhee and others have noted. One could argue, however, that Aristotle will take elements of it up in

The Double Meaning of Strife in Hesiod | 221

his equating the work of humans with the function of humans later in his *Nichomachean Ethics* (I, 7).

Gregory Nagy has made an extensive analysis of the concept of Strife in Homer and its aristocratic connotations. Nagy also appreciates the positive social function assigned by myth to the institution of blame. He recognized in Hesiod, too, the "social ambivalence of *Eris* (strife) as a prime theme of his *Works and Days*" (Nagy 19.2). Praising and blaming, he argues, are subsumed in the principle of competition. And, good or evil, *Eris* functions as a prime definition of the Human Condition (19.3) And, just as Nagy has honed in on the aristocratic influence, so, too, Dustin Gish has written of the value of the struggle of citizen-soldiers of Athenian Democracy and the many against the aristocratic critique in his reproduction of the Old Oligarch in his "Mis-Reading Direct Democracy as Mob Rule at the Founding: Popular Sovereignty and the Prospects for Good Government in Athens and America." Though Plato and other critics will be very influential in undermining the basis for democracy for centuries as mob-rule, in more recent years there has been a vigorous defense of the ability of ordinary citizens to defend their own business as well as the business of the Polis very well (to paraphrase Thucydides' Funeral Oration, 2.40) by Josiah Ober, Kurt Raaflub, Jennifer Roberts, and others.

AGONISM AND DEMOCRACY

Andreas Kalyvas's "The Democratic Narcissus: The Agonism of the Ancients Compared to that of the (Post)Moderns" advances the discussion by analyzing the "aristocratic value system which permeated and co-existed with the religious and martial qualities of the archaic *agon*. The aristocratic element is two-fold, first as a form of game oriented towards the selection of the Aristos" (18–19). One might see this in Odysseus' discus throwing against the young lads on Scheria as well as his contest against the suitors to string his bow in Homer's *Odyssey* (8.190, 21.410). In Kalyvas, "it is foremost a life and way of living one's life that stands apart from, and above, work and the exertion of physical labor for bare existence" (18–19). This ignores, one might notice, the work of slaves, who through their unwilling labor kept the society afloat. He continued that "ancient agonistic ethos exhibits contempt for the peaceful, everyday existence of the common people" (Golden 146–57). Kalyvas connects *agon* with the *demos* later by explaining that the enlargement of agonism to comprise and constitute the democratic *polis* evolved after a period of struggle with the aristocratic classes. He echoes Pericles (again in the *Funeral Oration*), that no one is kept by virtue of their social background from contributing to the Polis and making it better. Yet, Kalyvas acknowledged that agonistic politics can also equally "threaten the political association with corruption as it tends to instrumentalize and denigrate politics for one's private interests in a visceral quest for pre-eminence. This threat was a permanent reminder of the truth in the myth of Narcissus, his punishment . . . and the harmful potential of self-love." This insight, Kalyvas continued: "is powerfully evoked in Hesiod's story of the two forms of *Eris*, strife: the bad that fosters over-ambition, envy, and distrust, causing wars, bloodshed, and destruction and the other, the good *Eris* that stimulates rivalry and competition and promotes collective betterment through adversarial relations" (28). Even so, Kalyvas argued that "Notwithstanding these affinities and continuities, the current revival of *agon* in political theory does not suggest a nostalgic appeal to a pre-modern Greek past. It does not indicate yet another neo-classical revival. Quite the opposite. . . . It represents a 'de-Hellenization' of agonism, a considerable divestment of its ancient significations and a radical redefinition" (31).

Conclusion: The Democratic Legacy of Strife

Hesiod, as we have seen, was one of the inaugurators of the tradition of conceiving of qualities as pairs of opposition, in this case of good and evil strife. Was that productive for further political/social relations? Later pre-Socratic philosophers saw Strife as an unqualified good, as it created the tension necessary to challenge the status quo. Hence Heraclitus' idea that strife *is* justice. Empedocles then reconfigured the opposition, as between love, which brings us together, and strife, that tears us apart. Each has its part to play in human evolution. Both versions of Strife will play a contested role, as well, when Democrats are able to successfully persuade Aristocrats of their own valuable contributions to the Polis and successfully prevail over their resistance to sharing power. The double meaning of Strife as constructive in the pursuit of excellence and in challenging unjustified Hegemons will have many followers in its later version as *Areté*. Destructive strife will bring on the endless wars that characterized the ancient world. Because of this, the cooperative virtues, exemplified by Empedocles and later Antigone's dealing in love, will not be as resonant. Brotherly love might have preserved Hesiod's family had not the destructive competitiveness of his brother brought it down. Both love and hate will also play a central role in bringing down the tyranny of Hippias and his brother Hipparchus, but it will result in the establishment of the Athenian Democracy, also a mixed but unrivaled blessing.

Notes

1. See von Wilamowitz-Moellendorff, Sinclair, Rowe, and Verdenius.
2. See Blok and Mason, Uglione, and Loraux, *Tragic*, *Children*, and *Mothers*.
3. Jean-Jacques Rousseau, even before Adam Smith, accounts for the Origin of Inequality in his *Second Discourse* as exactly the comparison people make to each other in their early history. No one wants the other to get the better of him, so they strive to be better. Darwin and Social Darwinists make use of the "survival of the fittest," though as Nietzsche noted, they were not always the fittest (Steinmann 15). Immanuel Kant, however, has a more benign view of this competition in that he thinks it can also produce culture.
4. Hannah Arendt will similarly distinguish labor, work, and action in her *Human Condition*. Adriano Tilgher's *Homo Faber, Work through the Ages*, and David Wolfsdorf's "Hesiod, Prodicus, and the Socratics on Work and Pleasure" explore these distinctions as well.
5. Or certainly by thinkers like Marx, Ruskin, or Tolstoy much later. Most recently, Matthew Crawford, also a philosophy PhD, has praised skilled craftsmanship in his *Shopcraft as Soulcraft: An Inquiry into the Value of Work*.
6. In Plato, see particularly his *Charmides* especially in Critias' distinctions between doing *(prattein)*, working *(ergazesthas)* and making *(poiein)*.

Works Cited

Arendt, Hannah. *The Human Condition*. U of Chicago P, 1998.
Bartlett, Robert C. "An Introduction to Hesiod's *Works and Days*," *Review of Politics*, vol. 68, 2006, pp. 177–205.
Blok, Josine, and Peter Mason, editors. *Sexual Asymmetry. Studies in Ancient Society*. J. C. Gieven, 1987.
Benardete, Seth. *The Argument of the Action: Essays on Greek Poetry and Philosophy*. U of Chicago P, 2000.
Calame, Claude. *Myth and History in Ancient Greece: The Symbolic Creation of a Colony*. Translated by Daniel W. Berman, Princeton UP, 2003.
Crawford, Matthew. *Shopcraft as Soulcraft: An Inquiry into the Value of Work*. Penguin, 2010.

Forbes, P. B. R. "Hesiod versus Perses." *The Classical Review*, vol. 64, 2009, pp. 82–87.
Freeman, Kathleen. *Ancillas to the Presocratics*. Harvard UP, 1983.
Gagarin, Michael. "*Dikē* in the *Works and Days*," *Classical Philology* vol. 68, 1973, pp. 81–94.
———. "Hesiod's Dispute with Perses," *Transactions of the American Philological Association* vol. 104, 1974, pp. 103–11.
———. "The Ambiguity of *Éris* in the *Works and Days*. *Cabinet of the Muses: Essays on Classical and Comparative Literature in Honor of Thomas G. Rosenmeyer*, edited by Mark Griffith and Donald Mastronarde, Scholars Press, 1990, pp. 173–83.
Gish, Dustin. "Mis-Reading Direct Democracy as Mob Rule at the Founding: Popular Sovereignty and the Prospects for Good Government in Athens and America," APSA, 2012.
Golden, Mark. *Sport and Society in Ancient Greece*. Cambridge UP, 1998.
Hawhee, Debra. "Agonism and *Arête*." *Philosophy and Rhetoric*, vol. 1, no. 3, 2002, pp. 185–207.
Hegel, Georg Wilhelm Friedrich. *Philosophy of History*, Dover Publications; Reissue edition, 2004.
Hesiod. *Theogony. Works and Days. Testimonia*, edited and translated by Glenn W. Most, vol. 57, Loeb-Harvard UP, 2018.
———. *Works and Days*, edited by T. A. Sinclair, Georg Olms Hildesheim, 1966.
Homer. *Odyssey*, edited by H. Rieu, translated by E. V. Rieu, introduced by Peter Jones, Penguin Classics, 2003.
Honig, Bonnie. *Political Theory and the Displacement of Politics*. Cornell UP, 1993.
Kalyvas, Andreas. "The Democratic Narcissus: The Agonism of the Ancients Compared to that of the (Post)Moderns." *Law and Agonistic Politics*, edited by Andrew Schaap, Ashgate, 2015, pp. 15–42.
Kant, Immanuel. "Conjectures on the Beginnings of Human History." *Political Writings*, edited and introduced by Hans Reiss, translated by H. B. Nisbet, Cambridge UP, 1991, pp. 221–34.
Loraux, Nicole. *Tragic Ways of Killing a Woman*, Harvard UP, 1987.
———. *Children of Athena: Athenian Ideas about Citizenship and Division of the Sexes*. Princeton UP, 1994.
———. *Mothers in Mourning*. Cornell UP, 1998.
Malthus, Thomas Robert. *An Essay on the Principle of Population*, Oxford World's Classics, 1999.
Marlowe, Christopher, *Doctor Faustus*. Norton Critical Edition, 2005.
Marx, Karl. "Moralizing Criticism and Critical Morality: A Polemic against Karl Heinzen," *Selected Essays*, 1844–1850. Translated by H. J. Stenning, Books for Libraries Press, 1968, pp. 134–70.
Nagy, Gregory. *The Best of the Achaeans: Concepts of the Hero in Archaic Greek Poetry*, Harvard UP, 1999.

Nietzsche, Friedrich. "Expeditions," *Twilights of the Idols and The Anti-Christ*. Translated by R. J. Hollingdale, edited by Michael Tanner, Penguin, 1990, pp. 78–115.
Ober, Josiah. *Political Dissent in Democratic Athens*. U of California P, 1998.
Olstein, Katherine. "Pandora and Dike in Hesiod's *Works and Days*," *Emerita* vol. 48, 1980, pp. 295–312.
Plato. *Charmides*. Translated by R. K. Sprague. *Plato: Complete Works*, edited by John M. Cooper and D. S. Hutchinson, Hackett, 1997, pp. 668–92.
Raaflub, Kurt. "Democracy." *A Companion to the Classical Greek World*, edited by Konrad Kinzel, Oxford UP, 2006.
Roberts, Jennifer. *Athens on Trial: The Anti-Democratic Tradition in Western Thought*. Princeton UP, 1994.
Rousseau, Jean-Jacques. *The Discourses and Other Early Political Writings*, edited and translated by Victor Gourevitch, Cambridge UP, 1997.
Rosenmeyer, Thomas G. "*Hesiod and Historiography*." *Hermes* vol. 85, 1957, pp. 257–85.
Rowe, C. J. *Essential Hesiod*. Bristol Classical Press, 1978.
Smith, Adam. *An Inquiry into the Wealth of Great Nations*, edited by Edwin Cannon, Methuen, 1904.
Solmsen, F. *Hesiod and Aeschylus*. Cornell Studies in Classical Philology, 1949.
Steinmann, Michael. "Nietzsche, Darwin, and the Greeks: On the Aesthetic Interpretation of Life." *Agonist*, vol. 9, 2015, pp. 1–42.
Strauss Clay, Jenny. *Hesiod's Cosmos*. Cambridge UP, 2003.
Teggart, Frederick J. "The Argument of Hesiod's Works and Days," *Journal of the History of Ideas*, vol. 8, 1947, pp. 45–77.
Tilgher, Adriano. *Homo Faber, Work through the Ages*. Gateway, 1930.
Thucydides. *History of the Peloponnesian War*. Translated by Walter Blanco, edited by Walter Blanco and Jennifer Tolbert Roberts, Norton Critical Editions, 1998.
Uglione, Renato, editor. *Atti del convegno natzionale di studi su la donna nel mondo antico*, Conference proceedings, Torino, 1986.
Verdenius, W. *A Commentary on Hesiod, Works and Days*. Leiden, 1985.
von Wilamowitz-Moellendorff, Ulrike. *Hesiodos Erga*, Weidmannsche Buchhandlung, 1928.
Weil, Simone. Iliad *Poem of Force*. Translated by Mary McCarthy. *Chicago Review*, vol. 18, 1965, pp. 5–30.
West, Martin L., editor and translator. *Greek Epic Fragments*. Loeb-Harvard UP, 2003.
Wilson, John R. "*Eris* in Euripides." *Greece & Rome*, vol. 26, 1979, pp. 7–20.
Wolfsdorf, David. "Hesiod, Prodicus, and the Socratics on Work and Pleasure," edited by Brad Inwood. *Oxford Studies in Ancient Philosophy*, vol. 35, Oxford UP, 2008, pp. 1–18.
Zarecki, Jonathan P. "Pandora and the Good *Eris* in Hesiod," *Greek, Roman, and Byzantine Studies*, vol. 47, 2007, pp. 5–29.

The Myth of Er and Pamphylia's Polyglossia

Nickolas Pappas

Could the journeying that Socrates tells of in the *Republic*'s myth of Er carry philosophical significance? Does it contribute, for example, to a reading of the myth as universalist? Afterlife journeys may promise to erase ethnic difference, but a closer look at real-life Pamphylia complicates that expectation. Pamphylia was polyglot, both Greek and non-Greek; if the myth treats those two groups differently, it may be delivering more than one message. On this reading, Pamphylia as the diverse audience for Er's call to justice lets Plato divide types of justice unequally among the world's population.

The Soul's Journey

After all its fresh and astonishing discussions, the *Republic* finishes with a vacuous figure of speech. "We shall do well," Socrates says of the just, "both here and in the thousand-year journey," by which he means the long time away from embodied life that a soul spends after dying and before coming back to be born (10.621d). Death is a πορεία "journey." This same noun had appeared earlier in the myth of Er (10.615a), as had the related verb πορεύεσθαι "travel," to describe what Er had done in the otherworld among dead souls (10.614b–c).

Death-as-journey might be more imaginative than life-as-journey. Living people move around; it takes some finesse to imagine far-off destinations for someone who's lying motionless. But still, the metaphor is old by the time Plato is writing the *Republic*.¹ "I'm wandering [ἀλάλημαι] in the house of Hades," the shade of unburied Patroclus complains to dreaming Achilles (*Il.* 23.74). Even within Plato's corpus, the image has grown familiar. Other dialogues describe the after-death experiences of souls as travel, emigration, and the like: the *Phaedo* especially (see 67b, 80d, 81a, 82b, 107d, 113–14), but the *Gorgias* (523a–b) and the pseudo-Platonic *Axiochus* (361b) too.

Rather than assume that Plato contents himself with a shopworn metaphor, I wonder what philosophical function πορεία might be performing as the fifth-to-last word of the *Republic*, maybe as a comment on the dialogue's argument. For one thing, the word picks up on something that really is a cliché, that Cephalus had said in Book I about his contemplation of death. In old age Cephalus worries about having defrauded anyone or owing worship to a god, in which case one might ἐκεῖσε ἀπιέναι "depart for that place" in a state of fear (1.331b).

"Going *there*," Cephalus says, as uninformed about what happens in the transition from life to death as this same sentence demonstrates him to be about justice, with his fantasy that it is a virtue one can obtain through well-placed reimbursements. The myth of Er turns Cephalus's vague object of dread into a science-fictionalized geography, and his unhelpful "depart for that place" into an itinerary both astronomical and minute, in which a millennium's reward or punishment (10.615a) is followed by seven days in a meadow (10.616b), then four days of travel to see the spindle of the solar system, another day to reach it (10.616b–c). So the first moral of the story may be that non-philosophers should not speak of death's voyage, any more than they ought to pronounce on justice. Philosophy gives content to those platitudes.

Ethnicity

Socrates does not expand the tale of death merely to upstage Cephalus. If the reference to a journey can be circling back to Book I to deepen a thought that had appeared there superficially—another manifestation of the *Republic*'s ring composition²—then the metaphor's elaboration may also be addressing some other aspect of the dialogue in this concluding moment. How could the journeying that departed souls do contribute to some other side of the *Republic*'s account of justice?

It surely matters that travel implies other lands. Today, Plato's readers tend to notice something that earlier readers downplayed: the persistence of Greek and Athenian chauvinism even in passages that speak favorably of the βάρβαρος or ξένος. The *Republic* contains allowances that the best city might come into existence in foreign lands (6.499c–d), but such promises are fleeting compared to the consistency with which the improved city is conceived as Greek (5.470e), or the way in which the city commits itself to enslaving non-Greeks (5.469b–c). Whole foreign nationalities are described as lacking the rationality that has to characterize a good city (4.435e–436a). Such disappointing language threatens to make the loftily imagined city of the *Republic* register as one more provincial Greek town. At best it is promoting the pan-Hellenism that developed alongside anti-Persian sentiment during the fifth century.[3]

The philosopher plays a distinct role in this tug-of-war between embrace of the alien and retreat to the local. The *Republic*'s philosophers are ultra-native in some respects, even presented as the *only* natives—as when, after having taken over the city, they reassign its adults to farm labor outside the walls, leaving only themselves inside with children who are ten and under (*Republic* 7.540e–7.541a).[4] But Socrates also calls philosophers a ξενικόν σπέρμα "foreign planting" in the soil of an existing Greek city, altered by that culture until they take on an ἀλλότριον ἦθος "other characteristics" (6.497b). In this passage anyone but the philosopher is more likely to belong in the city. By studying elevated realities the philosopher becomes κόσμιός τε καί θεῖος "well-ordered and divine" to the extent that a human can be (6.500c–d), and that divine quality again implies the philosophers' failure to belong in the city. Aristotle's observation comes to mind, that someone naturally ἄπολις "without a city" is either a miserable kind of human or above humanity (Aristotle *Politics* I.2 1253a2–4).[5] And the *Republic*'s cave pictures Plato's best-case philosopher as a combination of exile and émigré, then alienated foreigner, back for a long visit but pining for the newfound home that lies out up in the sunlight (7.514a–7.517a).[6] When permitted to philosophize, these escapees feel as though they have ἀπῳκίσθαι "moved" to the isles of the blessed (7.519c).

If spiritual dislocation by the philosopher counteracts nativism, so that one's true foreignness waits to be discovered across an ontological border, the travel spoken of in the myth of Er may problematize the *Republic*'s provincialism too. Is the land of souls a place you can move to?

The question is not whether spiritual dislocation demonstrates that the philosopher understands what it is to be foreign. That would be a philosophical pretension to foreignness and condescending to a foreigner's experience. The question is rather whether the *Republic* uses the category of the foreign and its associations in portraying the philosopher: associations like peculiar speech, friendlessness, divided loyalties, inexpertise about local custom, and on the positive side, knowledge of alternative practices and intimacy with the gods.[7]

If not the result of encounters with actual non-Athenians, the philosopher's otherworldly investigations emulate distance from local attachment. And so, if death constitutes a journey from the world, it ought to render everyone foreign in this philosophical way. As the *Republic* understands the philosopher in part through the lens of the alien, its closing myth must be understanding all souls through that same lens. On this reading death combats provincialism by making every soul a traveler, somewhat as death in the *Meno* obliterates the distinction between free and slave.[8] Even if the πλῆθος "multitude" can never philosophize (6.494a), philosophers capable of leading a city to justice might be found among all the world's multitudes.

Along such lines, the myth of Er might contain a rebuttal to provincialism. Call this an interpretive hypothesis. Reincarnation on the scale the myth promises incorporates all animals (10.620d). Judgment operates globally, under the administration of gods who owe no favors to wealthy Athenians. And the long stays in hell and heaven, the campout with souls pitching tents (κατασκηνᾶσθαι, 10.614e) on the underworld's meadow, and the observation of all the planets from a vantage point unlike anything found in life (10.616c–10.617b) trivialize ethnic loyalties and attachments. The peregrinations of the perished undo any ethnic orientation, as the *Republic*'s city would like to have done. Where does the soul find a home? If no answer really fits, we may have to call every human soul, not only the philosopher, a foreigner.

Pamphylia

By the later fifth century, Greeks had come to include non-Greeks in their underworld. Aeschylus's *Persians* puts Darius in Hades. His near-contemporary Polygnotus produced a painting at Delphi of the mythical dead that—according to the exhaustive description in Pausanias (*Description of Greece* 10.25–31)—included Marsyas the Phrygian and many Trojan characters (Vermeule 36–37). In the myth of Er ethnicity enters with Pamphylia, at the time of the dialogue's writing a region within the Persian Empire, whose cities had contributed funds and ships to the Empire's assault on Greece.[9]

The name of this region appears to combine πᾶς "all" with φῦλον "tribe, breed, nation," in which case, etymologically speaking, Pamphylia was *all nations*. Here is Er on behalf of all people, in that case, and selected to report back to everyone about the fate that awaits us all. It is tempting to interpret the name along such lines. But by the same reasoning one can infer that someone from Cleveland (originally "Cleaveland") represents the spot where the land is cleaved apart, unless it's where the land cleaves together. A little geographical etymology goes a long way. Cleveland may have other meanings unrelated to the contranym in its name.

Etymology fails as a reading of Er's Pamphylia, first, because even in antiquity other origins existed for the name. Herodotus credits the founding of the region to the Dorian tribe Πάμφυλοι, while Ephorus derives that tribe's name from Pamphylos, the son of the Dorian king Aegimius.[10] But even supposing that Pamphylia does take its name from the multiplicity of nations it comprises, what follows about a Pamphylian's story? Depending on what we can deduce about the actual place Pamphylia in Plato's day, we may take the myth of Er *either* as a univocal admonition to be shared among the earth's peoples, *or* as a multiple message, one part maybe even undermining another, the elements traveling together seeking different audiences. Socrates implies that the entirety of the story comes to more than his summary (10.615a). Its complex of details may well aim at still other auditors.

Pamphylia lay along the southern coast of Asia Minor, where local languages were Anatolian. Herodotus calls its people descendants of those who came from Troy with Amphilochos and Calchas, seers on the Greek side of the Trojan War. (But τῶν ἐκ Τροίης ἀποσκεδασθέντων "those scattered from Troy" could also refer to Trojans who left their defeated city.)[11] Pausanias, writing centuries later, likewise calls Pamphylians Greek.[12] A mention in Thucydides implies nothing either way.[13] Some Pamphylian cities are listed on Athenian inscriptions among other allies.[14] But such lists also included Carian cities, so inclusion on them did not make a city Greek.

Other literary evidence makes Pamphylia seem more foreign. Most generally, Euripides has Dionysus describe the part of Asia lying along the salty sea, where as he puts it, "Greeks mix with barbarians" (*Bacchae*

17–19). And there is an extant *periplous* or circumnavigational geography of the Mediterranean, referred to as the work of "pseudo-Skylax," and dated to the middle of the fourth century. Pseudo-Skylax assigns the more clearly Greek cities in Pamphylia, Phaselis, and Perge to neighboring Lycia. As his tour continues, he names Pamphylia by its cities including Side, which he calls a colony of Kyme (*Periplous* 101).[15]

The reference to Kyme carries extra significance in light of a later comment. The *Anabasis*, Arrian's chronicle of Alexander, says of Side that the Greeks from Kyme who settled there went on to "forget" their native Greek and to speak in a version of the foreign language previously dominant there (1.26.4). Pseudo-Skylax seems to be confirming that the Greeks were not indigenous to the area; Arrian sees them as not remaining linguistically Greek. Greek "colonization" in Pamphylia had limited success.

I share Stephen Halliwell's sense that Pamphylia is part of "Plato's way of giving an exotic but deliberately imprecise aura to the myth" (171). I only think that is not the last word. Some parts of Pamphylia qualify as Greek, but others do not, and the "exoticism" in the place name may extend to the greater exoticism of its combining Greek with foreign.

The mixing, as linguistic phenomenon, is attested from other sources. A Biblical reference to Pamphylia occurs in Acts of the Apostles, which reports Jews in Jerusalem, at Pentecost (2.1), from numerous foreign regions (2.5). All these visitors marveled that the Galilean apostles could speak in the visitors' native languages (2.6–9), and some of them came from Pamphylia (2.10). No one would have remarked on the apostles' speaking Greek. At least by this time, some centuries after Plato, and despite the spread of Greek around the eastern Mediterranean, "Pamphylia" could be expected to represent "non-Greek."

Available inscriptions reinforce the sense of a non-Greek linguistic community in Pamphylia, despite the inscriptions themselves being Greek. Christina Skelton identifies orthographical and grammatical features that point to the ongoing dominance of Anatolian languages in Pamphylia. Certainly, as she concludes, the Greek language was spoken in Pamphylia in the least normal way of all that era's dialects. Greek would have been a second language for more people than it was native. For one thing, Pamphylian Greek appears not to have used articles. Moreover the "consonant inventory," Skelton writes, "appears less Greek than Anatolian" (114). The Pamphylians likely saw themselves as possessing a "mixed Greek-Anatolian heritage" (118), and were correct to do so (125).

The Pamphylian names given in Plato's myth likewise bespeak a populace not identified entirely with the Greek language. Er's own name has a foreign sound. Halliwell's notes to Book X summarize popular proposals—that the name "Er" is Hebrew,[16] or that it is Iranian, even specifically that as an Iranian name it alludes to Zoroaster, from whom Colotes the Epicurean accused Plato of plagiarizing the story. Halliwell withholds judgment but concludes that Plato did not expect his readers to take the name as Greek (170–71). Greek proposals for its meaning go back to Plutarch, even though "Er" does not sound like a Greek name.[17] Pierre Destrée reads Er as a ἥρων "hero," with convincing criticisms of rival Greek etymologies, but he spends less time on non-Greek interpretations of the name, expressing doubt that the myth's universal message would warrant importing a foreign name (567). By the same token, Er's foreignness suits the myth perfectly if (as I argue) the myth deliberately distinguishes among ethnicities.

The other Pamphylian character, Ardiaeus, also has a non-Greek name. The myth makes him a horrid tyrant from a thousand years earlier who finds that his torments in Hades will not end. Ardiaeus is taken to have been Plato's invention (Grainger, appendix 1). The case for seeing him as non-Greek, if anything, exceeds that for Er. Even if Plato follows Herodotus in believing that Pamphylian Greeks of his time had descended from participants in the Trojan War, those descendants would not have been living in the region long enough to establish a tyranny a thousand years before him. (The myth depicts other heroes from Troy now having completed their millennium in Hades. They would have been the contemporaries of Ardiaeus not his progenitors.)

The *Republic*'s symmetry suggests a second reason. When Socrates concludes his defense of justice, he comes back to the ring of invisibility that Glaucon described, with which Gyges seized the throne of Lydia. "The soul ought to act justly whether it has Gyges' ring or doesn't" (10.612c). The *Republic*'s defense of justice closes where it began, and the myth of Er may be read as a continuation of that closure, with a look at the putative freedom from punishment that tyrants enjoy. And suitably, where Gyges begins his rise to tyranny when a cavern opens for him (2.359d), Ardiaeus faces the terror of his sentence when the mouth of hell denies him exit (10.615e).

Gyges hailed from Asia Minor, appropriately, for the Greeks spoke as if tyranny had originated in Asia. Despite the plentiful presence of tyrants in Greek cities, the stereotype of the βάρβαρος that developed in classical literature made tyranny the defining constitutional form in foreign lands (E. Hall). Ardiaeus, native to Asia, and called "the Great" as Persian kings were, thus makes most sense as an ethnic non-Greek.

Types of Justice

The mixed population in Pamphylia is the one that Er's body comes back to and makes up the audience for his story when he comes to on the pyre. Can this diverse group draw divergent morals from the myth?

Again, take the Gyges story as foil to the myth of Er.[18] Glaucon includes details that he passes over—very likely failing to see their significance—but that anticipate the *Republic*'s diagnosis of tyrannical pathology: Gyges' gratuitous adultery with the queen; the ring's appearance on a body inside a decoy-horse, which suggests that the ring had brought that previous owner to seek lethal sexual gratification after the manner of Pasiphaë, which is what boundless lust comes to in tyrannical souls. Thus Glaucon passes along elements of the refutation that Socrates will enlarge upon in Book 9. One hearer's evidence that everyone loves injustice shows another hearer why they should not (Pappas 112–14). The myth of Er likewise supports distinct interpretations. "Beyond the boundaries of this life, justice is rewarded"—that's *always* the upshot, but as "justice" means more than one thing, the upshot does as well.

Pamphylian ethnic identity bears on the polysemy in the myth. The two ethnicities present in the story align with the two forms of justice that it reinforces, which emerge in the myth's two parts: judgment regarding one's past life, selection of the life to come. First, and insofar as Hades is the place where life ends, it offers thousand-year rewards and punishments. The justice reinforced here consists in obedience to good laws. Souls receive reward or punishment for (respectively) εὐεργεσίας "good deeds" (10.615b) or ὅσας ἠδίκησαν "whatever unjust deeds" they had committed (10.615a). They do not need to understand what made an action just or unjust, or how justice and its absence comport themselves within a soul, as Glaucon and Adeimantus asked Socrates to show (2.366e). The first phase of death concerns itself with justice in the ordinary sense: what Cephalus and Polemarchus had thought they were talking about, in Book I, with their attempts to characterize social virtue (1.331c–1.336a).

It would oversimplify things to contrast this ordinarily conceived justice with a single philosophical alternative from the *Republic*. The *Republic* keeps reframing and reconstruing justice.[19] Nevertheless, the change in direction signaled by Plato's brothers' challenges to Socrates—the change that issues in the *Republic*'s analysis of soul—does mark the major discontinuity between ordinary and philosophical conceptions of justice. On one hand we find law-abiding behavior, on the other attention to the person's unseen constitution. Non-philosophers, lacking as they do any idea that justice has an invisible meaning, can look at a pathological human being and see only the splendid outward show (9.588d–e). Even within the well-constituted city, the military class possesses only a πολιτικήν "political, civic" courage (4.430c), while the many practice a type of moderation that consists in nothing better than obedience to authorities (3.389d–e). Non-philosophers are excluded from virtue (Bobonich 43).

Attention to the soul, which is to say philosophical attention, means care and tendance for the soul's internal relations. It also means awareness of the soul's complexity and dynamics. That attention comes into play in the latter part of the myth; for insofar as Hades is the place where life begins, it offers options for the next embodiment among which a soul can choose.

When Socrates comes to the choices of new lives, he interrupts his narration to underscore the moral. "Glaucon, my friend, *there* is the total danger for humans" (10.618b). This need to choose a good life explains why people need to study "this" (10.618c), i.e., what life-circumstances do to a soul. "By considering the nature of the soul [πρός τήν τῆς ψυχῆς φύσιν ἀποβλέποντα]" (10.618d), one can make oneself ready to identify the best subsequent life to live. Even someone like Orpheus, whom the Greeks consider an expert about the soul's future (2.364e), is subjected to the regime of expertise (10.620a). Orpheus will do well if trained in philosophy, not otherwise. Righteous law-abiding behavior will bring the great thousand-year reward, but it will not guarantee aptitude at this additional task—as justice of the kind practiced by Cephalus falls short of the self-harmonizing soul justice that the *Republic* goes on to disclose.

It is a commonplace among the *Republic*'s readers to see the resemblance between Cephalus and the quick-choosing soul who grabs up a tyrant's life and then laments its decision (10.619b–c). That reading yet again is encouraged by the dialogue's ring-composition. Socrates says that this soul, whom Bunyan might have called "Quick-to-Choose," had passed a life in virtue, then a millennium in heaven, before his reckless decision to live next time as a tyrant. But that soul's virtuous life had been passed in a "well-ordered" city, and Socrates would not offer such a description for the Athens that Cephalus occupied. In fact, and despite its care to give names to other characters, the myth of Er divulges nothing about this doomed soul. And yet Quick-to-Choose shares something with Cephalus when Socrates explains his life, ἔθει ἄνευ φιλοσοφίας ἀρετῆς μετειληφότα "sharing in virtue by habit, without philosophy" (619c–d). Cephalus agonizing over unredeemed debts also slips away as soon as dialectic shows its face (1.331d): it was habit without philosophy for him too.

Whoever Quick-to-Choose may have been, this soul's hapless choice shows the difference between the two justices reinforced in the myth. Unphilosophical justice suffices for long years in the heavens but will not guarantee wise life-choosing. If anything, the opposite is true. Centuries of joy have a soporific effect, and most law-abiding citizens finish their millennium's reward so flabby-minded that they fail their otherworldly philosophy exam; while the souls emerging dirty from long correction underground will cast a shrewd eye over the awaiting lives (10.619d). What it takes to choose wisely for the future has little to do with what it took to live justly in the past. Virtue obtained through habit, without philosophy, will not be able to attend to the soul that is philosophy's special subject.

Mark McPherran provisionally draws the sad conclusion that most souls seesaw between justice and injustice as one life yields to the next, except for those monstrous tyrants who never escape their underground torments, and except for the blessed philosophers savvy enough to pick a philosophical life on every go-round. You may find McPherran's reading pessimistic, but he is right that the conditions for success in the myth's first phase differ from the conditions for success in its second. In both cases justice pays; but that is habitual justice in one instance, philosophical and soul-attentive justice in the other.

Souls' Ethnicities

I described Quick-to-Choose as the myth's central character, for the myth tells a complete otherworld story only about that one character. We find out what kind of life the soul had lived, and what happened to it during the initial judgment, and what would be happening next with its re-embodiment. For no one else is all that information supplied. At the same time, Quick-to-Choose is the only character who remains unidentified: no name, no ethnicity. Er is a Pamphylian, although he takes no part in the other world's activities; Ardiaeus, the other Pamphylian, experiences hellish torments, but because he cannot escape them he does not go through the choice of lives.

At the other end of the spectrum, the mythical names that Socrates goes through—Orpheus to Odysseus—take up lives to enter. As if they had never undergone reward or punishment, these souls choose κατὰ συνήθειαν . . . τοῦ προτέρου βίου "according to what they were accustomed to in their previous lives" (10.620a). Ajax is motivated by his mistrust of humans, Atalanta by her love of athletics (10.620b). Not one choice made by these souls is affected by the punishment or reward they experienced, despite what Socrates himself put forward as the critical factor in decisions about the future. From this part of the myth you might infer that for the old Greek heroes the afterlife is not about punishment or reward so much as it is about their better or worse insights into justice and the soul.

Why is it that when the myth focuses on one species of justice, it limits that justice to either Greek or non-Greek? If philosophical justice exhibits its value in one's sagacious selection of the next life, the myth evidently expects that only from Greeks. Only to them does the moral apply that Socrates enunciates, that one ought to take pains while alive to learn soul-inquiry. This is not to say that all Greeks possess philosophical justice, only that it is expected of them and not of others.[20]

So Er wakes at his own wake and finds himself home in Pamphylia. He reports his experiences. Pamphylia being the place it is, his story reaches non-Greek Pamphylians as the reassuring news that they will not have to see Ardiaeus again. The moral order in the greater world ensures that every injustice is punished. Foreigners listening can take away this practical reinforcement that had seemed to motivate Cephalus.

But Greeks live in Pamphylia too, and they too hear Er's story. The name of Ardiaeus draws a blank with them; the Trojan-War names hold their interest. For Greek heroes, evidently the last great act (before becoming someone else) is to look into lives and gauge what a life does to the soul living it. Heroes philosophize. In this way, a single story brings distinct messages to the different peoples of Pamphylia. Rather than occlude ethnicity, the journey after death lets the *Republic* differentiate among them.

The purpose of digging into ethnic details in the myth of Er is not to bring an accusation against Plato, nor even to interrupt the logic of xenophobia, as important as that is to do. Another benefit, where understanding the *Republic* is concerned, derives from reading this kind of confrontation as part of a portrayal of the foreign as the ignorant, when ignorance comes to mean the absence of philosophy. I have the ignorance in mind for which Socrates calls dialectic the only remedy, when he says in Book VII that ἡ διαλεκτική μέθοδος "the system or science of dialectic" is the only kind of inquiry that can rescue the eye of the soul when it is buried ἐν βορβόρῳ βαρβαρικῷ "in foreign filth" (7.533d).

Where the foreign seems unphilosophical, the unphilosophical at home takes on a foreign character, as if some of the city's own people lose their legitimacy as citizens by failing to understand the philosophical justification for the regime. The alien who fails to know our ways encourages us to see the one who fails to know our ways as alien. Here you may think of everyone who faces expulsion from the *Republic*'s city, from the playwrights who generate ignorant mimetic verse and get turned away at the gates (3.398a–b), to old-timers who have to go out into the farmland after the revolution, for fear they will not adopt the new political philosophy (7.540e–541a).

The city of the *Republic* would hardly be the only society that designated some locals as outsiders and so recreated a confrontation with foreigners even within demographic confines. But it is one society that the *Republic*'s argument stipulates as unified, coming together in the first place when πολλοί "many" are gathered together εἰς μίαν οἴκησιν "into one dwelling" (2.329c), and continuing to identify itself as a unity by contrast with all those other cities that contain multitudes (4.422e). A city hardly deserves the name, according to the *Republic*, when it fails to maintain its unity. The act of vesting power in the city's philosophers, whose knowledge and concern apply to the city as a whole, promises a synoptic self-governance unlike the self-interested rival factions found in all other communities. But when expertise itself defines creates a new species of foreigner, the quest for a political unity grounded in knowledge seems to transform itself into a civic order whose citizens are foreigners to one another.[21]

Notes

1. Vermeule, in her unmatched survey of Greek portrayals of death, can write of "the natural belief that the dead went on a journey from the burial house to a lower world" (56).

2. The *Republic* seems to contain endless evidence for the symmetrical principles of organization that bring the final books to take up topics introduced in the opening books. Its "ring-composition" is widely spoken of, though as Barney observes ("Ring-Composition in Plato") discussions can be hard to find in the secondary literature.

3. On representations of foreigners in the fifth century, see E. Hall.

4. The *parergon* to the *Theaetetus* contains another such depiction of the philosopher. The premier examples of philosophers inquire into what a human being is but ignore their own neighbors to such an extent that they scarcely know whether the neighbors are human (174b). In other words, the archetypal philosopher might be the only person in town, hence the only citizen.

5. I am grateful to Shant Shahrigian for reminding me of this line in connection with Plato's *Republic*, as well as for quoting Nietzsche: "To live alone one must be a beast or a god—so says Aristotle. That leaves out the third case: one must be both—a philosopher." Nietzsche, *Twilight of the Idols* "Sayings and Projectiles" (3).

6. On the cave and the philosopher as foreigner, see LeMoine (5, 56–87, esp. 79–82).

7. At times the dialogues compare foreigners to gods by reason of their age. Ascribing words to non-Greek languages resembles the Homeric practice of calling them divine words, because foreigners are older than Greeks: *Cratylus* 425e, and see 391e–92a. Socrates also says in the *Cratylus* that sun and moon and such are many foreigners' gods and had once been for Greeks (397c–d). The further away some people live, the further in the past. Already for Homer the Ethiopians far to the south maintain a fellowship with the gods that everyone else had lost: *Od.* 1.21–23, 5.281–87; also see *Il.* 1.423–24, 23.206–07.

8. Plato *Meno*: otherworldly experience of all souls, 81b–c; the slave's typical Socratic session, 84a, c. On the humanization of the *Meno*'s slave, see DuBois. Note however that the *Meno*'s slave is Greek, even born in the household: 82b, 85e. That dialogue does not efface ethnic difference and even insists on it. Meno comes from Thessaly (70a–b), and we learn from Xenophon that he betrayed his fellow Greeks to the Persian king (*Anabasis* 2.6.28–29).

9. Herodotus' most specific information about Pamphylia locates it in the Empire. Pamphylia belongs to one of the tax districts that Darius creates (*Histories* 3.90.1), and supports the fleet invading Greece with thirty ships, albeit equipped Ἑλληνικοῖσι ὅπλοισι "with Greek weaponry" (7.91).

10. Herodotus *Histories* 5.68.2; Ephorus fragment 15. For discussion, see J. Hall.

11. Grainger cites Herodotus *Histories* 7.91, Strabo *Geography* 14.4.3. Strabo repeats the information in Herodotus but adds that Mopsos—another seer—was a founder. The record on Amphilochos is confused: Herodotus himself credits Amphilochos with having founded a city near Syria (3.91.1), far from Pamphylia,

while Thucydides says he returned to Greece to found a new Argos, which then had its own history of losing and regaining its Greek language (*Peloponnesian War* 2.68.3–5). As for Calchas, the post-Homeric *Nostoi* has him going to the very different Asian site of Colophon (*Nostoi* fr. 1 = Proclus *Chrestomathy* 2).

12. Pausanias *Description of Greece* 7.3.7. But note that this passage is speaking not of the people in Pamphylia but of those people *from* that region who settled in Erythrae, up in Ionia. That those Pamphylians are Greek does not prove all the Pamphylians are too.

13. Thucydides mentions Pamphylia in connection with the battle at Eurymedon, a river he locates in that region. He does not describe Pamphylia's people or ethnicity: *Peloponnesian War* 1.100.1.

14. The inscription IG I³ 71 of the Delian League contains [Π]έργε "Perga" and [Σ]ίλλυ[ον] "Sillyon" (col. II, 113–14), and the more uncertain [Ἀσπεν]δος [ἐμ Παμφ]υλίαι "Aspendos in Pamphylia" (col. II, 156–57). *Searchable Greek Inscriptions*, consulted 6/11/2022.

15. For date of pseudo-Skylax, see Shipley.

16. Er's name appears twice in the Hebrew Bible: Gen.38.6, Chron. 4.21. This could be a coincidence; still Keren Freidenreich tells me that "Er" in Hebrew can mean "one who wakes." To those around Er in this world, the astonishing event about him would have been just his return to consciousness twelve days after apparent death (10.614b).

17. Plutarch offers the main ancient etymology for Er's name. In *Why the Oracles Cease to Give Answers*, one character explains "Er" as "a place in the *aêr* [air, atmosphere]" where souls go: *Moralia* 740b–c. On Plutarch and etymologies of names see on Isis, *Moralia* 351f (Hilton 66).

18. Keren Freidenreich is developing her own reading of the stories as bookends to the *Republic*'s argument. The observations she has made thus far prompted me to look back to Gyges in these remarks about Er, although her reading proceeds along different lines from mine.

19. See the provisional or incomplete nature of justice as disclosed through the tripartite structure of the city and soul: 4.435d, 6.504b. An ontological step remains from soul-justice to the form of justice, which is justice in its orientation to the good.

20. Harold Tarrant asked me about Orpheus's Thracian identity. This may have been a late development in biographies of Orpheus, for Plato's mentions of him and Thamyris never call them Thracian. Orpheus's status as poet implies that he was known as a Greek cultural hero and certainly that he spoke Greek. I hope to expand on this point on a future occasion.

21. This discussion grew out of a paper on the myth of Er that I read at the Society for Ancient Greek Philosophy in 2018. Tony Preus sat in front of me as I read, attentive and supportive, and engaged with me about the paper's

arguments. In light of Tony's many labors on behalf of SAGP, and in support of the study of ancient philosophy, I am grateful for this chance to contribute to a volume in his honor.

Works Cited

Barney, Rachel. "Ring-Composition in Plato: The Case of *Republic X*." *Cambridge Critical Guide to Plato's Republic*, edited by Mark McPherran, Cambridge UP, 2010, pp. 32–51.

Bobonich, Christopher. *Plato's Utopia Recast: His Later Ethics and Politics*. Oxford UP, 2002.

Destrée, Pierre. "Who is Plato's Soldier Er? A note on ΗΡΩΣ ΤΟΥ ΑΡΜΕΝΙΟΥ, ΤΟ ΓΕΝΟΣ ΠΑΜΠΗΥΛΙΟΥ (*Resp.* 614B3-4)." *Classical Philology*, vol. 115, no. 3, 2020, pp. 566–77.

DuBois, Page. "The Slave Plato." *Slaves and Other Objects*. U of Chicago P, 2003, pp. 153–69.

Grainger, John D. *The Cities of Pamphylia*. Oxbow Books, 2009.

Hall, Edith. *Inventing the Barbarian: Greek Self-Definition through Tragedy*. Clarendon, 1989.

Hall, Jonathan M. *A History of the Archaic Greek World, ca. 1200–479 BCE*. 2nd ed., Wiley Blackwell, 2014.

Halliwell, Stephen. *Plato: Republic X*. Aris & Phillips, 1988.

Hilton, Collin Miles. *Plutarch Reading Plato: Interpretation and Mythmaking in the Early Empire*. 2020. Bryn Mawr College, PhD dissertation.

LeMoine, Rebecca. *Plato's Caves: The Liberating Sting of Cultural Diversity*. Oxford UP, 2020.

McPherran, Mark L. "Virtue, Luck, and Choice at the End of the *Republic*." *Cambridge Critical Guide to Plato's Republic*, edited by Mark McPherran, Cambridge UP, 2010, pp. 132–46.

Packard Humanities Institute, *Searchable Greek Inscriptions*. epigraphy.packhum.org/text/72

Pappas, Nickolas. *Plato's Exceptional City, Love, and Philosopher*. Routledge, 2021.

Shipley, Graham. *Pseudo-Skylax's Periplous: The Circumnavigation of the Inhabited World. Text, Translation, and Commentary*. Bristol Phoenix, 2011.

Skelton, Christina. "Greek-Anatolian Language Contact and the Settlement of Pamphylia." *Classical Antiquity*, vol. 36, 2017, pp. 104–29.

Vermeule, Emily. *Aspects of Death in Early Greek Art and Poetry*. U of California P, 1979.

Between *Numen* and *Nous*

Bachelard on the Awakening of Consciousness

Eileen Rizo-Patron

While we were discussing Gaston Bachelard's allusions to what he called the "*noumenal* dimension" hidden within the heart of phenomena in *Earth and Reveries of Repose* (8–43), Prof. Anthony Preus raised the question that launches this essay: "Shouldn't we say that the imagery Bachelard explores in that book is based on *numinal* intuitions (>Lt. *numen*) rather than on *noumenal* ideas (>Gk. *nous*)?[1] Before addressing this important question directly, let us note that Bachelard's understanding of the *noumenon* was more akin to a Platonic "Idea" that the intellect may be able to tune into under special circumstances (*New Scientific* 5–6), than to Kant's unknowable "in-itself."[2]

But in order to distinguish between the *noumenal* and the *numinal* (or *numinous*) in Bachelard's own thinking, we must examine the meaning and sources of these two distinct modes of intuition, and then consider their possible interactions as he explored the workings of human consciousness in his philosophical works. This was, in fact, one of the questions that Bachelard grappled with throughout his career—even though he did not explicitly deploy the terms *numen* and *nous*, used here for heuristic purposes. Nonetheless, in his earlier *Dialectic of Duration* (134n2) he had cited Rudolf Otto's critique of Henri Bergson in *The Idea of the Holy* (112n1) for confounding a rational conception (i.e., *noumenon*) with an intuition that bears the force of a religious or aesthetic feeling (i.e., *numen*).[3] When offering a hindsight snapshot of his own findings in this same book, however, Bachelard was himself left with this provocative question: "Between *pure thought* and *pure poetry*, we have suddenly found links . . . correspondences. We have moved not just from one meaning to another, but from meaning to soul. . . . Might poetry then not be a mere accident, a detail, a diversion of being? Could it be the very principle of creative evolution?" (*Dialectic* 22)

Etymological Sources

As we proceed to examine the etymological roots of the Latin term *numen* (pl. *numina*; adj. *numinal, numinous*) and the Greek *noumenon* (>Gk. *noein*; pl. *noumena*; adj. *noumenal*), let us keep in mind the fluid associations and mutations that language undergoes as it traverses time, space, and cultures, for—as Bachelard often noted—imagination and usage are the forces that induce the formation of words which later may be officially ratified (*Earth-Will* 118; *Earth-Repose* 66; *Reverie* 110).

The Latin *numen* is defined in the *Merriam-Webster Dictionary* as a "divine force" usually identified with a natural phenomenon, object, or place. Etymologically, it is said to be related to *nuo+men* "a nodding with the head," suggesting an "assent to divine influence (Erasmus 415)."[4] But some scholars claim that the Greek term *noumenon* (denoting "an influence apprehensible by the mind") migrated into Early Latin as *noumen*—likely implying the "force of an idea"—only later to take the form of *numen* as a "divine force" in Classical Latin.[5] It was Rudolf Otto who centuries later coined the adjective *numinous*, in *The Idea of the Holy*, as a "category of value" that described those intuitions experienced as a shock or flash of revelation capable of disarming both heart and mind, exposing them to advents of mystery, searing beauty, divine grace, or horror—depending on the attitude or mental state of the subject (7, 52–61).[6]

Parsing Bachelard's "*Noumenon*"

Unlike some interpretations of the Platonic Idea or Form, however, Bachelard's *noumenon* was not necessarily "immutable." It seemed, rather, to pick up on the dynamic sense of the Greek verb *noein*, and its middle-passive present participle, connoting "a thing being known."[7] Allusions to the noumenal in his writings could in fact range from the infinite microphysical or microgeometrical potentials of thought ("Noumenon" 80–83; *New Scientific* 6; *Philosophy* 27, 51–53, 81, 89), to ideal insights that emerge as "glimmers of enlightenment" from dark zones of the world-psyche (*Instant* 3; *Reverie* 126), to the endlessly resonating semantic depth of words—whether literary or scientific (*Earth-Repose* 8–9). Bachelard even coined the term *bibliomenon* to suggest purely intellectual intuitions, not based on empirical precedents but that are nonetheless recognized and shared through the written word (*Activité* 13–14).[8] Most important, he regarded the *noumenon* as a "vibrant idea" that harbors dynamic and *generative* capacities. As early as 1931 he defined a microphysical *noumenon* as a "center of radiation capable of generating phenomena" ("Noumenon" 76). And years later, he would further qualify it as a "*nougonal noumenon*" (>Gk. *nous* + *gonia*)—namely, an idea with the power to spawn new ideas (*Rationalisme* 109–10). This potential, which has its ancient Greek antecedent in Anaxagoras' "seeds of *Nous*,"[9] might help explain how the early Latin *noumen*—if understood as an "idea force"—could lend itself to be transmuted into *numen* as a "divine force" in classical Latin, whereupon it donned its more explicitly "religious" slant. It is this connotation that Rudolf Otto seemed to pick up on when he unfolded the nature of the *numinous* in *The Idea of the Holy*, arguing that it is no mere subjective feeling or impression, but an actual phenomenon that addresses the self: a *numen praesens* which may alight as a shock, a warning, a gift, a call (11ff).

The Instant: Between *Numen* and *Nous*?

The text that jumpstarted Bachelard's lifelong exploration of the relations between *numen* and *nous* in the awakening of consciousness was *Intuition of the Instant*, Bachelard's first book on what he regarded as the discontinuous nature of time,[10] inspired by the lyrical power and ideas of Gaston Roupnel's philosophical novel *Siloë*.[11] In his introduction to this early work, Bachelard was already alluding to apparent interactions between *numen* and *nous* via the dynamic interface he discovered between inspiration and reason:[12] "Whether it comes from suffering or whether it comes from joy, we all experience as human beings a moment of illumination at some point in our lives: a moment when we suddenly understand our own message, a moment when knowledge, by shedding light on passion, detects *at once* the rules and relentlessness of destiny—a truly synthetic moment when decisive failure, by rendering us conscious of the irrational, becomes the success of thought" (*Instant* 3). These suggestive lines are followed by a series of clues that Bachelard will proceed to unpack and examine critically—not only in *Intuition of the Instant* but throughout his career, from a number of disciplinary and contextual perspectives (epistemological, psychological, rhythmanalytical, pedagogical, poetic, etc.). His allusion to an affective experience in this passage is immediately accompanied by reason's recognizant retrieval as it reflects on the event, potentially opening the way to understanding one's "message." A dialectical motion thus becomes evident in that "synthetic moment" of illumination between *numen* and *nous*, triggered by the initial shock on consciousness. While a powerful intuition such as this might not need to be experienced more than once in a lifetime to keep *resonating* in memory as a destinal summons, human nature tends to avoid it or otherwise twist it to inflate the ego, in which case it may take several "knocks" for one to wake up to its implications. Even then, it seems to act but as a turning point—surely one among many to come—whereupon the conscious work toward human awakening might resume its progress, again and again, along an "anagenetic" spiral of becoming (>Gk. *ana* + *genesis*: rising birth):[13] "Intellectual courage consists in actively and vitally preserving this instant of nascent knowledge, of making it the unceasing fountain of our intuition, and of designing—with the subjective history of our errors and faults—the model of a better, more illumined life" (*Instant* 4).

Before overviewing Bachelard's proposed models, however, we should note that Bachelard's reading of *Siloë*'s "guiding idea" (*Instant* 5)—unlike Roupnel's rhapsodic narrative of human redemption—actually took the shape of a polemic against Bergson's theory of "continuous time," a polemic he would keep sharpening in later works. Nonetheless, toward the conclusion of *Intuition of the Instant*, he admitted being struck by the realization of the shortfalls of his own restricted rationalistic approach:[14] "While reading *Siloë*, we were keenly aware that we were contributing, by our own commentary, an assortment of loaded contradictions. But sympathy with the work soon encouraged us to trust the lessons we drew from our own errors" (*Instant* 57). It is this very recognition that would launch Bachelard toward a deeper exploration of a series of disciplines of waking consciousness which in his *Intuition of the Instant* he labeled as "pedagogies of discontinuity" (*Instant* xii, xv-n11, 33).

Approaches to the Noumenal

In *Earth and Reveries of Repose*, Bachelard lamented the fact that many contemporary philosophers after Kant had tended to disregard the entire realm of noumenal potentiality that happened to be unveiled by the new twentieth-century sciences of quantum physics and noumenal chemistry, often dismissing the glimmers of enlightenment that can emerge from hidden zones of the universe and the psyche, thus "condemning human beings to remain on the phenomenal plane" (*Earth-Repose* 7). Paul Dirac's microphysical discovery of "negative mass" and "negative energy" through "mathematical dreaming," I suspect, not only introduced him to the "surrational potentials of reverie" (*Philosophy* 28–33) but seems to have begun stirring a speculation in him regarding a possible relation between anagogic (>Gk. *ana* + *agein*, to lead upwards) and poetic reveries, as modes of *breaking through* and *beyond* epistemological and affective obstacles, respectively, even if proceeding from opposite poles of the psyche (intellectual heights vs. depths of the soul).[15] It was the advent of those new sciences, which boldly traverse the realms of "pure thought" and "matter," that must have triggered such *questions* regarding crossovers or correspondences between "noumenal intuitions of negative mass" and the "elemental poetic reveries" he would soon start exploring in his long series on "the imagination of matter."[16] Although science and poetry adopt entirely different methods to probe such hidden energies—that is, through abstract intellectual formulations (*Philosophy* 32) *versus* sympathetic image-soundings through "the vibratory aspect of our being" (*Air* 84, *Space* 14)—both approaches, I would argue, are predicated upon the axiomatic presence of a hidden force-field in which human beings are immersed—body, mind, and soul—and within which humanity aspires to *participate* creatively. In fact, such intense aspiration had already been expressed in the *Dialogues of Plato*—most powerfully in the *Symposium* (212a–b) and the *Republic* (490a–b), which address, each in its own way, the *potential* for human beings ultimately to "participate" in the *generation* of pure truth and beauty by "commingling" with the gods, yet only once having undergone an arduous process of education for the refinement of mind and soul.[17]

So, in *Earth and Reveries of Repose*, Bachelard would venture to offer four (independent, yet intertwining) pedagogical paths by which he believed this elusive "noumenal" realm might be tapped into—not only in the *hard sciences* but also, rather urgently, when it comes to the *human sciences* (given the psycho-social and political climate he had been living through around World War II).[18] These pedagogies could be summarily paraphrased as (1) practices of purification through the examination of consciousness accompanied by the recognition and rectification of error (objective and subjective); (2) pedagogies of discontinuity, including a rhythmic dialectics that takes note of being's need for concealment amid bursts of disclosure, or stages of intense action *versus* letting go; (3) pedagogies of provocation that encourage contradiction and clashes of interpretation through polemical debate—guided by the powers of *animus*; and (4) disciplines of lucid reverie marked by an "approach of open wonder" in the face of unprecedented experience, with its deliberate adoption of an attitude of non-knowing and deep listening—guided by the powers of *anima* (*Space* xxxii–iii; *Reverie* 65–67, 95).[19]

Bachelard's Pedagogies of Waking Consciousness

> The unexamined life is not worth living.
>
> —Plato, *Apology* (38a5–6)

Examination of Consciousness and Recognition of Error

Whereas in the *Formation of the Scientific Mind* and in the *Philosophy of No* Bachelard traces epistemological obstacles to the attainment of "objective knowledge," in *Psychoanalysis of Fire* (and his subsequent works from 1942–1948) he will delve into an exploration of obstacles of subjective affect and culturally shared "complexes of the elemental imagination" (fire, water, air, and earth). These distinct branches of study illustrate, via specific examples, Bachelard's double pedagogy of mind and soul purification through the examination of consciousness and conscience, accompanied by the recognition of objective and subjective error. He expresses the value of these processes, rather movingly, writing toward the end of his *Psychoanalysis of Fire*:

> To admit one has erred is to pay the most signal homage to the perspicacity of one's mind. By so doing we re-live our education, intensify it, illuminate it with converging rays of

light. We also externalize, proclaim and teach it. . . . But how much more intense this is when our objective knowledge is the knowledge of the *subjective*, when we discover in our own heart the human universal, when, after having honestly psychoanalyzed our study of self, we integrate the rules of morality with the laws of psychology. Then the fire that was consuming us suddenly enlightens us. (*Fire* 100–1)

Such self-vigilance is made possible by our capacity for self-abstraction from natural habits, drives, cultural routines, or from any kind of ideological identity with which we might become inordinately attached.[20] It facilitates the recognition of limiting prejudices (subjective, objective, individual, collective), hence the release of the *cogito* along what he will call time's "vertical axis" (which cuts across the horizontal axis of transitive time) as a series of awakenings.[21]

PEDAGOGIES OF DISCONTINUITY: RHYTHMIC DIALECTICS

But self-vigilance is not simply a matter of intellectual self-abstraction, as Bachelard also notes in his *Dialectic of Duration*. It is necessarily linked to a rhythmic dialectics where the psyche needs to alternate between exertion and rest, attitudes and perspectives, to allow itself a balanced process of renewal, sublimation, and growth. This entails the ongoing admission of the limits of *nous* (reason) and our need to remain open to sudden blows of *numen* (however elating or painful) that may descend upon us at any moment. This rhythmic dialectics—so crucial to Bachelard's notion of "pedagogies of discontinuity" (*Intuition* xvn11, 33)—is also illustrated in his recognition of necessary alternations between mystical tension and relaxation (*Air* 121), between dreaming in *anima* and thinking in *animus* (*Reverie* 55–95), between the therapeutic activation vs. reduction of complexes (*Lautréamont* 69), including the ability to forgive oneself for falling prey to unhelpful habits and drives (*Dialectic* 147). For, the mere *awareness of stumbling blocks* can often have a paralyzing effect, so that moving beyond them must depend on the deployment of focused energy and positive feeling (*Lautréamont* 90–91). Bachelard will thus describe anagenetic becoming—psychic awakening that follows a path of sublimation toward an ideal—as rhythmically punctuated by breaks between inspired resumptions (*Dialectic* 47, 91, 102).

Pedagogies of Polemical Provocation

An evident antecedent to Bachelard's pedagogical approach in this case—particularly in some of its variations we will visit below—was the Socratic Method, through its exercise of critical questioning, dialogue, and debate.[22] It is certainly a precursor to Bachelard's incessant questioning of our underlying assumptions and axioms, in order to discover epistemological and affective obstacles that hinder human access to truth. As did Socrates, Bachelard insisted that "truth is the daughter of discussion, not of sympathy"—much less of complicity. In his view, human beings suffer individually *and* collectively "from an incapacity to make [their] thoughts mobile" (*Philosophy* 114). In Bachelard's words, *la tête bien faite* (the made-up mind) "needs to be remade." If incapable of mutating it suffers, for humankind is essentially "a mutating species" (*Formation* 26).

In *Philosophy of No*—the text that best summarizes his polemical philosophy—Bachelard will propose that, in the face of rational impasses, the mind has the potential to rise to *noumenal* heights—notably in scientific work—through the practice of a "dialectical surrationalism" he there describes as an anagogically mathematizing reverie that "ventures into thought, that thinks while it ventures, that seeks an illumination of thought by thought, and finds a sudden intuition beyond the veils of informed thought" (32).[23] Thanks to its synthetic agility, he celebrates mathematics here as a "model language" that helps promote dialectical thinking (32, 113), while drawing detailed examples from microphysics, noumenal chemistry, and microgeometry that tackle contradictions to promote progress in scientific thought (34–89).

Inspired by Alfred Korsybski's *Science and Sanity* and his pedagogical work in American classrooms,[24] here Bachelard will also advocate the cultivation of critical-semantic agility in young students via exercises in semantic-contradiction, or what Korsybski calls a "non-Aristotelian logic," to help attune their minds to a living logos revealed in "instants of nascent knowledge," over against the tendencies of language to inculcate fixed definitions, strict linear thinking, and mental automatism through repetition and conceptual sedimentation (*Philosophy* 110–14).

In defense of deploying Korsybski's "non-Aristotelian logic of contradiction" in language classrooms to stimulate brain-growth in children, Bachelard claims that—particularly in those cases where mental obstacles have been instilled by repetitive programming or affective complexes—the mind needs to be *stunned* by some "critical impasse" before it can be broken open to novel thinking (*Philosophy* 109-10). So, beyond the proposed practice of "non-Aristotelian logic" in elementary education, Bachelard will suggest the importance of teaching a diversity of languages and literary cultures from a young age to promote the expansion of consciousness,[25] even though—given the cultural climate at the time (late 1930s-1940s)—this had seemed a remote possibility (112). In fact, Bachelard wrote: "He [Korsybski] foresaw an American nation—and no doubt all nations—very soon afflicted by an epidemic of schizophrenia, . . . [which] would develop somehow at the level of the language centers. It would come from a lack of synchronization between the evolution of reality and society, on the one hand, and the evolution of language" (*Philosophy* 113). This is a prognosis we are, alas, finding confirmed through the tendency toward technological reduction (at times weaponization) of sociopolitical language so prevalent in our days.

Looking back on this section, however, I would argue that, although "mathematical reverie" is lauded in the *Philosophy of No* as the best way to promote agility in abstract relations among ideas and in dialectical thinking, anagogic reverie cannot be restricted to mathematical language—as Bachelard will even here suggest, despite himself, by invoking the "*ars poetica* of physics" (32). In his subsequent books, on the elemental imagination, he will indeed reveal that "poetic reverie" can just as well lead to flexible new ways of thinking through the exercise of the so-called "unreality principle" of imagination, which—interwoven with the "reality principle" of perception in a healthy psyche—encourages the lucid entertainment of *possibilities*, rather than the premature dismissal of contradictions, hence helping promote a dialectic of *values* capable of stimulating anagenetic evolution (*Water* 23; *Air* 7; *Earth-Repose* 60-67, 82; *Reverie* 81, 160-62).

Oneiric Values and Lucid Reverie

The above remarks bring us back to Rudolf Otto's description of the *numen* as a "category of *value*"—distinct from a "category of reason" (7). As it turns out, right on the heels of Bachelard's overview of proposed approaches to *noumenal* insight in *Earth and Reveries of Repose*, he would interject the startling caveat that "Any theory of the knowledge of reality that discards *oneiric values* ultimately divorces itself from the *vital interests* that give *impetus to knowledge itself*" (8, emphasis added). Since this particular work had been devoted to exploring the powers of elemental reverie through poetic imagery, he would defer elaborating on his thesis regarding the sources of "knowledge" to a subsequent work on epistemology (which we will address below). Nonetheless, the implication here is that reason itself is essentially linked with "oneiric values" (>Gk. *oneiros* = dream).

So our question here is: what is the nature of those "oneiric values" on which reason depends, and what are some key examples? While it is clear that our innate desire for the ideal of pure Truth is what constantly impels reason to revise and surpass its own paradigms—a value exemplified by the philosopher's unrelenting quest for truth in Books VI and VII of Plato's *Republic* and by humanity's never-ending scientific efforts to understand the hidden workings of our universe—it is the desire for pure Beauty, lauded by Diotima in Plato's *Symposium*, that gives flight to aesthetic ventures to tune into the hidden symphonies of Being. One might infer that both quests for ultimate Truth and Beauty are moved by an innate—if forgotten—desire for the Good beating deep in our hearts—a value that, if awakened, seems to feed virtue and fuel moral action, as proposed in Plato's *Meno* (80d, 85c–88d).

All such values seem to point us toward a flickering *numinous-noumenal* force-field that needs to be tuned into via various modes of attentive reverie—anagogic, elemental, poetic—that can break through (and beyond) already instituted rational or aesthetic categories, enabling the mind to respond to a subtler and deeper call. Although throughout most of his works Bachelard emphasizes the role of "formal causality"—intellectual or aesthetic—in human awakenings (*Intuition* 61, 63; *Dialectic* 123, 133, 134; *Lautréamont* 85, 88–89), he will also suggest that such formal causes are oriented by some purpose (however penumbral) that can usher human consciousness either toward an anagenetic or a catagenetic fate (*Lautréamont* 88; *Water* 142; *Air* 112). Hence the importance of becoming increasingly conscious of what he had called the "oneiric values" that motivate life and thought.

Crucial, in this regard, is Bachelard's growing recognition that "poetic reverie" (unlike daydream) is not a slackening of thought in passive submission to libidinal forces—as he appeared to imply in his brief description of the "Orpheus complex" in the *Dialectic of Duration* (152), and in his description of "ordinary reverie" in the *Philosophy of No* (32)—but rather a lucid mode of "thinking-dreaming" capable of both diving into the obscure "infrared" zones of the psyche to emerge as "intensified awareness" (*Lautréamont* 84–86; *Water* 18; *Reverie* 5–6; 127–28), and of rising to rarefied "ultraviolet" heights of illumination and moral courage

(*Lautréamont* 86–88) as illustrated in Nietzsche's "ascensional reveries" explored in *Air and Dreams* (140–45). The verticality of reverie needs to allow this dialectic of depths and heights (*Intuition* 61), or to welcome both movements (of undoing and sublimation) in *uno actu*, as proposed by the poet and polymath Novalis (*Air* 107–09, 144, 263).

Interestingly, later in the *Poetics of Reverie*, Bachelard will discover that even in those instants when we are able to reverberate to the slightest "variations" in poetic imagery, consciousness may experience "micro-awakenings," which nonetheless bear enduring and significant implications: "Every instance of new awareness (*prise de conscience*) is an increment to consciousness, an added light, a reinforcement of psychic coherence. Its swiftness or instantaneity may hide that growth from us. But there is a growth of being in every *prise de conscience*" (5, translation amended).[26]

In this regard, Hans-Georg Gadamer would make a pertinent remark in his *Truth and Method*, suggesting that access to *noumenal* ideality might potentially be opened by a fleeting *numinous* intuition of "beauty as radiance": "[Such beauty] appears suddenly; and just as suddenly disappears again. If we must speak with Plato of a hiatus (*chorismus*) between the world of the senses and the world of ideas, this is where it is and this is where it is also overcome" (438). Plato's hiatus, in this case, is none other than what Bachelard had called the *instant* as the simultaneously destructive/redemptive locus of discontinuous time.

Toward a *Noumenological* Account of Becoming?

Before we close, I would like to address Bachelard's attempt at a synoptic account of how thought is able to rise through various levels of the cogito, on its way to releasing the mind from the automatism of natural attachments, emotional reactions, and habits of thought (individual and collective), thus helping reawaken consciousness to the hidden wisdom of the soul (*Dialectic* 108–12; cf. *Instant* 58–63; *Rationalisme* 79–81).

Taking his cue from quantum physics in the *Dialectic of Duration*, Bachelard associated what in *Intuition of the Instant* he had called "the eternal return of reason" with discontinuous moments of qualitative becoming: "Qualitative becoming is . . . a quantum becoming. It has to move through a dialectic, going from the same to the same via the other" (*Dialectic* 102). This suggests that what he calls "intellectual time"—if indeed punctuated by numinous moments of noumenal illumination—has more to do with quantum pulses and leaps than it does with the coherence of discursive rational continuity. Although he admits that such leaps and ruptures do not suffice to clarify the superimposition of our temporal experiences at the several levels of the living body, mind, and soul, he claims they help us realize that time springs up and rebounds rhythmically at several simultaneous levels of consciousness which manifest as different frequencies. Thus he argues that, while riddled with lacunae, the pulse of time has a depth or density which—depending on each individual's state of mind and soul—might either be inwardly experienced as a cacophony of voices, burdened by "ill-made durations" (21), or be harmoniously coordinated by an underlying rhythm conducive to the awakening of wisdom, and the repose of the soul (102).

Beyond the basic level of the Cartesian cogito (*I think, therefore I am*), which in his view unfolds along the horizontal axis of phenomenal time (*Dialectic* 109), Bachelard specifically proposes that the human cogito is able to rise to a second level (*I think that I think*) whereupon it can observe its thinking modes, and even rise to a third level (*I think that I think that I think*) that embarks consciousness beyond "*phenomenological* description" toward a "*noumenological* description" which offers what he calls "the first adumbration of vertical time"—namely, the axis of liberation, perpendicular to transitive time, which brings on an awakening of the *moral person* (108–11; cf. *Instant* 62–63).

Many years later, after having devoted himself to exploring the poetic imagination for about a decade (1938–48), Bachelard returns to matters of epistemology in *Le Rationalisme Appliqué* (1949), where he will further hone in on the possibility of accessing higher (or deeper) orbits of consciousness through acute self-vigilance and rectification of our modes of knowing, and further discuss what he recognizes to be rationalism's "transcendent vocation" (80). But now, resuming his description of the stages of cogito proposed in his earlier *Dialectic of Duration*, he will label the ones corresponding to $(cogito)^1$, $(cogito)^2$, and $(cogito)^3$, as first-, second-, and third-degree "surveillance of consciousness"[27] (*Rationalisme* 77–81), and ultimately include a radiant realm of open-ended potentiality, accessible via a "fourth-degree surveillance of consciousness" corresponding to the meditative zone of $(cogito)^4$ which, in his earlier texts, he had alluded to as exceedingly elusive, and difficult to attain (*Dialectic* 100):[28]

> During *special reveries*, we may find heightened instances of lucidity of fourth-degree surveillance that occur at radically

discontinuous moments, when the thinking being is suddenly *surprised to think*. . . . At such moments, we get the impression that what calls to be addressed is *a doctrine of births*. . . . When we allow ourselves to be led by true poets, we get the feeling that we need to admit the presence of a "fifth element"—a luminous, ethereal element that would be the dialectical element of the four "elements of imagination" we explored systematically and meditated upon for many years. (*Rationalisme* 81, my translation and emphasis)

Here Bachelard seems to be "divining" the presence of a poetic logos that serves as a backdrop for the dialectics of the four classical elements of nature and imagination[29] and—I submit—even for his surrational dialectics. It clearly anticipates the "substance of inspiration" he will cite later in his career, in the *Poetics of Reverie* (1961), as an essence "irreducible to any physical substance" (7). Also, in the *Poetics of Reverie* Bachelard will reiterate that the light of the "cogito of reverie" is a "glimmer that does not know its origin," or that "rebounds from unfathomable depths" (126). Although he admits that—unlike the professor's cogito—it does not immediately translate into "certainty," its light presents itself as the "force of an idea" that, I dare suggest, resurrects the earlier-cited classical Latin notion of *noumen* (transitional term between the Greek *noumenon* and the Latin *numen*) that Bachelard had found so powerfully illustrated in Roupnel's *Siloë*: "At the root of his contemplative redemption, we believe, lies a *force* that enables us to accept life in a single act, with all its intimate contradictions. In placing absolute nothingness at both edges of the instant, Roupnel must have been led to such intensity of consciousness that the entire image of a destiny was legible, in a sudden glimmer, within the very act of mind and spirit" (*Instant* 56, emphasis added). Even in the *Dialectic of Duration*—despite its argument tending to favor intellectual or formal causality above a determinative final causality (110–11)—Bachelard admitted that the intellect ultimately needed to "give way" to some form of finality (91) which, rather than emerging from the discursive chain of duration, tends to come as a subtle voice, a sudden glimmer, or a lightning burst from a pulsating logos that cuts unexpectedly into the logos of ratio (102).

For Bachelard, as we have seen, such voices or flashes of insight can be intuited in the heart as "oneiric values" that empower the intellect to re-envision paradigms and re-organize its priorities in the pursuit of knowledge (*Earth-Repose* 8; cf. *Instant* 56–57; *Reverie* 126). For they are moments when one's life message is suddenly *brought into focus* (*Instant* 3)—revelations that can hence serve as a navigating compass, orienting human reason toward the promotion of the soul's well-being and the fulfillment of its urgent moral purposes.

Notes

1. This discussion was triggered by my essay "Sounding the Noumenal in the Phenomenal: Bachelard and Arguedas."

2. A key legacy of Plato's philosophy is the notion that *noumena* and the *noumenal* world are "objects of the highest knowledge, truths, and values." In his transcendental aesthetic, Immanuel Kant would adopt the Platonic Idea as a "*noumenon*" contrasted with a "*phenomenon*," giving it his own interpretation(s) in the *Critique of Pure Reason* (A254, 271). See Honderich 657.

3. Bachelard's reference to *The Idea of the Holy*—albeit brief—indicates his acquaintance with the French translation (*Le Sacré*, 1932) of Otto's original *Das Heilige* (1920), which directly explored the notion of the *numinous* vis-à-vis rationality.

4. See also "Numen," Wiktionary. en.wiktionary.org/wiki/numen

5. See Riccioli (47). Also at: en.wiktionary.org/wiki/numen

6. Although Bachelard generally avoided using theological terminology, he explored spiritual experiences from the perspectives of philosophical aesthetics, myth, depth-psychology, and contemplative reverie, including Eastern meditation practices. See Kearney, "Vertical Time: Bachelard's Epiphanic Instant" (57–58) and Kotowicz on Bachelard vis-à-vis aspects of Buddhist thought (137–40, 155).

7. See "Noumenon," at en.wikipedia.org/wiki/Noumenon_(disambiguation)

8. Such *bibliomena* could include, for instance, ideas and values such as those inscribed in the U.S. Constitution which—while conceived to be self-evident—serve as "ideals" for human society to strive toward as it faces the specific challenges of each historical period.

9. See www.encyclopedia.com/people/philosophy-and-religion/philosophy-biographies/anaxagoras.

10. Bachelard's second book on time, *Dialectic of Duration*, further develops Roupnel's thesis of temporal discontinuity (18–20), in an argument against Bergson's notion of continuous duration.

11. *Siloë* traced the journey of human consciousness from its elemental origins to its metaphysical destiny. Although its title is inspired on the pool of Siloam (John 9:7), Roupnel insisted that *Siloë* was not intended as a biblical reference but was left open to each reader's interpretation (*Siloë* 8). Bachelard associated the

springs of Siloam with the "renewal of rational freshness" (*Instant* 3), and with what he called "the very sources of the person" (*Dialectic* 18).

12. As we will see, Bachelard would continue to grapple with the tensions between *nous* and *numen* throughout his writings in the guise of intellectual vs. oneiric intuitions, anagogic vs. poetic reveries, etc. (*Instant* 3–5, 55–57; *Dialectic* 22; *Earth-Repose* 19; *Space* xx–xxi).

13. Subject to a temporal dialectics, human beings are constantly undergoing, in Bachelard's view, either anagenetic or catagenetic transformations—that is, toward evolution or degradation (*Dialectic* 132, 142; *Lautréamont* 88–90). In *Water and Dreams* he will claim that "anagenetic duration" is a matter of progressive growth associated with work, and the will to produce (108).

14. As we shall see below, Bachelard will persist in promoting the virtues of *polemical reason* not only in his epistemological works, but even in his poetic studies, where he acclaims the Promethean ideal as a powerful "culture complex" expressed as a defiance against the gods, in the effort to help humanity gain intellectual mastery over nature (*Fire* 7–12; *Fragments* 65–89). I examine the ambivalences of this struggle in "Bachelard's Subversive Hermeneutics: A Reading of 'Lightning' in Shelley's *Prometheus Unbound*" (362).

15. In *Philosophy of No*, Bachelard trenchantly contrasts "anagogic reverie" with "natural reverie," which he there described as passively following the seductions of the libido (32). But he was soon to discover that "poetic reverie" can be a *lucid discipline* capable of delving deep into the psyche to emerge as "intensified awareness" (*Water* 18; *Reverie* 5, 6, 127–28).

16. In the *Psychoanalysis of Fire*, Bachelard had tackled "fire complexes" under a harsh light, not initially sympathetic to flights of reverie. However, midway through that book he underwent a subtle turn in attitude regarding their potential. Significantly, right after finishing the *Philosophy of No* in 1940—the year he was hired as Chair of the History and Philosophy of Science at the Sorbonne—he shocked the academic world by plunging head-on into his series on elemental reveries: *Water and Dreams*, *Air and Dreams*, *Earth and Reveries of Will*, and *Earth and Reveries of Repose*.

17. Here I cite from the Jowett translations of the *Republic* 490a–b: "The keen edge will not be blunted, nor the force of his desire abate until [the seeker] have attained the *knowledge* of the true nature of every essence by a *sympathetic and kindred power in the soul,* and by that power drawing near, mingling and becoming incorporate with very Being. Having thus *begotten* mind and *truth*, he will have knowledge and will live and grow truly" (355); and the *Symposium* 212a: "In that *communion* only, beholding beauty with the eye of the mind, he will be enabled to *bring forth beauty*, not representations of beauty, but realities . . . and bringing forth and nourishing true virtue to become the friend of God . . ." (218).

18. Given the prescribed limits of this essay, we will here offer only a synoptic view of Bachelard's proposed ways "to design and illustrate the model

of a better, more illumined life" (*Instant* 3) as elaborated in subsequent essays throughout his career.

19. While Bachelard long professed to keep both *animus* vs. *anima* modes of intuition sharply distinguished (*Reverie* 211–12), he would keep grappling with their interaction in his explorations of waking consciousness (*Reverie* 93). Dr. Anthony Preus is nonetheless right in noting that the realm accessed through "poetic wonder" might best be described as "numinous" than "noumenal."

20. Such self-abstraction implies a capacity to place our ostensible identities (or the roles we play in life—political, personal, ethnic, religious, etc.) in a gentler, less judgmental perspective.

21. Below we will trace the stages of this expanding consciousness by addressing what Bachelard calls a "*noumenological* description" of subjective experience *(Dialectic* 108–12; *Rationalisme* 79–81; cf. *Intuition* 58–63).

22. Most of Bachelard's proposed pedagogies, in fact, have undeniable antecedents in the Platonic Dialogues. Specifically, his works on the examination of objective error can be traced back to Plato's teachings in Book VII of the *Republic* regarding the seeker's emergence from the "cave of shadow appearances" to encounter the source of Truth or noumenal light (Book VII). And his works on facing "subjective error" or on purifying affective consciousness could be traced back to Diotima's teachings on the sublimation of human desire, guided by divine Love, to attain a vision of Beauty in Plato's *Symposium* (212b). Thanks to Diotima's guidance, Socrates realized that reaching a state of communion with divine Love and Beauty's radiance at the core of being is *essential* to the ultimate fulfillment of right-living or *politeia* itself—given that it involves the harmonious order of socio-political relationships in a polis (*Symposium 212a*).

23. Translation slightly amended. Waterston translates Bachelard's "*rêverie anagogique*" as "anagogical dreaming," erasing an important distinction between *rêve* (dream) and *rêverie* (reverie) that Bachelard will explicitly clarify in his later *Poetics of Reverie* (11).

24. Alfred Korsybski was an American philosopher, author of *Science and Sanity*. Original and later editions are cited here: www.biblio.com/science-and-sanity-by-alfred-korzybski/work/97190.

25. At higher-education levels this practice is extended by deliberately promoting critical discussions regarding pressing issues of the time through "a plurality of interpretations" (*Philosophy* 100, 121), with the teacher even playing "devil's advocate" (as did Socrates) to help promote dialectical thinking. On the importance of promoting such thinking, see also Paul Ricœur, *Conflict of Interpretations: Essays in Hermeneutics I*; even the ancient Greek philosopher Heraclitus on the essential tensions and contradictions of the "ever-living Logos" (see Kahn 192, 267ff).

26. Bachelard's "*prise de conscience*" (translated by D. Russell as "awareness") implies actively *taking something offered to consciousness*, something "objective" alluded to by Rudolf Otto as a *numen* in *Idea of the Holy* (11).

27. These stages cannot but bring to mind the analogously expanding orbits of consciousness in Diotima's account of the pursuit of true Beauty as radiance in Plato's *Symposium* (210a–212a).

28. On the possible dangers of entering this "meditative zone" (which might recall the state of mind of priestesses at the Delphic oracles), see Bachelard's 1955 essay on Balzac's *Séraphîta*, partly inspired by Swedenborgian mysticism (RD 93–99), including Balzac's own comments about his experience writing his short novel (*RD* 95, 95n6).

29. Bachelard was a neo-Presocratic Ionian thinker, by temperament, as Kotowicz notes: the "four elements were as real to him as they were to the early Greeks; he dwelled in a hylozoic world and thought like an atomist" (156). However, his understanding of the ever-living logos drew not only on Ionic cosmic principles but was ultimately rooted in the dialectical tensions of the "inner, personal world of the psyche," as was Heraclitus' doctrine (Kahn 20–21). And while Bachelard's idealism was quite Platonic, Bachelard was still a pre-Platonic thinker in that his world was one "before philosophers entered the arena of politics and power" (Kotowicz 156).

Works Cited

Bachelard, Gaston. *Activité Rationaliste dans la Physique Contemporaine*. PUF, 1951.

———. *Air and Dreams*. Translated by Edith and Frederick Farrell, Dallas Institute Publications, 1988. Trans. of *L'Air et les songes*. José Corti, 1943.

———. *Dialectic of Duration*. Translated by Mary McAllester Jones, Clinamen, 2000 Trans. of *La Dialectique de la durée*. Boivin & Cie. Éditeurs, 1936.

———. *Earth and Reveries of Repose*. Translated by Mary McAllester Jones, Dallas Institute Publications, 2011. Trans. of *La Terre et les rêveries du repos*. José Corti, 1948.

———. *Earth and Reveries of Will*. Translated by Kenneth Haltmann, Dallas Institute Publications, 2002. Trans. of *La Terre et les rêveries de la volonté*. José Corti, 1947.

———. *Formation of the Scientific Mind*. Translated Mary McAllester Jones, Clinamen, 2002. Trans. of *La Formation de l'esprit scientifique*. Vrin, 1938.

———. *Intuition of the Instant*. Translated by Eileen Rizo-Patrón, Northwestern UP, 2013. Trans. of *L'Intuition de l'instant: Essai sur la Siloë de Gaston Roupnel*. Éditions Stock, 1932.

———. *Lautréamont*. Translated by Robert Scott Dupree, Dallas Institute Publications, 1986. Trans. of *Lautréamont*. José Corti, 1939.

———. *New Scientific Spirit*. Translated by Arthur Goldhammer, Beacon, 1984. Trans. of *Le Nouvel esprit scientifique*. PUF, 1934.

———. "Noumenon and Microphysics." Translated by Bernard Le Roy, *Philosophical Forum*, vol. 37, no. 1, 2006, pp. 75–84. philpapers.org/rec/BACNAM-2. Trans. Of "Noumène et Microphysique" (1931), *Études*, edited by G. Canguilhem, J. Vrin, 1970, pp. 11–24.

———. *Philosophy of No*. Translated by G. C. Waterston, Orion Press, 1968. Trans. of *Philosophie du non*. PUF, 1940.

———. *Poetics of Reverie*. Translated by Daniel Russell. Beacon, 1969. Trans. of *Poétique de la rêverie*. PUF, 1960.

———. *Poetics of Space*. Translated by Maria Jolas, Beacon, 1969. Trans. of *Poétiquede l'espace*. PUF, 1957.

———. *Psychoanalysis of Fire*. Translated by Alan C. M. Ross, Beacon, 1964. Trans. of *Psychanalyse du feu*. Librairie Gallimard, 1938.

———. *Rationalisme Appliqué*. 4th ed., PUF, 2004.

———. *Right to Dream*. Translated by J. A. Underwood, Dallas Institute Publications, 1988. Trans. of *Droit de rêver*. PUF, 1970.

———. *Water and Dreams*. Translated by Edith Farrell. Pegasus Foundation, 1983. Trans. of *L'Eau et les rêves*. José Corti, 1942.

Erasmus, Desiderius, *Collected Works of Erasmus*. U of Toronto P, 1985.

Gadamer, Hans-Georg. *Truth and Method*. Translated by Sheed & Ward Ltd., edited by Garrett Barden and John Cumming, Crossroad, 1985.

Honderich, Ted. *Oxford Companion to Philosophy*. Oxford UP, 1995.

Kahn, Charles H. *Art and Thought of Heraclitus*. Cambridge UP, 1979.

Kearney, Richard. "Vertical Time: Bachelard's Epiphanic Instant." *Adventures in Phenomenology: Gaston Bachelard*, edited by Eileen Rizo-Patron et al., SUNY Press, 2017, pp. 49–61.

Korsybski, Alfred. *Science and Sanity*. Science Press, 1933. Institute of General Semantics, 1948.

Kotowicz, Zbigniew. *Gaston Bachelard: Philosophy of the Surreal*. 2016. Edinburgh UP, 2018.

Meriam-Webster Dictionary. www.merriam-webster.com/dictionary/numen

Otto, Rudolf. *Idea of the Holy*. Translated by John W. Harvey, Mansfield, Martino, 2010. Trans. of *Das Heilige*, Vierte Auslage, Breslau, 1920.

Plato. *Apology. Collected Dialogues of Plato*, edited by Edith Hamilton and Huntington Cairns, Bollingen Series LXXI. Princeton UP, 1989, 3–26.

———. *Meno. Collected Dialogues of Plato*, edited by Edith Hamilton and Huntington Cairns, Bollingen Series LXXI. Princeton UP, 1989, pp. 353–84.

———. *Republic. Dialogues of Plato*, edited by Justin D. Kaplan. The Jowett Translations, Washington Square, 1972, pp. 235–386.

———. *Symposium. Dialogues of Plato*, edited by Justin D. Kaplan. The Jowett Translations, Washington Square, 1972, pp. 161–234.

Riccioli, Giovanni Battista. *Prosodia Bononiensis Reformata*. Venice: Typis Seminarii Patavii, 1714. (Original publication, Venice: Antonium Bortoli, 1707)

Ricœur, Paul. *Conflict of Interpretations: Essays in Hermeneutics I*, edited by John Ihde, Northwestern UP, 2007.

Rizo-Patron, Eileen. "Sounding the Noumenal in the Phenomenal." *Bachelard Studies*, edited by Jean-Phillippe Pierron, vol. 1, 2020, pp. 159–70. mimesisjournals.com/ojs/index.php/bachelardstudies/issue/view/52

———. "Bachelard's Subversive Hermeneutics: Role of Lightning in Shelley's *Prometheus Unbound*." *Religion and the Arts*, vol. 10, no. 3, 2006, pp. 355–73.

Justice, Accountability, and Its Limits in Plato's *Republic* I

Anne-Marie Schultz

Most readers of Plato regard the *Republic* as a sustained inquiry into the nature of justice (and injustice) on the individual and the political level. This view is not surprising given the project Socrates sets out in Book II after "Glaucon and the others begged [him] not to abandon the argument but to help in every way to track down what justice and injustice are and what the truth about their benefits is" (368c). Socrates suggests that they watch justice and injustice come into being in the city in speech (369a). Socrates describes a simple city of necessity (369a–71). He asks Glaucon and Adeimantus if they have glimpsed where justice came into being. Adeimantus says, "perhaps . . . it is in some need they have for one another" (371e). Socrates seems pleased and describes the city in further detail (372a–b). Glaucon interrupts this vision of justice grounded in mutual obligation: "You seem to make these men have their feast without relishes" (371c). Socrates then observes, "We are, as it seems, considering not only how a city, but also a luxurious city, comes into being" (372e). The rest of the *Republic* considers justice and injustice in the sick or "feverish" city (372e).

    I am not arguing against the well-established view that the *Republic* explores the nature of justice. Here, I consider Plato's philosophical masterpiece as a consideration of justice in terms of accountability and the limitations of this view of justice. This reconsideration arises from Socrates' expressed opinion that "the true city is . . . the one we just described"

(372e), which seems to contain a vision of justice as mutual need and accountability. To this end, I briefly define accountability and point to some relevant secondary literature. Second, I focus on how accountability arises in dramatic details of the opening scene. Third, I analyze Cephalus' and Polemarchus' definitions of justice. These passages can be interpreted in terms of individual and collective accountability. Fourth, I focus on the heated exchange between Thrasymachus and Socrates to show how Thrasymachus attempts to hold Socrates accountable for Athenian imperial injustices. Finally, I discuss aspects of Athenian history in the aftermath of the Peloponnesian War and how they may illuminate our own politically divisive times.

Accountability

Some might find my desire to read the *Republic* in terms of accountability problematic, because accountability seems to be such a contemporary ethical concept. However, the noun λόγος and the corresponding verb λέγειν convey a sense of accountability. One meaning of λόγος is "an account" and of λέγειν "give an account." With this association in mind, concerns about anachronism diminish significantly. The contemporary literature on accountability is quite large. I regard accountability as having three primary parts: First, it requires an understanding of mutual obligation to others. Second, it demands willingness to take responsibility for the results of our behaviors. Third, it involves taking action to repair the harm that arises from our actions. Accountability is both an individual and a collective process. For instance, someone might discover that their property is on unceded native land and decide to make a monthly payment to a charity supporting indigenous rights. Similarly, a university could offer discounted tuition to descendants of enslaved people who worked on the university grounds. Brendan Case notes, "Understandably, accountability is much on the public's mind these days, but most often in the negative, backwards-looking sense of increasingly fragile and sclerotic structures for holding wrongdoers accountable" (325). Case suggests that "We would perhaps do well, however, to pay greater attention to accountability, not only in these backwards-looking practices, but also as a forward-looking virtue, a disposition to live accountably in relation to those to whom one is rightly answerable" (325).

The Opening Scene

The *Republic* begins as Socrates narrates the events of the preceding day to an unnamed audience: "I went down to the Piraeus yesterday with Glaucon, son of Ariston" (327a). Though, as readers, we do not know exactly where Socrates is when he tells this narrative nor who his auditors are, we learn a great deal from this opening sentence. Socrates' first words link the narrative he will tell with tyranny by including Glaucon in his account. Jacob Howland's *Glaucon's Fate* reassesses the *Republic* in light of the fact that Glaucon died fighting with Critias and the Thirty Tyrants against the exiled Athenian democrats in the battle of Munychia in 404 BCE. Mark Munn notes, "It is a fair guess that among them was Glaucon son of Ariston, an older brother of Plato. Glaucon's valor in the battle at Megara six years earlier seems to have caught the eye of Critias, and his ambition to rise in politics was noticed by Socrates and later recalled by Xenophon. Glaucon, at any rate, was no longer named in the company of his brother a few years later, at the time of Socrates' trial" (239). The setting of the opening scene of the dialogue evokes the battle itself. Munn notes that Socrates and Glaucon are "walking back from the scene of a festal precession to the shrine of Bendis, certainly along the same road that soaked up the blood of the seventy devotees of Critias" (239). Munychia was the seat of power of the Thirty.

While neither the dramatic character, Socrates, nor the narrator, Socrates, knew about the horrors that Athens would suffer as a result of losing the war to Sparta, nor the rise of the Thirty, nor Glaucon's eventual fate, the historical Socrates, the historical author Plato, and the immediate reading and listening audience of the *Republic* certainly would have known what happened to Glaucon. Plato's choice to construct the *Republic* as a narrative that Socrates tells about himself and a tyrant orients our attention to the many ways that discussions of tyranny and examples of tyrannical behavior arise in the *Republic*. As Cinzia Arruzza aptly notes, "The *Republic* both begins and ends by addressing the problem of tyranny" (6). She asserts that "the critique of tyranny is a thread that runs through the entirety of the dialogue and decisively contributes to its overall structure" (6).

Accountability is intertwined with the problems of tyranny and tyrannical desire. The essence of tyranny is the unwillingness to be held accountable for one's thoughts, words, and deeds. The historical Glaucon was Plato's half-brother. By focusing on Glaucon and Socrates from the beginning of the dialogue, Plato asks us to consider if Socrates should be held accountable for Glaucon's turn to tyranny. Plato implicitly asks us to hold Glaucon accountable for his own actions as well.

Socrates continues, "I wanted to say a prayer to the goddess, and I was also curious to see how they would manage the festival, since they were holding it for the first time" (327a). Socrates' narrative remarks can be interpreted as an act of accountability.[1] He subjects both his activities and his city's religious practices for review. Socrates presents himself as being willing to obligate himself to a new goddess through the activity of prayer and to make assessments about its merits. Being able to acknowledge this possibility that long-standing practices are not necessarily the best way, or only way, lies at the heart of accountability. Socrates tells his unnamed narrative audience that "the procession of the local residents was a fine one and that the one conducted by the Thracians was no less outstanding" (327a). Socrates reports that after he said his prayers they were setting toward home, up the road by the long walls where they would pass by the hill of Munychia.

Socrates reports: "Polemarchus saw us from a distance as we were setting off for home and told his slave to run and ask us to wait for him" (327b). Polemarchus commands his slave to go after Socrates. The slave forcibly restrains Socrates and reports that "Polemarchus orders you to wait" (327b). Socrates tells the auditor, "I turned around, and asked where Polemarchus was. He's coming up behind you, he said, please wait for him" (327b). In his narrative about a tyrant, Socrates preserves the words of a slave. The slave speaks twice before Glaucon does. This prioritization of the slave's words over Glaucon's foreshadows that Glaucon will ultimately be enslaved by his tyrannical desire. Arruzza describes Plato's conception of the tyrant as one who has "lawless appetites, a strong sexual eros, greed, anger, violence, and impiety" (51). Glaucon immediately complies with the command, "Of course, we'll wait" (327b).

Polemarchus, Adeimantus, Niceratus, and some others catch up with them. Polemarchus observes, "Socrates, I guess you two are hurrying to get away to town" (327c). Socrates replies, "that's not a bad guess" (327c). Polemarchus tries to impose his will over Socrates' desire to get home.

> Do you see how many we are? he asked.
> I do.
> Well, you must either prove stronger than we are, or you will have to stay here.

Isn't there another alternative, namely that we persuade you to let us go?
But could you persuade us if we won't listen?
Certainly not, Glaucon said.
Well, we won't listen; you'd better make up your mind to that. (327c–e)

Polemarchus' response to Socrates' captures the current mood of the American nation. The possibility of listening to a competing political narrative seems vanishingly small. Mark Munn notes that a similar polarization of rhetoric occurred in Athens as the Peloponnesian War commenced: "After 431, the polarizing pressures of war tended to reduce the pursuit of intellectual arete to the pursuit of rhetorical skill itself" (79). Socrates appears amenable to the enticements of the torchlit horseback ride, the all-night festival, dinner, and conversation with young men (328a). Glaucon declares "so it seems we must stay" (328b). Socrates allows: "If it is so resolved, that is how we must act" (328b). Socrates holds himself accountable to the overall will of the group. They go to Cephalus' house.

Cephalus, Polemarchus, and Their Definitions of Justice

The theme of accountability to one another arises in Cephalus' opening words. He tells Socrates, "You don't come down to the Piraeus to see us as often as you should" (328c). Cephalus acknowledges his current physical state makes his ability to visit Athens difficult: "If it were still easy for me to walk to town, you wouldn't have to come here; we'd come to you" (328d). He holds Socrates accountable to their relationship: "you ought to come here more often. I want you to know that as the other pleasures, those connected with the body wither away in me, the desires and pleasure that have to do with speeches grow more" (328e). Cephalus also holds Socrates accountable to the young men. He tells Socrates, "Now do as I say; be with these young men now, but come regularly to us as to friends and your very own kin" (328c–d).

Socrates expresses delight in the opportunity to talk with Cephalus about the path and perils of old age (328e). Cephalus says his moderate well-being has arisen because he is no longer slave to his desires (328e–29d). Socrates wants him to say more. They discuss if it is easier for someone to act justly and fairly if they have money (330a–d). Socrates asks Cephalus, "What do you suppose is the greatest good that you have enjoyed from possessing great wealth?" (330d). Cephalus explains that it placates his fears that he will meet an unfavorable end "like the man who finds many unjust deeds in his life often even wakes from his sleep in a fright as children do" (330e). In this context, the first definition of justice arises. Socrates responds to Cephalus' reference to Pindar. He asks, "But as to this very thing, justice, shall we so simply assert that it is the truth and giving back what a man has taken from another, or is to do these very things sometimes just and sometimes unjust?" (331c). Though Socrates problematizes the definition of justice, it accords with a sense of being accountable for others both in terms of what we say and what we do. Socrates provides a counterexample of taking weapons from a friend and not returning them if the friend becomes insane (331c). Cephalus quickly agrees with Socrates, which undermines the first definition. Socrates remarks, "this isn't the definition of justice, speaking the truth and giving back what one takes" (331b). Polemarchus jumps in to defend the definition and Cephalus departs, saying, "I hand down the argument to you, for it is already time for me to look after the sacrifices" (331d).

Socrates asks Polemarchus, "What was it Simonides said about justice that you assert he said correctly?" (331e). Polemarchus' initial response seems to accord with a sense of accountability, "That it is just to give to each what is owed" (331e). After Socrates presses him, Polemarchus refines his definition as "the one that gives benefits and harms to friends and enemies" (332d). This definition seems to preclude genuine accountability. How can one recognize and make amends for the harms if the definition itself says it is permissible to harm enemies? Under this view, accountability seems to be nothing other than rewarding those who are "like us" and precludes the possibility of repairing harm that may have arisen to those who are not like us.

Polemarchus is often treated harshly in the literature, but perhaps unduly so.[2] In the *Phaedrus*, Socrates refers to Polemarchus in a favorable light. When Socrates atones for their previous errors in praising the non-lover, he tells Love, "If Phaedrus and I said anything that shocked you in our earlier speech, blame it on Lysias, who was its father, and put a stop to his making speeches of this sort; convert him to philosophy like his brother Polemarchus" (*Phaedrus* 275a–b). Socrates may be alluding to this nascent philosophical ability within Polemarchus in the *Republic* when he describes himself and Polemarchus as "being frightened and flustered as he [Thrasymachus] roared into our midst" (336c). At the beginning of Book V, Polemarchus and Adeimantus demand that Socrates defend his comments about women and children being shared in common (449a). Polemarchus' actions harken back to the beginning of the dialogue. Socrates reports, "But Polemarchus—he was sitting at a little distance from Adeimantus—stretched out his hand and took hold of his cloak from above by the shoulder, began to draw him toward himself, and, as he stooped over, said some things in his ear, of which we overheard nothing other than his saying, 'Shall we let it go or what shall we do?'" (449b). Polemarchus and Adeimantus hold Socrates accountable, refusing to let him off easy. Glaucon and Thrasymachus support "a resolution approved by all of us" (450a). Socrates, with some reservations, complies with their demands (450a–c). The historical fate of Polemarchus also shows the limits of his definition of helping friends and harming enemies. Polemarchus dies at the hands of the Thirty. Lysias describes the details of his brother's death: "Polemarchus received from the Thirty their accustomed order to drink hemlock, with no statement made as to the reason for his execution: still less was he allowed to be tried and defend himself" (12.17). Lysias elaborates, "When he was being brought away dead from the prison, although we had three houses amongst us, they did not permit his funeral to be conducted from any of them, but they hired a small hut in which to lay him out. We had plenty of cloaks, yet they refused our request of one for the funeral; but our friends gave either a cloak, or a pillow, or whatever each had to spare, for his interment" (12.18). While Polemarchus' definition of helping friends and harming enemies may capture what passes for justice in the real world, particularly in a politically divisive landscape like contemporary America, Polemarchus' definition and his demise point to the necessity of a higher standard to which we must be accountable other than our friends and political allies.

Thrasymachus

Thrasymachus' definition of justice moves away from justice as mutual accountability and need. He captures the essence of political tyrannizing words and deeds. Thrasymachus asserts that "the just is nothing other than the advantage of the stronger" (338c). Thrasymachus upholds the view on both the individual and collective level: "Each ruling group sets down laws for its own advantage, a democracy sets down democratic laws; a tyranny, tyrannic laws . . . and they declare that what they have set down—their own advantage—is just for the ruled, and the man who departs from it they punish as a breaker of the law and a doer of unjust deeds" (338e). He forcefully concludes: "the man who reasons rightly concludes that everywhere justice is the same thing, the advantage of the stronger" (339a).

Like Polemarchus, Thrasymachus is often treated harshly in the secondary literature.[3] However, several aspects of their exchange between Socrates and Thrasymachus contribute to a more sympathetic portrait of him. For example, Thrasymachus holds Socrates accountable for his argumentative tactics. Thrasymachus accuses Socrates of bearing false witness, calling him "a sycophant in arguments" (340d), accusing him of using excessive precision (340e). Socrates challenges him on this, "All right, Thrasymachus, so in your opinion I play the sycophant" (341a). Thrasymachus holds his ground: "You most certainly do" (341a). Socrates responds, "Do you suppose I ask as I asked because I am plotting to do harm to you in the argument?" (341b). Thrasymachus asserts his autonomy: "You won't get away with doing harm unnoticed and, failing to get away unnoticed, you won't be able to overpower me in argument" (341b).

Socrates' next narrative intervention highlights Thrasymachus' willingness to challenge Socrates' attempts to dominate him. Socrates reports, "When we came to this point in the argument, and it was evident to everyone that the argument had just turned around in the opposite direction, Thrasymachus, instead of answering, said, 'Tell me, Socrates, do you have a wet nurse?'" (343a). Socrates emphasizes that he is the questioner. Thrasymachus continues his assault: "she neglects your sniveling nose and doesn't give it the wiping you need" (343a). Socrates seems set on enraging Thrasymachus further. He feigns ignorance about Thrasymachus' remark about sheep and shepherds, saying, "Because of what?" (343a).

Thrasymachus accepts the challenge and applies his metaphor to the political realm: "And that is tyranny, which by stealth and force takes away what belongs to others, both what is sacred and profane, private and public, not bit by bit, but all at once" (344a). He concludes, "injustice, when it comes into being on a sufficient scale, is mightier, freer, and more masterful than justice, and as I have said from the beginning, the just is the advantage of the stronger, and the unjust is what is profitable and advantageous for oneself" (344c). Socrates describes the moment: "When Thrasymachus had said this, he had it in mind to go away, just like a bathman, after having poured a great shower of speech into our ears all at once. But those present did not let him and forced him to stay put and present an argument for what had been said" (344d). Those present become the stronger and exert their collective will over Thrasymachus. Socrates insults Thrasymachus with his narrative remarks by calling him a bath attendant, someone in a servile position in Athenian society (Gianfaldoni et al.). The dramatic events give support for Thrasymachus' argument in a way that the argument itself may not. Though Thrasymachus tries to exert his autonomy and leave the gathering, he is restrained by the stronger members of the party.

Thrasymachus' frustration evokes Polemarchus' original response to Socrates' offer of persuasion (327c). He questions the possibility of reasoned discourse: "How am I to persuade you, if you aren't persuaded by what I said just now? What more can I do? Am I to take my argument and pour it into your very soul?" (345b). Socrates does not respond directly. Instead, Socrates challenges him on the details of his previous argument: "But we also said that injustice is powerful, or don't you remember that, Thrasymachus?" (345c–47a). Socrates admits that "Thrasymachus did not agree to all of this so easily as I tell it now, but he dragged his feet and resisted, and he produced a wonderful quantity of sweat, for it was summer" (350d–e). Socrates tells a selective story. He omits much of Thrasymachus' struggle against Socrates' attempts to win the argument. At the same time, he emphasizes how hard Thrasymachus worked for his argument. Socrates illustrates his rhetorical victory over Thrasymachus by mentioning Thrasymachus' sweat and his blush (350d). Still, Thrasymachus does not give up. Thrasymachus responds to Socrates' challenge to remember what they said about injustice being mighty by imploring Socrates to "let me say as much as I want" (350d). Thrasymachus knows that Socrates tries to exert control over him through short speech. Thrasymachus knows his rhetorical strength lies in speech making. Socrates mentions his prowess in the *Phaedrus*. Socrates tells Phaedrus, "As to the art of making speeches, bewailing the evils of poverty and old age, the prize, in my judgment, goes to the mighty Chalcedonian. He it is also who knows best how to inflame a crowd, and once they are inflamed, how to hush them again with his words' magic spell, as he says himself" (267c–d).

Socrates' reference to Thrasymachus by his home city has some bearing on how to view their debate in the *Republic*. Debra Nails notes that "It was as a diplomat in Athens on behalf of Chalcedon that Thrasymachus' rhetorical skills were tested most significantly" (*People of Plato* 289). She explains, "Chalcedon had mounted an unsuccessful revolt against imperial Athens, and that his diplomatic need to prevent harsh reprisals against his native city gave potency and poignancy not only to Thrasymachus' position in *Republic* (CF 351B) but to the fervor with which he defended it" (289). Stephen White notes that Thrasymachus "was a consistent opponent of outside aggression and a champion of local autonomy" (309). Thrasymachus, in all likelihood, had Athens' imperialistic actions in mind as he listens to Socrates' query: "Would you say that a city is unjust that tries to enslave other cities unjustly, and has reduced them to slavery, and keeps many enslaved to itself?" (351b). Thrasymachus retorts, "It's this the best city will most do, the one that is most perfectly unjust" (351b). In 416 BCE, Athens acts in this exact manner when it subjugates Melos by putting all the men to death and enslaving all the women.[4] Thrasymachus tries to hold Socrates accountable for the imperialist actions of Athens.

Both Thrasymachus and Socrates would have known well that Socrates' city, Athens, debated the fate of Mytilene and its citizens after an unsuccessful revolt. The Mytilene Revolt from Athens occurred in 428 BCE. According to Nails, the dramatic date for the *Republic* is either 421 BCE or 411 BCE ("Dramatic Date" 383). If 421 BCE, this revolt would be on Thrasymachus' mind as he offers this definition of justice. If the later date, the auditors would have been aware of Mytilene and Melos in 416 BCE.[5] If the earlier dramatic date of the *Republic* is correct, Mytilene was only seven years before this conversation. The Athenian threat to Thrasymachus' city would have been even more immediate. Thrasymachus finally concedes, "Let that be your banquet, Socrates, at the feast of Bendis" (354a). Socrates acknowledges that he may have won because Thrasymachus stopped trying to overpower him with glorious rhetoric, "Given by you, Thrasymachus, after you became gentle and ceased to give me rough treatment" (354a). Socrates holds himself accountable for the flaws in his argumentative practices, comparing himself to "gluttons who grab at whatever is set before them" (354b) and apologizes for getting sidetracked by the consideration of whether "injustice is more profitable than justice" (354b). Book I ends with this aporetic lament: "So long as I do not know what the just is, I shall hardly know whether it is a virtue or not and whether the one who has it is unhappy or happy" (354c).

The Fall of Athens, the Thirty, and the Restoration of Democracy

The Peloponnesian War ended in 404 BCE. The terms of surrender for the Athenians were harsh. They had to dismantle the long walls, burn their ships, and lose their self-governance. Lysias writes, "Lysander sailed into your harbours, that your ships were surrendered to the Lacedaemonians, that the walls were demolished, that the Thirty were established, and that every conceivable misery befell the city" (13.34). Lysias describes some of their actions: "Not even in respect of the smallest fraction of our property did we find any mercy at their hands but our wealth impelled them to act as injuriously towards us as others might from anger aroused by grievous wrongs" (12.20). Sadly, Polemarchus and his family were merely one example of the violent actions of the Thirty. Lysias reports: "They sent many of the citizens into exile with the enemy; they unjustly put many of them to death, and then deprived them of burial; many who had full civic rights they excluded from the citizenship; and the daughters of many they debarred from intended marriage" (12.21).

A group of Athenian democrats backed by Spartan enemies from abroad fought them. Democracy was restored in 403 BCE. The *Apology* alludes to this historical context. After reporting the oracle's response, Socrates refers to Chaerephon's brother as a means of verifying his account because Chaerephon is dead. Socrates then remarks, "Gentlemen, do not make a disturbance at what I say" (21a). Why are the jurors responding in such emotional terms to Socrates' contextualization of the story he is about to tell? Socrates' reference to the exile under the Thirty and his reference to Chaerephon's death provide us with two clues.[6] Barry Strauss explains that when the Thirty began killing pro-democratic citizens, "those who survived financed an anti-oligarchic movement in the mountains outside Athens, with help from Sparta's rivals abroad. Within a year, the movement grew into an army. The democrats defeated the oligarchs in battle" (32). This happened only four short years before Socrates' trial. Socrates' remark challenges the current political peace by reminding them of how tenuous political self-governance is. No doubt, no one in the courtroom liked to be reminded of how recently democracy had been restored. The jurors would have been highly attuned to Socrates' reference in this context. On this point, Raaflaub notes, "Trained for decades in the skills of recognizing political allusions, the Athenians would have picked up hints of tyranny much more frequently and easily than we suspect" (72).

This profound civic conflict should shape our understanding of the inquiry into the nature of political justice in the *Republic*, particularly given the historical fates of Glaucon and Polemarchus, each dying on opposite sides of the conflict with the Thirty. Mallet explains, "In only half a century, the conception of conflict radically changed. Conflict was no longer about fighting an alien threat but about civil war, war between people sharing the same culture (or, even worse, people from the same city). This context forms the foundation of Plato's political thought and shows how urgent it was to define a new conception of war and peace for Athens in order to avoid a new era of conflicts" (Mallet 89). Somehow the Athenians were able to move ahead and be accountable to each other despite the great harm that members of the two factions imposed on each other. Despite the challenges of this deep factionalism, some level of political functionality did arise after democracy was restored. Childs notes, "Despite the ravages of the Peloponnesian war, Athens managed to assuage the horrors of political strife, to engage in foreign ventures, and especially to rebuild her economy. The Piraeus again became the major center of trade in the Aegean, as it had been under the Athenian empire of the fifth century" (21).

How were they able to accomplish this rapprochement? Several things are worth noting. First, as democracy was restored, the Athenians took an oath to harbor no grievance against each other with respect to public crimes that had occurred during the rule of the Thirty. As a result, "each side was able to set aside their differences and reconcile" (Löning 13). Second, a renewed emphasis on the importance of written law began to emerge. Munn explains, "The process of authorizing the *nomoi* of Athens now had in view not only the prospective work of the Athenian *demos* and its officers, but was also seen as the way of preserving the essential and time-tested practices of the Athenians against the possibility of future subversion" (269). Third, there were numerous jury trials about the harm that citizens inflicted on one another because personal crimes were not covered by the amnesty oath. By examining extant speeches from these trials, Munn maintains that "despite the fact that forgiveness was prominent in the rhetoric of reconciliation, Athenian juries were repeatedly subjected to emotional appeals to those recent events" (279). Fourth, Munn explains that the reunification was made more complex because "the Athenians were now two: those who had remained in the city during the reign of the Thirty, and those who had fought against them to return from exile" (295). He continues, "the reunification proceeded from the recognition that there were 'men of natural nobility' (*agathoi*) on both sides of the divide" (295). As we confront the divisive discord of our contemporary political landscape, we should hold fast to this possibility of recovering from divisive factional harm that the Athenians displayed.

Notes

1. On Socrates as narrator, see Schultz 2013 and 2020.
2. See Keyt, Weiss.
3. See Young, Barney, and Zalta.
4. On Athens and Melos, see Munn (119–20, 122); Thucydides (book 16).
5. For details of the debate about how Athens discusses its possible response, see Thucydides (3.25–28, 35–50).
6. On the Thirty, see Krentz and Raaflaub.

Works Cited

Arruzza, Cinzia. *A Wolf in the City: Tyranny and the Tyrant in Plato's* Republic. Oxford UP, 2019.

Barney, Rachel, and Edward N. Zalta. "Callicles and Thrasymachus." *The Stanford Encyclopedia of Philosophy*, fall 2017. plato.stanford.edu/archives/fall2017/entries/callicles-thrasymachus

Case, Brendan. "Accountability as a Sub-Type of Justice: 'Obedience' and 'Religion' in Aquinas's *Summa Theologiae*." *Studies in Christian Ethics*, vol. 24, no. 3, 2021, pp. 324–35.

Childs, William. *Greek Art & Aesthetics in the 4th Century B.C.* Princeton UP, 2018.

Eisikovits, Nir. "Transitional Justice." *The Stanford Encyclopedia of Philosophy*, edited by Edward N. Zalta, fall 2017. plato.stanford.edu/entries/justice-transitional

Franklin, V. P. "Georgetown Students Demonstrate How Reparations Can Be Made to African-American Students." *ACLU News and Commentary*, 22 May 2020. www.aclu.org/news/racial-justice/georgetown-students-demonstrate-how-reparations-can-be-made-to-african-american-students

Gianfaldoni, Serena, et al. "History of the Baths and Thermal Medicine." *Journal of Medical Science*, vol. 4, 2017, pp. 566–68.

Holan, Angie Drobnic. "In Context: Donald Trump's 'Very Fine People on Both Sides' Remarks (Transcript)." *PolitiFact*, 26 Apr. 2019. www.politifact.com/article/2019/apr/26/context-trumps-very-fine-people-both-sides-remarks

Howland, Jacob. *Glaucon's Fate: History, Myth, and Character in Plato's* Republic. Paul Dry Books, 2018.

Keyt, David. "Plato on Justice." *Socratic, Platonic and Aristotelian Studies: Essays in Honor of Gerasimos Santas*, Springer, 2011, pp. 255–70.

Krentz, Peter. *The Thirty at Athens*. Cornell UP, 1982.

Löning, Thomas Clark. *The Reconciliation Agreement of 403/402 B.C. in Athens: Its Context and Application*. Hermes Einzelschrift, 1987.

Lysias. "Against Eratosthenes." In *Lysias*. Translated by W. R. M. Lamb, Harvard UP, 1930, pp. 221–27.

Mallet, Joan-Antoine. "War and Peace in Plato's Political Thought." *The Philosophical Journal of Conflict and Violence*, vol. 1, no. 1, 2017, pp. 87–95.

Munn, Mark H. *The School of History: Athens in the Age of Socrates*. U of California P, 2000.

Nails, Debra. "The Dramatic Date of Plato's *Republic*." *The Classical Journal*, vol. 93, 1988, pp. 383–96.

———. *The People of Plato: A Prosopography of Plato and Other Socratics*. Hackett, 2002.

The New Yorker. "Ta-Nehisi Coates Revisits the Case for Reparations." *New Yorker*, 10 June 2019. www.newyorker.com/news/the-new-yorker-interview/ta-nehisi-coates-revisits-the-case-for-reparations

Peteet, John R., Charlotte V. O. Witvliet, and C. Stephen Evans. "Accountability as a Key Virtue in Mental Health and Human Flourishing." *Philosophy, Psychiatry, and Psychology*, vol. 29, no. 1, 2002, pp. 49–59.

Plato. *Apology*. *Plato: Complete Works*, edited by John M. Cooper, translated by G. M. A. Grube, Hackett, 1997, pp. 17–36.

———. *Phaedrus*. *Plato: Complete Works*, edited by John M. Cooper, translated by Alexander Nehamas and Paul Woodruff, Hackett, 1997, pp. 506–56.

———. *The Republic of Plato: Translated and with an Interpretive Essay*, edited by Adam Kirsch, translated by Allan Bloom, Basic Books, 2016.

Raaflaub, Kurt. "Stick and Glue: The Function of Tyranny in Fifth-Century Athenian Democracy." *Popular Tyranny*, edited by Kathryn Morgan, U of Texas P, 2003, pp. 79–94.

Rather, Dan, and Eliot Kushner. "The Coup Continues." *Steady*, 16 June 2022. steady.substack.com/p/the-coup-continues?r=ahi4w&s=r Move

Scanlon, Thomas. *What We Owe Each Other*. Harvard UP, 2000.

Schultz, Anne-Marie. *Plato's Socrates as Narrator: A Philosophical Muse*. Lexington, 2013.

———. *Plato's Socrates on Socrates: Socratic Self-Disclosure and the Public Practice of Philosophy*. Lexington, 2020.

Strauss, Barry. "The Classical Greek 'Polis' and Its Government." *A Companion to Ancient Greek Government*, edited by Hans Beck, Blackwell, 2013, pp. 22–37.

Thucydides. *The Peloponnesian War*. Translated by Steven Lattimore, Hackett, 1998.

Weiss, R. "Cephalus, Polemarchus, and Socrates on Justice." *Knowing and Being in Ancient Philosophy*, edited by D. Bloom et al., Palgrave MacMillan, 2022, pp. 221–35.

White, Stephen A. "Thrasymachus the Diplomat." *Classical Philology*, vol. 90, no. 4, 1995, pp. 307–27.

Young, Charles. "Polemarchus and Thrasymachus' Definition of Justice." *Philosophical Inquiry*, vol. 2, no. 1, 1980, pp. 404–19.

Beauty Dethroned?

Plato's Symposiasts on What We Love

Thomas M. Tuozzo

The topic of the after-dinner speeches in Plato's *Symposium* is Eros: that is, the god (and the experience) of being in love.[1] Socrates' speech is generally taken to offer the account of being in love that Plato wishes us to take most seriously. The strongest alternative view in the dialogue is certainly that offered by Aristophanes.[2] As we occasionally find elsewhere in Plato, the alternative, non-Socratic view is given a very strong and attractive presentation.[3] In what follows I shall be concerned to lay bare the grounds of that attractiveness and to argue that it is not specious: the Aristophanic account is a serious alternative to the Socratic one.

These two accounts of love differ in their view of what it is that attracts us when we fall in love. According to Socrates' speech (which he ascribes to the Mantinean seer Diotima), what attracts us is *beauty*. People fall in love with beautiful persons, often with physically beautiful persons. But central to Diotima's account is the claim that beauty in all its forms—including, of course, in the form of a beautiful character—may excite our love. The love occasioned by the beloved's beauty is a source of creative, generative energy: to use Diotima's open-ended phrase, love aims at reproduction in the beautiful. Now Diotima describes three ways such reproduction can take place. In the first, the generative energy of love takes the body as its focus, and the lover engenders physical children, thereby winning (if lucky) the sort of immortality that a string of descendants can bring. The second way takes the soul as its focus, and the lover engenders a noble character (in themselves and their beloved) whose expression in glorious actions may win them immortal renown. These first two ways of being in love are recognizable, traditional ways in which heterosexual and pederastic love had been conceptualized in Greek culture. Not so the third way, which Diotima treats as the revelation of a higher mystery. In this way of being in love, the generative energy produced is channeled into a rigorous philosophical regime devoted to understanding the beautiful, starting from beautiful bodies and proceeding upward, through beautiful characters, customs, and sciences, until the lover reaches the Form of Beauty itself. Such a use of love alone, we learn, produces *true* virtue; if any erotic practice can make us *truly* immortal, it is this.[4]

Diotima's teaching is clothed in some of Plato's most sublime rhetoric and has had enormous influence on European thought.[5] But it cannot compete with Aristophanes' speech when it comes to resonance in twenty-first-century mass culture. Aristophanes' myth of a primal division of our original nature into two incomplete halves, with the experience of love explained as our yearning to find and fuse with our other half, recurs as a leitmotiv in the film *Hedwig and the Angy Inch*, and figures prominently in the music video of Li'l Nas X's "Montero (Call Me by Your Name)." [6] Aristophanes' account of love speaks to our contemporaries' experience of being in love in a way that, it would seem, Socrates' account does not.

The fundamental difference between Socrates and Aristophanes concerns what it is that we love. As we have seen, beauty is at the very center of Socrates' account of being in love. Aristophanic love has so little to do with a concern for the beautiful that no form of the word for beautiful—*kalon*—is to be found in his entire speech.[7] This lexical fact should occasion more surprise than it usually does; elsewhere in the corpus Plato's Socrates treats it as a truism that love is of the beautiful.[8] Socrates, indeed, has Diotima point out the difference between her account of love and Aristophanes': she criticizes what is recognizably Aristophanes' account for construing love as a desire for "one's own" and "what belongs to one," instead of recognizing that, as she would have it, love is the pursuit, under the aegis of the beautiful, of what is *good* for one.[9] The non-appearance of beauty in Aristophanes' speech invites the reader to put into question the centrality of beauty in Socrates' account of love, and indeed, to reassess the role beauty plays in other encomia of love in the dialogue, as well. As it turns out, it is fair to say that *none* of the speakers that precede Socrates explicitly thematizes love's orientation toward beautiful objects. This is true even for Agathon's speech, where the beauty of love itself is dwelt on at length. The beauty Agathon emphasizes is precisely the beauty of *being* in love; in retrospect, we can see that the beauty that somehow results from or characterizes love, and not beauty as the instigator or object of love, is the major focus of the previous speakers, as well. Socrates' first order of business after Agathon's speech is to prove to him that love takes beauty as its object and so cannot, in fact, itself be beautiful. I shall start with the way beauty figures in Agathon's speech. I shall then backtrack to examine the way beauty figures in the earlier speeches, and then turn to the Aristophanic alternative in which beauty makes no explicit appearance.

Near the beginning of his speech Agathon tells us that Love is the "happiest, since most beautiful and most excellent" of all the gods (195a5–7). That is, it is Love's own beauty (along with his virtues) that takes center stage. And Agathon grounds Love's beauty in what appears to be one of Love's even more fundamental characteristics: his youthfulness. It is because he is the youngest of the gods that he must be the most beautiful, Agathon tells us, and he supports the claim that he is the youngest by pointing out that Love "hates old age and doesn't come a mile near it, but consorts always with the young and belongs with them. For the time-honored saying is right: like always sticks to like" (195b3–5). Later on in his speech Agathon does indeed tell us that Love takes what is beautiful things as it object. But he brings in this idea only incidentally in the course of discussing the first benefit the world received from the presence of Love. Citing Hesiod and Parmenides, Agathon tells us that, before Love was born, the gods, under the sway of Necessity, treated each other atrociously. The advent of Love produced peace and harmony among them. Agathon makes this point twice;[10] it is only the second time around that he mentions, as an aside, that the love that brought this about is love for beautiful things: "That is how the gods' quarrels were settled, once Love came to be among them—love of beauty, obviously, because love does not attach to ugliness. . . . Once this god was born, all good things came to gods and human beings alike—from loving beautiful things" (197b3–8). This is the comment Socrates singles out in his refutation of Agathon, in order to refocus the discussion of love squarely on its taking beauty as its object, which then serves as the foundation for Diotima's entire account of love.

Let us now turn to the previous speeches: how do they understand the relationship between love and beauty? Here it is useful to recall that the Greek term *to kalon* has a much broader range than the English translation "beautiful." It applies as naturally to moral values as to physical good looks, and does not, in moral contexts, have the figurative or analogical flavor that the English term "beautiful" does. It is for this reason that translators often prefer different English terms in those contexts (e.g., "noble," "admirable"). Now in the speeches of Phaedrus, Pausanias, and Eryximachus, it turns out that *kalon* occurs in its moral sense, to describe the morally desirable products of love or the morally praiseworthy way of being in love, far more often than in its physical sense. The beauty, whether moral or physical, *of the beloved*, that is, of the object of love, is seldom mentioned in those speeches.

The first speaker, Phaedrus, focuses (like Agathon and most of the other symposiasts) on pederastic love. The main topic of his speech is the great benefit such love brings about for both lover and beloved. Love fosters "that which ought to serve as a guide for their whole lives for those men who plan to live beautifully / nobly (*kalōs*)," namely, "shame (*aidōs*) at disgraceful things, and ambition (*philotimian*) for beautiful / noble ones (*tois kalois*)" (178c5–d2). Both shame and love of honor (*philotimia*) involve a concern for the esteem of others, and it seems that, for Phaedrus, the pederastic relationship promotes these attitudes by establishing the lover and the beloved as a kind of privileged audience to each other's behavior, someone whose esteem they value more than that of anyone else (see 178d4–e3). Being in a lover–beloved relationship makes one wish to appear as good as one can in the eyes of the other (where Phaedrus understand this "good" in the manner of the heroic tradition, as courageous). Phaedrus does not explain why being in such a relationship has this effect on lover and beloved. But one natural explanation is that it does so because each of the two has been, and realize that they have been, *chosen* by the other as worthy of being in the relationship. The lover fell in love with this particular youth and set about wooing him; the youth in turn eventually decided to accept him as his lover and so became his beloved. Each, we may suppose, is concerned to show himself worthy of the choice that the other has made.[11] And since each is concerned to prove his worthiness by demonstrating his courage, one may also suppose each considers that he was chosen by the other at least in part because of his perceived possession (or promise) of courage. That is, because of the quality of his character (if also because of his good looks).

Phaedrus does not explicitly state that the lover is attracted to the beloved's beautiful character. He does mention, very obliquely, the beauty of the beloved, and when he does so, it seems pretty clear that he has physical beauty in mind. Phaedrus illustrates the courage-inspiring quality of love by citing two mythological examples: Alcestis, who courageously died in place of her husband, and Achilles, who courageously died in avenging the death of Patroclus. The cases are complementary: Alcestis is an example of a lover who dies for her beloved; Achilles, an example of a beloved who dies for his lover. Phaedrus makes a point of defending his assignment of the roles of beloved to Achilles and lover to Patroclus, an assignment which, as he notes, conflicts with what was apparently the traditional view. As Phaedrus puts it: "Aeschylus is talking nonsense when he says that Achilles was Patroclus' lover, [Achilles] who was more beautiful not only than Patroclus but also than all the heroes put together; and still beardless, and so much younger, as Homer says" (180a4–6). Here the fact that Achilles was more beautiful than Patroclus is taken as evidence that the former was the beloved. From this we can infer that love does, indeed, take what is beautiful as its object. And given that (like Agathon) Phaedrus associates this beauty with youth, there can be no doubt that he has Achilles' physical beauty in mind. Given the rest of the speech's emphasis on virtue, this implicitly raises the question of the relative roles of moral and physical beauty in the love relationship.

Phaedrus' speech focuses on the ennobling effects a love relationship has on its participants, without mentioning what they actually do as lover and beloved. Pausanias makes that activity, and the proper way to engage in it, the focus of his account. The conceptual underpinning of Pausanias' speech is the claim that no human action, considered only in itself, is either beautiful/noble (*kalon*) or shameful—it all depends on how it is done. This is true of drinking, singing, and conversing (180e4–181a); it is also true of the activity involved in love, namely, having sex.[12] The beautiful way in which a love affair can be conducted is the kind of beauty that Pausanias is most concerned with. Some people in love are only concerned with having sex, and don't care about doing it beautifully or nobly; these are those who follow the common or Pandemian eros. Pausanias characterizes such lovers as indiscriminate in their pursuit of sex; he does not indicate that they have any particular interest in physical beauty.[13] The followers of heavenly or Uranian eros, on the other hand, seek to satisfy their sexual desire in a noble or beautiful fashion. They do not crudely look for young boys to have sex with and then discard, but rather they wait for the youth to begin to grow a beard. This is because, in the case of younger boys, "it is not clear where they will end up as concerns the virtue or vice of body and soul" (181e2–3). Uranian lovers look for someone old enough and intelligent enough to talk to, one whom the lover will be able to teach the things a good man needs to know. The Uranian lover does, of course, want sex from the relationship, but it is sex located within a broader context in which he also helps mold the beloved's character. The Pandemian lover approaches sex the way the gourmand approaches eating—indiscriminately, and with no concern for the manner in which they consume what they do. The Uranian lover, on the other hand, is like the gourmet—the person with whom he has the sexual relationship must be of a certain quality (i.e., intelligent and capable of moral growth), and the sex take place within a relationship that respects and foster that quality. There is no more reason to deny the legitimacy of the distinction between the two kinds of love, or to question the sincerity of the Uranian lover, than there is to deny the distinction between gourmet and gourmand, or that between lush and connoisseur of wine. Nonetheless, just because Pandemian eros does indeed count as a kind of love, it is true that, for Pausanias, love *as such* is not concerned with virtue or nobility—either that of the boy or that of the lover. Love, as such, is concerned simply with sex. The concern with virtue is an additional, beautiful refinement that the Uranian lover adds on.

Pausanias, as we have seen, makes no explicit reference to the physical beauty of the beloved. In the next speech, that of Eryximachus, physical beauty is marginalized even further. While at the beginning of his speech Eryximachus does describe love among humans as directed toward beautiful people (*pros tous kalous*, 186a4), this seems a merely conventional way of referring to human love, with which Eryximachus is not himself primarily concerned. For he immediately generalizes Pausanias' two kinds of love and raises them to principles operative throughout the cosmos. Exemplifying them first in his own field of medicine, Eryximachus notes that bodies can be either healthy or diseased, and insists that bodies of each sort is characterized by its own distinctive kind of love. It is noble (and beautiful) to gratify the love of a healthy body, and that love is itself noble. It is base to gratify the base love of a diseased body (186b2–d1). It is the task of medicine, and indeed of expertise everywhere, to instill the noble kind of love where it is missing, and to remove the base kind of love. As it transpires, the noble kind of love characterizing healthy bodies is that in which the opposites within the body—hot, cold, and so on—are "friendly to and love one another" (186d5–6). And quite generally, good and healthy states, whether of human bodies, the weather, or anything else, are states in which opposites have been harmonized and are in agreement. Bad or diseased states, on the other hand, are those in which opposites remain at odds with one another and commit outrage on one another (cf. *ho meta tēs hubreōs erōs*, 188a7). The love that characterizes such states is, apparently, the love of excess on the part of each of the opposites, a love that produces disharmony and disorder (cf. 188b3–5).

Given the stark contrast between the noble and the base kinds of love, one might have expected Eryximachus to recommend indulging only the noble kind of love. It comes as something of a surprise then that, when he turns once again to the love between human beings, Eryximachus offers the following advice:

> Ultimately the same rule applies: one ought to gratify orderly people, and those who aren't orderly yet in such a way as to make them so, and one ought to guard their love, which is the noble, heavenly love, the Love of the Uranian Muse. But the common love, that of the Polyhymnian Muse, this must be prescribed carefully to those to whom we prescribe it, so that one may reap its pleasure (*tēn . . . hēdonēn autou*) without instilling any debauchery. . . . (187d4–e3)

Here we see that the base love, too, has something to recommend it: pleasure. Whereas Pausanias had thought that the pleasures of sex could be pursued, within the context of Uranian love, in a refined way such that it promotes the beloved's virtue, Eryximachus appears to think that the order-and-harmony-preserving love is quite distinct from the disharmony-promoting-yet-pleasant love. Like Pausanias, Eryximachus thinks that a good love affair will include the pleasures of sex within the context of a pursuit of virtue or harmony; but Eryximachus thinks of the two aims as fundamentally opposed, and such as must be combined with great care.

In Eryximachus' speech, physical beauty has all but dropped out of the analyses of love. Instead, physical pleasure and virtuous orderliness have become the two ends of (what are now) two different kinds of love, kinds of love that are, accordingly, in tension with one another. Aristophanes' speech changes the conceptual landscape entirely. Aristophanes rejects the division of love into two, and makes both sexual pleasure and virtue inessential to the nature of love. He explicitly treats as absurd the idea that when in love a person is simply concerned with attaining sexual pleasure (192c7–8). As we shall see, he also treats being in love as being, at best, orthogonal to a concern with virtue, and at worst, as leaning toward vice. Instead, he analyzes being in love as a yearning for completion, for the recovery of a lost, primaeval wholeness. As earlier noted, Aristophanes develops this account by means of a myth. The original state of human beings was very different from our current state. Humans were complete, with their completeness reflected in the sphericity of their physical bodies. That completeness, however, did not manifest itself in static or tranquil contentment. Rather, it was a condition of energetic activity and self-assertion: these self-contained humans made so bold as to scale heaven and attack the gods. For their impiety Zeus split them in two. Humans' original spherical completeness, it turns out, had all along also had a specifically double aspect, as though in anticipation of their eventual punishment. Each had two faces, four arms and four legs, and two sets of genitalia. Spherical man had two sets of male genitalia, spherical woman two of female, and the spherical hermaphrodite, one of each. Split down the middle, each resulting half is radically incomplete, and experiences an overwhelming desire to find their other half and restore their primeval wholeness. When they find their other half, they drop everything and cling to it, attempting to fuse together to regain their former wholeness.

One of the features of Aristophanes' account that is particularly appealing to moderns, I believe, is its virtually total erasure of the distinction between the lover and the beloved. And with that distinction disappears the asymmetrical ascription of beauty and youth, or indeed of any other qualities that might be deemed objectively and impersonally desirable, to the beloved. And it is not accidental, I think, that the disappearance of any mention of beauty or youth is accompanied by a divorce between erotic yearning and sex. That there is such a complete divorce is a central feature of Aristophanes' account. Human beings felt the yearning for completeness that constitutes being in love even before sex was invented, as it were. As Aristophanes tells it, the newly split half-humans would cling to their other half so desperately as to neglect everything else, and began to die off. To keep that from happening, Zeus had Hermes turn their genitals around so that these would come into contact, almost by accident, during their embrace; the resulting orgasm would provide some relief from their yearning and allow humans to attend to the other business of life they had neglected. Sexual satisfaction is thus, in psychoanalytic terms, only an inadequate substitute for the longed-for completion, and provides only a temporary respite.

As I mentioned, this divorce of sexual desire from the experience of being in love goes hand in hand with the rejection of beauty, youth, or any other general quality as the proper object of love. Sexual desire can, perhaps with some little difficulty, be assimilated to other physical desires, and assigned a natural object, as thirst has drink for its object and hunger has food. If we look for a comparable value-neutral description of the object of sexual desire, the speeches we have looked at so far in the *Symposium* suggest "youth"; if for a value-laden term, they suggest "beauty." But on Aristophanes' account, eros is directed to no such general object. Each person's appropriate love interest is quite literally *sui generis*: it is that which particularly completes them. Further, Aristophanes' account also explicitly rejects the connection between love and reproduction that will figure so importantly in Socrates' speech. When having Hermes turn genitalia around so that humans could find temporary respite from their longing, Zeus decided to use one of the three resulting pairings of genitalia for procreation. Prior to that point, humans sowed their seed directly into the earth. The connection between being in love and reproduction is as accidental, on Aristophanes' account, as the connection between being in love and having sex.

The fact that it frees being in love from service to some greater end at least in part explains, I suggest, the appeal of Aristophanes' account to modern readers. On this view, the value of being in love cannot be reduced to some general good thing it provides us; the person who is the proper object of love is just that quite specific person who completes one. In this regard, Aristophanes' account supplies what has often been thought to be missing from Socrates' account, from at least the time of Vlastos's famous article: namely, prizing the individuality of the one loved. In principle, only the one person will do. And certainly this does seem to capture something about the experience of being in love, something that is at the very least obscured when love is thought to be directed at some generally characterizable end.

Let me close by addressing two Platonic criticisms that the *Symposium* offers of this account of love. Plato insinuates the first of these into Aristophanes' speech itself. The original humans, in the fullness of their being, impiously attacked the gods; does the path to completeness necessarily lead to wickedness? Here a response is possible within the terms of Aristophanes' myth itself. Aristophanes explains the sphericity of the first humans as follows: "Now here is why there were three kinds. . . . The male kind was originally an offspring of the sun, the female of the earth, and the one that shared in both was an offspring of the moon, because the moon shares in both. They were spherical, and so was their motion, because they were like their parents" (190a9–b5). The wholeness of the heavenly bodies and the earth do not necessarily lead to disorderly motions; indeed, the regularity of their motions and the beauty of their choreography is insisted on by characters throughout the Platonic corpus. This suggests that the power that comes from completeness need not lead to vice. The completed loving couple may well devote themselves to a project that is primarily neither virtuous nor vicious, but distinctively their own.

The second Platonic criticism, which is suggested by Diotima's implicit criticism of the Aristophanic account of love, is related to the first. Diotima remarks:

> Now there is a certain story . . . according to which lovers are those people who seek their other halves. But according to my story, a lover does not seek the half or the whole, unless, my friend, it turns out to be good as well. I say this because people are even willing to cut off their own arms and legs if they think they are in bad condition. I don't think individuals embrace what is their own (*to oikeion*), unless someone calls that which is good "one's own" or "what belongs to one." That's because what everyone loves is really nothing other than the good. (205d10–206a2)

Diotima criticizes the Aristophanic account for failing to show how love is related to the human good. And this criticism does point to a second, striking lexical fact about Aristophanes' speech. As mentioned above, words for "beauty" are entirely absent from that speech. Forms of the word for "good" (*to agathon*), as it turns out, are almost as rare. There is only one significant use of the term,[14] and that occurs in Aristophanes' peroration: "I say that the way our human race would become happy is if we fully achieve our love and each of us find our very own darling, thereby returning to our original nature (*tēn archaian physin*). And if this is the best thing (*ariston*), then necessarily what is nearest to that in the present circumstances is best: and that is to find a darling who is naturally congenial to us (*kata noun autōi pephukotōn*)" (193c2–8). Throughout his speech Aristophanes had emphasized that the goal of love is the restoration of our original nature. He took for granted that such a restoration would be a good thing, and only explicitly articulates the thought here, when discussing the second-best option—finding not our true other half, but someone who is naturally congenial to us.[15] The value of what love does for us—even in the second-best case—is rooted in the normativity of our essential nature. In her critique, Diotima omits any mention of nature, and instead uses the more value-neutral term, "what belongs to one" (*to oikeion*).¹⁶ Doing so allows her to raise the question of how good getting what belongs to one really is. As she points out, as people are willing to part with the legs and arms they have if it is good to do so, what is so good about trying to get four more?

Indeed, though Diotima does not do so, we could develop a further criticism on this point. If the Aristophanic lover were *indifferent* to their good, and retained what they happened to possess (and sought more of the same) without regard to what is in fact good, they would be in the grips of a self-destructive narcissism. But if we understand "one's own" as what returns one's original nature, nothing of this sort follows. In particular, there is no reason to think that the whole to which the Aristophanic lover aspires is an inward-looking, narcissistic one. The original spherical humans cooperated with each other (in, admittedly, an impious attack on the gods). A fulfilled loving pair may very well choose to turn their powers to some other, non-vicious, outward-facing project. In finding each other, Aristophanic lovers experience a mutual quickening of their natural powers—how they use that power is up to the lovers themselves.¹⁷

Notes

1. This is, I think, the easiest way to narrow down the polysemy of the English "love" to produce a rough match for the Greek *eros*. An *erastes* is someone who is in love, not necessarily one whose love is reciprocated—and so not necessarily a lover (as the term is commonly used today). All translations are my own, with the benefit of consulting published translation, especially Nehamas and Woodruff.

2. For all its interest, Alcibiades' speech does not so much present a rival view to Socrates' as a plaintive objection to it.

3. A notable example is Protagoras' Great Speech at *Protagoras* 320d–328d.

4. For a defense of this reading of Socrates' speech, see Tuozzo.

5. Particularly as mediated through Ficino's Neo-Platonic interpretation of it in his Renaissance commentary on the dialogue.

6. The Aristophanic story is recounted in "The Origin of Love," a song (with animation) featured in *Hedwig and the Angry Inch* (www.youtube.com/watch?v=_zU3U7E1Odc). Plato's Greek describing our original scission is pictured inscribed on the Tree of the Knowledge of Good and Evil in "Montero (Call Me by Your Name)" (www.youtube.com/watch?v=6swmTBVI83k). Aristophanes'

even-handed treatment of different sexual orientations makes his account especially attractive to lesbians and gay men, though I suspect that the conceit resonates far more broadly.

7. Many commentators do not note the absence of the term from Aristophanes' speech. For honorable exceptions, see Konstan (120), who notes it while cataloguing occurrences of the word in the different speeches, and Halliwell (10). The latter recognizes that Aristophanes' account is incompatible with making objective beauty the proper object of love, and proposes that the absence of the term is Aristophanes' attempt to paper over a tension in his account.

8. At *Charmides* 167c5–e7, the beautiful is treated as the special object of love in the way color is of sight and sound of hearing.

9. See 205e5–7, where Diotima uses the expressions *to heautōn* and *oikeion . . . kai heautou* to characterize what the object of love is on the Aristophanic account. Aristophanes does not use a locution of this sort until the very end of his speech, at 193d2.

10. First near the beginning of his speech (195b6–c6), and then again just before breaking into his Gorgianic peroration (197b3–9).

11. One might offer a similar account of such cases as Achilles' braving death for the sake of Patroclus after the other has already died. The beloved's concern here is to vindicate, before the eyes of the world and perhaps especially in his own estimation, the worth that the other's choice of him for an erotic relationship had implied.

12. He uses the transparent euphemism, "doing the deed" (*diapraxasthai*, 181b5).

13. He comes closest to doing so when, in explaining why the relationship with such a lover is not lasting, he says: "As soon as the bloom of the body, which he was in love with, ceases, 'off he flies'" (183e3). Here it is more properly youth, rather than physical beauty as such, that seems to attract the Pandemian lover.

14. The only other occurrence is at 191e7–192a2, where Aristophanes says that the boys who are "slices of the male" are the best (*beltistoi*) because they are most manly/courageous by nature.

15. Unlike some, I do not believe that the fact that we were, in fact, never part of a spherical whole, and that it therefore makes little sense to think of finding our unique matching half, vitiates Aristophanes' account of love. The myth gives vivid expression to the enlivening experience of falling in love with someone who seems to complete one; it is a mistake to press its details too literally.

16. Aristophanes himself had used this word only once, again in the peroration, at 193d2.

17. It is a pleasure to offer this essay to Tony Preus, whom I have known for many years, in recognition of his myriad contributions to ancient philosophy. An earlier version of the essay was delivered at the Ancient Philosophy Society meeting in Spokane, Washington, in April 2023. I wish to thank the audience

there for their questions, and especially my commentator, Van Tu, for her very helpful comments. I would also like to acknowledge the helpful comments of an anonymous reviewer for the press.

Works Cited

Halliwell, Stephen. "Eros and Life-Values in Plato's *Symposium*." *Plato in Symposium. Selected Papers from the Tenth Symposium Platonicum*, edited by Michael Erler and Mario Tulli, Academia Verlag, 2016, pp. 3–13.

Konstan, David. *Beauty: The Fortunes of an Ancient Greek Idea*. Oxford UP, 2014.

Plato. *Symposium*. Translated by Alexander Nehamas and Paul B. Woodruff, *Plato: Complete Works*, edited by John M. Cooper, Hackett, 1989, pp. 83–104.

Tuozzo, Thomas M. "Saving Diotima's Account of Erotic Love in Plato's *Symposium*." *Ancient Philosophy*, vol. 41, no. 1, 2021, pp. 83–104.

Vlastos, Gregory. "The Individual as Object of Love in Plato." *Platonic Studies*, 2nd ed., Princeton UP, 1981 [1973], pp. 3–42.

Forms as Causes in *On Coming to Be and Passing Away* II.9

William Wians

In a passage that comes late in *On Coming to Be and Passing Away*, Aristotle argues that Platonic Forms as described in the *Phaedo* are inadequate to serve as the cause of coming into being and passing away (*On Coming to Be* II.9, 335b7–24).[1] An adequate account—something "everyone dreams of"—must be able to explain one of the fundamental facts of generation: the generator does not always generate, but only at some times and not at others. Platonic Forms, Aristotle argues, cannot explain why this is so.

Aristotle's anti-Platonic argument in II.9 has attracted steady scholarly attention.[2] But while offering valuable insights into the argument itself, scholars have paid less attention to the chapter's overall structure, within which the anti-Platonic argument is just one stage. By considering the argument as part of a larger whole, my essay will accomplish two things. First, it will show how the chapter identifies two necessary conditions for an adequate account of coming into being in nature. The first condition emerges from the anti-Platonic argument. But the chapter goes on to show that a second condition must also be satisfied. This condition is found in the strictly materialist account Aristotle rejects in the continuation of II.9. Taken together, the two arguments point toward a sufficient condition—which the chapter refers to only indirectly as "a third cause"—that no predecessor has recognized.[3] The essay's second accomplishment will be to shed light on the chapter's overall place within Aristotle's comprehensive science of nature. Doing so will identify a further shortcoming of the Platonist position, while also revealing the precise way in which II.9

is preliminary to II.10, with which II.9 forms a larger sequence. Though II.10's account lies outside the scope of this essay, it is there that Aristotle provides his own explanation of the coming into being of perishable things.

I will divide II.9 into five stages of unequal length.[4] (1) the chapter begins with a brief but crucial framing section that carefully delimits what is to follow (335a24–28); (2) a second stage states how the material and, much more briefly, the formal causes are to be understood in the context of the investigation announced in the framing section (335a28–b7); (3) the third section reviews two previous attempts to account for coming into being, one derived from the *Phaedo*, the other from unnamed materialists; (4) the fourth stage consists largely of the anti-Platonic argument (335b7–24); and (5) the final and longest stage turns to certain materialists who claim a source of motion resides in the matter (335b24–336a10). The chapter concludes with a brief reminder that Aristotle has dealt with causes and their natures elsewhere.

The Framing Section (335a24–28).

Aristotle begins by locating the task that will occupy chapters II.9–10, and the approach to be followed: "Since some things are of a nature to come-to-be and to pass away, and since coming-to-be actually takes place in the region about the center, we must discuss the number and the nature of the sources (*archai*) of all coming-to-be alike; for we shall more easily form a theory (*theôrêsomen*) about the particulars when we have first grasped the universals (*tô katholou*)" (335a24–28; translations are from Forster, lightly revised).[5] The opening observation that some things come into being and perish identifies a defining assumption of the science of nature.[6] At the same time, it states half of an implied contrast: there are natural things that are *not* generated and that do *not* pass away, that is, perceptible eternal things. The next lines remind his audience of a main point from II.8: "the mixed bodies," which are made up of the simple bodies earth, water, air, fire, occupy the terrestrial center of Aristotle's finite, spherical cosmos (II.8, 334b31–32). Taken together, the lines precisely locate the present investigation within one branch of the science of nature, namely the investigation of those things that are sensible and perishable, occupying the sublunary realm (see *Physics* II.7, 198a21–31).

If coming-to-be in the middle region of the cosmos is a fact, then (recalling the language of *Posterior Analytics* II.1–2) the task remaining is to discover the reason why (*to dioti*). This leads to the final line of the framing stage. Aristotle will first take stock of the "universals," which will then make theorizing about particulars easier.

What Aristotle has in mind is not immediately clear.[7] On my reading, the argument of the chapter counts as *logikos*.[8] A *logikos* argument operates outside the boundaries set by a science's proper principles and often serves as preliminary to establishing principles. For that reason, it can be called dialectical in one sense of that term. In Aristotle's treatises on nature, a *logikos* argument often precedes a *phusikos* argument, that is, an argument proper to the science of nature. This is the pattern found in the two chapters making up the sequence of II.9–10: a *logikos* analysis in II.9 treats causes in general, followed by a *phusikos* argument in II.10 that supplies Aristotle's own position.

Matter and Form (335a28–b7)

II.9's second stage begins by claiming that the *archai* discovered in the terrestrial realm will be the same in kind as those in the eternal realm: "These sources (*archai*), then, are equal in number to and identical in kind (*tô(i) genei*) with those which exist among both eternal and primary things" (335a28–29).[9] By "both eternal and primary things," Aristotle refers to the celestial bodies and lower spheres on the one hand and the outmost sphere, that is, the first heaven (*prôtos ouranos*) of Aristotle's universe and its movement, on the other (*De Caelo* I.9, 278b10–15; II.6, 288a13–17; II.12, 292b18–25; *Metaphysics* XII.7, 1072a19–23). The passage therefore is claiming that the same *archai* can be found in all moveable things, whether eternal or perishable.[10]

While saying the same *archai* operate in both eternal and non-eternal regions makes Aristotelian etiology philosophically economical, the claim immediately gives rise to one of the central problems of II.9. Why if the principles are the same in kind do they operate differently in the region made up of things that come into being?[11] Just because these things are perishable and not eternal, the principles must apply to them in a different way. A proper account must explain how the same principles apply differently to the two different sorts of natural things.

What Aristotle says—and does not say—next deserves more notice than it has received. In proceeding to identify what the "same number and kinds" of *archai* are, he says: "For there is one [*archê*] in the sense of material, a second in the sense of form (*morphê*), and the third too must (*dei*) be present also; for the two are not enough to generate things which come-to-be, just as they are not enough in the case of primary things either" (335a29–32).[12] What should be noted is that Aristotle does not name the third kind of *archê*. Obviously enough, he must be referring to what has come to be called the efficient cause, and many commentators speak as if Aristotle had done so directly.[13] Remarkably, however, at no point in II.9 does Aristotle refer directly to the efficient cause (we shall in fact find three instances of such indirection). And if we look ahead to the closing lines of the chapter, we see that Aristotle speaks as if only two causes, the material and the formal, had been discussed in the chapter, with no mention of the efficient cause, not even indirectly: "We have given a general account of the causes in a previous work, and we have now distinguished between the matter and the form" (336a13–14; my translation).[14] As a summary of what II.9 has accomplished, it implies that the efficient cause has yet to be dealt with.[15] Indeed, not until the continuation of the sequence in II.10 does Aristotle speak of the cause of motion directly, using formulas familiar from other works.[16] We shall return to Aristotle's indirection with regard to the "third cause" shortly.

The next ten lines speak of the material cause of coming into being (335a32–b7). Aristotle does not, as one might expect, speak of the elements or primary pairs of opposites that had occupied Book II's attention to this point. Instead, and consistent with the announced purpose of dealing with causes generally before turning to particulars, he lays the groundwork for what is to follow by presenting a conceptual analysis of matter in relation to coming-to-be. He explains that "cause" in the sense of matter pertains to things that have a capacity (*dunaton*) either to be or not to be, including things that can come-to-be and pass-away.[17] Things with this capacity differ from things that exist by necessity, such as eternal things. "This, then, is the cause of things that are generated in the sense of matter" (335b5–6).[18]

In contrast to the ten lines devoted to the material cause, the formal cause receives only a single compressed, somewhat puzzling mention in the continuation of the passage: "Whereas cause, in the sense of the 'for the sake of which' (*to hou heneken*) is their shape and form (*morphê kai eidos*); and this is the definition of the essential nature of each of them (*ho logos ho tês hekastou ousias*)" (335b6–7).[19] The statement implies that, at least among things that come into being and pass away, the final cause is not distinct from a thing's form, which is contained in the statement of a thing's being.[20] In a well-known passage from the *Physics*, Aristotle in fact asserts the coincidence in natural things of formal and final causes, along with the cause of motion as well (*Physics* II.7, 198a22–27).[21] This makes the indirection noted above all the more puzzling. Having linked the efficient cause to the other non-material causes in the *Physics*, why does Aristotle not remind the reader of his having done so here, just as *Coming to Be* reminds the reader of many other previous discussions in the *Physics*? Again, the lack of speaking directly of the cause of motion is notable.

Two Earlier Accounts (335b7–17).

The ten lines of what I'm marking as the third stage refer to two earlier attempts to identify the cause of coming-to-be. It begins with another indirect reference to the cause of motion: "But a third must also be present, of which everyone dreams but never puts into words" (335b7–8).[22]

A moment's reflection shows that the third stage should not be regarded as a typical "survey of predecessors." Though Aristotle speaks of "everyone," he identifies just two schools of thought. Platonists have placed the cause of coming-to-be and passing away in the Forms (335b9–16).[23] Unnamed materialists have sought the cause in the material sources of things (335b16–18). Aristotle has chosen two opposing representative types to carry through the previous stage's distinction between form and matter, just as he will develop the opposition between the two camps in the fourth and fifth stages of the chapter.

The Platonic position comes not from the *Timaeus*, which has been singled out repeatedly in *Coming to Be*, but from the *Phaedo*.[24] In that dialogue, Socrates introduces the Forms in response to Cebes' argument that the soul undergoes many incarnations but is nevertheless not immortal. Socrates says that what is required to prove the soul's immortality is precisely "a thorough investigation into the cause (*tên aitan*) of *geneseôs kai phthorâs* (*Phaedo* 95e10–96a1). There follows the famous "philosophical autobiography" of Socrates, which contains its own indictment of materialists, leading in turn to an account of the Forms as causes.

The theory as Aristotle reports it is this (335b9–16). Socrates distinguishes between two sorts of entities: Forms and those things said to partake of Forms. Each item of the latter sort is said to exist in virtue of the Form, and to come into being and pass away as it participates or ceases to participate in the Form. This implies, Aristotle says, that Forms are the cause of *geneseôs kai phthorâs*, just as one reads in the *Phaedo*.

Aristotle's statement of the materialist position is much briefer: "On the other hand, some have thought that the matter in itself was the cause; for it is from this, they said, that movement (*kinêsis*) arises" (335b16–17).[25] Scholars have suggested a variety of predecessors as Aristotle's target.[26] In the chapter's final stage, I will offer evidence that Aristotle is targeting the Atomists. But because he is *not* providing anything like a comprehensive survey of predecessors here, identifying a specific target is not the point. Rather, having named form and matter in the chapter's second stage as two of the three types of causes that must be sought, he now selects two representative but opposing prior theories, one of which misunderstands form and the other matter. In doing so, he maintains the focus at the general or *logikos* level of causes. Criteria for an adequate account will emerge from the opposition between the two parties.

We should also note that the two predecessor accounts are not strictly comparable. The theory in the *Phaedo* seeks to account for coming into being and passing away. It does not speak of motion. The materialists, on the other hand, do speak of motion. As Aristotle makes explicit later, they make coming into being a consequence of the motion inherent in matter. This will also become important in our analysis of the final stage of the chapter.

The Anti-Platonic Argument

The first line of the fourth stage marks the transition to Aristotle's criticisms of the two positions: "But neither of these schools of thought is right" (335b17–18). In this section, I will consider the anti-Platonic argument.

Aristotle advances two criticisms of the *Phaedo* theory. First, the theory does not explain why Forms generate only intermittently: "For if the Forms are causes (*aitia*), why (*dia ti*) do they not always (*aei*) generate continually but only intermittently, since both the Forms and the partakers in them (*methektikoi*) are always (*aei*) there?" (335b18–20).[27] Both Forms as generators and the things that partake of them are present are "always there." But whenever a non-rational agent and patient are present, a potency will be actualized (cf. *Metaphysics* IX.5, 1048a5–7). Generation, therefore, should be continuous.[28] As implied by the *dia ti*, what is needed is something else—a further *aitia*—that is *sufficient* to explain the fact that coming into being happens intermittently and not continuously.

This last point can be stated more generally. Any adequate account of causes in nature and their role in coming into being must account for one of the fundamental phenomena of generation: the generator does not always generate, but only at some times, not at others. The failure of the Forms is not one that is internal to a rival account, as for instance, is the contradiction with which Aristotle charges Empedocles at I.1 (315a2–19). The argument in II.9 points to the *insufficiency* of Platonic Forms as the cause of coming into being. Implied in Aristotle's criticism is a requirement that any account, including his own, must satisfy.[29]

Aristotle's second criticism of the *Phaedo* theory draws attention to cases where something other than the form itself is the cause: "Furthermore (*eti*), in some cases we see that something else is the cause (*to aition*); for it is the physician who implants (*empoiei*) health and the scientific man scientific knowledge, although health itself and science itself exist and also the participants in them; and the same is true of the other operations carried out in virtue of a special faculty (*dunamis*)" (335b20–24).[30] As so often when he analogizes between art and nature, Aristotle uses the analogy to distinguish aspects of causality that in nature coincide. Though health can be produced naturally, the physician produces it in the patient artificially as the product of the medical art, which is to say as the result of the form—form as Aristotle understands it, not a Platonic Form—resident in the physician's soul (the same point is made using the same example at *Metaphysics* VII.7, 1032a32–b14). The examples serve to make clear a need to distinguish both in art and in nature between the form that is imparted and the agent that imparts it, even when in nature they coincide. The insufficiency of Platonic Forms is not that they are unmoved (so is Aristotelian form), but that they are *choristos*, a criticism familiar from many passages in the corpus.[31]

The Anti-Materialist Argument (335b24–336a12)

In the final stage of II.9, Aristotle turns to the other dreamers, the materialists, and in doing so implies a second necessary condition that any account of coming-to-be must satisfy. He begins with a telling contrast between their approach and that of the Platonists: "On the other hand, if someone were to say that it was the matter that caused coming-to-be due to its movement, he would speak in a way more appropriate to natural science (*phusikôteron*) than those who speak in the way just mentioned" (335b24–25; transl. Reeve).[32] By his use of the comparative adjective *phusikôteron*, Aristotle implies the materialist approach, though ultimately mistaken, is nevertheless more appropriate to a science of nature than the Platonic account. As an earlier contrast at I.2, 316a5–14 makes clear, the materialists referred to must be the Atomists.[33] There are those, the earlier passage says, who "inquire [into coming-to-be] by the dialectical method." The context makes clear this approach is that of the Platonists. Their dialectical approach is contrasted to that of Democritus (and of Leucippus, mentioned earlier), who was "convinced by arguments germane to the subject and founded on the study of nature" (316a13–14).[34] Because of their focus on the material dimension of nature, they are more properly *physiologoi* than the Platonists. Motion is a central concern of the study of nature (*Metaphysics* XII.1, 1069a37; *Physics* II.7, 198a28–31), and a failure to adequately name its cause must count as a fatal deficiency. The materialists end in the wrong place, but in contrast to the Platonists, they begin appropriately, within the sphere of natural philosophy. Aristotle's remark, then, has to do with the proper way to investigate coming-to-be. The matter must be included in any account of change in nature.

This is why the incommensurability of the two positions noted above is important. Plato's account, as Williams puts it, sought to explain generation "in terms of something that has nothing to do with movement" (184). The materialists, by contrast, reason in a way that is in accordance with the investigation into nature in that they seek to understand motion first, from which coming into being is one result. This reveals what the materialists get right: motion is prior to coming into being.

What the materialists get wrong is the nature of matter in relation to the cause of motion. They mistakenly locate the source of motion (and therefore of coming-to-be) in the matter itself. But as stated in II.9's second stage, it is the nature of matter not to move but to be moved. Whatever powers matter may have, that which "alters and changes [something's] shape is more a cause (*aitiôteron*) of coming to be" (335b26–27; translation Reeve), and this is true both in nature and in art. Again, the comparative form of the adjective is significant. Matter is not *adunaton*. It has its own proper potency.[35] A correct understanding of matter therefore depends on correctly understanding its *dunamis*, which is to be moved in specific ways.

This leads to another indirect reference to the efficient cause: "To move, that is to act, is the function of another power" (335b30–31). As with the previous indirect references, Aristotle must be referring to the cause of motion. This makes what he says next seem like a non sequitur. The materialists failed because "they omit the more authoritative cause (*kuriôteron aitian*); for they exclude the essence and the form (*morphê*)" (335b34–35; my translation).[36]

Even with the identification of formal, final, and moving causes in *Physics* II.7 in mind, what Aristotle says here is puzzling. It seems as if he is letting in by the window what he threw out at the door at the previous stage.[37] But this is not the case. What he rejected in the anti-Platonic argument was, precisely, Platonic Forms and the accompanying vague notion of participation. Here it is a governing form of any sort, and with it a final cause, that is being excluded by the materialists.[38]

In fact, it is the materialists who, in their dream state, surreptitiously readmit a banished entity. As he says in his final objection, "Moreover also, when they do away with the formal cause, the powers (*dunameis*) which they attribute to bodies and which enable them to brings things into being are too instrumental (*lian organikas*) in character" (336a1–3).[39] For the third time in the anti-materialist argument, one must take notice of a comparative form, *lian organikas*. Materials, whether in art or nature, have their own *dunameis*, derived ultimately from their being composites of the hot, cold, wet, and dry, just as the materialists would say.[40] They are, therefore, capable of being organs or instruments of a sort. But relying simply on the hot or cold to bring things together or to separate them ignores more specific causal connections. The basic capacities of matter are aimless without a more authoritative cause governing them.

Once again, Aristotle employs an analogy of art to nature to distinguish causes that in nature coincide. In the anti-Platonic argument, the analogy pointed to the need for a temporally specific agent to explain the intermittent causation of the omnipresent form. Now Aristotle uses it to show the need for a more governing cause that puts in motion the potentially instrumental matter toward an end-directed use. Relying only on the innate capacity of the matter, he says, would be like attributing cutting to the saw and not to the carpenter. Without the carpenter, the saw does not cut. Without the form, the *dunamis* in the matter is not moved to come into being. The matter is imbued with *dunameis* to be moved in a specific way, but another cause is responsible for the actual coming into being.

Conclusion

Platonic Forms are incapable of explaining why coming into being happens intermittently and not continuously. The materialists exclude formal cause altogether and locate motion in the material makeup of natural things themselves. But because matter qua matter is a *dunamis* not to move but to be moved, their account fails to account for why coming into being happens at all. There must be a third cause capable of moving the matter.

Aristotle concludes II.9 by saying "But we have ourselves dealt with causes in general in a previous work,"[41] and in doing so brings to a close the *katholou* investigation of causes in the realm of things that come to be promised at the start of the chapter. His own account of the causes of coming into being and passing away comes in II.10. The ultimate causes of coming into being turn out to be the same as those for eternal things, just as the second stage of II.9 had claimed at 335a28–29. The difference in the middle region of the cosmos is due to the sun's moving along the ecliptic, making the motion of the sun the efficient cause of coming into being. However implausible his account is to a modern understanding, Aristotle preserves the philosophical economy of his account of the cosmos, while satisfying the necessary conditions for any account of coming into being that emerged in II.9.[42]

Notes

1. In translating the title *Peri Geneseôs kai Phthoras* as *On Coming to Be and Passing Away*, I follow Joachim and now Reeve in preference to *On Generation and Corruption*, the title given to his translation in the landmark Ross and Smith and retained in the *Revised Oxford Aristotle*. To my ear, the word "corruption" has lost whatever sense of passing out of being it may have had a century ago, and more importantly obscures the connection to one of the three sorts of substance identified at *Metaphysics* XII.1, 1069a30–31, where *phthartê* is typically translated as perishable or destructible; see also the threefold division of scientific subjects at *Physics* II.7, 198a28–31.

2. The two most recent papers devoted to *On Coming to Be* II.9 of which I am aware are Mouzala and Huismann. For earlier attention paid to the chapter, particularly for Aristotle's understanding of Platonic Forms, see Annas, Bolton, Fine, and Mueller.

3. For Tuozzo, the lesson of II.9 is that an "adequate interpretation of Aristotelian efficient causation must do justice to its associations with both

matter and form" (450). I agree, and would add that in Aristotle's view, his predecessors had only dimly perceived the efficient cause at all. Perhaps their lack of recognition is reflected in a fact to be noted: Aristotle never in II.9 refers to the efficient cause directly.

4. My divisions are meant for convenience of analysis. The points at which I've divided the text are influenced by the insights found in Netz. While chapter divisions are a post-Aristotelian innovation, they make perfect sense with regard to II.9 and 10.

5. Ἐπεὶ δ' ἐστὶν ἔνια γενητὰ καὶ φθαρτά, καὶ ἡ γένεσις τυγχάνει οὖσα ἐν ᾧ περὶ τὸ μέσον τόπῳ, λεκτέον περὶ πάσης γενέσεως ὁμοίως· πόσαι τε καὶ τίνες αὐτῆς ἀρχαί ῥᾷον γὰρ οὕτω τὰ καθ' ἕκαστον θεωρήσομεν, ὅταν περὶ τῶν καθόλου λάβωμεν πρῶτον.

6. Though the fact that some things come into being may seem obvious, it was precisely this fact that the Eleatics denied. See, for example, *Physics* VIII.1, 250b15–18. See also Joachim (247).

7. Mouzala (124–25) follows Joachim and Philoponus in taking the distinction to be between an investigation at the generic level vs. the specific level, which is not inconsistent with the position I am adopting with regard to the sequence formed by *GC* II.9–10.

8. My claims in this paragraph derive from Zingano.

9. Εἰσὶν οὖν καὶ τὸν ἀριθμὸν ἴσαι καὶ τῷ γένει αἱ αὐταὶ αἵπερ ἐν τοῖς ἀιδίοις τε καὶ πρώτοις·

10. On the special nature of the contrast presented here between the number and kinds of causes, see Williams (180–81).

11. A similar question is the basis for the tenth aporia in *Metaphysics* III (1000b4–1001a1).

12. ἡ μὲν γάρ ἐστιν ὡς ὕλη, ἡ δ' ὡς μορφή. Δεῖ δὲ καὶ ἣν τρίτην ἔτι προσυπάρχειν· οὐ γὰρ ἱκαναὶ πρὸς τὸ γεννῆσαι αἱ δύο, καθάπερ οὐδ' ἐν τοῖς πρώτοις.

13. See for example Joachim (247, 248), and Tuozzo, Mouzala, and Huismann. It is a tendency that goes back at least as far as Philoponus. Williams is careful to follow Aristotle in referring only to "third cause" throughout his commentary on II.9.

14. Ἡμῖν δὲ καθόλου τε πρότερον εἴρηται περὶ τῶν αἰτίων, καὶ νῦν διώρισται περί τε τῆς ὕλης καὶ τῆς μορφῆς.

15. Both Forster (312) and Joachim (253) take the passage to refer only to what I'm calling the second stage. My essay shows why it is better to take the phrase as referring to the entirety of II.9.

16. Like the translation "corruption," "efficient" seems to me to have lost its relevant sense to modern ears. More important, it is not close to the phrases Aristotle himself uses in referring to this cause. Familiar formulations are found at, for example, *Physics* II.3, 194b30: "The primary source of the change or rest";

195a8: "the other cause from which the motion comes"; 195a10: "the principle of motion"; II.7, 198a26: "the primary source of motion"; 198a33: "the primary moving cause"; *Metaphysics* I.3, 983b28–29 and 984a25: "the starting point from which the movement derives"; 4, 985a12: "the starting point of movement"; V.2, 1013b29–30: "that from which the change or rest from change first starts."

17. At 335b1–5, Aristotle makes clear that things that come into being and pass away are a subset of things that can both be and not be.

18. Διὸ καὶ ὡς μὲν ὕλη τοῦτ' ἐστὶν αἴτιον τοῖς γενητοῖς . . .

19. . . . ὡς δὲ τὸ οὗ ἕνεκεν ἡ μορφὴ καὶ τὸ εἶδος τοῦτο δ' ἐστὶν ὁ λόγος ὁ τῆς ἑκάστου οὐσίας.

20. The final cause of coming into being and passing away is addressed at II.10, 336b25–337a7. For the problematic language of imitation in that passage, see Johnson (146–49).

21. Lewis develops a far-ranging argument that loosens the connection between the efficient cause on the one hand and formal/final causes on the other, linking efficient causes with the material cause throughout Aristotle's natural philosophy (see further Tuozzo 450). Lewis's position as I understand it is not inconsistent with my interpretation of *GC* II.9.

22. Δεῖ δὲ προσεῖναι καὶ τρίτην, ἣν ἅπαντες μὲν ὀνειρώττουσι, λέγει δ' οὐδείς. Following Rashid and Reeve in reading τρίτην ("a third") in place of Joachim's τὴν τρίτην ("the third").

23. I capitalize Forms when referring to Plato's account as Aristotle criticizes it, and "forms" or "form" in reference to Aristotle's own formal cause. For a detailed working through of Aristotle's reference to the *Phaedo* theory, and particularly to the distinction between mover and that which is moved, see (in addition to earlier articles cited in note 2) Tuozzo (451–54); Mouzala (130–41).

24. Guthrie draws attention to the shift (244, n2).

25. Οἱ δ' αὐτὴν τὴν ὕλην ἀπὸ ταύτης· γὰρ εἶναι τὴν κίνησιν.

26. See Joachim (249); Reeve (163n287).

27. Εἰ μὲν γάρ ἐστιν αἴτια τὰ εἴδη, διὰ τί οὐκ ἀεὶ γεννᾷ συνεχῶς, ἀλλὰ ποτὲ μὲν ποτὲ δ' οὔ, ὄντων καὶ τῶν εἰδῶν ἀεὶ καὶ τῶν μεθεκτικῶν;

28. Huismann (671) identifies the key premise of Aristotle's argument as what modern logicians would call an indifference premise—what scholars of ancient philosophy might know better as an *ou mallon* argument. Applied to the argument in II.9, he takes Aristotle to mean the following: "if Forms and their participants are always present, there is no more reason for Forms to generate always than for Forms to generate intermittently." On indifference arguments in ancient philosophy and beyond, see Makin.

29. A point made also by Mouzala (126).

30. ἔτι δ' ἐπ' ἐνίων θεωροῦμεν ἄλλο τὸ αἴτιον ὄν· ὑγίειαν γὰρ ὁ ἰατρὸς ἐμποιεῖ καὶ ἐπιστήμην ὁ ἐπιστήμων, οὔσης καὶ ὑγιείας αὐτῆς καὶ ἐπιστήμης καὶ τῶν μεθεκτικῶν· ὡσαύτως δὲ καὶ ἐπὶ τῶν ἄλλων τῶν κατὰ δύναμιν πραττομένων.

31. Huismann (665) cites the *Metaphysics* passage to argue that the expert and not the expert's art is effectively causal, and that the expert as efficient cause can be moved even as they impart motion. While this may be true in the case of the expert, this certainly isn't true of the efficient cause of coming into being and perishing Aristotle identifies in II.10.

32. Forster translates *phusikôteron* as "in accordance with the facts of nature." Both the revised Oxford translation and Williams render it as "more scientific." When Kupreeva translates Philoponus' quoting of this passage (Philoponus 282.6–7), she renders the term as "more in accordance with the study of nature," noted by Mouzala (142).

33. Neither Joachim nor Reeve notices the relevance of 316a5–14. Williams does note the earlier passage but does not use it to identify Aristotle's target here (184).

34. Δημόκριτος δ' ἂν φανείη οἰκείοις καὶ φυσικοῖς λόγοις πεπεῖσθαι.

35. Nicely brought out by Forster's translation of *aitiôteron* as "more potent a cause."

36. καὶ ὅτι παραλείπουσι τὴν κυριωτέραν αἰτίαν· ἐξαιροῦσι γὰρ τὸ τί ἦν εἶναι καὶ τὴν μορφήν. Williams notes the non sequitur (184).

37. A charge noted and rebutted by Williams (184–85).

38. Tuozzo suggests that Aristotle may use *morphê* for form here in order to lexically distinguish his efficient cause from the Platonic Forms he had earlier discussed, for which he used *eidos* (452).

39. Ἔτι δὲ καὶ τὰς δυνάμεις ἀποδιδόασι τοῖς σώμασι, δι' ἃς γεννῶσι, λίαν ὀργανικῶς, ἀφαιροῦντες τὴν κατὰ τὸ εἶδος αἰτίαν. Joachim takes the argument at 336a1–12 as being directed against Pythagorean materialists (251–52). The point with regard to materials that are "too instrumental" remains the same.

40. "It is clear, then, that the necessity in natural things is that which is spoken of as matter and the motions of this" (*Physics* II 9, 200a30–2).

41. A reference to *Physics* II, 3 and 7.

42. This essay derives from a comment I was pleased to give on a paper by Tyler Huismann at the APA Central Division meeting, February 24, 2018, in Chicago. I owe a special thanks to David Reeve for sharing with me the pre-publication proofs of his *Aristotle's Chemistry*.

Works Cited

Annas, Julia. "Aristotle on Inefficient Causes." *The Philosophical Quarterly*, vol. 32, 1982, pp. 311–26.

Barnes, Jonathan, editor. *The Complete Works of Aristotle, The Revised Oxford Translation*. Princeton UP, 1984.

Bolton, Robert. "Plato's Discovery of Metaphysics: The New *Methodos* of the *Phaedo*." *Method in Ancient Philosophy*, edited by Jyl Gentzler, Clarendon, 1998, pp. 91–111.

Duke, E. A., et al., eds. *Platonis Opera* I. Clarendon, 1995.

Fine, Gail. "Forms as Causes: Plato and Aristotle." *Mathematik und Metaphysik bei Aristoteles*, edited by Andreas Graeser, Haupt, 1987, pp. 69–112.

Forster, E. S., translated with notes. *On Sophistical Refutations* and *On Coming-to-be and Passing Away*. With D. J. Furley, *On the Cosmos*, Loeb-Harvard UP, 1955.

Guthrie, W. K. C. *A History of Greek Philosophy VI: Aristotle, an Encounter*. Cambridge UP, 1981.

Huismann, Tyler. "Aristotle on How Efficient Causation Works." *Archiv für Geschichte der Philosophie*, vol. 104, no. 4, 2022, pp. 633–87.

Joachim, Harold H. *Aristotle, On Coming-to-be and Passing-away (De Generatione et Corruptione). A revised text with introduction and commentary.* Clarendon, 1922.

Johnson, Monte R. *Aristotle on Teleology*. Clarendon, 2005.

Lewis, Frank. "Teleology and Material/Efficient Causes in Aristotle." *Pacific Philosophical Quarterly*, vol. 69, 1988, pp. 54–98.

Makin, Stephen. *Indifference Arguments*. Blackwell, 1993.

Mueller, Ian. "Platonism and the Study of Nature (*Phaedo* 95e ff.)." *Method in Ancient Philosophy*, edited by Jyl Gentzler, Clarendon, 1998, pp. 68–89.

Mouzala, Melina G. "Aristotle's Criticism of the Platonic Forms as Causes in *De Generatione et Corruptione* II 9. A Reading Based on Philoponus' Exegesis." *Peitho. Examina Antiqua*, vol. 1, 2016, pp. 123–47.

Netz, Reviel. "The Aristotelian Paragraph." *Proceedings of the Cambridge Philological Society*, vol. 47, 2001, pp. 211–32.

Philoponus, John. *On Aristotle on Coming-to-Be and Perishing 2.5–11*. Translated by I. Kupreeva, Duckworth, 2005.

Rashed, Mohammed. *Aristotle: De la Génération et la Corruption*. Les Belles Lettres, 2005.

Reeve, C. D. C. "Aristotle's Chemistry. On Coming to Be and Passing Away." *Meteorology* I.1–3, 4.1–12. Hackett, 2023.

Ross, W. D., ed. *Aristotle's* Metaphysics. Clarendon, 1924.

———. *Aristotle's* Physics. Clarendon, 1936.

———. *Aristotle's* Prior and Posterior Analytics. Clarendon, 1949.

——— and John A. Smith, eds. *The Works of Aristotle Translated into English*. Clarendon, 1908–30.

Tuozzo, Thomas. "How Dynamic Is Aristotle's Efficient Cause?" *Epoché: A Journal for the History of Philosophy*, vol. 15, 2011, pp. 447–64.

Williams, Christopher J. F. *Aristotle's De generatione et corruptione*. Clarendon, 1982.

Zingano, Marco. "Ways of Proving in Aristotle." *Reading Aristotle: Argument and Exposition*, edited by William Wians and Ronald Polansky, Brill, 2017, pp. 7–49.

Contributors

D. Z. Andriopoulos has published countless articles and anthologies in Ancient Philosophy. His anthologies exemplify his dedication to organizing and publishing honorary works for his colleagues. Andriopoulos edited *Philosophical Inquiry* and served as lead editor of *Politeia: International Interdisciplinary Philosophical Review*. Andriopoulos served as a professor of philosophy at the Aristotle University of Thessaloniki throughout most of his career, and he also spent part of his tenure at the University of Missouri in Kansas City.

Martha C. Beck is Professor of Philosophy at Lyon College and earned her PhD from Bryn Mawr College. Beck has authored many articles and sixteen books, including *Looking for the Ancient Greeks: Damasio, Aristotle and Human Flourishing* and *Using the Greek Goddesses to Create a Well-Lived Life for Women* (both from Cambridge Scholars Press, 2018). Beck's focus on the legacy of ancient Greek civilization in the era of globalization has led her to teach in Prague and Greece, and, in 2012, 2017, and 2022, to teach and work with colleagues in Indonesia. More on Beck's work can be found on her YouTube channel.

Rose M. Cherubin is Associate Professor of Philosophy and affiliate faculty in African and African American Studies and in Women and Gender Studies at George Mason University, where she has also served as Director of Graduate Programs. She received her BA from The School of Visual Arts and her PhD from the CUNY Graduate Center. Cherubin's research areas include justice, truth, and what-is and their relationships in early Greek thought and in Alain Locke. Her publications include "Sex, Gender, and Class in the Poem of Parmenides: Difference without Dualism?" (2019)

and "Alētheia from Poetry into Philosophy: Homer to Parmenides" in Wians's *Mythos and Logos* (SUNY, 2009).

Meredith Trexler Drees is an Associate Professor and Chair of the Department of Religion and Philosophy at Kansas Wesleyan University. Her book *Aesthetic Experience and Moral Vision in Plato, Kant, and Murdoch: Looking Good/Being Good* (Palgrave Macmillan, 2021) examines the relationship between ethics and aesthetics and presents an extended version of Iris Murdoch's moral vision. She was awarded a research fellowship in 2022–2023 at the University of Notre Dame to continue her work in this area.

Mateo Duque is Assistant Professor of Philosophy at Binghamton University. He received his PhD from the Graduate Center, The City University of New York (CUNY). His areas of research include Ancient Greek philosophy (particularly Plato) and aesthetics. He is the co-editor with Gerald Press of *The Bloomsbury Handbook of Plato*. His most recent publications are "'Οὐκ ἔστιν' (141e8): The Performative Contradiction of the First Hypothesis" and "Two Passions in Plato's *Symposium*: Diotima's *To Kalon* as a Reorientation of Imperialistic *Erōs*."

Howard Engelskirchen is a retired professor of law and philosophy who, for a memorable moment, was a hiking companion of Dr. Preus over miles and miles of upstate New York's Finger Lakes Trail. His thesis *The Aristotelian Marx and Scientific Realism* (SUNY Binghamton 2007), modified and developed, became *Capital as a Social Kind: Definitions and Transformations in the Critique of Political Economy* (Routledge, 2011). His work on Aristotle and Marx continues.

Myrna Gabbe is an Associate Professor in the Department of Philosophy at the University of Dayton. She holds a PhD from the University of Pennsylvania. Her past research focused on Aristotle's *De Anima* and the Peripatetic commentaries on it. Currently, she focuses on Aristotle's zoological texts, with a particular interest in his reproductive anatomy and physiology.

Hyun Höchsmann is affiliated with East China Normal University, Shanghai. Mingling the study of philosophy with art history and literature at Ludwig-Maximilians Universität and University of London, she drank at the fountains of the Sorbonne. Her research efforts range over Greek philosophy, philosophy of music, Eastern philosophy, Walter Benjamin, and Gilles Deleuze. Her publications include "Cosmology, *psyche*, and *ātman* in the *Timaeus*, the *R̥gveda*, and the *Upaniṣads*," "Porphyry's Extension and Restriction of Plato's Views on Justice," and "Harmony of the Spheres in Pythagoras and Zhuangzi."

Anne J. Mamary is Professor of Philosophy at Monmouth College in Monmouth, Illinois. Her PhD in Philosophy, Interpretation, and Culture is from SUNY Binghamton, where she studied Greek and Greek philosophy with Tony Preus. Her recent publications include "How Do You Know His Name is Gabriel?" (*Journal for Critical Animal Studies*, 2020) and "Ruddy Stargazers: Centaurs, Philosophers, and a Life Worth Living" in Finamore and Nyvlt's *Plato in Late Antiquity, the Middle Ages, and Modern Times* (Prometheus Trust, 2020). She is editor of *The Alchemical Harry Potter* (McFarland, 2021).

Phillip Mitsis is the Alexander S. Onassis Professor of Hellenic Culture and Civilization at New York University and Academic Director of the Institute for Verdi Studies. He writes on ancient philosophy and its influence on early modern philosophers, and on Greek and Roman literature. Recent publications include *Natura Aut Voluntas. Recherches sur la pensée politique et éthique hellénistique et romaine et son influence* (2020) and, as editor, *The Oxford Handbook of Epicurus and Epicureanism* (2020).

Mark Moes completed an MA in philosophical theology at the Aquinas Institute of Theology and a doctorate in philosophy at the University of Notre Dame. In 2022, he retired from the position of Professor of Philosophy at Grand Valley State University in Michigan, specializing in Ancient Philosophy. He is author of *Plato's Dialogue Form and the Care of the Soul* and articles on ancient philosophy and philosophy of medicine. He is currently doing research on two connected projects: a book on Plato's *Republic*, and a book on the whole corpus of the published writings of Alasdair MacIntyre.

Parviz Morewedge received his PhD from UCLA. He taught for fifty-seven years at UCLA, Cornell, Columbia, Rutgers, Fordham, and at SUNY and CUNY and has lectured/held seminars across the country and the world. He has authored or edited fourteen books and seventy essays. Morewedge was a Senior Research Engineer at GM's Computer Division and a UN consultant for Iran, Syria, Russian Federation, PRC, Uzbekistan, Tajikistan, Belarus, and the Kyrgyz Republic. He directed *Global Scholarly Publications* for forty years and co-organized the International Conference on Ancient and Medieval Philosophy with Anthony Preus and John P. Anton for thirty-six. Morewedge and spouse Professor Rosmarie T. Morewedge have a son, Carey K. Morewedge, and two grandsons, Ivan and Vladan Cikara-Morewedge.

Joyce M. Mullan is a Teaching Assistant Professor of Philosophy in the College of Arts and Letters at Stevens Institute of Technology in Hoboken, New Jersey. Her research focuses on Ancient and Enlightenment Ethical and Political Theory, and she has presented widely and on a wide variety of topics at philosophical and political sciences conferences. Her published work includes "To Whom Do we Owe the Truth in Fanon and Gandhi" (*Review Journal of Philosophy and Social Science*, 2009) and "Humanity and *Humanitas* in Rousseau and Kant" in *Misery and Dignity of Humanity* (Seneca Institute, 2006).

Nickolas Pappas is Professor of Philosophy at the Graduate Center of the City University of New York. He is the author of books and articles, mainly on ancient philosophy, including the *Routledge Guidebook to Plato's Republic*; *The Philosopher's New Clothes* (Routledge); and *Plato's Exceptional City, Love, and Philosopher* (Routledge). Pappas wrote "Plato's Aesthetics" for the *Stanford Encyclopedia of Philosophy*. His new research investigates the Platonic figure of the foreigner, with special emphasis on the *Republic*.

Eileen Rizo-Patron earned a PhD in Comparative Literature from Binghamton University. She co-edited *Traversing the Heart: Journeys of the Interreligious Imagination* with Richard Kearney (Brill, 2010) and translated Gaston Bachelard's *Intuition of the Instant* into English (Northwestern UP, 2013). Rizo-Patron organized an international congress on the centennial anniversary of novelist José Maria Arguedas at the Catholic University in Lima, Peru and co-edited the 3-volume series *José María Arguedas: La Dinámica de los Encuentros Culturales* (PUCP, 2013). Rizo-Patron is editor of *Adventures in Phenomenology: Gaston Bachelard* (SUNY, 2017) and serves on the editorial board of the tri-lingual *Études Bachelardiennes*.

Anne-Marie Schultz is Professor of Philosophy at Baylor University. She also serves as Undergraduate Program Director and recently received the designation of Master Teacher. Schultz is the author of *Plato's Socrates as Narrator* (Lexington, 2013) and *Plato's Socrates on Socrates* (Lexington, 2020) and numerous articles on Plato, Augustine, and the Scholarship of Teaching and Learning.

Thomas M. Tuozzo is Professor of Philosophy at the University of Kansas. He received his PhD in Classics and Philosophy from Yale University and has been a visiting professor at Emory University and the University of Michigan. He has published articles on Platonic and Aristotelian moral psychology and metaphysics, as well as a book, *Plato's Charmides: Positive Elenchus in a "Socratic" Dialogue* (Cambridge UP, 2011). His current research focuses on ancient views of love, Platonic metaphysics, and ancient theories of causation.

William Wians has taught philosophy at Merrimack College since 1997. He also teaches graduate courses at Boston College, and has taught at Boston University, the University of Chicago, and the University of Notre Dame, where he received his PhD. Recent publications include three edited collections: *Logos and Muthos: Philosophical Essays in Greek Literature* (SUNY, 2009); *Logoi and Muthoi: Further Philosophical Essays in Greek Literature* (SUNY, 2019); and *Reading Aristotle: Argument and Exposition*, co-edited with Ronald Polansky (Brill, 2017).

Name Index

Adey, Glyn, 64
Aeschylus, 63n12, 64, 134, 225, 230, 281
al-Biruni, Abu Rayham, 207n6
Alderman, Harold, 41
al-Fārābī, Abu Nasr, 198–99, 207
Algar, Hamid, 208
al-Ghazālī, Abū Ḥāmid, 201, 205, 207n7
Ali Khalidi, Muhammad, 207
al-Majūsī, Ali ibn al-Abbas, 202
al-Nasafī, Azīz al-Dīn, 207n8, 208
al-Tusi, Nasir al-Din, 206n2
Améry, Jean, 178n17, 179
Anacreon, 146
Anaximander, 121–27, 128n9, 129
Annas, Julia, 80n8, 81, 300n2, 303
Apel, Karl-Otto, 61, 64, 65
Archer-Hind, Richard D., 118, 129
Arendt, Hannah, 8, 211, 223n4
Arieti, James A., 155, 158, 163
Aristotle, 2, 4, 10, 13, 26n8, 26n11, 30–53, 62–63n6, 64, 65, 66, 94n10, 99, 100–107, 110–12, 113n4, 114, 121, 125, 129, 142, 147, 166, 170, 171, 174, 177n5, 177n10, 179, 198, 199, 203, 206n4, 208, 215, 220, 229, 239n5, 291–300, 300n1, 300–301n2, 301n13, 301n16, 302n17, 302n21, 302n23, 302n28, 303n31, 303n33, 303n38, 303n42, 303, 304, 305, 306, 309
Arruzza, Cinzia, 265, 266, 275
Asmis, Elizabeth, 71, 72, 81
Athanassakis, Apostolos, 117, 129
Austin, Emily A., 25n2, 26n11, 27, 93n2, 95
Avicenna, 208

Bachelard, Gaston, 243–56, 256n1, 256n3, 256n6, 256n10, 256n11, 257nn12–16, 257n18, 258nn19–20, 258nn22–23, 258n26, 259nn28–29, 260, 261, 308
Badawi, Abdurrahman, 208
Bakhtiar, Laleh, 208
Baltzly, Dick, 41
Balzac, Honoré de, 259n28
Barden, Garrett, 260
Barnes, Corey L., 64 n17, 64n19, 64
Barnes, Jonathan, 114, 118–20, 120n3, 128, 129, 208, 303
Barney, Rachel, 97, 239n2, 241, 275n3, 275
Bartlett, Robert C., 93n2, 95, 213, 215, 218, 223
Beck, Hans, 278
Bell, Jeremy, 163
Benardete, Seth, 62n1, 62n3, 64, 215, 223

311

Benton, Gregor, 114
Bergson, Henri, 243, 246, 256n10
Berman, Daniel W., 223
Bernal, Martin, 206n3, 208
Bernard, Mary, 163, 259
Bettelheim, Charles, 103, 114
Bianchi, Emanuela, 53, 63n6, 64
Bihbanhani, A. Musavi, 208
Blanco, Walter, 225
Blok, Josine, 223n2, 223
Bloom, Alan, 41, 276
Bloom, D., 276
Blossner, Norbert, 184, 194
Bobonich, Christopher, 235, 241
Bolton, Robert, 300n2, 304
Bonitz, Hermann, 118, 129
Bossi, Beatriz, 91, 92, 95
Bostock, David, 119, 128n4, 129
Boudouris, K. J., 164
Bowden, Hugh, 129n13, 129
Boyce, Mary, 207n11, 208
Brann, Eva, 150, 151, 154, 160, 163
Bremer, John, 150, 154, 163
Brennan, Tad, 97
Brisson, Luc, 91, 95, 96, 97, 139, 140, 144n7, 144n10, 144n12, 145, 147
Brittain, Charles, 97
Brochard, Victor, 51, 64
Brock, Roger, 25n3, 27
Buchman, David, 207
Buck, Christopher, 65
Bundy, Elroy L., 140, 141, 145n16
Burkhardt, Jacob, 133, 139, 141, 142, 145
Burke, Edmund, 165, 172, 173, 177n2, 179
Burkert, Walter, 127, 129
Burnet, John, 128n5, 129, 147
Burnyeat, Myles, 193n8, 194
Bury, R. G., 26n11, 27, 66, 92, 97
Bywater, Ingram, 96

Cairns, Huntington, 42, 260
Calame, Claude, 223
Calder, W. M., 147
Calvo, Tomas, 144n10, 145, 147
Campos, Daniel, 93n2, 95
Candiotto, Laura, 95, 97
Canguilhem, G., 260
Cannon, Edwin, 225
Carone, Gabriela Roxana, 95
Carpenter, Amber Danielle, 93n2, 95
Carter, Jacoby Adeshei, 64, 65
Carver, Terrell, 114
Case, Brendan, 264, 275
Cassin, Barbara, 61, 64n20, 65
Cherubin, Rose, 64n19, 65, 305
Childs, William, 274, 275
Cicero, 116, 129, 215
Clayton, Barbara, 150, 154, 160, 163
Clower, William, 202, 209
Coles, Andrew, 129
Cooper, John M., 42, 82, 95, 97, 163, 225, 276, 289
Corbin, Henry, 198, 201, 207n11, 208
Coxon, P. W., 209
Crawford, Matthew, 223n5, 223
Crotty, Kevin, 132, 145
Cumming, John, 260
Curd, Patricia, 44, 45, 65
Currie, Bruno, 145n17, 145

Damad, Mir, 199, 200, 205, 208
Darwin, Charles, 223n3, 225
Davidson, Donald, 93n3, 95
de Beauvoir, Simone, 53, 178n17, 179
Delbos, Victor, 64
Delcomminette, Sylvain, 93n2, 95
Del Forno, Davide, 145
Demos, Marian, 144n6, 145
Dennett, D. C., 86, 96
Derrida, Jacques, 87, 96
Descartes, René, 58, 61, 65
Destrée, Pierre, 233, 241

De Vries, G. J., 25n2, 27
Dibaji, Ibrahim, 208
Diels, Hermann, 65, 145
Dillon, John, 95, 96, 97
Dillon, Matthew, 26n9, 27
Dimas, Panos, 93n2, 96
Dimock, George E., 65
Diogenes Laertius, 129n12, 170, 179
Diogenes the Cynic, 170
Dirac, Paul, 247
Di Teresi, Christopher, 63n13
Dorandi, T., 179
Dorter, Kenneth, 41
DuBois, 239n8, 241
Duke, E. A., 304
Dupree, Robert Scott, 259
Dussel, Enrique D., 61, 64n20, 65
Dutt, Clemens, 114
Dybikowski, James, 93n2, 96

Eisikovits, Nir, 275
Emlyn-Jones, Christopher, 66
Empedocles, 5, 121–27, 128n10, 129n12, 129, 142, 211–12, 222, 297
Engels, Friedrich, 5, 112, 113n3, 114
Engelskirchen, Howard, 103, 112n1, 114
Erler, Michael, 289
Euclid, 207n6
Euripides, 16, 135, 144n5, 214, 225, 231
Evans, C. Stephen, 276
Evans, Matthew, 26n16, 27, 93n2, 96

Farrell, Edith, 259, 260
Farrell, Frederick, 259
Fendt, Gene, 156, 159, 163
Ferrari, G. R. F., 26n7, 27, 72–73, 79n7, 81, 192n2, 193n11, 194
Fine, Gail, 300n2, 304
Finger, Stanley, 202, 209
Fisher, Betty J., 65

Fletcher, Emily, 26n15, 27, 93n2, 94n4, 96
Forbes, P. B. R., 215, 224
Forster, Edward S., 64, 292, 301n15, 303n32, 302n35, 304
Fort, Jeff, 147
Forte, Joseph, 93n2, 96
Fränkel, Hermann, 140, 145
Franklin, V. P., 275
Frede, Dorothea, 26nn11–12, 28, 89, 93nn2–3, 96, 97
Freidenreich, Keren, 240n16, 240n18
Frisby, David, 64
Frixione, Eugenio, 202, 209

Gadamer, Hans-Georg, 253, 260
Gagarin, Michael, 217, 224
Galen of Alexandrea, 202
Gallop, David, 118, 119, 129
Garner, John V., 93n2, 96
Gerson, Lloyd, 201, 208
Gianfaldoni, Serena, 271, 275
Gill, Christopher, 97
Gill, Mary Louise, 107, 113n4, 114
Gilson, Étienne, 200, 208
Giménez Salinas, José Antonio, 93n2, 96
Gish, Dustin, 221, 224
Glazebrook, Trish, 51, 65
Goehr, Lydia, 85, 96
Goldhammer, Arthur, 259
Goldstein, J. H., 27
Gordimer, Nadine, 66
Gosling, J. C. B., 89, 93n3, 97
Gourevitch, Victor, 225
Graeser, Andreas, 304
Graham, Daniel W., 44, 50, 65
Grainger, John D., 233, 239n11, 241
Greenfeld, Howard, 66
Gregory, Andrew, 122, 126, 128nn6–8, 129
Gregory, Justina, 95n12, 96

Griffith, Mark, 224
Griswold, Charles, 81n19, 82
Grube, G. M. A., 42, 82, 87, 97, 276
Gruner, Cameron O., 208
Gurtler, Gary Michael, 179
Guthrie, W. K. C., 302n24, 304

Habermas, Jürgen, 61, 65
Hackforth, Reginald, 26nn11–12, 27, 28, 89, 93n3, 121, 128nn3–5, 129
Hall, Edith, 234, 239n3, 241
Hall, Jonathan M., 239n10, 241
Halliwell, Stephen, 16, 17, 145n19, 146, 232, 233, 241, 288n7, 289
Haltmann, Kenneth, 259
Hamilton, Edith, 42, 260
Hampton, Cynthia M., 93n2, 94n8, 96
Harris, Leonard, 64, 65
Harrison, S. J., 147
Harte, Verity, 26n13, 27, 93n2, 96
Harvey, John W., 260
Havelock, Eric A., 144n4, 145n21, 146
Heaney, Seamus, 143, 146
Hedrick, Charles, 144n3, 146
Heffernan, George, 65
Hegel, Georg Wilhelm Friedrich, 207n11, 224
Heraclitus, 63n15, 121, 134, 145n21, 212, 222, 258n25, 259n29, 260
Herodotus, 231, 233, 239nn9–11
Herrmann, F. G., 56
Hesiod, 8, 37, 134, 142, 211–25, 223n4, 279
Highet, G., 146
Hilton, Collin Miles, 240n17, 241
Holan, Angie Drobnic, 275
Hollingdale, R. J., 225
Homer, 6, 15, 27, 30, 37–41, 62n4, 65, 85, 132, 134, 135, 137, 142, 146, 149–63, 212, 213, 219, 221, 224, 239n7, 239–40n11, 281, 306
Honig, Bonnie, 224

Hornblower, Simon, 141, 144n5, 144n7, 146
Hourani, George Fadlo, 208
Howland, Jacob, 151, 153, 156, 162n3, 163, 265, 275
Huggard, E. M., 208
Huismann, Tyler, 300n2, 301n13, 302n28, 303n31, 303n42, 304
Hutchinson, D. S., 42, 95, 97, 225

ibn Isḥāq, Ḥunayn, 202
Ihde, John, 261
Inwood, Brad, 82, 124, 125, 128n10, 129n11, 129, 178–79n18, 225
Ionescu, Cristina, 93n2, 96
Irigaray, Luce, 157, 263
Irwin, Terrence, 80nn7–8, 82
Izutsu, Toshihiko, 208

Jaeger, Werner, 64, 131, 140, 141, 143, 144n1, 145n15, 146
Jankélévitch, Vladimir, 178n17, 179
Jesus Christ, 172, 173, 177n2, 196
Joachim, Harold H., 300n1, 301nn6–7, 301n13, 201n15, 302n22, 302n26, 303n33, 303n39, 304
Johannitius (see ibn Isḥāq), 202
Johnson, Barbara, 96
Johnson, Monte R., 302n20, 304
Johnstone, Henry W., 66
Jolas, Maria, 260
Jones, Henry Stuart, 65
Jones, Mary McAllester, 259
Jones, Peter, 224
Jones, Russell E., 96
Jongkind, Dirk, 178n13, 179
Journée, Gérard, 62n5, 65

Kahn, Charles, 80n7, 82, 258n25, 259n29, 260
Kalin, Ibrahim, 208, 209
Kallen, Horace, 59

Name Index | 315

Kalyvas, Andreas, 8, 211, 221, 222, 224
Kamtekar, Rachana, 193n8, 194
Kant, Immanuel, 176, 178n16, 179, 197, 207n7, 223n3, 224, 243, 247, 256n2, 306, 308
Kaplan, Justin D., 260
Kaufmann, Walter, 209
Keith-Spiegel, Patricia, 25n1, 26n14, 27
Kennedy, George Alexander, 82
Kessler, Charles, 209
Keyes, Clinton W., 129
Keyt, David, 275n2, 275
Khayyām, Omar, 207n6, 209
Khomeini, Ruhollah, 198, 208
Kinzel, Konrad, 225
Kirk, Geoffrey Stephen, 141, 146
Kirsch, Adam, 276
Kisner, Matthew J., 209
Koehnken, Adolf, 145n17, 146
Komjathy, Louis, 67, 79n1, 82
Konstan, David, 96, 176, 178, 179, 288, 289
Korsybski, Alfred, 250, 251, 258n24, 260
Kosman, Aryeh, 106, 111, 113n4, 114
Kotowicz, Zbigniew, 256n6, 259n29, 260
Kranz, Walther, 65, 145
Kraut, Richard, 81
Krentz, Peter, 275n6, 275
Kuhn, K. H., 209
Kupreeva, I., 303n32, 303
Kushner, Eliot, 276

LaFrentz, Grace, 161, 163
Lamb, W. R. M., 209, 276
Lattimore, Richmond, 144n2, 147
Lattimore, Steven, 276
Lear, Gabriel Richardson, 72, 82, 96
Le Bon de Beauvoir, Sylvie, 179

Lee, Edward N., 114
Leibniz, Gottfried Willhelm, 205, 206n2, 206n4, 207n12, 208
LeMoine, Rebecca, 239n6, 241
Lenhardt, Christian, 65
Le Roy, Bernard, 260
Lesses, Glen, 80n5, 82
Levaniouk, Olga, 150, 154, 160, 162, 163
Levin, Susan B., 95n12, 96
Lévi-Strauss, Claude, 145n18, 146
Lewis, Frank, 302n21, 304
Liddell, Henry George, 65
Lisi, Francisco L., 932n, 96
Lloyd, A. C., 28
Lloyd, Janet, 147
Locke, Alain L., 3, 43–66, 63n8, 63n12, 63n15, 64n19, 305
Long, A., 118, 128n2, 129
Löning, Thomas Clark, 274, 275
Loomis, David Eugene, 192n3, 194
Loraux, Nicole, 223n2, 224
Lorenze, Hendrick, 80n6, 82
Lovibond, Sabina, 93n2, 97

MacKenna, Stephen, 209
MacLean, Paul, 193n8, 194
Maimonides, Moses, 206n4
Makin, Stephen, 302n28, 304
Mallet, Joan-Antoine, 273, 274, 276
Malthus, Thomas Robert, 214, 224
Marcos de Pinotti, Graciela E., 93n2, 97
Marlowe, Christopher, 214, 224
Maslov, Boris, 145n21, 146
Mason, Peter, 223n2
Mastronarde, Donald, 224
Marx, Karl, 4, 5, 99–114, 112–13nn2–4, 207n11, 223n5, 224, 306
McCarthy, Mary, 225
McCoy, Marina, 152, 163
McGhee, P. E., 27

McKenzie, Roderick, 65
McLaughlin, Andrew, 93n2, 97
McPherran, Mark L., 236, 241
Meikle, Scott, 99, 101, 110, 112, 114
Memmi, Albert, 63n9, 66
Mendieta, Eduardo, 65
Migliori, Maurizio, 93nn2–3, 97, 145
Miller, Mitchell, 7, 25, 26, 27, 62, 66, 181–94, 193n5, 193n7
Miller, Thomas, 176n1, 179
Moes, Mark, 193n4, 194
Mohaghegh, Mehdi, 208
Molé, Marijan, 208
Montin, Karin, 163
Mooradian, Norman, 93n2, 97
Moore, Christopher, 135, 146
Morewedge, Parviz, 201, 206n2, 207n6, 207n9, 208
Morgan, Catherine, 141, 144n5, 144n7, 146
Morgan, Kathryn, 139, 146, 276
Morreall, John, 25n1, 26n14, 27
Morris, Ian, 132, 136, 146
Morris, T. F., 41
Moses, 196, 205
Moss, Jessica, 69, 80n5, 82, 93n2, 97
Morrow, Glenn, 42
Most, Glenn W., 216, 224
Mourelatos, Alexander P. D., 54, 62n2, 66, 114
Mouzala, Melina G., 300n2, 301n7, 301n13, 302n23, 302n29, 303n32, 304
Mueller, Ian, 300n2, 304
Muniz, Fernando, 93n2, 97
Munn, Mark H., 265, 267, 274, 275n4, 276
Murray, Augustus T., 65

Naas, Michael, 163
Naddaf, Gerad, 134, 139, 144n7, 145, 146

Nagy, Gregory, 86, 97, 221, 224
Nails, Deborah, 178n12, 179, 271, 272, 276
Nehamas, Alexander, 42, 87, 97, 163, 276, 287n1, 289
Nestle, Wilhelm, 142, 146
Netz, Reviel, 301n4, 304
Newman, John K., 138, 139, 144n11, 146
Nicholson, Graeme, 82
Nicholsen, Shierry Weber, 65
Nietzsche, Friedrich, 197, 206n5, 209, 223n3, 225, 239n5, 253
Nightingale, Andrea W., 25n3, 27, 144n6, 146
Nisbet, H. B., 224

Oakes, Jeffrey, 209
Ober, Josiah, 144n3, 146, 221, 225
O'Donohue, Andrew, 41
Ogihara, Satoshi, 93n2, 97
Olstein, Katherine, 213, 216, 219, 220, 225
Otto, Rudolf, 243, 244, 245, 251, 256n3, 258n26, 260

Palmer, John Anderson, 44, 66
Pappas, Nickolas, 41, 234, 241, 308
Parmenides, 43–66, 62nn1–2, 62–63n6, 80n10, 169, 170, 182, 279, 305, 306
Parry, Richard, 93n2, 97
Partee, Morriss Henry, 42
Pausanias, 230, 231, 240n12, 280, 281, 283
Pearson, Nancy, 208
Peck, Arthur L., 64
Peller, Gary, 64n20, 66
Pender, Elizabeth E., 144n6, 146
Pendergast, Richard, 193n9, 194
Penner, Terry, 93n2, 97
Perks, Lisa G., 25n2, 26n14, 28

Name Index | 317

Peteet, John R., 276
Philoponus, John, 301n7, 301n13, 303n32, 304
Pierron, Jean-Phillippe, 261
Pindar, 5–6, 131–47, 144n2, 145nn14–15, 212, 268
Planinc, Zdravko, 154, 156, 161, 163
Plato, 2, 3, 4, 5, 6, 7, 8, 9, 10, 13–28, 25n5, 26nn11–12, 26n14, 29–42, 63n12, 66–82, 80n5, 80n7, 80–81nn10–14, 81n17, 81n20, 83–98, 94n5, 95n12, 115–29, 131–47, 149–64, 162nn2–3, 165–79, 176n1, 177nn2–7, 177n10, 178n12, 178nn14–15, 178n17, 181–94, 193n11, 198, 205, 207n10, 209, 218, 220, 221, 223n6, 225, 227–41, 239n2, 239nn5–6, 239n8, 239n18, 239n20, 243, 244, 247, 248, 252, 253, 256n2, 257n17, 258n22, 259n27, 259n29, 260, 263–76, 277–89, 287–88n6, 291–304, 300n2, 302n23, 303n38, 306, 307, 308, 309
Plotinus, 195, 201, 208, 209
Plumwood, Val, 52, 53, 64n20, 66
Plutarch, 233, 240n17, 241
Polansky, Ronald, 304, 309
Pomeroy, Sarah B., 157, 163
Porphyry, 201, 307
Powell, Barry, 27
Pradeau, Jean-François, 93n3, 97
Preddy, William, 66
Preus, Anthony, 162n5, 170, 179, 243, 258n19
Pritzl, Kurt, 194
Prodicus, 223n4, 225
Pseudo-Skylax, 232, 240n15, 241

Raaflub, Kurt, 221, 225
Race, William H., 147
Radt, Stephan L., 147
Ranta, Jerrald, 42

Rashed, Mohammed, 304
Rather, Dan, 276
Reeve, C. D. C., 42, 82, 298, 300n1, 302n22, 302n26, 303n33, 304
Reidy, David A., 93n2, 97
Reiss, Hans, 224
Renault, Olivier, 97
Richardson, Nicholas James, 144n7, 147
Ricœur, Paul, 65, 258n25, 261
Rieu, E. V., 41, 224
Rieu, H., 224
Rizo-Patrón, Eileen, 259, 260, 261, 308
Roberts, Jennifer Tolbert, 221, 225
Rose, Peter W., 140, 141, 145n14, 145n21, 147
Rosenmeyer, Thomas G., 147, 215, 224, 225
Ross, Alan C. M., 260
Ross, William D., 64, 300n1, 304
Rossetti, Livio, 44, 50, 66
Roupnel, Gaston, 245, 246, 255, 256nn10–11, 259
Rorty, Richard, 65, 114
Rowe, C. J., 223n1, 225
Rudolph, Kurt, 205, 209
Russell, Daniel C., 26n11, 28, 96, 258n26 260
Rutter, Keith N., 96

Sallis, John, 151, 163n6, 164
Santas, Gerasimos, 82, 275
Sappho, 6, 146, 149, 163
Sardo, Peymen Adeli, 208
Sartre, Jean-Paul, 66
Sassi, Maria Michela, 128n9, 129
Saunders, Trevor J., 91, 97
Sauvé Meyer, Susan, 177n8, 179
Scanlon, Thomas, 276
Schaap, Andrew, 224
Schadewaldt, Wolfgang, 140, 145n16, 147

Schultz, Anne-Marie, 275n1, 276, 309
Scott, Robert, 65, 209
Sedley, David, 118, 128n2, 129, 144n10, 147
Setaioli, Aldo, 66
Sextus Empiricus, 62n1, 66
Shelly, Cameron, 25n2 26n14, 28
Shipley, Graham, 240n15, 241
Shorey, Paul, 163, 209
Sider, David, 66
Sigelman, Asya C., 147
Silk, Michael, 147
Silverthorne, Michael, 209
Simmons, Margaret A., 179
Simpson, Lorenzo C., 61, 64n20, 66
Sinclair, T. A., 223n1, 224
Skelton, Christina, 232, 241
Slings, S. R., 179
Smith, Adam, 215, 223n3, 225
Smith, C. U. M., 202, 209
Smith, John A., 300n1, 304
Smyth, Herbert Weir, 64
Snell, Bruno, 136, 139, 144n2, 147
Socrates, 2, 3, 4, 5, 6, 7, 8, 9, 10, 11, 13–28, 26n6, 26n10, 26n16, 29–42, 65, 67–82, 79–80n4, 80n5, 80n11, 83–98, 115–29, 135, 136, 138, 140, 149–64, 166, 168, 169, 170, 172, 176–77n1, 177n2, 179, 181–94, 193n10, 194n12, 220, 227–41, 239n7, 250, 258n22, 258n25, 263–76, 275n1, 277, 278, 279, 285, 287n2, 287n4, 295, 309
Solmsen, F., 213, 225
Sommerville, Brooks A., 93n2, 97
Spinoza, Benedict de, 205, 206n2, 206n4, 209
Sprague, R. K., 225
Steiner, Dorah, 139, 147
Steinmann, Michael, 223n3, 225
Stenning, H. J., 224
Stern, J., 147

Stewart, Jeffrey C., 63n12, 66
Stratton, George, 66
Strauss, Barry, 273, 276
Strauss Clay, Jenny, 216, 225
Suhrkamp, Heikki Nyman, 147

Tanner, Michael, 225
Tarrant, Harold, 240n20
Teggart, Frederick J., 216, 225
Thein, Karel, 93n2, 98
Theophrastus, 46, 47, 48, 50, 52, 54, 66, 125
Thesleff, Holger, 178n12, 179
Thomas, Dylan, 143, 147
Thucydides, 175, 219, 221, 225, 231, 239–40n11, 240n13, 275nn4–5
Thummer, Erich, 145n17, 147
Tihanyi, Catherine, 145
Tilgher, Adriano, 223n4, 225
Trépanier, Simon, 123, 128n10, 129
Tulli, Mario, 289
Tuozzo, Thomas M., 26n11, 28, 92, 98, 287n4, 289, 300–301n3, 301n13, 302n21, 302n23, 303n38, 304

Uglione, Renato, 223n2, 225
Underwood, J. A., 260
Usher, M. D., 158, 164

Vahabzadeh, Bijan, 207n6, 209
Valditara, L. M. Napolitano, 145
Verdenius, W., 223n1, 225
Vermeule, Emily, 231, 238n1, 241
Vernant, Jean-Pierre, 132, 137, 147
Vlastos, Gregory, 114, 128n8, 129, 177n2, 179, 285, 289
Vogt, Katja Maria, 93n2, 98
von Wilamowitz-Moellendorff, Ulrike, 223n1, 225
von Wright, Georg Henrik, 147

Walzer, Richard, 207

Waterston, G. C., 258n23, 260
Waugh, Joanne, 157, 164
Weil, Simone, 225
Weiss, R., 275n2, 278
White, Stephen A., 272, 276
Whiting, Jennifer, 93n2, 95n11, 98
Wians, William, 179, 304, 306
Widengren, Geo, 205, 209
Williams, Christopher J. F., 298, 301n10, 301n13, 303n32, 33, 36, 37, 304
Williams, Peter J., 178n13, 179
Wilson, Emily, 163
Wilson, John R., 214, 225
Wilson, R. McLachlan, 209
Winch, Peter, 147
Wittgenstein, Ludwig, 138, 142, 145n20, 147
Witvliet, Charlotte V. O., 276

Wolfsdorf, David, 220, 223n4, 225
Wolfson, Henry Austryn, 206n4, 209
Wolkow, Benjamin, 117, 129
Woodruff, Paul, 42, 87, 97, 163, 276, 287n1, 289
Woods, Michael, 80n7, 82

Xie, Ming, 66

Young, Charles, 275n3, 276
Young, David, 145n17, 147

Zaehner, Robert Charles, 203, 206n4, 209
Zalta, Edward N., 208, 275n3, 275
Zarecki, Jonathan P., 216, 225
Zeno, 44, 50, 51–52, 65
Zeyl, Donald J., 91, 97
Zingano, Marco, 301n8, 304